THE CULT OF THINNESS

THE CULT OF THINNESS

SECOND EDITION

Sharlene Nagy Hesse-Biber
Boston College

New York   Oxford
OXFORD UNIVERSITY PRESS
2007

Oxford University Press, Inc., publishes works that further Oxford University's
objective of excellence in research, scholarship, and education.

Oxford New York
Auckland   Cape Town   Dar es Salaam   Hong Kong   Karachi
Kuala Lumpur   Madrid   Melbourne   Mexico City   Nairobi
New Delhi   Shanghai   Taipei   Toronto

With offices in
Argentina   Austria   Brazil   Chile   Czech Republic   France   Greece
Guatemala   Hungary   Italy   Japan Poland   Portugal   Singapore
South Korea   Switzerland   Thailand   Turkey   Ukraine   Vietnam

Copyright © 2007 by Oxford University Press, Inc.

Published by Oxford University Press, Inc.
198 Madison Avenue, New York, New York 10016
http://www.oup.com

Oxford is a registered trademark of Oxford University Press

Library of Congress Cataloging-in-Publication Data
Hesse-Biber, Sharlene Nagy.
 The cult of thinness / by Sharlene Nagy Hesse-Biber.—2nd ed.
  p. cm
 Rev. ed. of: Am I thin enough yet? 1996.
 Includes bibliographical references and index.
 ISBN-13: 978-0-19-517878-4 (alk. paper)
 ISBN-10: 0-19-517878-5 (alk. paper)
  1. Body image. 2. Leanness—Psychological aspects. 3. Eating disorders—Social
aspects. 4. Women—Psychology. I. Hesse-Biber, Sharlene Nagy. Am I thin enough yet?
II. Title

BF697.5.B63H47 2007
306.4'613—dc22

                                                                    2006045301

Printed in the United States of America
on acid-free paper

To my strong-willed daughters, Sarah Alexandra and Julia Ariel,
and
in memory of two pioneering women—my sister, Janet Green Fischer, and
my sister-in-law, Carol B. Biber, Ph.D.

Contents

Acknowledgments

Many in the Boston College community contributed generously to this project. My thanks go first to the students of Boston College who shared their thoughts and opinions with me in replying to the questionnaire and intensive interviews. I want to express my heartfelt appreciation to several resource experts, whose names will remain anonymous, for their opinions on a wide range of issues dealing with women's body image. Thanks also to the Office of Research Administration of Boston College who provided me with the opportunity to apply for research grants to support this project.

Kate Kruschwitz was instrumental in helping to make my academic writing more accessible to a wider audience

Special thanks go to several graduate and undergraduate research assistants, in particular, to Emily Barko, Cooley Horner, Faith Kirkpatrick, Ximena Ramirez, Melissa Ricker, Belen Molinuevo, and Ingrid Wulczyn, for providing invaluable feedback on book chapters and for helping with the editorial revisions of the chapters and the daunting task of gathering accurate statistical data. In addition, Emily Barko and Ximena Ramirez provided important feedback on the images selected for the book; I have included some of Emily's original collages gathered from popular women's magazines.

Many others supported and assisted in this project, and I am particularly grateful to Steve Vedder and Jodi Wigren. I want to thank Peter Labella and Sean Mahoney, social science editors at Oxford University Press, for their enthusiastic support as well as the hard-working efforts of the editorial staff at Oxford University Press, in particular, Lisa Grzan and Chelsea Gilmore.

I am grateful to my daughters, Sarah Alexandra and Julia Ariel, for their patience, humor, love, kindness, and enthusiastic support for my combining my work and family life. Thanks also go to my mother, Helene Stockert, and my sister, Georgia Gerraghty, for their care, support, and great cooking.

I want to express my sincere appreciation to my husband, Michael Peter Biber, for "hanging in there" while I spent many hours on this project. His support, love, and understanding were crucial during all phases of this writing project.

Brookline, Massachusetts

THE CULT OF THINNESS

Introduction

My research interest in the topic of women's body image and weight issues began years ago, when the director of the Counseling Center at Boston College asked me to help find out why the Center was overwhelmed with female students with eating problems. The situation had been getting worse over the past few years. Numerous cases of bulimia (compulsive binge eating, often followed by self-induced vomiting) and anorexia (obsession with food, starvation dieting, and severe weight loss) appeared every week.

As the author of a previous study on female student career and lifestyle aspirations, as a professor of sociology and women's studies, and as a faculty advisor at Boston College, I was fascinated by the fact that eating disorders were much more common among women.[1] I wanted to understand why such problems had recently exploded. Although bulimia and anorexia are individual diagnoses, one can assume that broader factors are at work when the incidence of a disorder suddenly increases.[2] Was something going on in our society to foster such behavior?

Over the next several months I began researching the field of eating disorders, as this was neither a topic I had previously studied, nor an issue I had experienced. But the problem did not strike home until one of the sophomores I was advising came into my office in tears. Janet broke into sobs and said to me, "I don't know what I am going to do. I'm too fat for the cheerleading squad."

Janet was fairly tall (5′ 8″) with a medium build. She weighed 125 pounds. She told me that when she showed up for the coed cheerleading tryouts, there had been a public weighing at the gym. All female applicants had to line up and get weighed, and if they were over the 115-pound limit they were rejected without a chance to demonstrate their skills. Janet had been starving herself for days, hoping to make the weight cut, but had failed.

A policy like this sends a clear message—there is an "ideal" body image a woman must conform to if she wants to become a cheerleader. Society expects to find petite women on a college cheerleading squad, "girls" whom male cheerleaders can tumble and lift in cheerleading routines. The cultural message is the same for other popular collegiate groups such as sororities and high-status cliques: A thin woman is a "valued" woman.

Compare Janet with her contemporary at that time, Doug Flutie, Boston College's Heisman trophy-winning football hero who has since gone on to a successful career in professional football. He too fought a cultural belief—that football requires big men. Flutie is only 5′ 9″ and well below the weight of the typical quarterback. However, through skill and agility, he shattered the stereotype of the tall, rangy quarterback. Cheerleading does not offer a similar opportunity to women. It was possible for Doug Flutie to become a "Little Big Man," but not for Janet to become a "Big Little Woman."

It is no wonder that American women are obsessed with thinness. They are exhorted to strive for a physical ideal that is laden with moral judgment. Slenderness represents restraint, moderation, and self-control—the virtues of our Puritan heritage. Our culture considers obesity "bad" and "ugly." Fat represents moral failure, the inability to delay gratification, poor impulse control, greed, and self-indulgence.

The slim figure has also come to represent health as well as beauty. It is promoted in advertisements for the multimillion-dollar beauty industry, the pharmaceutical industry, and the food industry. Bookstores are full of advice on losing weight, flattening the stomach, getting rid of cellulite, and dressing to look more slender. Twenty years ago, there were 300 diet books in print,[3] while in 2004 "Amazon.com listed 439 books concerning weight loss" in that year alone! In fact, "the number of diet books seems to have doubled consistently every four years since 1992. . ."[4] Today, there are even more. Some of the best sellers include Dr. Robert Haas's *Eat to Win* (over 2 million copies in print), Harvey and Marilyn Diamond's *Fit for Life* (3 million in print), and William Dufty's *Sugar Blues* (over 1 million in print.) More recent books include Dr. Arthur Agatston's *The Southbeach Diet: The Delicious, Doctor-Designed, Foolproof Plan for Fast and Healthy Weight Loss*, and Robert Atkins's *Dr. Atkins' New Diet Revolution*, which earned $6 million in 2001 alone.[5]

The Cult of Thinness provides an in-depth look at American women's obsession with their bodies and the societal forces that propel them to engage in widespread social, political, and economic rituals to obtain a slender figure. This book is an extension and revision of my earlier, award-winning book *Am I Thin Enough Yet?* (Oxford, University Press, 1996). *The Cult of Thinness* offers young women, parents, clinicians, and educators an in-depth look at the growing problems of body image and eating disorders, which occur 10 times more frequently in women than in men, by examining the lives of young women who are already touched by body image and eating issues.

Since the 1960s, the ideal body type for women has become steadily slimmer and less curvaceous than in the 1950s, the era of Marilyn Monroe's bosomy beauty. In the 1970s, visitors to Mme. Tussaud's London wax museum rated Twiggy (the original "waif" model) as the "most beautiful woman in the world."[6] A recent study of measurements of fashion models and Miss America pageant winners from the 1920s to the present reveals a growing gap in body image measurements between these idealized images and young women's body measurements in the general population. *Playboy* centerfold models' measurements have followed suit over the past five decades, with all of these idealized bodies now below normal weight. The study also notes that 25% of fashion models now meet the American Psychiatric Association's diagnostic criteria for anorexia nervosa.[7]

Fueling this trend are large-scale market interests that exploit women's insecurities about their looks. American food, weight loss, and cosmetic industries thrive on the purchases made to attain the unattainable goal of physical perfection. The slim and flawless "cover girl" is an icon created by capitalism for the sake of profit. Millions of women pay it homage.

But why are women especially vulnerable to eating disorders? Influenced by patriarchal institutions, from the conventional family to schools and the media, girls as young as 7 and 8 years old learn that the rewards of our society go to those who conform, not simply on the level of overt behavior, but on the level of biology.[8]

To understand this disturbing social phenomenon, I initiated a survey of 395 students (282 females and 113 males) concerning their eating habits, diets, and attitudes toward self, family, friends, and school. I included interviews with experts in the health care and fitness industries as well.

I also conducted an in-depth study of 60 college-age women over an 8-year period. I spent an average of 3 hours interviewing each one, and was able to talk with many of them again during the course of their college careers. I followed a few of these women through graduate school and beyond. (Names and events have been altered to protect each person's anonymity.) Their stories comprise a critical part of this book and led to its title, *The Cult of*

Thinness. I chose such a dramatic metaphor because the basic behavior associated with being in a cult—ritualistic performance and obsession with a goal or ideal—is also characteristic of many modern women.[9] I hope to convey the intense, day-to-day involvement which the pursuit of thinness demands. The body rituals women practice, and the extent to which they sacrifice their bodies and minds to this goal, seem to create a separate reality for its followers. An extensive interview with Anna, a woman who had actually been a member of a religious cult, helped me to see the many parallels (chapter 1).

In the course of investigating this cult, I examine why women place such a high premium on their bodies (chapter 2), and I investigate how body perceptions differ among men and women, and how weight has become a primary definer of women's worth and identity. Historically, women have always gone to great lengths to transform themselves to meet the changing cultural requirements of femininity. In this book I trace the mind/body dualism in Western cultural thought, which casts women in the role of the body and men in the role of the mind. I show how dominant social and economic interests, sometimes characterized as "patriarchal" and "capitalist," shape this dualism. The essence of the term "patriarchy" is literally "rule of the father."[10] In the context of modern times and for the purposes of this study, patriarchy can be defined as a "system of interrelated social structures, and practices in which men dominate, oppress and exploit women."[11] In this study, I examine the various manifestations of patriarchy as they have evolved within and between social and economic institutions. We will find that one major manifestation of patriarchy is the primary image of women as good wives and mothers and objects of decorative worth. I define the basic nature of capitalism as a political/economic system based on the principle of a competitive, free market economy. These interests have made big business out of women's preoccupation with their bodies. Aided by advertising and mass media, the Cult of Thinness generates enormous profits for the food, diet, and health industries (chapters 3 and 4).

For me, the most poignant research data comes from the case studies of young women's lived experiences. Judged either by outward appearances or by the standards set by the Metropolitan Life Insurance's ideal weight chart, few of the students I interviewed would be characterized as overweight. Anyone might look at them and see "normal," successful female coeds—indeed, the women themselves also commented on this fact, except for those who were clearly anorexic. Yet all were very concerned about their weight, and some were truly obsessed by it. *Their* testimonies show how the Cult of Thinness promotes eating disorders. In chapters 5, 6, and 7 their voices tell us about their dissatisfactions with their bodies, their concerns with food, and the cultural pressures they feel. They tell us why the pursuit of thinness has become their consuming issue.

For the most part, the women I interviewed were young adults from white upper-middle- and middle-class families. But I also discovered how the Cult's message is spreading to other populations, for example, preteens, adolescent boys, and adult males. We also examine the growing issues of weight and eating problems among women of color as well as gays and lesbians, groups that appeared to be formerly untouched by the Cult of Thinness (chapter 8).

Ultimately, we need to look for ways to break free from the Cult. It is important to say at the outset that I am not advocating that women give up the pursuit of beauty and fashion entirely. Adornment of the body as well as beauty and fashion rituals form an integral part of all human cultures. But current beauty and fashion trends that advocate attaining ultra-thinness, at any price, are unrealistic. Given that most women's bodies do not naturally fit the thin ideal, these trends are destructive to women's health, self-esteem, and economic and social advancement within society.

The final chapter of this book evaluates the range of therapies and personal and collective action available to help women overcome their weight obsessions and eating problems. Many of them provide a new framework for envisioning femininity and personal power, for overcoming body insecurity, and for strengthening the inner self. Others involve changing the cultural environment itself.

The Cult of Thinness offers important lessons and solutions to eating problems and eating disorders that can be garnered from young women whose lives were exposed to decades of extreme pressures within American society to be thin. Along the way, the reader is provided with important self-help tips to tackle the growing problems of body image issues that young women and new recruits to the Cult of Thinness continue to encounter.

Throughout my analysis I provide examples of women who resist becoming cult victims. Women can abandon their cultural baggage. They can reject the culturally dictated ideal, and transform it into their own image. There *are* alternatives to the Cult of Thinness.

Notes

1. The reported ratio of female to male anorexics and bulimics is 10 to 1. See: Richard A. Gordon, *Anorexia and Bulimia: Anatomy of a Social Epidemic* (Cambridge, MA: Basil Blackwell, 1989), 32, and Lock et al., 2001. It is estimated by the National Eating Disorders Association (NEDA) that in the United States alone "as many as 10 million females and 1 million males are fighting a life and

death battle with an eating disorder such as anorexia or bulimia. Approximately 25 million more are struggling with binge eating disorder (Crowther, Wolf, & Sherwood, 1992; Fairburn et al., 1993; Gordon, 1990; Hoek, 1995; Shisslak, Crago & Estes, 1995)" (NEDA; http://www.nationaleatingdisorders.org). Anorexia carries the highest mortality rate of any mental illness, approximately 20%. These data account only for those individuals who are clinically diagnosed; they exclude those individuals who manifest subclinical diagnoses or who refuse to seek help or lack access to medical care.

Currently, eating disorders are showing up in adolescent girls, and are no longer confined to a particular class, ethnic group, or gender, as the medical literature previously described (Abrams and Stormer, 2002; Altabe, 1998; Atlas, Smith, Hohlstein, McCarthy, and Kroll, 2002; Barry and Grilo, 2002).

Anorexia has a significant mortality rate. The American Anorexia/Bulimia Association estimates that 10% of those with a clinical diagnosis of anorexia may die (http://www.aabainc.org/general/anorexia.html). . . . "The American Anorexia and Bulimia Association [AABA] (2001) estimates that five million U.S. women suffer from some form of eating disorder, 15 percent of Americans have eating disordered attitudes, and 1,000 people will die each year from eating disorders. Furthermore, one percent of teenage girls will develop anorexia, and up to ten percent of those may die due to the illness annually." See: E. Grace Lager and Brian R. McGee, "Hiding the Anorectic: A Rhetorical Analysis of Popular discourse Concerning Anorexia." *Women's Studies in Communication,* 26 (2003). Accessed from Questia.com. Bulimia is estimated to be 4-5 times more prevalent than anorexia but harder to diagnose, since many bulimics are of normal weight and/or overweight, and usually hide their binge- and purge-behaviors, making diagnosis elusive unless they seek help on their own. The number of women dying from bulimia is difficult to estimate, but the one estimate suggests that 1-3% of adolescents are afflicted with this disorder (DSMIV; American Psychiatric Association, 1994). Bulimic symptoms can have serious medical consequences such as kidney failure and congestive heart failure (Boskind-Lodahl and White, 1978, pp. 141–144). There are combinations of anorexia and bulimia known as "bulimarexia"; this disorder may cause the greatest health risks (Boskind-Lodahl and White, 1978).

2. A range of research studies in the United States and elsewhere (primarily in affluent Western cultures) document the increase in eating disorders from the early 1960s to the 1990s. Gordon claims that the rates of eating disorders in the general population "increased by a factor of at least two" (p. 152). While some have speculated that the rise in eating disorders may be a result of greater awareness and detection, the vast numbers of clinical research data "make such an interpretation unlikely" (p. 153). See: Richard A. Gordon, "A Sociocultural Interpretation of the Current Epidemic of Eating Disorders," in *The Eating Disorders,* ed. B.J. Blinder, B.F. Chaiting, and R. Goldstein (New York: PMA Publishing, 1988), 151–163.

The rates of anorexia nervosa and bulimia, while increasing, are still not high in the general population. However, these disorders are especially high in the female adolescent student population, which is thought to be at greatest risk. Some researchers estimate that in the United States 1 in every 200-250 women between the ages of 13 and 22 suffers from anorexia nervosa, and that between 20% and 30% of college women control their weight through vomiting, diuretics, and laxatives. See: Steven Levenkron, *Treating and Overcoming Anorexia Nervosa* (New York: Warner Books, 1983), 1; Susan Squire, *The Slender Balance: Causes and Cures for Bulimia, Anorexia, and the Weight-Loss/Weight-Gain Seesaw* (New York: G.P. Putnam's Sons, 1983).

Research suggests that the prevalence of eating disorders continues to increase in frequency. See: Katherine A. Halmi, "Anorexia Nervosa: Demographic and Clinical Features in 94 Cases," *Psychosomatic Medicine*, 36, no. 1 (1974): 18–26; Dolores J. Jones, Mary M. Fox, Haroutum M. Babigan, and Heidi E. Hutton, "Epidemiology of Anorexia Nervosa in Monroe County, New York: 1960 1976," *Psychosomatic Medicine*, 42, no. 6 (1980): 551–558; R. E. Kendall, D. J. Hall, Anthea Hailey, and H. M. Babigan, "The Epidemiology of Anorexia Nervosa," *Psychological Medicine*, 3 (1973): 200–203; J. A. Sours, "Anorexia Nervosa: Nosology Diagnosis, Developmental Patterns, and Power-Control Dynamics," in *Adolescence: Psychological Perspectives.*, ed. Gerald Caplan and Serge Lebovici (New York: Basic Books, 1969), 105–215.

In fact, the rate of women's problems with food may be *underestimated.* My research on college-educated women reveals that eating disorders exist along a continuum from very severe cases to more mild, subclinical cases (while women in this category do not fulfill all the diagnostic criteria for bulimia and anorexia, they are still obsessed with weight issues, such as binge eating, fasting, extreme dieting, and the like). These students' eating issues would not be diagnosed as abnormal. See: Sharlene Hesse-Biber, "Eating Patterns and Disorders in a College Population: Are College Women's Eating Problems a New Phenomenon?" *Sex Roles*, 20, no. 1/2 (1989): 71–89; and Sharlene Hesse-Biber, "Report on a Panel Longitudinal Study of College Women's Eating Patterns and Eating Disorders: Noncontinum versus Continuum Measures," *Health Care for Women International*, 13, no. 4 (1992): 375–391.

3. A Hillel Schwartz, *Never Satisfied: A Cultural History of Diets, Fantasies and Fat* (New York: Free Press, 1986), 240.

4. A Canadian Broadcasting Corporation (CBC), "CBC Witness: Diet Wars," December 5, 2001, www.cbc.ca. Also see: Dan Ackman, "The Global Epidemic in Diet Advice," Forbes.com. (http://www.forbes.com/business/healthcare/2005/05/03/cx_da_0503topnews.html)

5. "America's Most Famous Diet Gurus," 2005, Forbes.com, http://www.forbes.com/careers/2005/04/06/cx_/rlh_0406dietgurus.html.

6. D.M. Schwartz, M.G. Thompson, and C.L. Johnson, "Anorexia Nervosa and Bulimia: The Socio-cultural Context," *International Journal of Eating Disorders*, 1 (1982): 20-36. See also: A. Morris, T. Cooper, and P.J. Cooper, "The Changing Shape of Female Fashion Models," *International Journal of Eating Disorders*, 8, no. 5 (1989): 593–596.

7. These data are from Carol Byrd-Bredbenner, Jessica Murray, and Yvette R. Schlussel. "Temporal Changes in Anthropometric Measurements of Idealized Females and Young Women in General," *Journal of Women and Health*, 41, no 2 (2005), 13–29.
8. Having internalized this message, modern women exert on themselves a subjection of the body equal to the institutional oppression described by Michel Foucault. See: M. Foucault, *Discipline and Punish: The Birth of the Prison*, trans. Alan Sheridan, (New York: Vintage Books, 1979). See also: S. Bartky, "Foucault, Femininity and the Modernization of Patriarchal Power," in *Feminism and Foucault*, ed. I. Diamond and L. Quinby (Boston: Northeastern University Press, 1988), 61–88.
9. For a description of cult behavior, see: Max Weber, *The Sociology of Religion* (Boston: Beacon Press, 1963). See also: R. Stark and W.S. Bainbridge, *The Future of Religion: Secularization, Revival and Cult Formation* (Berkeley: University of California Press, 1986).
10. Sylvia Walby, in her book *Theorizing Patriarchy*, notes that the term has been used to refer to societies in which men ruled because of their position as head of the household. See: Max Weber, *The Theory of Social and Economic Organization* (New York: Free Press, 1947); C. Pateman, *The Sexual Contract* (Cambridge: Polity Press, 1988). See also: S. Walby, *Theorizing Patriarchy* (Cambridge, MA: Basil Blackwell, 1990).
11. This definition is taken from the work of Sylvia Walby. She presents one of the most comprehensive theoretical discussions of the term. See: S. Walby, *Theorizing Patriarchy* (Cambridge, MA: Basil Blackwell, 1990), 20.

Bibliography

Abrams, L. S., & C. C. Stormer. "Sociocultural Variations in the Body Image Perceptions of Urban Adolescent Females." *Journal of Youth and Adolescence*, 31, no. 6 (2002): 443–450.

Ackman, Dan. "The Global Epidemic in Diet Advice," 05/03/05. Forbes.com http ://www.forbes.com/business/healthcare/2005/03/03/cx_dg_0503topnews.html.

Altabe, M. "Ethnicity and Body Image: Quantitative and Qualitative Analysis." *International Journal of Eating Disorders*, 23 (1998): 153–159.

American Psychiatric Association. *Diagnostic and Statistical Manual of Mental Disorders* (4th ed.). Washington, DC: American Psychiatric Association, 1994.

Atlas, J. G., G. T. Smith, L. A. Hohlstein, D. M. McCarthy, & L. S. Kroll. "Similarities and Differences between Caucasian and African American College Women on Eating and Dieting Expectancies, Bulimic Symptoms, Dietary Restraint, and Disinhibition." *International Journal of Eating Disorders*, 32 (2002): 326–334.

Attie, I., & J. Brooks-Gunn. "Weight concerns as chronic stressors in women." In *Gender and Stress*, ed. R. Barnett, L. Biener, & G. Baruch, pp. 218–252. New York: Free Press, 1987.

Barry, D. T., & C. M. Grilo. "Eating and Body Image Disturbances in Adolescent Psychiatric Inpatients: Gender and Ethnicity Patterns." *The International Journal of Eating Disorders,* 32, 3 (2002): 335–343.

Bartky, S. "Foucault Femininity and the Modernization of Patriarchal Power." In *Feminism and Foucault,* ed. I. Diamond & L. Quinby, pp. 61–88. Boston: Northeastern University Press, 1988.

Boskind-Lodahl , M. & W. C. White. "The Definition and Treatment of Bulimarexia in College Women—A Pilot Study." *Journal of the American College Health Association,* 27, no. 2 (October 1978): 84–97.

Byrd-Bredbenner, C., J. Murray, & Y.R. Schlussel. "Temporal Changes in Anthropometric Measurements of Idealized Females and Young Women in General." *Journal of Women and Health,* 42, no. 2 (2005): 13–29.

Canadian Broadcasting Corporation (CBC). "CBC Witness: Diet Wars." http.//www.cbc.ca/ (accessed December 5, 2001).

Crowther, Janis H., E. M. Wolf, and N. E. Sherwood. "Epidemiology of Bulimia Nervosa." In *The Etiology of Bulimia Nervosa: The Individual and Familial Context,* ed. J. H. Crowther, D. L. Tennenbaum, S. E. Hobfoll, and M. A. P. Stephens. Philadelphia: Hemisphere Publishing Corporation, 1992.

Forbes, Inc. "America's Most Famous Diet Gurus." http://www.forbes.com/ 2005/04/06/cx_lrlh_0406dietgurus_print.html (accessed December 8, 2005).

Foucault, M. *Discipline and Punish: The Birth of the Prison,* trans. A. Sheridan. New York: Vintage Books, 1979.

Garner, D.M., P. E. Garfinkel, D. Schwartz, & M. Thompson. "Cultural Expectations of Thinness in Women." *Psychological Reports,* 47, no. 2 (1980): 483–491.

Gordon, R. A. *Anorexia and Bulimia: Anatomy of a Social Epidemic.* Cambridge, MA.: Basil Blackwell, 1989.

Gordon, R. A. "A Sociocultural Interpretation of the Current Epidemic of Eating Disorders." In *The Eating Disorders,* ed. B.J. Blinder, B.F. Chaiting, & R. Goldstein, pp. 151–163. New York: PMA Publishing, 1988.

Halmi, K. A. "Anorexia Nervosa: Demographic and Clinical Features in 94 Cases." *Psychosomatic Medicine,* 36, no. 1 (1974): 18–26.

Hesse-Biber, S. "Eating Patterns and Disorders in a College Population: Are College Women's Eating Problems a New Phenomenon?" *Sex Roles,* 20, nos. 1/2 (1989): 71–89.

Hesse-Biber, S. "Report on a Panel Longitudinal Study of College Women's Eating Patterns and Eating Disorders: Noncontinuum versus Continuum Measures." *Health Care for Women International,* 13, no. 4 (1992): 375–391.

Hoek, H.W., & D. van Hoeken. "Review of the Prevalence and Incidence of Eating Disorders." *International Journal of Eating Disorders,* 34 (2003): 383–396.

Jones, D. J., M. M. Fox, H. M. Babigian, & H. E. Hutton. "Epidemiology of Anorexia Nervosa in Monroe County, New York: 1960-1976." *Psychosomatic Medicine,* 42, no. 6 (1980): 551–558.

Kendall, R. E., D. J. Hall, A. Hailey, & H. M. Babigian. "The Epidemiology of Anorexia Nervosa." *Psychological Medicine,* 3, no. 2 (1973): 200–203.

Levenkron, S. *Treating and Overcoming Anorexia Nervosa*. New York: Warner Books, 1983.

Morris, A., T. Cooper, & P.J. Cooper. "The Changing Shape of Female Fashion Models." *International Journal of Eating Disorders*, 8, no. 5 (1989): 593–596.

National Eating Disorders Association. "Statistics: Eating Disorders and Their Precursors." http://www.nationaleatingdiosrders.org

Pateman, C. *The Sexual Contract*. Cambridge: Polity Press, 1988.

Schwartz, D.M., M.G. Thompson, & C.L. Johnson. "Anorexia Nervosa and Bulimia: The Socio-cultural Context." *International Journal of Eating Disorders*, 1, no. 3 (1982): 20–36.

Schwartz, H. *Never Satisfied: A Cultural History of Diets, Fantasies and Fat*. New York: Free Press, 1986.

Shisslak, C.M., M. Crago., and L.S. Estes. "The Spectrum of Eating Disturbances." *International Journal of Eating Disorders* 18, no. 3 (1995): 209–219.

Sours, J.A. "Anorexia Nervosa: Nosology Diagnosis, Developmental Patterns, and Power-Control Dynamics." In *Adolescence: Psychological Perspectives*, ed. G. Caplan & S. Lebovici, pp. 185–215. New York: Basic Books, 1969.

Squire, S. *The Slender Balance: Causes and Cures for Bulimia, Anorexia, and the Weight-Loss/Weight-Gain Seesaw*. New York: G.P. Putnam's Sons, 1983.

Stark, R., & W.S. Bainbridge. *The Future of Religion: Secularization, Revival and Cult Formation*. Berkeley: University of California Press, 1986.

Walby, S. *Theorizing Patriarchy*. Cambridge, MA: Basil Blackwell, 1990.

Weber, M. *The Sociology of Religion*. Boston: Beacon Press, 1963.

Weber, M. *The Theory of Social and Economic Organization*. New York: Free Press, 1947.

Wiseman, C. V., J. J. Gray, J. E. Mosimann, & A. H. Ahrens. "Cultural Expectations of Thinness in Women: An Update." *International Journal of Eating Disorders*, 11, no. 1 (1992): 85–89.

ONE

A Cult Grows in America

Ever since I was 10 years old I always wanted to be the thinnest, the prettiest. 'Cause I thought, if I look like this, then I'm going to have so many boyfriends, and guys are going to be so in love with me, and I'll be taken care of for the rest of my life.

—Delia, college senior

What's Wrong with This Picture?

Pretty, vivacious, and petite, Delia was a picture of fashionable perfection when she first walked into my office. Her tight jeans and fringed Western shirt showed off her thin, 5' frame; her black cowboy boots and silver earrings completed a presentation that said, *"Look at me!"*

The perfect picture, however, has a serious price. Delia has come to me to talk about her *"problem."* She is bulimic. In secret, she regularly binges on large amounts of food, then forces herself to vomit. It has become a powerful habit, one that she is afraid to break because it so efficiently maintains her thin body. For Delia, as for so many others, being thin is everything.

I mean, how many bumper stickers have you seen that say "No Fat Chicks"? Guys don't like fat girls. Guys like little girls. I guess because it makes them feel bigger and, you know, they want somebody who looks pretty. Pretty to me is you have to be thin and you have to have, like, good facial features. My final affirmation of myself is how many guys look at me when I go into a bar.

Delia's Story

Delia is the eldest child, and only girl, in a wealthy Southern family. Her father is a successful dentist and her mother has never worked outside the home. Her

FIGURE 1.1 My Inspiration Collage, 2005.

parents fought a lot when she was young—her father was an alcoholic—and they eventually divorced. According to Delia, both parents doted on her.

> I've never been deprived of anything in my entire life. I was spoiled, I guess, because I've never felt any pressure from my parents to do anything. My dad would say, "Whatever you want to do, if you want to go to Europe, if you want to go to law school, if you don't want to do anything . . . whatever you want to do, just be happy. No pressure."

He was unconcerned about her weight, she said, but emphasized how important it was to be pretty. Delia quickly noticed this message everywhere, especially in the media.

> I am so affected by *Glamour* magazine and *Vogue* and all that; I'm looking at all these beautiful women. They're thin. I want to be just as beautiful. I want to be just as thin. Because that is what guys like.

When I asked what her mother wanted for her, she recited, "To be nice and pretty and sweet and thin and popular and smart and successful and have everything that I could ever want and just to be happy." "Sweet and pretty and thin" meant that from the age of 10 she was enrolled in a health club and learned to count calories. Her mom, who at 45 is "beautiful, gorgeous, thin," instructed her on how to eat:

> "Only eat small amounts. Eat a thousand calories a day; don't overeat." My mom was never critical, like "You're fat." But one time, I went on a camping trip and I gained 4 pounds and she said, "You've got to lose weight." I mean, she watched what I ate. Like if I was going to get a piece of cake she would say, "Don't eat that."

At age 13 she started her secret bingeing and vomiting. "When I first threw up I thought, well, it's so easy," she told me. "I can eat and not get the calories and not gain weight. And I was modeling at the time, and I wanted to look like the girls in the magazines."

Delia's preoccupation with thinness intensified when she entered high school. She wanted to be a cheerleader, and was tiny enough to make it. "When I was 16 I just got into this image thing, like tiny, thin. . . . I started working out more. I'd just fight eating because I was working out all the time, going to aerobics two or three times a day sometimes, eating only salad and a bagel, and like, no fat. I just got caught up in this circle."

College in New England brought a new set of social pressures. She could not go running every day because of the cold. She hated the school gym, so she stopped working out and gained 4 pounds her freshman year. Her greatest stress at college had nothing to do with academics. "The most stressful thing for me is whether I'm going to eat that day, and what am I going to eat," she told me, "more than getting good grades."

After freshman year Delia became a cheerleader again.

> Going in, I know I weighed like 93 or 94 pounds, which to me was this enormous hang-up, because I'd never weighed more than 90 pounds in my entire life. And I was really freaked out. I knew people were going to be looking at me . . . and I'm like, "I've got to lose this weight." So I would just not eat, work out all the time. I loved being on the squad, but my partner was a real jerk. He would never work out, and when we would do lifts he'd always say, "Delia, go run. Go run, you're too heavy." I hadn't been eating that day. I had already run 7 or 8 miles and he told me to run again. And I was surrounded by girls who were all so concerned about their weight, and it was just really this horrible situation.

College life also confirmed another issue for Delia, a cultural message from her earliest childhood. She did *not* want to be a breadwinner. She put it this way:

> When I was eight I wanted to be president of the United States. As I grew older and got to college I was like, "Wow, it's hard for women." I mean, I don't care what

people say. If they say the society's liberated, they're wrong. It's still really hard for women. It's like they look through a glass window *(sic)*. They're vice presidents, but they aren't the president. And I just figured, God, how much easier would it be for me to get married to somebody I know is going to make a lot of money and just be taken care of. . . . I want somebody else to be the millionaire.

Delia said she lived by three simple rules. To the Duchess of Windsor's dictum "You can never be too thin or too rich," she added "Be confident and be funny" and "You eat to live, not live to eat." She ignored the fact that not eating, or getting rid of what she had eaten, controlled her life.

Anna's Story

> *I really kind of learned from a very young age to surrender*
> *myself to other people's will, desire, and wants*
> —Anna, religious cult member for 12 years

Anna entered a religious cult in her early 20s.

He *[cult leader]* said he would take care of us. We could forget everything that had happened to us, that had caused us pain in our lives and we would now be fine. I think I was feeling kind of lost—the experience of being out on my own was difficult. The way that I think of it now is that I climbed back into Daddy's lap and it seemed very comforting that there was someone who had this spiritual vision about my destiny who was going to be my guide and tell me what to do. . . . I think other people who met him and even other women who met him who were more independent than I was just said, "Screw this, I'm not about to do this kind of thing." He didn't suck in everybody that came his way.

Anna's descriptions of her total immersion in the separate and controlled reality of a spiritual cult are chilling:

We really became this very separate group of people, because our leader made that happen. He separated us from our families, and made us feel very bound to each other and to him, and different from everybody else. . . . I was attached to the leader and the whole way of life. In some ways it is not unlike being a nun or a priest or a monk or something except that we were not living celibate lives if we were married. It is just a very protected base. . . .

But remaining in those ranks means constant vigilance. It demands adherence to certain beliefs (which may seem quite bizarre to outsiders) and the practice of specific rituals. Most religious cults center on a spiritual leader who defines the path, and who threatens exile, or worse, to those of his flock who stray. Anna commented:

Our guru considered himself infallible. He was beyond feedback, so that if I looked at him and saw something I didn't like, he told me that I was projecting, that he was merely a mirror for my own shortcomings. . . . He was really good at playing upon your weaknesses as a way to keep people bound to him, and I felt that the only reason my life had value was because of him and what this way of life had given me. Subconsciously, I thought I would die if I left him. . . . He basically said that we should expect that if we left, our entire lives would go down the tubes, and he said that everything that we had learned and gained from the day that we walked into the cult would disappear when we left. I am embarrassed to say that I actually believed it. It took me a really long time to realize that was entirely impossible. I got hit on the head. It doesn't make sense now.

Anna's journey is not that different from Delia's, whose single-minded pursuit of thinness and beauty has many parallels to a religious cult. In both cases, a group of individuals is committed to a life defined by a rigid set of values and rules. They seem obsessed with the path to perfection, which, though unattainable, holds out compelling promises. In following their ideals, they usually feel that they are among "the chosen." Members of true cults frequently isolate themselves from the rest of the world, and develop a strong sense of community, acceptance, and even salvation.

As one religious cult expert notes,

Cults seek to replace a lost community and a lost idealism. . . . They offer community, meaning, and spiritual direction, serving as ad hoc rites of passage in a society where traditional institutions seem to be failing. . . . They are not subject to control by the larger group, and many of them do not want to reintegrate their members back into the larger group—quite the reverse. They deliberately maintain members in a kind of limbo, permanently suspended from the surrounding environment.[1]

The Cult of Thinness

Young women like Delia invest in thinness with the same intense, moment-to-moment, day-to-day involvement as religious cult members devote to their beliefs. They may not answer to a single leader, but bow instead to powerful economic, social, and cultural forces that define and value females in terms of their physical attributes.

This Cult of Thinness is enveloping American society. Conservative estimates put the number of young women and girls with eating disorders between 5 and 10 million.[2] Estimates of body dissatisfaction among women range upward to 56%.[3] Younger kids are joining the diet craze: An estimated 40% of 9- and 10-year-old kids say they "sometimes" or "very often" diet.[4]

The American population is spending $50 billion dollars each year buying diet-related products.[5]

Being female is the primary criterion for membership in the Cult of Thinness. The object of worship is the "perfect" body. The primary rituals are dieting and exercising with obsessive attention to monitoring progress—weighing the body at least once a day and constantly checking calories. The advertising industry and the media provide plenty of beautiful-body icons to worship. There are numerous ceremonies—pageants and contests—that affirm this ideal.

There are plenty of guides and gurus along the way. Often it is the mother who initiates the young novice into the secrets of losing weight. Some of the most revered oracles have celebrity as their major qualification. Kirstie Alley, Jessica Simpson, Oprah Winfrey, and Anna Nicole Smith are among those who advise their fans on the virtues or pitfalls of certain diets and exercises. Other sages have medical qualifications and have produced "sacred texts." Dr. Atkins's diet, the Scarsdale Diet, the Pritikin Diet, the South Beach Diet, and the Miami Mediterranean Diet were produced by best-selling diet doctors. Some diet gurus are psychologists with special phone-in hours for those who have fallen off their diets, or a special "intensive care" line for those in dire need,[6] or motivational audiotapes for their patients.

The Christian dieting industry sees women's problems with food as a "spiritual hunger"—the problem with food is the problem of the soul, and if you put your spiritual life in order, the weight loss will follow.[7] Presbyterian minister Charlie Shedd published the first Christian dieting book, *Pray Your Weight Away,* in 1957, and since that time many spiritual diet books have followed.[8] Probably the most popular is Gwen Shamblin's *Weigh Down Diet.*[9] While the program may bring Christians who follow it closer to God, Christian nutritionist Pam Smith notes that "'People come away from it with no understanding of what they need for health. Who wouldn't want to hear that you can eat biscuits and gravy and it doesn't matter because somehow it's going to work? But there is no self control; rather, people are saddled with the anarchy of whatever, whenever, however.'"[10]

Diet clubs and 12-step weight loss programs introduce even more fervor for shedding pounds. Their meetings are filled with conversion stories of how so-and-so "saw the light" and lost pounds, or fell from grace by eating "forbidden" foods. There are recommended penances, as well as weekly support groups and telephone chains to help the backsliders. One researcher who attended over 90 group-diet meetings compares them to quasi-religious experiences. She notes:

> These dieters labeled overweight as a sinful deviation, buttressed by the religious argot of saint, sinner, angel, devil, guilt, confession and absolution. Some

stated that they had innocently caught this sin, as rather passive and helpless illness victims. Others claimed that they had actively acquired their sinful state— as "almost criminals," hanging their heads in shame, they assumed the responsibility for their fat "misdemeanors" or "felonies." [11]

Those who have experienced the shared sacrifice of the cult create a "sacred" environment. Their common lifestyle brings them together and drives a wedge between them and the rest of society, which may come to be viewed as "profane." Thin is sacred. Thin is beautiful and healthy; thin will make you happy. Salvation awaits those who attain the ideal body; if you are female, thin will get you a husband. Fat is profane. To be fat is to be ugly, weak, and slovenly; to be fat is to have lost control, be lazy, and have no ambition. Achieving the proper weight is not just a personal responsibility, it is a moral obligation. Those who indulge in gluttony and sloth do not want to be among the "saved." [12]

Just as there is a range of faith among the devotees of any religion, the women I interviewed can be positioned along a continuum. [13] The most avid members of the Cult of Thinness engage in bizarre practices more characteristic of fringe cult movements, like the followers of Reverend Moon or Jim Jones or more currently, movements of scientology or of Kabbalah, today often considered cults, or at the very least, cult-like. These rituals surrounding anorexia, bulimia, and exercise addiction carry the risk of emotional and physical damage, or even death.

A Dangerous Tool

Members of the Cult of Thinness use whatever strategies they can find to strive for the ideal body. Delia believed that it was her appearance that would lead her to her goal of marrying a millionaire. Her eating disorder was a tool for accomplishing this end. [14]

The concept of "tool" is important to understanding the increase in eating disorders among American females. Delia's behavior was a straightforward means of meeting the stringent standards of beauty dictated by her culture. What a clinician would view as pathological, Delia saw as utilitarian, along the same lines as cosmetic surgery. When I asked her how she was going to deal with her eating "problem" she replied:

> I have no idea. I mean, I don't see it going away. I guess it's kind of sick. Once I lose 5 pounds, I'll be really happy with my body, but I will always be working and eating right and exercising to keep the 5 pounds off because that is very, very important to me. And however contradictory and sick and overrated and vain and anything else you can say about it, it's the truth. My bulimia, my exercising and even abstaining from food, they're tools for me to lose weight.

Economic and career achievement is a primary definition of success for men. Of course, men can also exhibit some self-destructive behaviors in pursuit of this success, such as workaholism or substance abuse. As we shall see, they are increasingly joining this cult. Delia's upbringing and environment defined success differently. She was not interested in earning $500,000 a year, but in marrying the guy who does. She learned to use any tool she could to stay thin, to look good, and to have a shot at her goal.

No wonder she was reluctant to give up her behavior. She was terrified of losing the important benefits of her membership in the Cult of Thinness. She knew she was hurting psychologically and physically, but in the final analysis, being counted among "the chosen" justified the pain.

> God forbid anybody else gets stuck in this trap. But I'm already there, and I don't really see myself getting out, because I'm just so obsessed with how I look. I get personal satisfaction from looking thin, and receiving attention from guys.

I told Delia about women who have suggested other ways of coping with weight issues. There are even those who advocate fat liberation, or who suggest that fat is beautiful. She was emphatic about these solutions:

> Bullshit. They live in la-la land. . . . I can hold onto my boyfriend because he doesn't need to look anywhere else. The bottom line is that appearance counts. And you can sit here and say, "I feel good about myself twenty pounds heavier," but who is the guy going to date?

A Woman's Sense of Worth

A woman's sense of worth in our culture is still greatly determined by her ability to attract a man. Body weight plays an important part in physical attraction. In research studies which asked people what attributes are most indicative of "positive appearance," weight was a key factor.[15] Social status is largely a function of income and occupation, which generally remains easier for men to achieve. Even a woman with a successful and lucrative career may fear that her success comes at the expense of her femininity. Feminist writer Naomi Wolf asserts:

> . . . For every feminist action there is an equal and opposite beauty myth reaction. In the 1980s it was evident that as women became more important, beauty too became more important. . . . Women's minds are persuaded to trim their desires and self-esteem neatly into the discriminatory requirements of the workplace, while putting the blame for the system's failures on themselves alone.[16]

FIGURE 1.2 A Woman's Sense of Worth: Borgata Babe, Borgata Hotel and Casino, 2005.

As women enter the labor market, weight again may have a role in determining their desirability for certain jobs [17] As recently as 2005, servers and bartenders at the Borgata Hotel Casino & Spa in Atlantic City, New Jersey, have been forced to step on a scale to keep their jobs there. Milford (2005), of *The News Journal*, writes:

> In February, the casino instituted a policy that says the so-called "Borgata Babes" can risk losing their job if they gain more than 7 percent of their baseline body weight and fail to lose it during a three-month leave of absence. For someone who weighs 110, that means 7.7 pounds. One of the attorneys representing a Borgata employee notes that women "are more likely for biological reasons to gain weight at certain times. What's more, it's harder for women to lose weight than it is for men. And, women weigh less than men, meaning their start weight gives them less wiggle room. For example, a 7 percent weight gain for a man who weighs 180 pounds is 12.6 pounds."[18]

In short, in compliance with the new Borgata weight policies, the less you weigh when you are hired—the less of a range you receive to gain weight in order to keep your job.

Trisha Hart and Renee Gaud are two Borgata employees who are upset with the casino's new weight policy and have filed lawsuits against Borgata.

> Hart, 28, of Wenonah, who was a 5-foot-9-inch, 144-pound size 6 when she was hired, said she lost 15 pounds and dropped to a size 0 costume because of an eating disorder and pressure from her superiors to lose weight. Her bosses commended and encouraged her when she lost weight, the complaint states. . . . Gaud, 35, of Mays Landing, who said she suffers from hypothyroidism, was a 5-foot-9 size 4 when she was hired in June 2003 but gained weight because of her condition, according to her complaint, filed April 19. When she asked for a bigger dress, the complaint alleges she was told: "Borgota Babes don't go up is size."[19]

Borgata Hotel Casino and Spa does not intend to back down, nor apologize, for its new policies. In fact, "The Borgata staunchly defends its weight policy. 'When people are putting a brand out there, they want a certain association with that brand,' Borgata chief operating officer Larry Mullin said. 'We've tried to elevate the position to be more than just somebody who serves a drink at a casino. It's an important part of what we offer here.'"[20] Apparently, Borgata is interested in "more than just somebody who serves a drink at [their] casino;" indeed, it seems Borgata has "elevated" this position to a "certain female body that serves."

Yet another example of an industry that often places demands on women to conform to particular physical appearance norms is the airline industry. Until recently, it created guidelines for flight attendants, a job considered to be women's work, which required a 5'5" inch female flight attendant to weigh 129 pounds or less. Every year dozens of flight attendants who could not meet these weight guidelines were fired. This begs the following questions: Who makes the rules? Is safety the only guideline? Can't a flight attendant be agile at 140 or 150 pounds? Is a weight limit a legitimate way of ensuring a safe flight? The Equal Employment Opportunity Commission (EEOC) and the Association of Professional Flight Attendants challenged these guidelines with a lawsuit, but a weight limit, though higher, continues to be in effect.

Cultural messages on the rewards of thinness and the punishments of obesity are everywhere. Most women accept society's standards of beauty as "the way things are," even though these standards may undermine self-image, self-esteem, or physical well-being. Weight concerns or even obsessions are so common among women and girls that they escape notice. Dieting is not considered abnormal behavior, even among women who are not overweight. But only a thin line separates "normal" dieting from (culturally induced) disordered eating.[21]

Culturally Induced Eating Disorders and the Cult of Thinness

There are several ways to view eating disorders. Early theories rely on what I have termed "individualistic" explanations. One theory assumes that an eating disorder is a reflection of a woman's psychosexual development. Women with eating disorders are said to fear oral impregnation and reject their sexuality.[22] Refusing food is one of the ways that an adolescent girl can gain some control and autonomy over the frightening changes in her body and her life. Psychotherapy is usually the treatment.

Another view has focused on biological causes. This view links eating disorders with depression, which may be caused by a chemical or metabolic defect, especially in women.[23] Drugs, sometimes in the form of hormones, are considered a dependable, quick, and inexpensive treatment.

Relatively recent thinking sees an eating disorder as the result of family dynamics. A power struggle between child and parent, especially the mother, leads to rejection of the mother as a role model.[24] This theory emphasizes relations between people rather than conflict within a person, and places little importance on wider factors outside a family unit. It is treated with family therapy.

These alternative views imply that the solution to an eating disorder lies within the individual or the family unit. Since the problem centers there, the person or family is also the target for change. Clearly, it is important to help individuals or families overcome their personality and even chemical "deficits" by identifying those at risk. But this approach often amounts to "blaming the victim."[25]

In Delia's history, evidence of psychological trauma might help us understand how her eating problem arose. She describes her dysfunctional family life when she was growing up:

> I think I first threw up in the hope of getting attention, because that was the year before my dad went into treatment for his alcoholism. Things were really bad at my house, as far as my parents fighting. If I could catch their attention that I was throwing up, maybe they wouldn't fight. . . .

But it did not have that effect. Amidst the emotional turmoil at home, she discovered the potent physical comfort of bingeing. By making herself vomit, she found a way to "eat her cake and get rid of it too." And she learned to keep it a secret. "Nobody knew."

There *are* psychological reasons for some of the eating problems occurring in young college women like Delia. Yet that perspective does not answer deeper questions: Why does Delia express her psychological distress through her body? If she had grown up in another era, would her distress manifest itself in another way, like Victorian hysteria, for example? Why does she continue this behavior, even when Mom and Dad have resolved their marital issues and her father has been a recovering alcoholic for many years? Why has this problem mushroomed at this point in history for so many women of her race, age, and class?

There are important economic and social forces behind Delia's growing "body trouble." The food, diet, fitness, and beauty industries, aided by the media, have systematically pressured many girls like Delia into believing their salvation lies in self-improvement, self-control, and achieving the ultra-slender body ideal. Social and cultural forces within the family, school, and peer group often join in by reflecting and amplifying these thinness messages.

The Cult of Thinness often includes "rewards" and "punishments" to urge women to shape their bodies toward the ideal. Delia comments on the enormous social rewards she receives for being in the "right" body; she gets male attention, her self-worth is bolstered, and she feels a sense of power and control. That potent experience points out the vast differences in how men and women feel about their bodies. A woman like Delia, who daily spends a great deal of time thinking about her body, is also amplifying the traditional mind/body split (woman as the body and man as the mind) within Western culture, as we shall see in chapter 2. She responds to thinness messages by "buying, trying, and complying" in an endless set of body rituals on the path to perfection.

Women may choose to spend thousands of dollars on body-work instead of investing in a purchase with a higher economic, educational, or intellectual return. In fact, by obsessively perfecting their bodies, they also are buying into a set of patriarchal values that may make them ever more dependent on men for approval and success.

Today's career-oriented, liberated woman is still exhorted to achieve "freedom and independence" through self-control: dieting, exercise, and beauty rituals. These ideals of freedom and independence are co-opted by those who stand to make millions of dollars on women's body insecurity. They couch the notion of women's freedom in purchasing terms: buy the fat-free candy bar promising thinness, the "free and clear" skin lotion promising an unblemished complexion, and the "freedom" bra promising to push up and artificially enlarge one's breasts. Women have "choices," but these are often limited to what color, what size bottle, and whether to use a credit or debit card.

Joining the Cult of Thinness is a process with a "continuum of participation." Individuals who have a healthy attitude toward food, weight, and body image are outside the spectrum. At one end of the continuum are the occasional dieters. At the other end are those who manifest both the *behaviors and personality characteristics* of "clinical eating disorders" like anorexia and bulimia.

Between these two poles is the growing population of "disorderly" eaters, who make up the Cult of Thinness membership. In my research on eating patterns and disorders among college students[26] I found an overwhelming number of women and some men with many of the *behavioral symptoms* associated with anorexia and bulimia. But few displayed the *psychological trauma* usually associated with clinical eating disorders. That is, they were obsessed with their weight and body image and often dieted, binged, and engaged in some behaviors associated with an eating disorder, such as fasting, using laxatives and diuretics, and even purging. But they did not demonstrate the psychological problems associated with full-blown eating disorders. We call these patterns of eating *"culturally induced"* eating disorders, which would not be diagnosed as abnormal on clinical measures, such as the Eating Disorders Inventory (EDI) and the Eating Attitudes Test (EAT). This type of eating has come to be known as "eating disorders not otherwise specified" (EDNOS).[27]

The Cultural Paradox

How is it that a thinness-worshipping nation is becoming fatter? The most recent statistics from the National Center for Health Statistics reveal that "30 percent of U.S. adults 20 years of age and older—over 60 million people—are obese." In addition, "the percentage of young people who are overweight has more than tripled since 1980. Among children and teens aged 6–19 years, 16 percent (over 9 million young people) are considered overweight."[28] The World Health Organization (WHO) states,

> According to the US Surgeon General, in the USA the number of overweight children has doubled and the number of overweight adolescents has tripled since 1980. The prevalence of obese children aged 6-to-11 years has more than doubled since the 1960s. Obesity prevalence in youths aged 12-17 has increased dramatically from 5% to 13% in boys and from 5% to 9% in girls between 1966-70, and 1988-91 in the USA.[29]

Obesity is in fact a rising global epidemic that affects all age and socioeconomic groups, and this "worldwide epidemic of obesity has been termed 'Globesity' by the WHO."[30]

Such data may seem to contradict our contention that we live in the shadow of a Cult of Thinness. Yet these two phenomena are not only congruent—they are inextricably linked. Our culture of fatness within our culture of thinness is

FIGURE 1.3 A Cultural Paradox Collage, 2005.

a paradox partly created by our capitalistic, weight-obsessed society. For example, the "fast-food industrial complex" has spread alarmingly across America, and beyond. Approximately 29% of Americans were getting their meals away from home in 1995, up from 1977, when only 16% consumed their meals outside the home.[31] It is estimated that 47.5% of the U.S. food dollar is spent on food prepared away from home.[32] In addition, according to Reed Mangels of the *Vegetarian Journal*, "The largest portion of calories from foods eaten away from home comes from fast food establishments . . . adults in general average 12% of calories from fast food, 10% from restaurants, and 11% from other places, including cafeterias, bars, others' homes, and vending machines. . . . Our reliance on convenience foods has serious health implications." [33] In addition, more Americans who eat at home are buying industrially prepared meals. As the global economy increasingly promotes commercialized and processed foods, individuals consume foods that are "high fat" and "energy dense," while low in most other forms of nutrition.[34]

Along with cheap and increasingly abundant food, we have a range of products (largely food- and drug-based) that promise we can lose weight quickly. However, these products frequently fail, creating the "rebound effect" when attempted weight loss results instead in weight gain, often accompanied by feelings of failure and low body-esteem. You can see the paradox at work in any supermarket checkout line—overweight Americans, their carts loaded with unwise choices, staring at skinny models on magazine covers promising the next "wonder diet."

Even though these consequences of dieting are common knowledge, the social accolades that a thin body promises supersede common sense, as "an end justifies the means" philosophy emerges. Furthermore, even when our common sense is readily available, we often learn to ignore our gut feelings and natural appetites in favor of a diet savior that promises us a better tomorrow.

Those who have joined the Cult are engaging in health-risking, even life-threatening behavior. At the very least, they are leading dissatisfied lives diminished by obsession. This volume offers young people, parents, clinicians, and educators an in-depth analysis of the Cult's origins. Looking at both sociocultural factors, such as capitalism and patriarchy, and individual factors, such as family and peer group influences, helps us understand why the Cult has spread so rapidly. New solutions to the problem of women's relationship with their bodies and food are suggested herein.

Notes

1. Willa Appel, *Cults in America: Programmed for Paradise* (New York: Holt, Rinehart and Winston, 1983), 11.
2. Janis H. Crowther, Eve M. Wolf, and Nancy E. Sherwood, "Epidemiology of Bulimia Nervosa," in *The Etiology of Bulimia Nervosa: The Individual and Familial Context*, ed. Janis H. Crowther, D.C. Tennenbaum, S.E. Hobfoll, and M.A. Stephens (Philadelphia: Hemisphere Publishing, 1992), 1–26. See also: C.M. Shisslak, M. Crago, and L.S. Estes, "The spectrum of eating disturbances," *International Journal of Eating Disorders*, 18, no. 3 (1995): 209–219. Thompson and Kinder (2003) note the number of women who have eating disorders outnumbers men by a ratio of 10 to 1. See: J.K. Thompson and B. Kinder, "Eating Disorders," in *Handbook of Adult Psychopathology*, ed. M. Hersen and S. Turner (New York: Plenum Press, 2003), 555–582.

   Thompson cites recent research results from a longitudinal study by Lewinsohn on the prevalence of eating disorders among young women who were followed for over 10 years. He notes: "Adolescent females were followed for more than 10 years and assessed periodically for the presence of eating disturbances. By age 24, 1.4% had anorexia nervosa and 2.8% had bulimia nervosa. Additionally, 4.4% met the criteria for a partial syndrome, similar to the subclinical diagnosis of eating disorder not otherwise specified." J. Kevin Thompson, "Preface: Eating Disorders and Obesity: Definitions, Prevalence, and Associated Features," in

Handbook of Eating Disorders and Obesity, ed. J. Kevin Thompson (Hoboken, NJ: John Wiley & Sons, 2004), xvi. See: P.M. Lewinsohn, *The Role of Epidemiology in Prevention Science,* Paper presented at the annual meeting of the Eating Disorders Research Society, Bernalillo, NM, December 2001.

3. Thomas F. Cash and Joshua I. Hrabosky, "Treatment of Body Image Disturbances," in *Handbook of Eating Disorders and Obesity,* ed. Kevin J. Thompson (Hoboken, NJ: John Wiley & Sons, 2004), 516. In fact, some research findings point to a worsening in the prevalence of body image dissatisfaction over the last quarter of a century for both sexes: As Cash and Hrabosky note:

    . . . the prevalence of body image dissatisfaction has worsened for *both* sexes over the span of 25 years. For example, the percentage of men dissatisfied with their overall appearance substantially increased between each period—15% in 1972, 34% in 1985, and 43% in 1996. The prevalence of women reporting overall appearance dissatisfaction also increased considerably over this period—23% in 1972, 38% in 1985, and 56% in 1996.

    Thomas F. Cash and Joshua I. Hrabosky, "Treatment of Body Image Disturbances," in *Handbook of Eating Disorders and Obesity,* ed. J. Kevin Thompson (Hoboken, NJ: John Wiley & Sons, 2004), 516.

4. Ann M. Gustafson-Larson and Rhonda Dale Terry, "Weight-Related Behaviors and Concerns of Fourth-Grade Children," *Journal of the American Dietetic Association,* 92, no. 7 (1992): 818–822.

5. Margo Maine, *Body Wars: Making Peace with Women's Bodies* (Carlsbad, CA: Gurze Books, 2000), 45.

6. Georgia Dullea, "Big Diet Doctor Is Watching You Reach for That Nice Gooey Cake," *New York Times,* December 1, 1991, p. 65(L).

7. Lauren F. Winner, "The Weigh and the Truth," *Christianity Today,* September 4, 2000, http://www.christianitytoday.com/ct/2000/010/1.50.html

8. Ibid.

9. Ibid.

10. Ibid.

11. Natalie Allon, "Fat Is a Dirty Word: Fat as a Sociological and Social Problem," in *Recent Advances in Obesity Research,* ed. A.N. Howard (London: Newman Publishing, 1975), 244–247. Allon's observations on one dieting organization spans 4 years.

12. For a discussion of the "sacred" and "profane" see Emile Durkheim, *The Elementary Forms of Religious Life,* trans. Joseph Ward Swain (New York: Collier Books, 1961), 52, 53.

13. The first-person accounts and some statistics in my book are based on data I gathered from a range of individuals. Part of this research is based on the original data I gathered from a longitudinal sample of college-age men and women concerning their eating patterns and disorders. The first data collection point consisted of a random sample of 395 sophomore students (282 females and 113 males) at a New

England university. Students responded to a questionnaire that covered eating habits, dieting, attitudes toward the self, family, friends, school, and related issues. We tapped the social, cultural, and psychological dimensions that affect students' attitudes about themselves and how these may relate to eating patterns. Included in the questionnaire were four different measures of eating disorders. Three of the measures are clinical tests that have been used in other research with student populations, which allowed us to compare our results with those studies. The measures are (1) the Eating Attitudes Test (EAT), (2) the Eating Disorders Inventory (EDI) (These two measures are used clinically to screen for anorexia and bulimia), and (3) a measure derived from the DSM-III criteria for bulimia. These three measures are scored to classify respondents as either normal or abnormal. The fourth measure was developed empirically in this study as a continuum measure to cover the entire range of eating patterns present in our sample. The measure allows us to identify patterns that lie anywhere between the extremes of normal and abnormal. We reinterviewed a subsample (second data collection point) of women respondents from this same study who were now in their senior year of college. We wanted to see what changes occurred in their eating attitudes and patterns from sophomore to senior years, as well as (third data point) 2 years post college. In addition, I conducted focus groups and one-on-one interviews with small convenience samples of ethnic group women at this same university, in order to expand my observations about ethnic minority women's weight and body issues. In addition, focus group interviews from a convenience sample of non-college-age women from different ethnic and class backgrounds, gay men and lesbian women, as well as preteen and adolescent girls from a range of class, race, and ethnic group backgrounds were also conducted over the course of 7 years from the mid-1990s until the present. Sharlene Hesse-Biber, *Am I Thin Enough Yet? The Cult of Thinness and the Commercialization of Identity* (New York: Oxford University Press, 1996).

14. Garfinkel's (1981) research supports this viewpoint. He notes that women's competitive striving for success can lead to the development of eating disorders in young women. See: Paul E. Garfinkel, "Some Recent Observations on the Pathogenesis of Anorexia Nervosa," *Canadian Journal of Psychiatry*, 26, no. 4 (1981): 218–222. See also: D.M. Garner and P.E. Garfinkel, "The Eating Attitudes Test: An Index of the Symptoms of Anorexia Nervosa," *Psychological Medicine*, 9, no. 2 (1979): 273–279.

15. See: T. Horvath, "Correlates of Physical Beauty in Men and Women," *Social Behavior and Personality*, 7 (1979): 141–151; T. Horvath, "Physical Attractiveness: The Influence of Selected Torso Parameters," *Archives of Sexual Behavior*, 10, no. 1 (1981): 21–24. See also: Sharlene Hesse-Biber, Alan Clayton-Matthews, and John A. Downey, "The Differential Importance of Weight and Body Image among College Men and Women," *Genetic, Social, and General Psychology Monographs*, 113, no. 4 (1987): 511–528.

16. Naomi Wolf, *The Beauty Myth* (New York: William Morrow, 1992, 28–29.

17. Esther D. Rothblum, "The Stigma of Women's Weight: Social and Economic Realities," *Feminism and Psychology,* 2, no. 1 (1992): 61-73.
18. Maureen Milford, "If You Don't Fit In—Watch Out," *News Journal,* June 20, 2005, http://www.delawareonline.com/apps/pbcs.dll/article?AID=/20050620/BUSINESS/506200301/1003
19. John Curran, "Servers File Discrimination Complaints over Casino Weight Limits," PhillyBurbs.com, April 27, 2005, http://www.phillyburbs.com/pb-dyn/news/104-04272005-481968.html
20. Suzette Parmley, "Weighty Conflict: A Casino and Its 'Borgata Babes' Are Facing Off," *Corvallis Gazette-Times,* June 6, 2005, http://www.gazettetimes.com/articles/2005/06/12/news/business/monbiz01.txt
21. Janet Polivy and C. Peter Herman, "Dieting and Binging: A Causal Analysis," *American Psychologist,* 40, no. 2 (1985): 193–201.
22. Hilde Bruch, *Eating Disorders: Obesity, Anorexia and the Person Within* (New York: Basic Books, 1973).
23. Harrison G. Pope and James I. Hudson, *New Hope for Binge Eaters: Advances in the Understanding and Treatment of Bulimia* (New York: Harper & Row, 1984).
24. Marlene Boskind-Lodahl and William C. White, Jr., "The Definition and Treatment of Bulimiarexia in College Women," *Journal of the American College Health Association,* 27 (1978): 84–86, 97.
25. William Ryan, *Blaming the Victim* (New York: Pantheon, 1971).
26. Sharlene Hesse-Biber, "Eating Patterns and Disorders in a College Population: Are College Women's Eating Problems a New Phenomenon?" *Sex Roles,* 20, no. 1/2 (1989): 71–89.
27. See: C. Norring, *Eating Disorders Not Otherwise Specified: Scientific and Clinical Perspectives on the Other Eating Disorders* (New York: Taylor & Francis, 2005). As Smolak and Striegel-Moore note, the category known as EDNOS in fact contains a variety of distinct subgroups:

    > The diagnosis of EDNOS includes several distinct subgroups: individuals whose eating disorder symptoms fail to reach the severity or duration threshold required for a diagnosis of AN [anorexia nervosa] or BN [bulimia nervosa], individuals with atypical eating disorders, and individuals whose clinical picture is marked by recurrent binge eating in the absence of the inappropriate compensatory behaviors that characterize BN. The latter clinical picture has been designated provisionally as BED, [binge eating disorder] an eating disorder in need of further study.

    Linda Smolak and Ruth H. Striegel-Moore, "Future Directions in Eating Disorder and Obesity Research," in *Handbook of Eating Disorders and Obesity,* ed. J. Kevin Thompson (Hoboken, NJ: John Wiley & Sons, 2004), 739.
28. Department of Health and Human Services, "CDC: Center for Disease Control and Prevention," http://www.cdc.gov/nccdphp/dnpa/obesity/
29. World Health Organization, "Obesity and Overweight," http://www.who.int/hpr/NPH/docs/gs-obesity.pdf

30. Gail Goldberg, "Obesity," *British Nutrition Foundation*, http://216.239.59.104/
search?q=cache:4gEWBajH_zYJ:www.nutrition.org.uk/upload/HP%25203
%2520obesity.pdf+gail+goldberg+obesity+british+nutrition+foundation+
globesity&hl=en
31. Biing-Hwan Lin, Joanne Guthrie, and Elizabeth Frazao, "The Diet Quality Balancing Act: Popularity of Dining out Presents Barrier to Dietary Improvements,"
Food Review, 21, no. 1 (1998): 2–10.
32. Reed Mangels, "Scientific Update: Review of Recent Scientific Papers Related to
Vegetarianism," *Vegetarian Journal*, 22, no. 1 (2003): par. 1, http://www.vrg.org/
journal/vj2003issue1/vj2003issue1scientific.htm
33. Ibid.
34. Gail Goldberg, "Obesity," *British Nutrition Foundation*, http://216.239.59.104/
search?q=cache:4gEWBajH_zYJ:www.nutrition.org.uk/upload/HP%25203%
2520obesity.pdf+gail+goldberg+obesity+british | nutrition+foundation+
globesity&hl=en

Bibliography

Allon, N. "Fat Is a Dirty Word: Fat as a Sociological and Social Problem." In *Re-
cent Advances in Obesity Research*, ed. A.N. Howard, pp. 244–247. London:
Newman Publishing, 1975.
Appel, W. *Cults in America: Programmed for Paradise*. New York: Holt, Rinehart and
Winston, 1983.
Berg, F.M. *Children and Teens Afraid to Eat*. Hettinger, ND: Healthy Weight Network,
2001.
Boskind-Lodahl, M. & W.C. White, Jr. "The Definition and Treatment of Bulimiarexia
in College Women." *Journal of the American College Health Association*, 27, no. 2
(1978): 84–86, 97.
Bruch, H. *Eating Disorders: Obesity, Anorexia and the Person Within*. New York:
Basic Books, 1973.
Cash, T.F., & J.I. Hrabosky. "Treatment of Body Image Disturbances." In *Handbook of
Eating Disorders and Obesity*, ed. J.K. Thompson, p. 515–541. Hoboken, NJ: John
Wiley & Sons, 2004.
Crowther, J.H., E.M. Wolf, & N.E. Sherwood. "Epidemiology of Bulimia Nervosa."
The Etiology of Bulimia Nervosa: The Individual and Familial Context. ed. J.H.
Crowther, D.L. Tennenbaum, S.E. Hobfoll, & M.A. Parris Stephens. Philadelphia:
Hemisphere Publishing, 1992.
Curran, J. "Servers File Discrimination Complaints over Casino Weight Limits."
PhillyBurbs.com, April 27, 2005. http://www.phillyburbs.com/pb-dyn/news/
104-04272005-481968.html
Department of Health and Human Services, "Overweight and Obesity: Home."
"Center for Disease Control and Prevention." http://www.cdc.gov/nccdphp/dnpa/
obesity/

Dullea, G. "Big Diet Doctor Is Watching You Reach for That Nice Gooey Cake." *New York Times,* December 1, 1991. p. 65(L).

Durkheim, E. *The Elementary Forms of Religious Life,* trans. J.W. Swain. New York: Collier Books, 1961.

Garfinkel, P.E. "Some Recent Observations on the Pathogenesis of Anorexia Nervosa." *Canadian Journal,* 26, no. 4 (1981): 218–222.

Garner, D.M., & P.E. Garfinkel. "The Eating Attitudes Test: An Index of the Symptoms of Anorexia Nervosa." *Psychological Medicine,* 9, no. 2 (1979): 273-279.

Goldberg, G. "Obesity." *British Nutrition Foundation.* http://216.239.59.104/search?q=cache:4gEWBajH_zYJ:www.nutrition.org.uk/upload/HP%25203%2520obesity.pdf+gail+goldberg+obesity+british+nutrition+foundation+globesity&hl=en

Gustafson-Larson, A.M., & R.D. Terry. "Weight-Related Behaviors and Concerns of Fourth-Grade Children." *Journal of the American Dietetic Association,* 92, no. 7 (1992): 818–822.

Hesse-Biber, S. *Am I Thin Enough Yet? The Cult of Thinness and the Commercialization of Identity.* New York: Oxford University Press, 1996.

Hesse-Biber, S. "Eating Patterns and Disorders in a College Population: Are Women's Eating Problems a New Phenomenon?" *Sex Roles,* 20, nos. 1/2 (1989): 71–89.

Hesse-Biber, S., A. Clayton-Matthews, & J.A. Downey, "The Differential Importance of Weight and Body Image among College Men and Women." *Genetic, Social and General Psychological Monographs,* 113, no. 4 (1987): 511–528.

Horvath, T. "Correlates of Physical Beauty in Men and Women." *Social Behavior and Personality* 7, no. 2 (1979): 141–151.

Horvath, T. "Physical Attractiveness: The Influence of Selected Torso Parameters." *Archives of Sexual Behavior,* 10, no.1 (1981): 21–24.

Lewinsohn, P.M. *The Role of Epidemiology in Prevention Science.* Paper presented at the annual meeting of the Eating Disorders Research Society, Bernalillo, NM, December 2001.

Lin, B.-H., J. Guthrie, & E. Frazao. "The Diet Quality Balancing Act: Popularity of Dining Out Presents Barrier to Dietary Improvements." *Food Review,* 21, no. 1 (1998): 2–10.

Maine, M. *Body Wars: Making Peace with Women's Bodies.* Carlsbad, CA: Gurze Books, 2000.

Mangels, R. "Scientific Update: Review of Recent Scientific Papers Related to Vegetarianism." *Vegetarian Journal,* 22, no. 1 (2003): par. 1. http://www.vrg.org/journal/vj2003issue1/vj2003issue1scientific.html

Milford, M. "If You Don't Fit In—Watch Out." *News Journal,* June 20, 2005. http://www.delawareonline.com/apps/pbcs.dll/article?AID=/20050620/BUSINESS/506200301/1003

Norring, C. *Eating Disorders Not Otherwise Specified: Scientific and Clinical Perspectives on the Other Eating Disorders.* New York: Taylor & Francis, 2005.

Parmley, S. "Weighty conflict: A Casino and Its 'Borgata Babes' Are Facing Off." *Corvallis Gazette-Times,* June 6, 2005. http://www.gazettetimes.com/articles/2005/06/12/news/business/monbiz01.txt

Polivy, J., and C.P. Herman. "Dieting and Binging: A Causal Analysis." *American Psychologist,* 40, no. 2 (1985): 193–201.

Pope, H.G., and J.I. Hudson. *New Hope for Binge Eaters: Advances in the Understanding and Treatment of Bulimia.* New York: Harper & Row, 1984.

Rothblum, E.D. "The Stigma of Women's Weight: Social and Economic Realities." *Feminism and Psychology,* 2, no. 1 (1992): 61–73.

Ryan, W. *Blaming the Victim.* New York: Pantheon, 1971.

Shisslak, C.M., M. Cargo, & L.S. Estes. "The Spectrum of Eating Disturbances." *International Journal of Eating Disorders,* 18, no. 3 (1995): 209–219.

Smolak, L., and R.H. Striegel-Moore. "Future Directions in Eating Disorder and Obesity Research." *Handbook of Eating Disorders and Obesity,* ed. J.K. Thompson, p. 738–754. Hoboken, NJ: John Wiley & Sons, 2004.

Thompson, J.K. "Preface: Eating Disorders and Obesity: Definitions, Prevalence, and Associated Features." In *Handbook of Eating Disorders and Obesity,* ed. J.K. Thompson, p. xii–xix. Hoboken, NJ: John Wiley & Sons, 2004.

Thompson, J.K., & B. Kinder. "Eating Disorders." *Handbook of Adult Psychopathology,* ed. M. Hersen & S. Turner, pp. 555–582. New York: Plenum Press, 2003.

Winner, L.F. "The Weigh and the Truth." *Christianity Today,* September 4, 2000. http://www.christianitytoday.com/ct/2000/010/1.50.html

Wolf, N. *The Beauty Myth.* New York: Anchor Books, 1992.

World Health Organization. "Obesity and Overweight." http://www.who.int/hpr/NPH/docs/gs-obesity.pdf

TWO

Men and Women: Mind and Body

*You know guys just sort of think you're stupid. Sure, I get a
lot of attention being blonde and female, but what society
really thinks of women is that intelligence doesn't even figure in. Just body and face. The time my mom asked me what
I was going to be when I grew up, I said I'd put myself on
the cover of a magazine. For men, it's the money they make,
not how they look. Nobody cares if a guy is a good father or
even a good person. He's the president of this company or
that, or the head doctor of such and such a hospital. It's his
job that counts.*

—Tracy, college sophomore

Our culture judges a man primarily in terms of how powerful, ambitious,
aggressive, and dominant he is in the worlds of thought and action. These are
qualities more of the mind than the body. A woman, on the other hand, is
judged almost entirely in terms of her appearance, her attractiveness to men,
and her ability to keep the species going. Her sexual body can even be quite
dangerous to a man on his way to success. She becomes a temptress distracting
him from his true work and the pursuit of rationality, knowledge, and power.

The split between mind and body is a central idea in Western culture. It
often frames our perceptions of what it means to be feminine and masculine.[1]
Well-known studies conducted by Paul Rosenkrantz [2] and his colleagues in the
1960s gave college students a list of extreme personality traits and their oppo-
sites: very passive versus very active; very illogical versus very logical; very
vain about appearance versus uninterested in appearance, and so on. The students were asked to ascribe each trait to either males or females, and to rank
each trait's social desirability. The findings from this study (and from others)
showed that traits most often associated with competence and social desirability were assigned to men, and those associated with having an "emotional" life
were assigned to women. Men were viewed as more independent than women,
more logical, more direct, more self-confident, and more ambitious. Women

were seen as being more gentle than men, more soft-spoken, more talkative, and more tender.

The problem with a dichotomy is that it provides no middle ground. If one trait is positive, then its opposite is negative—if a man is strong, then a woman is weak. But such a narrow view of human behavior ignores the reality that there are a range of traits common to both sexes.[3]

The college-age women I interviewed fully understood this mind and body gender stereotyping. Angela said:

> My body is the most important thing. It's like that's all I ever had because that's all everyone ever said about me. My mother would say that I am smart and stuff, but really they focused on my looks. And even my doctor enjoys my looks. He used to make me walk across the room to check my spine and he'd comment on how cute I walked, that I wiggled. Why comment on it at all?

She noted how difficult it is for women to be acknowledged for "male" attributes: "I think men are shocked when they see a gorgeous, really intelligent woman. You'll always hear about how 'gorgeous.' You don't hear or very rarely hear, 'She's a very intelligent woman.'"

As the Hydroxycut ad reveals (see Fig. 2-1), a woman's personality holds little importance once she achieves the ideal body—thus, we can surmise that when "the talk" centers on personality, it is only because she looks less than ideal.

Historical Roots of the Mind/Body Dichotomy

The notion of a split between mind and body dates back at least to ancient Greece. Aristotle, in the fourth century B.C., asserted that males were superior to women, whom he described as "monsters . . . deviated from the generic human type." Women were imperfect versions of the ideal form of humankind, "mutilated males," who were emotional and passive prisoners of their body functions.[4]

Scholar Donna Wilshire explains that Aristotle's world contained a variety of hierarchical dualisms: Soul ruled the body; reason was preferable to emotion. The Mind, which only a male could have, was said to be connected to the "divine" Soul. The female, therefore was incapable of reason:

> For him, Pure Mind ["Nous," only possible for males] is connected with "divine" Soul, which is supreme of all earthly things. The male Mind is therefore *higher* and *holier* than all matter, even higher than the beloved Apollonian [ideal, male] body; certainly the male Mind and Reason rule over and are "more divine" than the female body because she [being ruled by emotions and body functions] is not capable of Mind or Reason, and so on.[5]

Even Aristotle's theory of embryology states that all life (Soul) is contained in semen—the mother was merely a receptacle. All "true" babies were male babies, and a female child was considered a failure in the process.[6]

Aristotle's work powerfully influenced Christian doctrine. St. Augustine in the fifth century and St. Thomas Aquinas in the thirteenth century asserted the primacy of male over female. Thomas Aquinas stated, "As regards the individual nature, woman is defective and misbegotten, for the active force in the male seed tends to the production of a perfect likeness in the masculine sex."[7] His teacher, Albert the Great, went even further: ". . . one must be on one's guard with every woman, as if she were poisonous snake and the horned devil. . . . Her feelings drive woman toward every evil, just as reason impels man toward all good."[8] Her redemption from such evil did not lie in the development of her capacity to think, but in her duties as wife and mother.[9]

During the seventeenth century, the Enlightenment, knowledge required "objectivity."[10] A scientist was supposed to be detached from all emotional and personal considerations in order to ascertain "the truth." The very notion of the dispassionate scientist, whose mind transcended the body, defined science as a male pursuit.[11] The object of scientific knowledge, that is, nature, was female.

Sir Francis Bacon's description of the scientific process uses imagery that suggests a hunter (man) capturing and dominating prey (woman): ". . . you have but to hound nature in her wanderings and you will be able when you like to lead and drive her afterwards to the same place again. Neither ought a man to make scruple of entering and penetrating into those holes and corners when the inquisition of truth is his whole object."[12]

Because the body was considered to be of a lower order and in fact could interfere with the pursuit of the truth, women were viewed as incapable of scientific thinking. The medical literature of the time supported this view, replete with examples of the mind/body dichotomy, especially in theories of reproduction. During the nineteenth century, medical science claimed any type of mental work was too taxing to the female reproductive organs:

> Victorian scientists promoted the "cult of true womanhood,"[13] discouraged education for women because too much of women's energy would go to their brains, causing their reproductive organs to atrophy, and asserted that menstruation results in irrationality and loss of mental powers.[14]

Cultural rules have controlled women's bodies throughout history.[15] Our Anglo-American legal institutions, for example, created laws based on the biological differences between men and women. U.S. laws enacted at the turn of the century regulated the number of hours per day or week that women were allowed to work. Other laws prevented them from working at night or in certain occupations like mining or smelting. This "protective legislation" drove women out of certain jobs, while it gained reduced hours for men in those occupations where women remained. In addition, domestic relations laws (those concerning property rights, pension benefits, maternity leave policies, etc.) have reinforced the idea that women are reproducers (the reproductive body) and men are breadwinners (the rational mind).[16]

For those of us embedded in a particular society, it is sometimes difficult to see how culture controls women's bodies. In the United States today, women who diet or have their breasts enlarged and their tummies tucked regard this as an exercise of free will. But if we compare these practices with two historical examples, one from ancient China and the other from the Victorian era, we may gain a new perspective.

Ancient China and the Practice of Foot Binding

For 1,000 years, the Confucian philosophy of hierarchical patriarchal authority formed the basis of Chinese society. Males were considered higher than females, and the old had authority over the young. As Confucius, born in 551

B.C., wrote, "Women are, indeed, human beings, but they are of a lower state than men."[17]

Foot binding, one of the most dramatic examples of control over such "lower beings," originated around the tenth century, with court dancers who wrapped their feet to imitate pointed, sickle moons (not unlike toe shoes in Western ballet). The Chinese court and the upper class had always prized small feet in women: Now they copied this practice and took it to extremes. It became an important symbol of high status within Chinese society. In time, it filtered down to the masses as well.[18]

This custom lasted more than 1,000 years and served to virtually cripple women in the name of beauty and femininity. Little girls had their toes bent under into the sole, with the heel and toes bowed forcibly together, and wrapped tightly. The bones eventually broke and the foot could no longer grow. This severely deformed clubfoot, only a few inches long, became known as the "lotus" or "lily" foot. Walking on these stumps was painful, if not impossible.

One young girl described suffering intensely:

> I was inflicted with the pain of foot binding when I was seven. I was an active child but from then on my free and optimistic nature vanished. Mother consulted references in order to select an auspicious day for it. She shut the bedroom door, boiled water, and from a box withdrew binding, shoes, knife, needle and thread. "Today is a lucky day," she said. "If bound today, your feet will never hurt; if bound tomorrow, they will." She then bent my toes toward the plantar [the mid-region of the sole] with a binding cloth ten feet long and two inches wide, doing the right foot first, and then the left. She ordered me to walk, but the pain proved unbearable.
>
> That night, mother wouldn't let me remove the shoes. My feet felt on fire and I couldn't sleep, mother struck me for crying. On the following days, I tried to hide but was forced to walk on my feet. Mother hit me on my hands and feet for resisting. Mother would remove the bindings and wipe the blood and pus which dripped from my feet. She told me that only with removal of the flesh could my feet become slender.
>
> . . . Every two weeks, I changed to new shoes. After changing more than ten pairs of shoes, my feet were reduced to a little over four inches. I had been binding for a month when my younger sister started; when no one was around we would weep together.[19]

Why did women, especially mothers, continue a custom that inflicted such suffering?[20]

The bound foot, a symbol of feminine beauty, represented a woman's only prospects in life. Inheritance laws of Chinese society were male dominated. Unable to inherit property or pass on the ancestral name, a girl was an economic liability until she left to join her husband's family. A good match with prosperous in-laws offered a girl's parents a chance to recoup their investment.[21] While the bride's parents could gain social and economic status, the groom's parents acquired another source of labor, both productive and reproductive. Upper-class women did not work outside their homes, but even though foot-bound, they still performed household chores, made handicrafts, and attended to the needs of their extended families.[22] Even peasant families who dreamed of marrying into a higher class crippled their daughters accordingly. Only the poorest female field workers escaped.[23]

This custom lasted as long as it did because it reinforced the patriarchal authority of Chinese society. Foot binding supported society's belief in the dichotomy between mind and body, and supported dualistic thinking (men were superior and women inferior; men were valued and women devalued). Women followed a strict line of obedience, first to fathers, then to husbands, and finally to sons upon the death of the husband.[24]

> The minds of footbound women were as contracted as their feet. Daughters were taught to cook, supervise the household, and embroider shoes for the golden Lotus. Intellectual and physical restriction had the usual male justification. Women were perverse and sinful, lewd and lascivious, if left to develop naturally. The Chinese believed that being born a woman was payment for evils committed in a previous life. Footbinding was designed to spare a woman the disaster of another such incarnation.[25]

Foot binding also restricted female mobility and sexuality, which are potential sources of power and resistance for women in preindustrial societies. As Susan Greenhalgh notes in her research on women in Old China:

> The greatest threat to the family system came from the women because they married *in* from an *outside* family. Women marrying into the patriarchal family could disrupt its stability by offering dissenting opinions about the allocation of labor and goods within the family, or by simply refusing to accept patterns of authority and interaction already established, and returning to their natal homes.[26]

Along with their bound feet, girls had to embrace a set of personality traits: "chaste and yielding, calm and upright"; "not talkative yet agreeable" in speech; "restrained and exquisite" in appearance and demeanor; engaged in work which demonstrated her skills in "handiwork and embroidery."[27] Upper-class Chinese women, who spent a great deal of time and energy (and pain) on this feminine ideal, were unlikely to challenge the established order.

Sexuality, another threat, also had to be channeled. Binding limited the possibility of extramarital affairs, since the bound woman could not leave the home unaided. Finally, as a prominent aspect of feminine identity, the bound foot was an important part of sexual rituals—even a focal point of sexual excitement. "The tiny and fragile appearance of the foot aroused in the male a combination of lust and pity. He longed to touch it, and being allowed to do so meant that the woman was his."[28]

Foot binding in ancient China seems grotesque and cruel, but it can help us understand the current Cult of Thinness. Foot binding reflected the economic and social power structure of a patriarchal society, which defined women in terms of their bodies—"commodities" for domestic economic exchange and social control.

When societies make the transition from medieval or traditional political-economic systems, like ancient China, to modern systems, power within that society shifts from centralized authority to various institutional powers, including those controlled by patriarchal interests.[29] A dominant force in modern society, capitalism in its early form relied on the *external* control of women's bodies, as in the practice of corseting.[30] But over time this control has become more *internal,* through self-imposed body practices and rituals. Because modern women are also consumers, this focus on their bodies has created many multibillion-dollar industries.

The Rise of Consumer Culture and the Practice of Corseting

Women wore the corset in England, the United States, and Western Europe for most of the nineteenth century, when the rise of capitalism led to women's emerging roles as both consumer and commodity.

The image of the Victorian woman was, in part, a response to the dramatic changes that accompanied industrialization. Vast economic expansion created a large, prosperous middle class. Work became segregated from the home, where the middle-class woman was expected to stay, supported by a well-to-do husband.

She was also expected to be a fragile, pure creature, submissive to her spouse and subservient to domestic needs. Her decorative value, a quality that embraced her beauty, her character, and her temperament, defined her. This ideal, later referred to as the "cult of true womanhood," demanded uncompromising virtue.[31] Like the rich woman of ancient China, the Victorian woman became a prized showpiece, evidence of her husband's wealth. As managers of hearth and home, middle- and upper-class wives became the chief consumers of early capitalists' products.[32]

Instead of the clubbed "lotus" foot, the important symbols of beauty and status for women were paleness, fragility, and a tightly cinched waist. The waist had a special erotic significance symbolizing passivity, dependence, and, more perversely, bondage.[33] The proud husband encircling his wife's waist in his broad hands, notes one researcher, demonstrated power and control.[34] According to one French beauty writer, Pauline Mariette:

> The waist is the most essential and principal part of the woman's body, with respect to the figure. . . . The bee, the wasp . . . those are the beings whose graceful and slender waist is always given as the point of comparison. . . . The waist gives woman her jauntiness, the pride of her appearance, the delicacy and grandeur of her gait, the unconstraint and delight of her pose.[35]

To attain such an ideal, a tightly laced undergarment reinforced with whalebone, and later steel, constricted women's waists for many hours a day.[36] This pressure often caused pain and distorted the internal organs. One zealous mother laced her daughter's stays too tightly and killed her at the age of 20:[37] ". . . her ribs had grown into her liver, and that her other entrails were much hurt by being crushed together with her stays, which her mother had ordered to be twitched so straight that it often brought tears into her eyes whilst the maid was dressing her."[38] The following description is more common:

> I ordered a pair of stays, made very strong and filled with stiff bone, measuring only fourteen inches round the waist. With the assistance of my maid, I managed to lace my waist to eighteen inches. At night I slept in my corset. The next day my maid got my waist to seventeen inches, and so on, an inch every day, until she got them to meet. For the first few days, the pain was very great, but as soon as the stays were laced close, and I had worn them so for a few days, I began to care nothing about it, and in a month or so I would not have taken them off on any account. For I quite enjoyed the sensation, and when I let my husband see me in a dress to fit I was amply repaid for my trouble.[39]

A tight corset prevented women from moving around very much, which tended to make them dependent and submissive.[40] Like the family furniture, a wife was considered a possession. Indeed, many were nearly as immobile as furniture. "Accounts of nineteenth-century house fires reveal that women occasionally went up in flames with the household goods because of immobilizing corsets and skirts too full to run in."[41]

Why did women corset themselves so willingly? Like the women of ancient China, their identities and rewards depended on their body image. One historian commented: "In an age when alternatives to marriage for women were grim and good husbands scarce, the pressures to conform to the submissive ideal that men demanded were enormous."[42]

Patriarchal interests, which characterized women primarily as wives, mothers, and decorative objects, complemented an economy relying more and more on domestic consumption.[43] Capitalism motivated producers to create new needs and exploit new markets, most of which centered around the body and its functioning. Advertising was also crucial in helping to define women as the primary consumers. It promoted insecurity by encouraging women "to adopt a critical attitude toward body, self and life style." They rushed to purchase the latest household items, which were important symbols of being a good wife and mother. They flocked to buy beauty products, which were signs of a woman's femininity and ability to hold on to her man. As long as a woman viewed her body as an object, she was controllable and profitable.[44]

The Origins of the Cult of Thinness: From External to Internal Body Control

Nineteenth-century industrialization and mass production influenced body image in general for both sexes. In her book *Never Too Thin*, social historian Roberta Seid points out that for women, beauty was becoming democratized as ready-made clothing introduced the idea of standard sizes.[45] The machine age promoted a streamlined aesthetic. "While . . . slenderness had been associated with sickness and fragility, now many health authorities cautioned against overeating and excess weight."[46] New studies related obesity to premature mortality. By the turn of the century, technological innovation, efficiency, and economic growth reinforced the ideal of a slender body, providing metaphors for the desired human body. "To be as efficient, as effective, as economical, as beautiful as the sleek new machines, as the rationalized workplace. . . . It was these . . . developments that forged the society we know today and that established the framework for our prejudice against fat."[47] In general, Seid notes that men were not bound by the pressure to look slender. A new male image, the "self-made" man, arose with the coming of the Industrial Revolution and the Protestant ethic. The "self-made" man strives for upward mobility through hard work, ability, and thrifty ways, not his physical appearance.[48] In fact men's clothing remained relatively unchanged over many decades.[49]

Twentieth-century capitalism included the diet, beauty, cosmetic, fitness, and health industries. Along with modern patriarchy, it continues to control women into the twenty-first century through pressures to be thin.[50] Increasingly, modern woman achieves this new ideal not through the purchase of a corset or girdle, but through self-directed dieting and exercise. Taken to the extreme, this self-direction becomes an eating disorder.[51]

The shift from external to internal control was part of the ideology of "women's independence." As the nineteenth century drew to a close, middle-class women were increasingly involved in social reform, volunteer activities, and work outside the home such as teaching and nursing.[52] By 1870 more were entering college, and by the 1890s they were beginning to compete with men in such professions as law, medicine,[53] and journalism. A new interest in physical fitness led doctors to prescribe women's tennis, golf, swimming, horseback riding, and bicycling. Dancing was the rage. Suffragettes were marching for the right to vote. Women were becoming more physically mobile, and abandoning their tight corsets.[54]

Of course, the 1920s women's movement threatened the traditional view of how men and women focused their lives, and a predictable backlash followed. Just as women were demanding more "space" and equality, the culture's standards of attractiveness demanded that they shrink.[55] A slender female body, achieved though dieting, became the dominant image for most of the twentieth century.[56]

In effect, patriarchal and consumer interests co-opted and harnessed women's newfound independence. In order to attain the ultra-slender ideal, women began to purchase diet products and to spend enormous amounts of time and energy on their bodies.[57] These activities continue to divert economic and emotional capital away from other investments women might make, like political activism, education, and careers, which might empower women and change their thinking about mind and body.

Even during the first wave of feminism, the slim, youthful, albeit rather sexless "flapper" of the 1920s became the most important symbol of American beauty. She had a straight, boyish figure, and exposed her slender legs. As one historian notes, it was a trivialized image:

> On the one hand, she indicated a new freedom in sensual expression by shortening her skirts and discarding her corsets. On the other hand, she bound her breasts, ideally had a small face and lips . . . and expressed her sensuality not through eroticism, but through constant, vibrant movement. . . . The name "flapper" itself bore overtones of the ridiculous. Drawing from a style of flapping galoshes popular among young women before the war, it connoted irrelevant movement.[58]

Psychiatrist John A. Ryle observed that cases of anorexia nervosa increased during the Flapper Era, which he attributed to "the spreading of the slimming fashion" and "the more emotional lives of the younger generation since the War."[59] Researchers at a 1926 New York Academy of Science conference on adult weight reported an outbreak of eating problems, which they linked to a "psychic contagion." One physician described a significant increase in the number of women whose dramatic weight reduction led to mental breakdown and hospitalization.[60]

However, "the flapper along with the entire exuberant culture of the 1920s vanished into the abyss of the Depression and then the consuming preoccupations of the Second World War."[61] Hemlines fell in the 1930s, and the defined waist returned. The ideal woman of the 1930s still had plenty of curves, but overall she remained slim.

The late 1940s and 1950s saw a temporary interruption of a long-term trend toward slenderness. Political and social reaction after World War II drove many white middle-class women out of their war effort jobs and back to their kitchens[62] in a period of "resurgent Victorianism."[63] As the economy switched back to domestic production, it urged women again to focus on a consumer role. Young men used the G.I. Bill to pay for educations and buy first homes. The "family wage" was enough to support a family, and it also justified why women should be paid less. While women still went to college, their numbers in the professions declined and many opted to marry upon leaving school. Economic expansion and the rise of suburbia created the white middle-class housewife.[64]

To complete the picture of domestic bliss, American fashion in the 1950s revived the hourglass figure. The girdle, long full skirts, and even crinolines came back to create a silhouette not unlike the Victorian lady. Hollywood provided a busty new feminine image, first personified by Marilyn Monroe, and later carried to extremes by the "Mammary Goddesses" like Jayne Mansfield.[65]

The Ultra-Slender Ideal

Within a decade, however, thin was back in. This time, the super-slim body ideal met and merged with other social influences. These forces included a new feminist movement and changes in women's roles, the increasing power of the media, and rampant consumerism. As Seid says:

> The imperative to be thin became monolithic as fashion's decrees were reinforced and pushed by all cultural authorities—the health industry, the federal government, employers, teachers, religious leaders, and parents until the concept became so self sustaining, so internalized that no reinforcement was necessary.[66]

The women's movement of the 1960s offered alternative visions to the "happy housewife" of the 1950s. Women began to close the gap in higher education, and their numbers in the labor force, with and without children, increased dramatically. The contraceptive revolution gave women some increased control over their own fertility.[67]

Yet as women gained economic, social, and political resources with which to chart their own destinies, the pressure to shrink in body size returned.[68] The media began to play a dominant role in this pressure. In the 1960s, films were no longer the most important influence in defining beauty. Instead, television, the American fashion industry, and women's magazines became the arbiters of image. Fashion photography, showcasing clothing, demanded stick-thin bodies.[69] In the mid-1960s, a 17-year-old, 5'6", 97-pound British model entered the American fashion scene. Her name was Twiggy. She became an instant celebrity and many young women began to emulate her. Understandably, researchers point to this decade as the era of marked increase in eating disorders.[70]

Of course, another major fashion influence, the Barbie doll, had already arrived. Writing in the magazine *Smithsonian*, Doug Stewart notes, "If all the Barbies sold since 1959 were laid head to heeled foot . . . they would circle the earth three and a half times."[71] CNN reports that "more than a billion Barbies have been sold in 150 countries." CNN news reporter Aaron Brown offers this account:

> Barbie was invented in 1959 and then it was revolutionary. Ruth Handler insisted that her doll have breasts. Baby dolls had dominated the market until Barbie came along. Someone once figured out that had the original Barbie been human, she would have been about 5'6" and her figure would have been 39-18-33. Barbie was an immediate sensation. The company that sold the doll, Mattel, became an instant success story. Ruth Handler and a Barbie model even rang the closing bell at the New York Stock Exchange.[72]

Barbie demonstrates that while roles can change over time, one may never find relief from the Cult of Thinness. "She was a model in 1959, a career girl in 1963, a surgeon in 1973 and an aerobics instructor in 1984."[73] Her body image includes exaggerated breasts, impossibly long legs, nonexistent hips, and a waist tinier than a Victorian lady's. This is the "perfect figure" presented to little girls. Barbie's 2006 line includes dolls with such names as "Hard Rock Café Barbie Doll" and "Peppermint Obsession Barbie Doll," as well as "Maiko Barbie Doll" from Mattel's "World Culture/Dolls of the World Barbie Collection." The Mattel company describes her as having "white makeup, a traditional hairstyle, white socks and Japanese sandals, she's the picture of femininity."[74] The most current Barbies sold online, for example through Target stores, features them in professional dress; however, their femininity is always assured, as in the case of the new "Barbie Pet Doctor," which Mattel describes wearing a "cute printed lab coat."[75] If I were a bit more cynical, I might wonder who really *is* the pet.

Women's magazines also contribute to the obsession with image, fashion, and thinness. One researcher points out that

> women's magazines collectively comprise a social institution which serves to foster and maintain a cult of femininity. This cult is manifested both as a social group to which all these born females can belong, and as a set of practices and

beliefs: rites and rituals, sacrifices and ceremonies, whose periodic performance reaffirms a common femininity and shared group membership. In promoting a cult of femininity, these journals are not merely reflecting the female role in society; they are also supplying one source of definitions of, and socialization into, that role.[76]

Why are women who have gained some economic independence still expressing their self-reliance and inner control through these body rituals? An opposing view suggests that dieting and physical fitness are not methods for the subordination of women, but ways that women can feel powerful. After all, for many women, feeling fat means feeling powerless. However, by investing time, money, and energy on attaining a thin body, women may be substituting a momentary sense of power for "real authority." Some feminists take the argument even further, pointing out that being overweight is, itself, a way of expressing power. In *Fat is a Feminist Issue*, Susie Orbach notes that being overweight is one way to say "no" to feeling powerless. A fat person defies Western notions of beauty and challenges, in Orbach's words, "the ability of culture to turn women into mere products."[77] Kim Chernin says that in a feminist age, men feel drawn to and perhaps less threatened by women with childish bodies because "there is something less disturbing about the vulnerability and helplessness of a small child, and something truly disturbing about the body and mind of a mature woman."[78]

The fact remains that regardless of their economic worth, women are socialized to rely on their "natural" resources—beauty, charm, and nurturance—to attract the opposite sex.[79] The stakes of physical attractiveness for women are high, since appearance, including body weight, affects social success.[80] Research studies suggest that college-age women experience even a few extra pounds as a major problem in their lives. Women report more dissatisfaction with their weight and body image than men, and in fact many women willingly embrace the mind/body dichotomy, partly because the woman who invests herself in her body often reaps enormous rewards and benefits. Ignoring investments in one's body can mean the loss of both self-esteem and social status.[81]

I do not want to imply that all women are enslaved by bodily concerns (or that all men are the "enemy"). Throughout history, many women have found ways to resist or alter controlling social practices. For example, the exaggeratedly corseted Victorian figure drew attention to the waist and enhanced the bosom, and some women began to use it to express their sexuality. In time, political conservatives reacted to the way women subverted the intent of corseting. They decried the practice as a sign of loose morals.[82]

It would be hard to portray all women as "victims." Women frequently collude in promoting body rituals. Like the mothers who bound their daughters' feet or tightened their corsets, today's mom may recommend the latest diet and fitness club to her daughter. Many women try to cut deals with the system. For Delia, in the previous chapter, dieting for a culturally correct body was a way to catch a rich husband. For other young women, working out in the gym may build the confidence they need to compete with men in the work world.

In a way, women's bodies are cultural artifacts, continually molded by history and culture.[83] Subjected to such pressures, the "natural body" gets lost. What replaces it may be the bewigged eighteenth-century countess, the waspwaisted Victorian housewife, the leggy flapper, or the waif modeling Calvin Klein jeans. All are bodily reflections of the play of power within a society.[84]

In the next chapter, I examine this power play in the "body business." The marriage between patriarchy and capitalism brings both institutions enormous rewards. Without looking at this alliance, we lose an important piece of the Cult of Thinness puzzle.

Notes

1. See Michelle Zimbalist Rosaldo, "Women, Culture and Society: A Theoretical Overview," in *Women, Culture and Society*, ed. Michelle Zimbalist Rosaldo and Louise Lamphere (Palo Alto, CA.: Stanford University Press, 1974). See also: Shirley B. Ortner, "Is Female to Male as Nature Is to Culture?" in *Women, Culture and Society*, ed. Michelle Zimbalist Rosaldo and Louise Lamphere (Palo Alto, CA: Stanford University Press, 1974) p. 67–88. Both these authors note that women are symbolized as closer to nature and men are more closely identified with culture. Male activities are given preference over female activities.

2. Paul Rosenkrantz, Susan Vogel, Helen Bee, and Donald Broverman, "Sex-Role Stereotypes and Self-Concepts in College Students," *Journal of Consulting and Clinical Psychology,* 32 (1968): 287–291. See also: P.A. Smith and E. Midlarksy, "Empirically Derived Conceptions of Femaleness and Maleness: A Current View," *Sex Roles*, 12, no. 3/4 (1985): 313–328, R.J. Canter and B.E. Meyerowitz, "Sex-Role Stereotypes: Self-Reports of Behavior," *Sex Roles*, 10, no. 3/4 (1984): 293–306.

3. See: Nancy Jay, "Gender and Dichotomy," *Feminist Studies*, 7, no. 1 (1981): 37–56. See also: G. Lloyd, *The Man of Reason: "Male" and "Female" in Western Philosophy* (London: Methuen, 1984); Eleanor Maccoby and Carol Nagy Jacklin, *The Psychology of Sex Differences* (Palo Alto, CA.: Stanford University Press, 1974); Marion Lowe, "Social Bodies: The Interaction of Culture and Women's Biology," in *Biological Woman: The Convenient Myth*, ed. R. Hubbard, M.S. Henifin, and B. Fried, pp. 91–116 (Cambridge, MA.: Schenkman Publishing, 1982). See also: C.F. Epstein, *Deceptive Distinctions: Sex, Gender, and the Social Order* (New Haven, CT: Yale University Press, and New York: Russell Sage Foundation, 1988), chapter 4.

4. See: Aristotle, "Politicia" and "De Generatione Animalium," in *The Works of Aristotle,* trans. Benjamin Jowelt, ed. W.D. Ross and J.A. Smith (London: Oxford, 1921). Cited in Donna Wilshire, "The Uses of Myth, Image, and the Female Body in Re-Visioning Knowledge," *Gender/Body/Knowledge: Feminist Reconstructions of Being and Knowledge,* ed. Alison M. Jagger and Susan R. Bordo (New Brunswick, NJ: Rutgers University Press, 1989), 92–114.

5. Donna Wilshire, "The Uses of Myth, Image, and the Female Body in Re-Visioning Knowledge," in *Gender/Body/Knowledge: Feminist Reconstructions of Being and Knowledge,* ed. Alison M. Jagger and Susan R. Bordo (New Brunswick, NJ: Rutgers University Press, 1989), 92–114.

6. See: Nancy Tuana, "The Weaker Seed: The Sexist Bias of Reproductive Theory," in *Feminism and Science,* ed. Nancy Tuana (Bloomington: Indiana University Press, 1989), 147–171.

7. Thomas Aquinas, "Summa Theologiae," 1:92, in Anthony Synnot, *The Body Social: Symbolism, Self and Society* (New York: Routledge, 1993), 46.

8. Cited in Anthony Synnot, *The Body Social: Symbolism, Self and Society* (New York: Routledge, 1993), 45.

9. Dawn H. Currie and Valerie Raoul, "The Anatomy of Gender: Dissecting Sexual Difference in the Body of Knowledge," in *Anatomy of Gender: Women's Struggle for the Body,* éd. Dawn H. Currie and Valerie Raoul (Ottawa, Canada: Carleton University Press, 1992), 2–3.

10. Dawn H. Currie and Valerie Raoul, "The Anatomy of Gender: Dissecting Sexual Difference in the Body of Knowledge," in *Anatomy of Gender: Women's Struggle for the Body,* ed. Dawn H. Currie and Valerie Raoul (Ottawa, Canada: Carleton University Press, 1992), 11–34. Currie and Raoul note:

> Descartes maintained that the mind exists independently of bodily need and individual experience. He posited that, through the exercise of reason, the thinker could acquire a view of the world which transcends its point of origin. Knowledge achieved through Cartesian reason was thus called objective, in that it is severed from emotional and political considerations, and universal, in that it is able to assume a "bird's eye" view of the social world. (1–2)

11. Evelyn Fox Keller offers a psychoanalytic view of how science becomes a male pursuit. Objectivity is not inborn and requires the separation of self from others. The mother plays a crucial role in the child's development of a self. Fox Keller underscores this observation and notes that the motherly influence does not impact just daughters. Young boys are socialized by their mothers, resulting in feelings of insecurity that propel them to separate from the mother figure. Consequently, boys align themselves with their fathers for a different relationship and role model for their own development. She notes that over time this developmental task results in a firm somewhat exaggerated sense of autonomy and makes males more suited to the pursuit of objectivity. Girls, on the other hand, develop less of a sense of separation from the mother that may "complicate her development of autonomy by stressing dependency and subjectivity as feminine characteristics." See: Evelyn

Fox Keller, "Gender and Science," *Psychoanalysis and Contemporary Thought: A Quarterly of Integrative and Interdisciplinary Studies*, 1 (1978): 409–433. See also: Susan Bordo, *The Flight to Objectivity: Essays on Cartesianism and Culture* (Albany: State University of New York Press, 1987). Many of these ideas are theoretically grounded in Nancy Chodorow's work. See: Nancy Chodorow, *The Reproduction of Mothering: Psychoanalysis and the Sociology of Gender* (Berkeley: University of California Press, 1978).

12. Francis Bacon, quoted in Carolyn Merchant, *The Death of Nature: Women, Ecology and the Scientific Revolution* (New York: Harper & Row, 1989), 168.

13. The cult of the "True Woman" was typified by characteristics of purity, piety, domesticity, and submissiveness. See: Sharlene Hesse-Biber and Gregg Lee Carter, *Working Women in America: Split Dreams*, (2nd ed.). (New York: Oxford University Press, 2005), chapter 2.

14. Zuleyma Tang Halpin, "Scientific Objectivity and the Concept of 'The Other,'" *Women's Studies International Forum*, 12, no. 3 (1989): 288.

15. Ruth Berman notes that the dualist rationalism of Aristotle and Plato demonstrates how society's rulers limit and distort the understanding of even profound thinkers in their desire to maintain the status quo in their self-interest. Leaders have historically and currently used the practice of invoking an apparently natural hierarchy of human worth to justify widely disparate economic and social conditions. Ruth Berman, "From Aristotle's Dualism to Materialist Dialectics: Feminist Transformation of Science and Society," in *Gender/Body/Knowledge: Feminist Reconstructions of Being and Knowing*, ed. Alison M. Jagger and Susan R. Bordo (New Brunswick, NJ: Rutgers University Press, 1989), 224–255; *Body/Politics: Women and the Discourses of Science*, ed. Mary Jacobus, Evelyn Fox Keller and Sally Shuttleworth (New York: Routledge, 1990).

Many social theorists have remarked on the importance of the body as a central mechanism of social control. See: Michel Foucault, *Discipline and Punish: The Birth of Prison*, trans. Alan Sheridan (New York: Pantheon Books, 1977); Bryan S. Turner, *The Body and Society* (New York: Basil Blackwell, 1984); Mike Featherstone, Mike Hepworth, and Bryan S. Turner (Eds.), *The Body: Social Process and Cultural Theory* (Newbury Park, CA.: Sage Publications, 1991); Barry Glassner, *Bodies* (New York: Putnam, 1988); Susan R. Bordo, "The Body and the Reproduction of Femininity: A Feminist Appropriation of Foucault," in *Gender/Body/Knowledge: Feminist Reconstructions of Being and Knowing*, ed. Alison M. Jagger and Susan R. Bordo (New Brunswick, NJ: Rutgers University Press, 1989), 13–33.

16. See: Susan Lehrer, *Origins of Protective Labor Legislation for Women: 1905–1925*. (Albany: State University of New York Press, 1987). See also: Zillah R. Eisenstein, *The Female Body and the Law*. (Berkeley: University of California Press, 1988).

17. James W. Bashford, *China: An Interpretation* (New York: Abingdon Press, 1961), 128. Cited in Susan Greenhalgh, "Bound Feet, Hobbled Lives: Women in Old China," *Frontiers*, 2, no. 1 (1977): 17–21.

18. See: Wolfram Eberhard, "Introduction" in Howard S. Levy, *Chinese Footbinding: The History of a Curious Erotic Custom* (New York: Walton Rawls Publisher, 1966), 15–19; Susan Greenhalgh, "Bound Feet, Hobbled Lives: Women in Old China," *Frontiers,* 2, no. 1 (1977): 17–21.

19. Howard S. Levy, *Chinese Footbinding: The History of a Curious Erotic Custom* (New York: Walton Rawls publisher, 1966), 26–27.

20. C. Fred Blake notes that a mother who bound her daughter's feet considered it a sign of caring. Blake notes: "The 'tradition' could not have passed from mothers to daughters if not for mothers' credibility as 'caring.' The conundrum of a mothers' care consciously causing her daughter excruciating pain is contained in a single word, *teng,* which . . . refers to 'hurting,' 'caring,' or a conflation of both in the same breath" (682). See: C. Fred Blake, "Foot-binding in Neo-Confucian China and the Appropriation of Female Labor," *Signs: Journal of Women in Culture and Society,* 19, no. 3 (1994): 676–712.

21. Fei Hsiao-tung, *China's Gentry: Essays in Rural-Urban Relations* (Chicago: University of Chicago Press, 1953), 32, 84; Chow Yung-ten, *Social Mobility in China: Status Careers among the Gentry in a Chinese Community* (New York: Atherton Press, 1966). Both cited in Susan Greenhalgh, "Bound Feet, Hobbled Lives: Women in Old China," *Frontiers,* 2, no. 1 (1977): 7–21.

22. Anthropologist C. Fred Blake notes, however, that by binding women's feet Chinese society "masked" the real contribution of women's labor to the overall economy: "The material contributions that women made to the family were indeed substantial. They included women's traditional handiwork—making items like clothes and shoes—as well as their biological contributions in making sons for the labor-intensive economy" (700). He notes that binding women's feet, a symbol of their labor power, made it easier for the family system to take over their labor power (707–708). See: C. Fred Blake, "Foot-binding in Neo-Confucian China and the Appropriation of Female Labor," *Signs: Journal of Women in Culture and Society,* 19, no. 3 (1994): 676–712.

23. Anthropologist C. Fred Blake notes that " 'big feet' of ordinary women were demeaned as clumsy and crude and as a disaster to the natural foundation—the productivity—of the civilized world" (693). C. Fred Blake, "Foot-binding in Neo-Confucian China and the Appropriation of Female Labor," *Signs: Journal of Women in Culture and Society,* 19, no. 3 (1994): 676–712.

24. Susan Greenhalgh, "Bound Feet, Hobbled Lives: Women in Old China," *Frontiers,* 2, no. 1 (1977): 7–21. (See especially p. 12.)

25. See: Andrea Dworkin, *Woman Hating* (New York: Dutton, 1974), 103–104. Anthropologist C. Fred Blake points to several socialization processes which reinforced the mind/body dualism in Ancient China. He notes:

> Boys' and girls' modes of self-realization, of becoming their respective bodies in relationship to others differed completely. The boys' self-realization focused on the locutionary and literary power of the world. The girls' self-realization required her not merely to become, but to "overcome her body" by restricting the space it filled. . . . The difference was drama-

tized in innumerable little ways . . . for instance, a daughter having her feet bound might receive a writing brush from her mother. The writing brush was a powerful symbol of masculinity and the world of civil affairs. But unlike her brother, the little girl did not receive the brush with the hope that she might learn how to shape literary discourse. Instead, she grasped the "point" of the brush in the hope that her feet might acquire its "pointed" shape. (681)

C. Fred Blake, "Foot-binding in Neo-Confucian China and the Appropriation of Female Labor," *Signs: Journal of Women in Culture and Society,* 19, no. 3 (1994): 676–712.

26. Susan Greenhalgh, "Bound Feet, Hobbled Lives: Women in Old China," *Frontiers,* 2, no. 1 (1977): 13.

27. See: Susan Greenhalgh, "Bound Feet, Hobbled Lives: Women in Old China," *Frontiers,* 2, no. 1 (1977): 12. See also: Florence Ayscough, *Chinese Women Yesterday and Today* (Boston: Houghton Mifflin, 1937); C. Fred Blake, "Foot-binding in Neo-Confucian China and the Appropriation of Female Labor," *Signs: Journal of Women in Culture and Society,* 19, no. 3 (1994): 685.

28. Howard S. Levy, *Chinese Footbinding: The History of a Curious Erotic Custom* (New York: Walton Rawls Publisher, 1966), 32. For an extensive discussion of the erotic nature of the bound foot, see: Bernard Rudofsky, *The Kimono Mind* (New York: Doubleday, 1965).

29. Michel Foucault, *Discipline and Punish: The Birth of the Prison,* trans. Alan Sheridan (New York: Pantheon Books, 1977).

30. It is important to point out that males were also subjected to body rituals and practices. Early capitalism with its mechanization of production needed disciplined bodies to do the mundane work routines in the early factory system. Using the body as a central arena of disciplinary power and control allowed nineteenth-century capitalism to operate efficiently and profitably. As Dreyfus and Rabinow note: "Without the insertion of disciplined, orderly individuals into the machinery of production, the new demands of capitalism would have been stymied." Hubert L. Dreyfus and P. Rabinow, *Michel Foucault: Beyond Structuralism and Hermeneutics* (Chicago: University of Chicago Press, 1983), 135. A worker's body was equated with that of a machine (whereas women workers were considered a lower-paid category compared with males). In his approach known as "Taylorism," Frederick Taylor, founder of "scientific management," envisioned a worker as part of the machinery of production. Through the application of scientific principles, specifically the technique of "time and motion studies," he proposed to ascertain how to get the most efficiency out of a given worker, ignoring some of the humanistic aspects of work. See: Frederick Taylor, *Principles of Scientific Management* (New York: W.W. Norton, 1967).

31. Ann Gordon, Mari Jo Buhle, and Nancy Schrom, "Women in American Society: An Historical Contribution," *Radical America,* 5, no. 4 (July-August 1971): 3–66.

32. Kathryn Weibel, *Mirror, Mirror: Images of Women Reflected in Popular Culture* (New York: Anchor Books, 1977), 176–177. Kathryn Weibel argues that the

separation in roles fostered by the Industrial Revolution was reflected in the disparity in comfort and ornamentation between men's and women's clothes. The
Industrial Revolution generated a larger, relatively wealthy, middle class of men.
As has been the case historically, wives were expected to display the wealth of
their husbands, becoming more "ornamented" and more "stuffed-looking" as
middle class wealth increased during the nineteenth century.

33. Fashion historian Valerie Steele notes that "the vast majority of women of all
classes wore corsets and the degree of tightness varied according to design of
dress, social occasion and age, personality and figure of the individual woman."
See: Valerie Steele, *Fashion and Eroticism: Ideals of Feminine Beauty from the
Victorian Era to the Jazz Age* (New York: Oxford University Press, 1985), 162.
See also: Helen E. Roberts, "The Exquisite Slave: The Role of Clothes in the
Making of the Victorian Woman," *Signs: Journal of Women in Culture and
Society,* 2, no. 3 (1977): 554–569.

34. Kathryn Weibel, *Mirror, Mirror: Images of Women Reflected in Popular Culture*
(NewYork: Anchor Books, 1977), 180. While establishing links between social or
cultural influences and illness is difficult, it has been suggested that a form of anemia, known as chlorosis, reflected the cultural repression women experienced during the Victorian Era. Joan Brumberg notes that chlorosis, an illness characterized
by weakness, fainting, and passivity was widespread among young women in the
United States dating from 1870 to 1920. See: Joan J. Brumberg, "Chlorotic Girls,
1870–1920: A Historical Perspective on Female Adolescence," *Child Development,* 53, no. 6 (1982): 1468–1477. Other researchers suggest that rates of
classical conversion hysteria may be another example of the importance of cultural pressures, in this case an environment where sexual repression and dependency were primary characterizations of women's role. Donald M. Schwartz,
Michael G. Thompson, and Craig L. Johnson, "Anorexia Nervosa and Bulimia:
The Socio-Cultural Context," *International Journal of Eating Disorders,* 1, no. 30
(1982): 20–36.

35. Pauline Mariette, *L'Art de la Toilette,* (Paris: Librairie Centrale, 1866), 40–41.
Cited in Valerie Steele, *Fashion and Eroticism: Ideals of Feminine Beauty from the
Victorian Era to the Jazz Age* (New York: Oxford University Press, 1985), 108.

36. Lawrence Stone compares corset makers with those who practice orthodontia. He
notes that corset makers were "the affluent equivalents of the orthodontists of
the late twentieth-century America, who also cater for a real need as well as a
desire for perfection in a certain area thought to be important for success in life."
See Lawrence Stone, *The Family, Sex and Marriage in England 1500–1800* (New
York, Harper & Row, 1977). As cited in William Bennett and Joel Gurin, *The
Dieter's Dilemma: Eating Less and Weighing More* (New York: Basic Books,
1982), 183. Another researcher points out that many medical professionals were
not very aware and concerned with the effects of tight lacing. One historian
hypothesizes that women who fainted were not necessarily suffering from psy-
chosomatic illnesses, but the effects of tight lacing. See: Mel Davies, "Corsets and
Conception: Fashion and Demographic Trends in the Nineteenth Century,"
Comparative Studies in Sociology and History, 24, no. 4 (1982): 611–641.

37. William Bennett and Joel Gurin, *The Dieter's Dilemma: Eating Less and Weighing More* (New York: Basic Books, 1982), 183.
38. Lawrence Stone, *The Family, Sex and Marriage in England 1500–1800* (New York: Harper & Row, 1977). As cited in William Bennett and Joel Gurin, *The Dieter's Dilemma: Eating Less and Weighing More* (New York: Basic Books, 1982), 183.
39. *Englishwoman's Domestic Magazine*, 3d ser.4 (1868): 54. Cited in Helen E. Roberts, "The Exquisite Slave: The Role of Clothes in the Making of the Victorian Woman," *Signs: Journal of Women in Culture and Society*, 2, no. 3 (1977): 564.
40. See: Lorna Duffin, "The Conspicuous Consumptive: Woman as an Invalid," in *The Nineteenth Century Woman, Her Cultural and Physical World*, ed. Sara Delamont and Lorna Duffin (London: Croom Helm, 1978), 26–56; Barbara Ehrenreich and Deirdre English, *For Her Own Good: 150 Years of the Experts' Advice to Women* (Garden City, NY: Anchor Books, 1979); Helen E. Roberts, "The Exquisite Slave: The Role of Clothes in the Making of the Victorian Woman," *Signs: Journal of Women in Culture and Society*, 2, no. 3 (1977): 554–569; Thorstein Veblen, *The Theory of the Leisure Class* (New York: Random House, Modern Library, original work published 1899).

There are caveats on interpreting the corset as primarily a means for subordinating women. Valerie Steele notes:

> The idea that nineteenth century (male dominated) society forced women into submissive and masochistic behavior is not really substantiated by the sartorial and documentary evidence. Even though most women were economically dependent on men, and may have needed to conform to male ideals to a certain extent, women's self-images and sexuality were not completely male defined. . . . My own research, has indicated that the clothing of the Victorian woman reflected not only the cultural prescriptive ideal of femininity but also her own aspirations and fantasies. . . . The Victorian woman played many often contradictory and ambiguous roles, but she cannot be characterized as a prude, a masochist or a slave.

Valerie Steele, *Fashion and Eroticism: Ideals of Feminine Beauty from the Victorian Era to the Jazz Age* (New York: Oxford University Press, 1985), 100–101.

While many historians saw the corset as a means of socially controlling women, not all are in agreement with this thesis. One historian argues that those who opposed corseting in the nineteenth century were socially conservative males who felt tight-lacing was a symbol of women's resistance to male authority (579). From this perspective, tight-lacing provided women with a means to express their sexuality and to gain some degree of power over their oppressive situation. David Kunzel notes: "In vain the preachers threatened women who exposed their breasts with cancer of the breast. In vain the preachers and physicians threatened provocatively corseted women with every anathema, disease, and even death itself" (574). See: David Kunzle, "Dress Reform as Antifeminism: A Response to Helene E. Robert's 'The Exquisite Slave: The Role of Clothes in the Making of the Victorian

Woman,'" *Signs,* 2, no. 3 (1977): 570–579. See also: Valerie Steele, *Fashion and Eroticism: Ideals of Feminine Beauty from the Victorian Era to the Jazz Age* (New York: Oxford University Press, 1985), 161–191.

41. Kathryn Weibel, *Mirror, Mirror: Images of Women Reflected in Popular Culture* (New York: Anchor Books, 1977), 179.

42. Helen E. Roberts, "The Exquisite Slave: The Role of Clothes in the Making of the Victorian Woman," *Signs: Journal of Women in Culture and Society,* 2, no. 3 (1977): 564.

43. It is important to note that patriarchal interests were also threatened during early industrialism. Capitalism challenged patriarchal power by separating the home from the workplace. Ehrenreich and English (1979) note: "The household was left with only the most biological activities—eating, sex, sleeping, the care of small children . . . birth, dying and the care of the sick and aged." Furthermore, "It was now possible for a woman to enter the market herself and exchange her labor for the means of survival." See: Barbara Ehrenreich and Deidre English, *For Her Own Good: 150 Years of the Experts' Advice to Women* (Garden City, NY: Anchor Books, 1979), 10, 13, 27.

44. Mike Featherstone, "The Body in Consumer Culture," *Theory, Culture and Society,* 1, no. 2 (1982): 20. See also: Stuart Ewen, *Captains of Consciousness: Advertising and the Roots of the Consumer Culture* (New York: McGraw Hill, 1976); Joseph Hansen and Evelyn Reed, *Cosmetics, Fashions and the Exploitation of Women* (New York: Pathfinder Press, 1986); Heidi Hartmann, "Capitalism, Patriarchy and Job Segregation by Sex," *Signs: Journal of Women in Culture and Society,* 1, no. 3 (1976): 137–169.

45. Roberta Seid provides an excellent detailed historical analysis of American society's movement toward slenderness. See especially: chapter 5, Roberta Pollack Seid, *Never Too Thin: Why Women Are at War with Their Bodies* (New York: Prentice-Hall Press, 1989); see also: Stuart Ewen and Elizabeth Ewen, *Channels of Desire: Mass Images and the Shaping of the American Consciousness* (New York: McGraw-Hill, 1982).

46. Ibid., 85.

47. Ibid., 83.

48. Ibid.,115.

49. Ibid.,115.

50. Barbara Ehrenreich and Deidre English, *For Her Own Good: 150 Years of the Experts Advice to Women* (Garden City, NY: Anchor Books, 1979); Stuart Ewen, *Captains of Consciousness: Advertising and the Roots of Consumer Culture* (New York: McGraw-Hill, 1976); Joseph Hansen and Evelyn Reed, *Cosmetics, Fashions and the Exploitation of Women* (New York: Pathfinder Press, 1986); Heidi Hartmann, "Capitalism, Patriarchy, and Job Segregation by Sex," *Signs: Journal of Women in Culture and Society,* 1, no. 3 (1976): 137–169; Brett Silverstein, *Fed Up! The Food Forces That Make You Fat, Sick and Poor* (Boston: South End Press, 1984).

51. Sharlene Hesse-Biber, "Women, Weight and Eating Disorders: A Socio-Cultural and Political-Economic Analysis," *Women's Studies International Forum,* 14, no.

3 (1991): 173–191; Susan Bordo, *Unbearable Weight: Feminism, Western Culture and the Body* (Berkeley University of California Press, 1993).

52. Mary Frank Fox and Sharlene Hesse-Biber, *Women at Work* (Palo Alto CA: Mayfield Publishing, 1984), 19.

53. In the late 1800s, a large number of women entered medicine. The percentage of women in the 1893–1894 medical graduating classes in the Boston area was 23.7%. Women accounted for 17% of Boston's medical community. But, by the end of World War I, the numbers of women dropped off. See: Augusta Greenblatt, "Women in Medicine," *National Forum: The Phi Beta Kappa Journal*, 61, no. 4, (1981): 10–11.

54. For a detailed discussion of this transition, see: Lois Banner, *American Beauty*, (Chicago: The University of Chicago Press, 1983); and William Bennett and Joel Gurin, *The Dieter's Dilemma: Eating Less and Weighing More* (New York: Basic Books, 1982), especially chapter 7, titled "The Century of Svelte."

55. See: Susie Orbach, *Hunger Strike: The Anorectic's Struggle as a Metaphor of Our Age* (New York: W.W. Norton, 1986), 75.

56. Roberta Pollack Seid, *Never Too Thin: Why Women Are at War with Their Bodies* (New York: Prentice Hall, 1989).

57. Ibid.

58. See: Lois W. Banner, *American Beauty* (New York: Knopf, 1983), 279.

59. John A. Ryle, "Discussion of Anorexia Nervosa," *Proceedings of the Royal Society of Medicine*, 32 (1939): 735–737. It is important to note that documented cases of anorexia nervosa were cited in the medical literature well before this time. See: William Gull, "Anorexia Nervosa (Apepsia Hysterica, Anorexia Hysterica)," *Transactions of the Clinical Society of London*, 7 (1974): 22–28; and (English language translation) Ernest-Charles Lasegue, "On Hysterical Anorexia," *Medical Times and Gazette*, no. 2, September 6, 1873, 22–28. pp. 265–266; September 27, 1873, pp. 367–369. Historian Edward Shorter points out however: "It is only in the decade before the first world war that references to anorexia in aid of modish thinness and romantic acceptance begin to proliferate." Edward Shorter, "The First Great Increase in Anorexia Nervosa," *Journal of Social History*, 21, no. 1 (1987): 82. Roberta Pollack Seid notes that even though there was a "slenderness craze" during this time (which she dates from 1919 to 1935), the pursuit of thinness was very different from that of the post-1960s decades: "the craze did not create the hysteria or the terrible effects on women that we know today. The positive associations with plumpness were too recent and too well entrenched to be easily eradicated." See: Roberta Pollack Seid, *Never Too Thin: Why Women Are at War with Their Bodies* (New York: Prentice Hall, 1989), 97.

60. "Weight Reduction Linked to the Mind," *New York Times*, p. 6, February 24, 1926.

61. Richard A. Gordon, *Anorexia and Bulimia: Anatomy of a Social Epidemic* (Cambridge, MA: Basil Blackwell, 1990), 78.

62. See: William Bennett and Joel Gurin, *The Dieter's Dilemma: Eating Less and Weighing More* (New York: Basic Books, 1982), 207.

63. Lois W. Banner, *American Beauty* (New York: Knopf, 1983), 283.

64. This is amply documented in Betty Friedan, *The Feminine Mystique* (New York: Norton, 1963).
65. Historian Lois Banner notes that during the 1950s women's sports suffered a setback. Banner states: "With few exceptions, the kind of acclaim accorded to individual women sports stars in the 1920s and 1930s no longer existed, and the commercial women's swimming and basketball teams popular in these earlier decades faded from view. . . . In high schools and colleges, women's athletics similarly came to occupy a modest position vis-à-vis men's sports." Lois W. Banner, *American Beauty* (New York: Knopf, 1983), 285. During the 1950s, there was evidence of the flapper in the image of Debbie Reynolds and Sandra Dee. Sandra Dee played the popular Gidget, who was portrayed as looking for a husband and not serious about a career. See: Lois W. Banner, *American Beauty* (New York: Knopf, 1983), 283.
66. Roberta Pollack Seid, *Never Too Thin: Why Women Are at War with Their Bodies* (New York: Prentice Hall, 1989), 257.
67. Mary Frank Fox and Sharlene Hesse-Biber, *Women at Work* (Palo Alto, CA: Mayfield Publishing, 1984).
68. An empirical test of this theory on changing body image comes from a study by Silverstein, Perdue, Peterson, Vogel, and Fantini (1986). They studied the standards of bodily attractiveness across time and note that over the course of the twentieth century, as the proportion of American women who worked in the professions or who graduated from college increased, the standard of bodily attractiveness became less curvaceous. They note that this occurred especially in the 1920s and during the 1960s. Thinness may be considered a sign of conforming to a constricting feminine image (like corseting), whereas greater weight may convey a strong, powerful image. See: Brett Silverstein, Lauren Perdue, Barbara Peterson, Linda Vogel, and Deborah A. Fantini, "Possible Causes of the Thin Standard of Bodily Attractiveness for Women," *International Journal of Eating Disorders,* 5, no. 5 (1986): 135–144.
69. Lois W. Banner, *American Beauty* (New York: Knopf, 1983), 266–287.
70. Allan Mazur, "U.S. Trends in Feminine Beauty and Overadaptation," *Journal of Sex Research,* 22, no. 3 (1986): 281–303.
71. Doug Stewart, "In the Cutthroat World of Toy Sales, Child's Play is Serious Business," *Smithsonian,* 20, no. 9 (December, 1989,): 80.
72. Aaron Brown, "Look Back at Those Who Passed in 2002." *CNN NewsNight,* December 31, 2002, http://transcripts.cnn.com/TRANSCRIPTS/0212/31/asb.00.html
73. Doug Stewart, "In the Cutthroat World of Toy Sales, Child's Play is Serious Business," *Smithsonian,* 20, no. 9 (December, 1989): 72–84.
74. Mattel, Inc. "Doll Showcase: 2006 Line" from Barbie B Collector, 2005, http://collectdolls.about.com/ About, Inc. a part of the New York Times, Company. 2006.
75. Target. "Dolls + Accessories: Barbie, Target.com (2005).
76. Marjorie Ferguson, *Forever Feminine: Women's Magazines and the Cult of Femininity* (London: Heinemann, 1983), 184.

77. Susie Orbach, *Fat Is a Feminist Issue* (New York: Berkeley Press, 1978), 21.
78. See: Kim Chernin, *The Obsession: Reflections on the Tyranny of Slenderness* (New York: Harper & Row, 1981), 110.
79. Pauline B. Bart, "Emotional and Social Status of the Older Woman," in *No Longer Young: The Older Woman in America: Occasional Papers in Gerontology.* Ann Arbor: University of Michigan, Institute of Gerontology, 1975, 321; Daniel Bar-Tal and Leonard Saxe, "Physical Attractiveness and Its Relationship to Sex-Role Stereotyping," *Sex Roles,* 2, no. 2 (1976): 123–133; Peter Blumstein and Pepper W. Schwartz, *American Couples: Money, Work and Sex* (New York: William Morrow, 1983); Glen H. Elder "Appearance and Education in Marriage Mobility," *American Sociological Review,* 34 (1969): 519–533; Susan Sontag, "The Double Standard of Aging," *Saturday Review,* 55, no. 39 (1972): 29–38.
80. Sharlene Hesse-Biber, Alan Clayton-Matthews, and John Downey, "The Differential Importance of Weight among College Men and Women," *Genetic, Social and General Psychology Monographs,* 113, no. 4 (1987): 511–538.
81. R. Pingitore, B. Spring, and D. Garfield, "Gender Differences in Body Satisfaction. "*Obesity Research,* 5, no. 5, (1997): 402–409. See: M. Tiggemann, "Gender Differences in the Interrelationships between Weight Dissatisfaction, Restraint, and Self-esteem," *Sex Roles,* 30, no. 5–6 (1994): 319–330. The authors point out that feeling fat is related to women's self-esteem.
82. David Kunzle, "Dress Reform as Antifeminism: A Response to Helene E. Roberts' 'The Exquisite Slave: The Role of Clothes in the Making of the Victorian Woman," *Signs: Journal of Women in Culture and Society,* 2, no. 3 (1977): 570–579. The wearing of men's clothing in the 1930s and 1940s and the "Annie Hall" look in the late 1970s and early 1980s might be interpreted as a way women resisted the dominant fashion trends which sought to control them. In *The Language of Clothes* (New York: Vintage Books, 1983), historian Alison Lurie notes:

> The wearing of men's clothes can mean many different things. In the thirties, sophisticated actresses such as Marlene Dietrich in top hat and tails and elegantly cut suits projected sophistication, power and a dangerous eroticism. The slacks and sweaters of the war period, and the jeans and pants outfits of the sixties and early seventies, were serious gestures toward sexual equality. (229)

Lurie further points out how these images, especially the Annie Hall look, could turn into an "ironic antifeminist message," In her words: "Because they are worn several sizes too large, they suggest a child dressed up in her daddy's or older brother's things for fun, and imply 'I'm only playing; I'm not really big enough to wear a man's pants, or do a man's job'" (229).
83. Barbara Ehrenreich and Deirde English, *For Her Own Good: 150 Years of the Experts' Advice to Women* (Garden City, NY: Anchor Books); Zillah R. Eisenstein, *The Female Body and the Law* (Berkeley: The University of California Press, 1988); Emily Martin, *The Woman in the Body: A Cultural Analysis of Reproduction* (Boston: Beacon Press, 1987); Helena Michie, *The Flesh Made*

Word: Female Figures and Women's Bodies (New York: Oxford University Press, 1987); Gayle Rubin, "The Traffic in Women," in *Toward an Anthropology of Women*, ed. Rayna R. Reiter (New York: Monthly Review Press, 1975), 157–210; Bryan S. Turner, *The Body and Society* (New York: Basil Blackwell, 1984); Susan Bordo, "Anorexia Nervosa: Psychopathology as the Crystallization of Culture," in *Feminism and Foucault: Reflections on Resistance*, ed. Irene Diamond and Lee Quinby (Boston: Northeastern University Press, 1988), 87–117.

84. Michel Foucault, *Discipline and Punish: The Birth of Prison.* trans. Alan Sheridan. (New York: Pantheon Books, 1977).

Bibliography

Aquinas, T. "Summa Theologiae" 1:92. In *The Body Social: Symbolism, Self and Society,* edited by A. Synnot, pp. 43–46. New York: Routledge, 1993.

Aristotle. "Politicia" and "De Generatione Animalium." In *The Works of Aristotle,* trans. B. Jowelt, ed. W.D. Ross & J.A. Smith. London: Oxford, 1921.

Ayscough, F. *Chinese Women Yesterday and Today.* Boston: Houghton Mifflin, 1937.

Banner, L.W. *American Beauty.* New York: Knopf, 1983.

Bart, P.B. "Emotional and Social Status of the Older Woman." (p. 3–21) In *No Longer Young: The Older Woman in America* (Proceedings of the 26th Annual Conference on Aging), ed. P. Bart. Ann Arbor: University of Michigan, Institute of Gerontology, 1975.

Bar-Tal, D., & L. Saxe. "Physical Attractiveness and Its Relationship to Sex-Role Stereotyping." *Sex Roles,* 2, no. 2 (1976): 123–133.

Bennett, W., & J. Gurin. *The Dieter's Dilemma: Eating Less and Weighing More.* New York: Basic Books, 1982.

Berman, R. "From Aristotle's Dualism to Materialist Dialectics: Feminist Transformation of Science and Society." In *Gender/Body/Knowledge, Feminist Reconstructions of Being and Knowing,* edited by A.M. Jagger & Susan R. Bordo. New Brunswick, NJ: Rutgers University Press, 1989.

Blake, F.C. "Foot-binding in Neo-Confucian China and the Appropriation of Female Labor." *Signs: Journal of Women in Culture and Society,* 19, no. 3 (1994): 676–712.

Blumstein, P., & P.W. Schwartz. *American Couples: Money, Work and Sex.* New York: William Morrow, 1983.

Bordo, Susan. "Anorexia Nervosa: Psychopathology as the Crystallization of Culture." In *Feminism and Foucault: Reflections on Resistance,* ed. I. Diamond & L. Quinby, 87–118. Boston, MA: Northeastern University Press, 1988.

Bordo, S. "The Body and the Reproduction of Femininity: A Feminist Appropriation of Foucault." In *Gender/Body/Knowledge: Feminist Reconstructions of Being and Knowing.* ed. A.M. Jagger & S.R. Bordo. New Brunswick, NJ: Rutgers University Press, 1989. pp. 13–33.

Bordo, S. *The Flight to Objectivity : Essays on Cartesianism and Culture.* Albany: State University of New York Press, 1987.

Bordo, S. *Unbearable Weight: Feminism, Western Culture and the Body.* Berkeley: University of California Press, 1993.

Brown, A. "Look Back at Those Who Passed in 2002." CNN NewsNight Aaron Brown, December 31, 2002. http://transcripts.cnn.com/TRANSCRIPTS/0212/31/asb.00.html

Brumberg, J.J. "Chlorotic Girls, 1870–1920: A Historical Perspective on Female Adolescence." *Child Development,* 53, no. 6 (1982): 1468–1477.

Canter, R.J. and B.E. Meyerowitz. "Sex-Role Stereotypes: Self-Reports of Behavior," *Sex Roles,* 10, no. 3/4 (1984): 293–306.

Chernin, K. *The Obsession: Reflections on the Tyranny of Slenderness.* New York: Harper & Row, 1981.

Chodorow, N. *The Reproduction of Mothering: Psychoanalysis and the Sociology of Gender.* Berkeley: University of California Press, 1978.

Currie, D.H., & V. Raoul. "The Anatomy of Gender: Dissecting Sexual Difference in the Body of Knowledge." In *Anatomy of Gender: Women's Struggle for the Body,* ed. D.H. Currie & V. Raoul, pp. 1–34. Ottawa, Canada: Carelleton University Press, 1992.

Davies, M. "Corsets and Conception: Fashion and Demographic Trends in the Nineteenth Century" *Comparative Studies in Sociology and History,* 24, no. 4 (1982): 611–641.

Dreyfus, H.L., & P. Rabinow. *Michel Foucault: Beyond Structuralism and Hermeneutics.* Chicago: University of Chicago Press, 1983.

Duffin, L. "The Conspicuous Consumptive: Woman as an Invalid." *The Nineteenth Century Woman, Her Cultural and Physical World,* ed. S. Delamont & L. Duffin. London: Croom Helm, 1978.

Dworkin, A. *Woman Hating.* New York: Dutton, 1974.

Eberhard, W. "Introduction." In *Chinese Footbinding: The History of a Curious Erotic Custom,* by H.S. Levy, New York: Walton Rawls, 1966.

Ehrenreich, B., & D. English. *For Her Own Good: Years of the Experts' Advice to 150 Women.* Garden City, NY: Anchor Books, 1979.

Eisenstein, Z.R. *The Female Body and the Law.* Berkeley: University of California Press, 1988.

Elder, G.H. "Appearance and Education in Marriage Mobility." *American Sociological Review,* 34, no. 4 (1969): 519–533.

Englishwoman's Domestic Magazine, 3d ser. 4 (1868): 54. In H.E. Roberts, "The Exquisite Slave: The Role of Clothes in the Making of the Victorian Woman." *Signs: Journal of Women in Culture and Society,* 2, no. 3 (1977): 564.

Epstein, C.F. *Deceptive Distinctions: Sex, Gender, and the Social Order.* New Haven, CT: Yale University Press, and New York: Russell Sage Foundation, 1988.

Ewen, S. *Captains of Consciousness: Advertising and the Roots of Consumer Culture.* New York: McGraw Hill, 1976.

Ewen, S., & E. Ewen. *Channels of Desire: Mass Images and the Shaping of the American Consciousness.* New York: McGraw-Hill, 1982.

Featherstone, M. "The Body in Consumer Culture." *Theory, Culture and Society,* 1, no. 2 (1982): 20.

Mike Featherstone, M., Hepworth, & B.S. Turner (Eds.). *The Body: Social Process and Cultural Theory.* Newbury Park, CA: Sage Publications, 1991.

Ferguson, M. *Forever Feminine: Women's Magazines and the Cult of Femininity.* London: Heinemann, 1983.

Foucault, M. *Discipline and Punish: The Birth of Prison,* trans. A. Sheridan. New York: Pantheon Books, 1977.

Fox-Keller, E.F. "Gender and Science." *Psychoanalysis and Contemporary Thought: A Quarterly of Integrative and Interdisciplinary Studies,* 1 (1978): 409–433.

Fox, M.F., & S. Hesse-Biber. *Women at Work.* Palo Alto, CA: Mayfield Publishing, 1984.

Friedan, B. *The Feminine Mystique.* New York: Norton, 1963.

Glassner, B. *Bodies.* New York: Putnam, 1988.

Gordon, A., M.J. Buhle, & N. Schrom. "Women in American Society: An Historical Contribution." *Radical America,* 5, no. 4 (July-August 1971): 3–66.

Gordon, R.A. *Anorexia and Bulimia: Anatomy of a Social Epidemic.* Cambridge, MA: Basil Blackwell, 1990.

Greenblatt, A. "Women in Medicine." *National Forum: The Phi Beta Kappa Journal,* 61, no. 4 (1981): 10–12.

Greenhalgh, S. "Bound Feet, Hobbled Lives: Women in Old China." *Frontiers,* 2, no. 1 (1977): 12.

Gull, W. "Anorexia Nervosa (Apepsia Hysterica, Anorexia Hysterica)." *Transactions of the Clinical Society of London,* 7, no. 22 (1874): 22–28.

Hansen, J., & E. Reed. *Cosmetics, Fashions and the Exploitation of Women.* New York: Pathfinder Press, 1986.

Hartmann, H. "Capitalism, Patriarchy, and Job Segregation by Sex." *Signs: Journal of Women in Culture and Society,* 1, no. 3 (1976): 137–169.

Hesse-Biber, S. "Women, Weight and Eating Disorders: A Socio-Cultural and Political-Economic Analysis." *Women's Studies International Forum,* 14, no. 3 (1991): 173–191.

Hesse-Biber, S., A. Clayton-Matthews, & J. Downey. "The Differential Importance of Weight among College Men and Women." *Genetic, Social and General Psychology Monographs,* 113, no. 4 (1987): 509–528.

Hesse-Biber, S., & G.L. Carter. *Working Women in America: Split Dreams* (2nd ed.). New York: Oxford University Press, 2005.

Jacobus, M., E.F. Keller, & S. Shuttleworth. (Eds.). *Body/Politics: Women and the Discourses of Science.* New York: Routledge, 1990.

Jay, N. "Gender and Dichotomy." *Feminist Studies,* 7, no. 1 (1981): 37–56.

Kunzle, D. "Dress Reform as Antifeminism: A Response to Helene E. Roberts' 'The Exquisite Slave: The Role of Clothes in the Making of the Victorian Woman.'" *Signs: Journal of Women in Culture and Society,* 2, no. 3 (1977): 570–579.

Lasegue, E.C. "On Hysterical Anorexia." *Medical Times and Gazette,* September 6, 1873, pp. 265–266; September 27, 1873, pp. 367–369.

Lehrer, S. *Origins of Protective Labor Legislation for Women: 1905–1925.* New York: State University of New York Press, 1987.

Levy, H.S. *Chinese Footbinding: The History of A Curious Erotic Custom.* Albany: Walton Rawls Publisher, 1966.

Lloyd, G. *The Man of Reason: "Male" and "Female" in Western Philosophy.* London: Methuen, 1984.

Lowe, M. "Social Bodies: The Interaction of Culture and Women's Biology." In *Biological Woman: The Convenient Myth*, ed. R. Hubbard, M.S. Henifin, & B. Fried. Cambridge, MA: Schenkman Publishing, 1982.

Lurie, A. *The Language of Clothes.* New York: Vintage Books, 1983.

Maccoby, E., & C.N. Jacklin. *The Psychology of Sex Differences.* Palo Alto, CA: Stanford University Press, 1974.

Martin, E. *The Woman in the Body: A Cultural Analysis of Reproduction.* Boston: Beacon Press, 1987.

Mattel, Inc. "Doll Showcase: 2006 Line." From Barbie B Collector, 2005. http://collectdolls.about.com/gi/dynamic/offsite.htm?site=http://www.barbiecollector.com/showcase/product.asp%3Ftype=%26subtype=%26product%5Fid=1003533

Mazur, A. "U.S. Trends in Feminine Beauty and Overadaptation." *Journal of Sex Research*, 22 no. 3 (1986): 281–303.

Merchant, C. *The Death of Nature: Women, Ecology and the Scientific Revolution.* New York: Harper & Row, 1989.

Michie, H. *The Flesh Made Word: Female Figures and Women's Bodies.* New York: Oxford University Press, 1987.

Orbach, S. *Fat Is a Feminist Issue.* New York: Berkeley Press, 1978.

Orbach, S. *Hunger Strike: The Anorectic's Struggle as a Metaphor of Our Age.* New York: W.W. Norton, 1986.

Ortner, S.B. "Is Female to Male as Nature is to Culture?" In *Women, Culture and Society*, ed. M.Z. Rosaldo & L. Lamphere. Palo Alto, CA: Stanford University Press, 1974.

Pingitore, R.B. Spring, B. & D. Garfield, "Gender Differences in Body Satisfaction." *Obesity Research*, 5, no. 5, 1997: 402–409.

Roberts, H.E. "The Exquisite Slave: The Role of Clothes in the Making of the Victorian Woman." *Signs: Journal of Women in Culture and Society*, 2, no. 3 (1977): 564.

Rosaldo, M.Z. "Women, Culture and Society: A Theoretical Overview." In *Women, Culture and Society*, ed. M. Rosaldo & L. Lamphere. Palo Alto, CA: Stanford University Press, 1974.

Rosenkrantz, P., S. Vogel, H. Bee, & D. Broverman. "Sex-Role Stereotypes and Self-Concepts in College Students." *Journal of Consulting and Clinical Psychology*, 32, no. 3 (1968): 287–291.

Rubin, G. "The Traffic in Women." In *Toward an Anthropology of Women*, ed. R.R. Reiter, pp. 157–210. New York: Monthly Review Press, 1975.

Rudofsky, B. *The Kimono Mind.* New York: Doubleday, 1965.

Ryle, J.A. "Discussion of Anorexia Nervosa." *Proceedings of the Royal Society of Medicine*, 32 (1939): 735–737.

Schwartz, D.M., M.G. Thompson, & C.L. Johnson. "Anorexia Nervosa and Bulimia: The Socio-Cultural Context." *International Journal of Eating Disorders*, 1, no. 3 (1982): 20–36.

Seid, R.P. *Never Too Thin: Why Women Are at War with Their Bodies.* New York: Prentice-Hall, 1989.

Shorter, E. "The First Great Increase in Anorexia Nervosa." *Journal of Social History*, 21, no.1 (1987): 69–97.

Silverstein, B. *Fed Up! The Food Forces That Make You Fat, Sick and Poor.* Boston: South End Press, 1984.

Silverstein, B., L. Perdue, B. Peterson, L. Vogel, & D.A. Fantini. "Possible Causes of the Thin Standard of Bodily Attractiveness for Women," *International Journal of Eating Disorders*, 5 (1989): 135–144.

Smith, P.A., & E. Midlarksy. "Empirically Derived Conceptions of Femaleness and Maleness: A Current View." *Sex Roles*, 12, no. 3/4 (1985).

Sontag, S. "The Double Standard of Aging." *Saturday Review*, 55, no. 39 (1972): 29–38.

Steele, V. *Fashion and Eroticism: Ideals of Feminine Beauty from the Victorian Era to the Jazz Age.* New York: Oxford University Press, 1985.

Stewart, D. "In the Cutthroat World of Toy Sales, Child's Play is Serious Business." *Smithsonian*, 20, no. 9 (December 1989): 72–82.

Stone, L. *The Family, Sex and Marriage in England 1500–1800.* New York: Harper & Row, 1977. In *The Dieter's Dilemma: Eating Less and Weighing More*, by W. Bennett & J. Gurin. New York: Basic Books, 1982. p. 183.

Synnot, A. *The Body Social: Symbolism, Self and Society.* New York: Routledge, 1993.

Tang Halpin, Z. "Scientific Objectivity and the Concept of 'The Other.'" *Women's Studies International Forum*, 12, no.3 (1989): 288.

Target. "Dolls + Accessories: Barbie." 2005 http://www.target.com/gp/browse.html/ref=in_br_browse-box/602-7035194-9894235?%5Fencoding=UTF8&node=1041580

Taylor, F. *Principles of Scientific Management.* New York: W.W. Norton, 1967.

Tiggemann, M. "Gender Differences in the Interrelationships between Weight Dissatisfaction, Restraint, and Self-esteem." *Sex Roles*, 30 (1994): 319–330.

Tuana, N. "The Weaker Seed: The Sexist Bias of Reproductive Theory." *Feminism and Science*, ed. N. Tuana, p. 147–172. Bloomington: Indiana University Press, 1989.

Turner, B.S. *The Body and Society.* New York: Basil Blackwell, 1984.

Velben, T. *The Theory of the Leisure Class* New York: Random House, The Modern Library, 1899.

Weibel, K. *Mirror, Mirror: Images of Women Reflected in Popular Culture.* New York: Anchor Books, 1977.

"Weight Reduction Linked to the Mind." *New York Times*, p. 6 February 24, 1926.

Wilshire, D. "The Uses of Myth, Image, and the Female Body in Re-Visioning Knowledge." *Gender/Body/Knowledge: Feminist Reconstructions of Being and Knowledge*, ed. A.M. Jagger & S.R. Bordo. New Brunswick, NJ: Rutgers University Press, 1989.

THREE

Selling the Body Beautiful: Food, Dieting, and Recovery

*In my office is a stack of women's magazines: temples of
self-scrutiny, bibles of body loathing . . . several stories
are promoted, among them: "Burn 1,000 Extra Calories a
Week!," "Weight-loss News: You Don't Need Willpower,"
"One Great at-Home Pilates Move for Bikini Abs," "SPE
CIAL: New Ways to Stop Stress Eating," and "We Found the
Best 12 Moves for Your Abs, Butt, & Thighs." I look at this
and sigh. Weight, weight, weight; abs, butt, thighs. Any
woman with a modicum of self-awareness understands what
this material is intended to do. It is goddess worship, goddess religion for the consumer age, commandments chiseled
on skin and bone, and it's designed to whip us mere mortals
into a frenzy of inadequacy so potent it causes us to act, to
go forth and buy the magazine and the many products it
advertises. Thou shall be thin, the goddess commands. Thou
shall not have wrinkles. Thou shalt compare and contrast.*

—Caroline Knapp[1]

*I lived with two girls for two years. And when they spoke to
you they had to be standing in front of the mirror. One of my
roommates finally said to me "when we come in our room
we're hanging a towel over the mirror." Because they would
literally stand there and look at themselves at every angle in
the mirror the entire time. I'd say, "What is your problem?
Are you in love with yourselves, are you that concerned?"*

—Judy, college senior

*It makes me feel better when I look in the mirror. And it
shows me that I'm taking care of myself and it just makes me
feel better about myself.*

—Juliet, college junior

FIGURE 3.1 Today's the Day: Diet and Workout Collage.

> *I would see these thin girls in the magazines and say I want to be like that. I would look at myself in the mirror and I didn't like what I saw.*
>
> —Donna, college sophomore

A mirror, reflecting the virtual image of an object placed before it, is an analogy for how society fosters women's obsession with weight and body image. The reflection Judy, Juliet, and Donna observe in the mirror may be a true likeness, but their feelings about their bodies deeply distort their perceptions. Judy's roommates check the image obsessively; Juliet seeks in her reflection her own well-being; Donna fears she cannot measure up. Our society encourages women to see themselves as objects.

In this chapter, we can focus our own critical gaze on the mirror set up by capitalism and patriarchal interests, like corporate culture, the traditional family, the government, and the media. Viewing the greater structure framing and supporting this mirror, not just the bright reflective surface, prompts us to ask a different set of questions: not "What can women do to meet the ideal?" but "Who benefits from women's excessive concern with thinness?" "How is this obsession created, promoted, and perpetuated?"

There's No Business Like the Body Business, I: Profiting from Women's Bodies

Most women feel their bodies fail the beauty test, and the American health and beauty industry benefits enormously from continually nurturing feminine insecurities. If women are busy trying to control their bodies through dieting, excessive exercise, and self-improvement, they are distracted from other important aspects of selfhood that might challenge the status quo.[2] In the words of one critic, "a secretary who bench-presses 150 pounds is still stuck in a dead-end job; a housewife who runs the marathon is still financially dependent on her husband."[3]

In creating women's concept of the ideal body image, the cultural mirror is more influential than the mirror reflecting peer group attitudes. Research has shown women overestimate how thin a body their male and female peers value. In a research study using body silhouettes, college students of both sexes were asked to indicate an ideal female figure, the one which they believed to be most attractive to the same-sex peer and other-sex peer. Not only did the women select a thinner silhouette than the men did,[4] but when asked to choose a personal ideal, rather than a peer ideal, the women chose an even skinnier model. Women are also more self-critical than men. In another study, a woman was twice as likely to rate her attractiveness as low, between 1 and 3 (on a scale of 1 to 10), than a man was. In general, women are more accepting than men of flaws in their partners, but less than half of women believe that others consider them physically appealing.[5]

Let us look at just how the food and weight-loss industries keep consumers in a constant battle over what they eat, how they eat, and how much control they have over their own bodies. This struggle starts with the media depicting unreasonably "perfect" bodies as attainable and continues with the confusing profusion of beauty, diet, and "health" advice from profit-making corporations.

Advertising and Beauty Advice: Buy, Try, Comply

Capitalism uses the media to project the culturally desirable body to women. These images are everywhere—on TV, in the movies, on billboards, in print. Women's magazines, with their glossy pages of ads, advertorials (advertisements presented in the style of an editorial), and beauty advice, hold up an especially devious mirror. They offer women "help" while presenting a nearly impossible standard. As Nancy, one college student, noted in our interviews:

> The advertisement showed me exactly what I should be, not what I was. I wasn't tall, I wasn't blonde, I wasn't skinny. I didn't have thin thighs, I didn't

have a flat stomach. I am short, have brown curly hair, short legs. They did offer me solutions like dying my hair or a workout or the use of this cream to take away cellulite.

Women's beauty magazines such as *Vogue* and *Cosmopolitan* have always stressed the need for women to take an active interest in their looks. A 1957 article in *Vogue* titled "How to Look Like a Beauty" scolds "some women" for not caring.

Some women find beauty unnecessary, and will take the trouble to hide inherited good looks behind frowzy hair, fat, badly-chosen spectacles, and dreary clothes, feeling elemental and honest when they spurn artifice. . . . But the woman who finds it necessary to be beautiful comes to look like a beauty because there is a need in her. She will make up for a lack of inherited good looks with work, knowledge, time, fashion and any artificial aid that's appropriate. . . . Beauty is, very often, like any other ambition or drive—capable of realization of a degree in proportion to the need of satisfaction. . . . If her hair is a natural disaster, she goes to the very best hairdresser and gets the very best advice as well as the very best work that she can.[6]

Marsha, a sophomore, is quite clear about where she got her drive to be thin.

I think *Vogue* is a good example of society and I think it puts a great deal of pressure on women everywhere. It's a terrible thing to be guilty of, but if I'm with a friend and I see a woman that doesn't look good, I'll say something like "Look at her hair. She should do something with it. God! She's heavy there."

Marsha further noted,

I think magazines are really mixed up. In the same magazine you'll see a health focus up-date and they'll write up things like . . . it's important to have a good perception of yourself, not to worry too much about your looks and not to drive yourself into dieting. . . . But then you turn the page and there's Miss Jane who just had a make-over and this is what we did to her hair and face and wow doesn't she look better. . . .

The "Beauty Q&A" section of *Cosmopolitan's* website contains typical advice. One topic, "How to Slim a Chin," poses as a helpful tip from a beauty editor, but is also an endorsement for a New York makeup artist and Origins makeup (a Cosmopolitan advertiser).

Q: I'm super self-conscious about my chin because I think it looks too fat. Can I make my chin appear thinner with makeup?

A: The best way to minimize the shape of your chin is to shade it subtly with a sheer powder bronzer that's only one shade darker than your skin tone—use anything darker and you could end up merely drawing more attention. The key to applying the bronzer so that it's undetectable by even the closest of admirers lies in using the right tools and technique.

First, stroke a large blush-type brush on the powder, shake off all excess to prevent streaks, then sweep it under your whole chin area, blending down along your neck and up along your jawline. This will create the illusion of a shadow and make the area less noticeable. Try Origins Sunny Disposition, $17.50.

Another tip: focus on enhancing the facial features you do like in order to draw attention away from your chin, says New York City makeup artist Barbara Stone. Go for a bright pink blush or a bold new eye shadow.[7]

Not everyone is taken in, of course. One student I interviewed dismissed the images she saw in the advertising pages of magazines as "constructed people."

> I just stopped buying women's magazines. They are all telling you how to dress, how to look, what to wear, the type of clothes. And I think they are just ridiculous. . . . You can take the most gorgeous model and make her look terrible. Just like you can take a person who is not that way and make them look beautiful. You can use airbrushing and many other techniques. These are not really people. They are constructed people.

Computer-enhanced photography has advanced far beyond the techniques that merely airbrushed blemishes, added highlights to hair, and lengthened the legs with a camera angle.

Photos of models and movie stars are often so doctored that they end up looking drastically different from the subjects they are supposed to reflect. As a result, women may believe that the "perfect" body and face really do exist. For example, on the cover of the February 2003 issue of the UK *GQ*, Kate Winslet shows off a dramatically slimmed-down body. The editor of the magazine admitted that the photograph had been "digitally altered," but "no more than any other cover star."[8] Less than 3 months after Winslet's digital metamorphosis, Queen Latifah appeared in a print advertisement for *Chicago* as a shadow of her former self. Miramax, the distributor for the movie, claimed that Latifah's slimmed appearance was the result of a "ratio mistake."[9]

In the fashion industry, Pascal Dangin is employed to make just such "ratio mistakes." Dangin is the digital retoucher for some of the most famous photographers in Hollywood. Interviewed in the *New York Times*, Dangin plays mum.

The people who benefit from my work do not benefit from me talking about it. . . . Everybody wants to look good. . . . Basically we're selling a product—we're selling an image. To those who say too much retouching, I say you are bogus. This is the world that we're living in. Everything is glorified.[10]

But if those who criticize the faking of photos are "bogus," what adjective would you apply to the photos themselves?

Digitally altering photos, removing blemishes or fat from cover models and actors at the magazine editor's whim, has become commonplace. In addition to the legal issues that may arise from those who, like Kate Winslet, do not want their images altered, the industry is perpetuating the idea of physical perfection. Increasingly, each part of a woman's body is now under great pressure to be perfect. The models gracing magazine covers are touting an assortment of "parts" to make that perfect whole. A woman no longer wants to *be* Julia Roberts, she wants to have Julia Roberts's smile, Jennifer Lopez's derriere, Angelina Jolie's legs, and Halle Berry's face.

And who benefits from this idea? How much does it cost to be preoccupied with parts? Let us examine the cost to moisturize properly, from the bottom up. A foot cream from CVS Pharmacy ranges from $4.50 to $7.00. This is about the standard price for most lower-end lotions for each body part, with face creams generally running from $6.00 to $11.00 and up. For instance, if you purchase four different lotions—feet, legs, face, and hands—you've already spent at least $20.00.[11] But the possibilities are virtually endless. You can get a shimmer lotion for a special night out, and a specific cream for your heels, elbows, eye area, cuticles, and wrinkles. Even with lower-end products, it adds up to serious cash. At the high end, there's Chanel's list of "essential moisturizers," including Rectifiance Intense Anti-Age Retexturizing Cream, Rectifiance Intense Anti-Age Retexturizing Fluid, Eclat Originel Maximum Radiance Cream, and Age Delay Time-Fighting Rejuvenation Lotion, each costing at least $58.50.[12] What's more, Chanel barely competes with even higher-end lotions like La Prairie's "Skin Caviar Luxe Cream," at $580.00 for 3.4 ounces.[13] Obviously, it adds up to huge profits for cosmetic companies— as we divide up our bodies and spend, they conquer.

The fitness industry has also deconstructed bodies into individual parts to be sculpted and perfected. We buy different workout videos for our abs, our butts, and our thighs. Similarly, companies like Lean Cuisine package diet products into smaller, but more expensive, servings consumed more frequently. Specialized meals have created extra special profits for food companies.

The American woman's dissatisfaction with her looks is directly related to the American food and weight loss industries' corporate practices and advertising campaigns promoting image, weight, and body obsession.

There's No Business Like the Body Business, II: The American Food Industry–Fatten Up and Slim Down

> I pop back and forth, gain and lose, gain and lose. Last Christmas my mother put me on a strict diet. I dropped about 10 pounds. When I got back to school, I just ballooned. You can see these pictures of me in December, my face will be thin, and by January it'll plump up again.

Stephanie, a college sophomore, knows the yo-yo syndrome well. So do millions of other Americans. Obesity specialist Dr. Thomas Wadden says, "We're being fattened up by the food industry and slimmed down by the . . . diet and exercise industry. That's great for the capitalist system, but it's not so great for the consumer."[14]

There is a great disparity between the amount of money spent promoting the things we *should* be eating versus the amount of advertising dollars spent pushing food that can harm our general health and make us fat. The government's nutrition education budget simply cannot compete with the food industry's $30 billion advertising fund. The National Cancer Institute funded a $1 million "5-a-day" campaign to encourage people to eat their daily allotment of fruits and vegetables, but must compete for consumer appetites against a $500 million McDonald's campaign.[15] It is no surprise McDonald's wins.

It is not uncommon for the average American to have a diet cola in one hand and high-fat fries and a burger in the other. Food and weight loss are an inescapable part of contemporary culture. The media bombard us with images of every imaginable food—snack foods, fast foods, gourmet foods, health foods, and junk foods. Most of these messages target children, who are very impressionable, and women, who make the purchasing decisions for themselves and their families. At the same time women are subjected to an onslaught of articles, books, video tapes, audiotapes, and TV talk shows devoted to dieting and the maintenance of sleek and supple figures. No wonder disordered eating develops in such an environment. The conflicting images of pleasurable consumption and an ever-leaner body type give us a food consciousness loaded with tension and ambivalence.

Food juggernauts and their billion-dollar "fatten up/slim down" advertising budgets have come up with some pretty powerful examples of schizoid thinking. In one of my favorite advertisements, the Hershey Company invites us to savor the buttery toffee and chocolate of the waferlike Skor candy bar. It shows the ultra-thin bar in profile, its wrapper seductively pulled back. The copy reminds us that even a candy bar "can never be too rich or too thin." The 2005 advertisement for Carl's Jr. restaurants' "Spicy BBQ Burger" is another perfect example of a mixed message. Paris Hilton is the star of the advertisement, her supermodel figure in a very revealing bathing suit. She has a body that is unattainable for the vast majority of women. She is eating a large, calorie-loaded burger. It's a message loaded with irony—no one really believes Paris maintains her tiny shape on fattening burgers, but the impossible image becomes another cultural icon nonetheless.

Social psychologist Brett Silverstein explains that the food industry, like all industries in a capitalist system, is always striving to maximize profit, growth, concentration, and control—at the expense of the food consumer. "[It] promotes snacking so that consumers will have more than three opportunities a day to consume food, replaces free water with purchased soft drinks, presents desserts as the ultimate reward, and bombards women and children with artificially glamorized images of highly processed foods."[16]

Diet foods are an especially profitable segment of the business, as the next section of this chapter reveals.

How "Lite" and "Lo" Can You Go?

Consider a few statistics.

- Weight-loss product retail sales have increased almost 90% in the past 5 years.[17]
- In 2003, approximately 600 kinds of low- or no-carb (carbohydrate) product were sold in the United States—almost twice the total from 2002.[18]
- $132.3 million worth of liquid and powder weight-control products were sold in 2000, of which $42.1 million resulted from Ultra Slim Fast sales.[19]
- $71.1 million of weight-control snack bars were also sold in 2000, of which $6.1 million is attributed to Power Bar sales.[20]

In 1983, the food industry came up with a brilliant marketing concept, and introduced 91 new "lite" fat-reduced or calorie-reduced foods[21]—with phenomenal success. The consumer equated "lightness" with health. The food industry seemed to equate it with financial health—lite foods have lower production costs than "regular" lines, but they are often priced higher:

> Light beer had more water. (Coors, one model for Miller Lite, was so watery that detractors called it "Colorado Kool-Aid"). . . . The saccharin in diet drinks was cheaper than sugar. . . . Especially profitable were dairy analogs fabricated from inexpensive vegetable fats: margarine, egg substitutes, creamers, frozen dinners, "lite" cheeses."[22]

The Food and Drug Administration (FDA) has tightened its regulations on food labeling and what "lite" claims are made.

The next craze, low-carb diets, began in the 1970s but did not become widely accepted and popular until the late 1990s. Dr. Robert Atkins published the "Atkins Nutritional Approach" in his 1972 book. His approach, which involved a low-carbohydrate, high-protein, and high-fat diet, received harsh criticism from the medical world. All previous medical knowledge pointed to controlling fats and calories while eating a balanced, moderate diet of protein, vegetables, fruits, and breads and grains as the best way to lose weight. The FDA even released a food pyramid promoting this type of low-fat, high complex-carbohydrate diet.

With 59 million Americans decreasing their carbohydrate intake, the low-carb movement has spurred the food industry into adapting and creating products to fit the market.[23] In just 2 months at the beginning of 2004, 360 new products, all sporting a lower-carb label, debuted in stores around the country.[24] Finding a low-carb alternative to your favorite foods is becoming easier, as beer, candy, soda, and pasta companies release these altered versions. And they are doing well. In its first year, Michelob Ultra, the first nationally marketed low-carb beer, boasted sales of $156.1 million.[25] Russell Stover brand led the candy department with $52.5 million in low-carb sales in 2003.[26] In June 2004, Coca-Cola, the biggest nonalcoholic beverage brand, released its low-carb alternative, C2. Advertisements for the product claim it is for "people who don't compromise. It's not about what you can't have. It's about getting what you want. And having what you need."[27] Pepsi has already fought back with Pepsi EDGE, a low-carb cola.[28] SKYY Vodka even introduced a line that offers a premixed alcoholic drink that is low carb. The title of this product, SKYY Sport, suggests that consuming the beverage leads to a healthy body.

Carb-watching may be booming now, but will it be the answer to our weight-loss woes? Hard facts are difficult to come by, but initial studies suggest there is some truth to the weight loss industry's carbohydrate claims. Dr. Jeff Volek and Dr. Eric Westerman, of the University of Connecticut and Duke University respectively, argue that criticisms of the low-carb diet strategy are largely unproven and that more research should be done to determine whether controlling carbs will be the key to prolonged weight loss and general wellness.[29]

Even the government has been forced to reexamine its previous dietary recommendations. The Atkins Physicians Council has advised members of Congress that ". . . the existing Food Guide Pyramid[30] and future versions that might continue to rely solely on low-fat, portion-control, or calorie-counting approaches will not be helpful to many of the approximately 60% of our population who have been unsuccessful using these same strategies over the past few decades."[31] They are advocating for "The Atkins Lifestyle Food Guide Pyramid"[32] to become part of what the government releases in its nutrition guidelines recommendations.[33]

Giving the Atkins brand the stamp of government approval is dangerous for several reasons. It links a profit-driven corporation to the business of health, and instead of being just a method of losing weight, it is now threatening to become what it means to *be healthy*. Despite the possible validity of the diet's claims, Atkins remains a business, always seeking to increase profits. Similarly, popular food products, like Ocean Spray brand juice are jumping on the Atkins bandwagon so that you can still drink your juice while going "light" with "less carbs." Here, Ocean Spray promises to be big on taste—but tiny on the body (see fig. 3.2).

Will Americans abandon their love of pasta and bread? Will the French fry cease to be their favorite food? Will we reverse the obesity trend and turn from a nation of calorie counters into carbohydrate counters? Or will the weight

FIGURE 3.2 Less Carbs, Lighter Bikini Body. *(Ocean Spray Cranberries, Inc.)*

problems Americans face continue to be much more complicated than one magic food component? If history tells us anything, the carbohydrate craze will pass just as the other trends have. In its wake will be a population eager for the new "quick fix" for weight loss "freedom," even though freedom is the opposite of what we get. Once again, "health concern" will mask the profit motive.

Power Play

Just as the cult member loses free agency as he or she sinks deeper into the cult, this new way of eating takes power from the consumer. Dieting has become a way of life. Eating is no longer a natural process, but something to be regulated and scrutinized. More people rely on corporate products and messages to help them in this regulation; we turn to the "100-calorie snack-pack" or the meal replacement bar to "keep us in check." Like cult members, we allow corporations claiming to know what is good for us to tell us what, when, and how to eat. What we lose is not weight, but control over our lives. We are increasingly dependent on a force concerned not with our bodies, minds, and hearts, but with the dollars in our wallets.

Every time the consumer falls for another obesity cure, he or she loses time, money, and energy on bogus products and unrealistic diets. This "magic cure" is so elusive because it simply does not exist. Obesity is a problem too multifaceted and complex to be solved by a single pill or diet regimen.

The Obesity Epidemic

The National Center for Health Statistics report for 1999-2002 indicates that 65% of Americans are overweight, with 30% considered obese.[34] James O. Hill, a doctor with the Center for Human Nutrition and the University of Colorado Health Science Center, cited in a business journal titled *Beverage Aisle*, states that these numbers depart drastically from figures from 25 years ago, when less than half of American adults were overweight. Even more worrisome, however, are his projected figures for 2008, when an estimated 73% of American adults will be overweight and just under 40% of American adults will be obese.[35]

Of course, corporations do not care if you are thin, fat, or average, as long as you buy their products. In creating the consumer demand for diet and junk fare at the same time, the food industry has favored mixed marriages and strange bedfellows. ConAgra (best known for its line of frozen Banquet dinners) sells Morton and Chun King as well as (through Beatrice) Clark Bars and La Choy and Rosarita products, none of which would be identified as "health food." However, ConAgra also introduced, through Beatrice, Healthy Choice reduced-calorie frozen dinners[36] and teamed up with Thompson Pharmaceuticals to sell Ultra Slim-Fast, an extremely popular liquid diet.[37] Have you eaten too many Clark Bars and Morton frozen dinners? Two meals a day of Ultra Slim-Fast and one Healthy Choice frozen dinner will help you lose weight and help ConAgra make more money.[38]

"Behind the phantasmagoria of food brand names presented on television and in modern supermarkets, there are fewer and fewer processors and marketers gaining more and more control over dinner,"[39] says Jim Hightower, author of *Food Profiteering in America*. Economist Lois Therrien explains, "The economic imperative driving consolidation is the search for growth. The volume of food sold in the U.S. is rising by only about 1 percent a year. Combine this with the skyrocketing cost of rolling out new products, and it's easier, and cheaper, to buy market share than build it."[40]

The connection between consolidation and profit is quite clear. In 1999, four companies—Kellogg's, General Mills, Kraft Foods, and Quaker Oats—had a little over 90% of the dollar share of ready-to-eat cereal in America. Kellogg's and General Mills each sold over $2 billion worth of cereal; Kraft's sales amounted to over $1 billion; and Quaker sales amounted to about $700 million.[41] Their market shares do not seem to have changed dramatically since then.

An advertisement for "Special K" cereal contains the slogan "Big white box. Smaller blue jeans," and concludes with "The prize is inside." Evidently, Kellogg's would like us to believe that eating this product promises a smaller fitting pair of pants; hence, the purported weight loss is the prize.

As the opportunities to sell us diet and junk food simultaneously have multiplied, the bottom line is clear. Consumer health never has been the priority, and companies profit from the confusion. Even companies producing research reports on different diets seek to profit by offering a service, like MarketData Enterprise's Bestdietforme.com, which determines which diet is best for you based on your purchase of a personal questionnaire. The health of the American people is being bought and sold to the highest bidders. Furthermore, when industry compensates doctors and health professionals for their endorsement, how do we know whom to trust?

Unfortunately, it is not only adults who are losing out to the corporations of America.

The Latest Target: Kids

Nowhere is the corporate drive for profit more evident and more disturbing than in local schools. As schools have struggled to survive deep funding cuts,

FIGURE 3.3 The Prize is Inside. *(Kellog's.)*

a corporate solution is becoming increasingly popular. By invading the cafeteria, showing up on textbook covers, providing scoreboards, and parading their colors on school buses, corporations are helping schools provide needed goods and services to their students. But what long-term effects does it have and why are corporations so interested in students?

Kids have enormous buying power. They have a whopping $167 billion worth of direct buying power, with their indirect influence thought to be triple that figure.[42] Companies want to make sure that their products are getting a piece of the action. What better advertising venue than a place kids are required to be 180 days a year? And even better, what if you could get a school to give you exclusive access for advertising? Innovations like Channel One media and Coca-Cola pouring rights (exclusive access to school market) have become widespread.[43]

The Channel One television program is broadcast in 12,000 middle and high schools across the country "featuring stories on breaking news and in-depth issues that affect the world, the nation, and specifically, America's teenagers."[44] Altogether, nearly 8 million students watch Channel One News in the mornings.[45] Schools benefit from free televisions, but the profit for

Channel One is $30 million for advertising annually. It is not hard to envision the effects of all that advertising when students are required to watch the advertisements (no channel surfing or powering off) of the latest junk foods and soda pop.[46]

Pouring rights, giving beverage companies exclusive access to a school's students, is another example of corporate takeover. One estimate states that up to 62% of schools have contracts, according to the soft drink association.[47] Fortunately, schools and parents are beginning to fight back, but with an opponent like the mammoth Coca-Cola Company and the immediate funding needs in our schools, it is an uphill battle. The following excerpt from *Consuming Kids* by Susan Linn is a good example of the damaging influence of corporations in our schools:

> A school principal sent me an "educational" poster about nutrition put out by the Frito-Lay company. . . . "Did you know," the poster says, "Cheetos, Doritos and other Frito-Lay snacks give you the bread/brain power that the food pyramid says you need? That means that you can include Frito-Lay snacks along with toast, spaghetti, rice and crackers as part of a nutritious diet!". . . The poster arrived at the school accompanied by the following note:

> Dear Cafeteria Manager:
>   Frito-Lay is tapping into the popularity of Pokémon for its latest promotion, and we want you to benefit from it. Enclosed you'll find a colorful poster for your cafeteria—with a nutrition message for kids about the Food Guide Pyramid.
>   The poster uses the Pokémon characters to capture kids' attention, and then lets them know that Frito-Lay products can be an important part of snacking right—as in the familiar Food Pyramid—because Frito-Lay snacks can help them meet their daily Bread/Grain requirements.
>   Display this poster in your cafeteria. It'll make the lunchroom a more fun and interesting place for your students, tell a story about nutrition and help build your cafeteria sales.[48]

Recent figures show that both boys and girls are getting a significant portion of their daily caloric intake from the sugar found in soda—8% for girls, and 9% for boys.[49] This undoubtedly plays a factor in kids' weight gain; they will choose high-sugar junk food when it is available. Furthermore, branding plays a huge part in what motivates kids, who then influence parents, to make purchasing decisions. In addition to the immediate problem of having corporate influence in our public schools, the effect that sugar has on behavior and learning capabilities in schools has yet to be fully researched. The consumption of high amounts of sugar is thought to be "involved in many common health problems: hypoglycemia, diabetes, heart disease . . . gout, hyperactivity, lack of concentration, depression, anxiety, and more."[50] The two- to threefold increase in childhood obesity in the past 20 years,[51] accompanied by the fact that nowadays one out of three American kids (born in 2000) will develop type 2 diabetes,[52] threatens our population's future. The invasion of schools by food corporations has high stakes.

There's No Business Like the Body Business, III: The Diet and Weight-Loss Industry—We'll Show You the Way

Americans are spending a startling $50 billion a year in the pursuit of weight loss.[53] Here are some statistics:

- Between 90% and 95% of diets fail.[54]

- U.S. companies spent $118 million on diet program advertisement in 2003. (Weight Watchers alone spent $93 million.)[55]

- Although only 9% of Americans are on an actual diet, 43% are adhering to an organized eating program and 82% are restricting their consumption of some type of food.[56]

- "More than 90 percent of weight lost on diets in the United States is regained."[57]

- "Of the more than 3,000 people in the National Weight Control Registry who have lost at least 30 pounds and kept it off for a year, only 9 percent maintain their weight without exercise."[58]

Increasingly, American women are told that they can have the right body only if they consume more products. They can change the color of their eyes with tinted contacts; they can have tanned skin by using self tanning lotion. They can buy cellulite control cream, spot firming cream, even contouring shower and bath firming gel to get rid of the "dimpled" look. One diet pill, called Meridia, is supposed to allow the consumer to "lose weight and actually keep it off." Meridia's accompanying pamphlet for patients says, "The most common side effects include headache, dry mouth, anorexia, constipation and insomnia."[59] The side effects may outweigh the benefits.

Many women believe that in order to lose weight they need to buy something—a pill, a food plan, or membership in a self-help group. The journey to creating the right body often begins with the purchase of a diet book. Today, some best-selling books include *The South Beach Diet: The Delicious, Doctor-Designed, Foolproof Plan for Fast and Healthy Weight Loss*, *The Rice Diet Solution*, *The Shangri-La Diet*, and *Ultrametabolism: The Simple Plan for Automatic Weight Loss*.[60]

In 2005, *The South Beach Diet*, *The South Beach Diet Good Fats/Good Carbs Guide*, and *The South Beach Diet Dining Guide* sold over 3 million copies.[61] *Dr. Phil McGraw's The Ultimate Weight Solution* sold a little over 1 million copies.[62] True adherents of the Cult of Thinness consider their diet books as bibles. Each book trumpets the true path to health and happiness and holds up a mirror reflecting only its own narrow world of correct behavior. Some books open with compelling personal conversions, others with sermons preached to the dieter. Some prescribe certain daily rituals of food preparation, food combination, food measuring, eating, and weighing-in. They warn dieters to follow the recipes carefully and never "sin" by going off the diet.

If following the diet book does not work, many find hope in formalized diet programs.

There are currently more than 17,000 different diet plans, products, and programs from which to choose.[63] Typically, these plans are geared to the female market. They are loaded with promises of quick weight loss and delicious low-calorie meals. Three of the most popular programs are Jenny Craig, Weight Watchers, and LA Weightloss.

Testimonials and before-and-after pictures are the primary marketing methods. "Our client Terry lost 92 lbs.," says the Nutri-Systems brochure. We see a "before" picture of Terry, overweight and slouching, clasping her hands together. Next we see Terry in a leotard, 92 pounds thinner, standing tall with her hands on her hips (she now has a waist). There are more happy faces of women who have lost weight and who are now able to do things such as bicycling or even going out on a date with a handsome man. The promise is "a happier, healthier life."

The typical weight loss plan can cost anywhere between $26 and $2,100 (per 3 month program)—and above,[64] though one of the best-known programs, Weight Watchers, is considerably less. Like its many clones, Weight Watchers is loosely run and mostly consists of a weigh-in class rooted in "group support, behavior modification, healthful eating, and exercise." Nowadays, the Weight Watchers program costs $27 to register and $13 for each weekly meeting. Currently, each week 1½ million people attend 46,000 meetings in 30 countries. That is almost 35 million people attending a year. These meetings brought in $392.4 million for the fiscal year ending in January 2004. In 2001, Weight Watchers made the move to the Internet, creating WeightWatchers.com, which offers users a way to participate in the program without attending meetings. This online version of the Weight Watchers program costs $49.95 for the first month and $16.95 after that. The website also offers an opportunity for those who do attend meetings to get supplemental help and information through the "etools" program, which costs $12.95 each month. Between the sale of products, Internet activity, meetings, and other sources, Weight Watchers brought in a net income of $174.4 million in 2005.[65] Weight Watchers' and the other commercial diet centers' success has been threatened recently by the surge of interest in the low-carbohydrate approach to dieting. Weight Watchers reported a decrease in participation at meetings in North America, which they attribute to the surge of popularity of Atkins-like diets. Another long-existing diet aid, Slim-Fast, has been experiencing a struggle in sales as well.[66] The endurance of the low-carbohydrate movement remains to be seen.

Comprehensive diet centers with more personally supervised medical and nutritional attention are also popular. Among the most highly supervised programs are the Very Low Calorie Diets such as Optifast, Medifast, or Health Management Resources. They are usually run by hospitals on an outpatient basis, with a standard regimen costing from $840 to $2,100.[67] Medifast reported revenue of $8.3 million for the first quarter of 2005.[68] By serving "300 dieters annually, a typical hospital could increase its revenues by more than $800,000 a year."[69] One such program, Optifast, costs from $1,800 to $2,000 for a 3-month program[70] and has treated over 1 million people since 1974.[71] Very Low Caloric Diets usually consist of powdered drinks that are supposed to completely substitute for meals. There have been a number of deaths attributed to them,[72] and it is generally agreed that they carry some medical risks.

Americans are still spending $12 billion every year on dietary aids, enhancers, supplements, and the like, despite the serious health risks and proven false advertising associated with them. There are a variety of reasons for using dietary supplements, but often they are advertised as a quick and easy way to either bulk up your muscles or slim down your waist. In recent years, drugs like ephedrine have resulted in serious injury and death, prompting government inquiries and bans on certain substances. Though these bans were a blow to the industry, there are always new substances and "miracle cures" waiting in the wings. The industry recently has offered vitamin and mineral supplements for those on low-carbohydrate diets. They range from "EAS Carb DynamX Capsules" and "1-EZ Diet Carb Suppressor" to more mainstream "Centrum Carb Assist" and "One-A-Day CarbSmart."[73] The Atkins brand also has a variety of supplements, allowing the brand to further profit in the carbohydrate supplement industry it spawned.

Thin Promises

Many programs promise weight reduction that is not only fast, but permanent. For instance, the brochure from the Jenny Craig Weight Loss Center reads:

> We listen to you. We work with you. We care about you and your success . . .
> that's what makes the Jenny Craig Program so unique. And its results are so

long lasting. You see, my program does more than help you lose weight quickly and easily. It teaches you how to keep your weight off.

The Diet Workshop promises an even speedier loss if you join one of its Quick Loss Clinics. By making a firm 6-week commitment, the dieter is rewarded by a loss of up to 20 pounds.

However, there is virtually no data available to support the weight loss industries' claims. In fact, it has recently been noted that "many people who complete a commercial diet will regain one-third of their lost weight after one year, two-thirds or more after three years and most, if not all, in three to five years. Many do not complete the program."[74] Medical research has come up with a theory that

> body weight may be regulated by a biologic set point system in the hypothalamus that "defends" a particular weight by maintaining energy balance and food consumption at certain levels. . . . Traditional diets often fail to reduce weight because the lower food intake sets off a "starvation reaction," in which the basal metabolic rate and overall activity level are decreased.[75]

FIGURE 3.4 The Proof is in the Jeans. *What's more, while Jenny Craig "teaches you how to keep your weight off," Medifast virtually "does it for you."* (*Medifast.*)

This research indicates that to lose weight you must (1) increase basal metabolic rate (aerobic exercise is one way) and (2) change the composition of your diet rather than restrict overall intake.

Some of the young women I interviewed echoed these observations.

> When I was really heavy at 17, I actually joined Weight Watchers. I lost 8 pounds with them. Then I just decided I didn't like that structure, weigh your food and this and that. I came off and I was caught up in this new job and getting ready to go away to school. I ended up losing more weight. And then again six or seven months ago I joined some diet group. I figured it would be an incentive getting weighed once a week. And I did lose 10 pounds relatively quickly and consciously. But recently I put it back on.

Another told me:

> In high school I tried the Scarsdale diet. It worked to a point but then I decided I just lost my energy instead of losing weight. So now I really believe that there is probably a certain weight that I will never go below. Maybe I could be five to ten pounds less than I am now, but I would have to change my whole eating habits, reduce portions, or give up drinking. So that might happen, but I don't do any of these trick diets any more.

Many of these diets require the participant to fixate on food to a great extent, creating an obsession with eating. One Vermont company called Weight Wizards produces a "foodmeter," which shows graphically how many calories are consumed for breakfast, lunch, dinner, and snacks. There is even a "color me thin weight loss kit." Many of the women I talked with mentioned this fixation.

> My little sister went on a diet, and she wanted me to go on one with her, so I said OK, I would this 1 week. I didn't really want to lose the weight. I just said I'd do it because she just wanted some moral support. After a week I said you're on your own. I never would have eaten this little. I became so hungry. How can I live on just pieces of toast? I never thought about food so much before I went on this diet. Whenever I'm hungry I eat. And if I'm not, I don't.

Julia joined a weight loss clinic program and became more and more obsessed with losing weight:

> It's just a starvation diet and they give you vitamins and you go in everyday and weigh. The focus was crazy. It was extreme. [The focus was on Julia losing weight for the next 3 months.] Fine, I could lose the weight, but then now that I've gained the weight back what does that mean? You put all this energy into losing weight, now that you've gained it back does that mean you're a screw up?

"Screwing up" is exactly what the industry is counting on. Failure becomes a personal, isolated problem that *you* or *me* or *she* has with control. This perpetuates a dependence on programs, books, pills, and so on to help women with their "control problem." Some diet companies are concerned with the problem of gaining weight back and have developed "maintenance" products. Maintenance programs are often expensive and their long-term outcomes are unproven. What can be proven are bigger profits and longer dependence on their programs. The discourse surrounding diets is frightening as well. The Atkins website offers help in persuading your family, your friends, and even your doctor that "Atkins knows best." It offers scientific evidence to give your doctor with convincing talking points. It also urges dieters to remember that "right now, weight loss is your destiny."[76] This kind of vocabulary raises questions about just what Atkins is advertising for—a lifestyle, a diet, a religion, a cult?

Kandi Stinson, author of *Women and Dieting Culture: Inside a Commercial Diet Group,* did a participatory research project in which she actually took part in one of the standard diet programs. Her findings reinforce the parallel between diet and an almost religious or cultlike experience. During her meetings she experienced a discourse of good versus evil along with other concepts like temptation, confession, and sacrifice. In a group weight-loss atmosphere, the "good" dieter is one who resists eating that piece of cake at the party or perhaps avoids going out with friends after work because of the greater risk of "falling" from the plan.[77] Dieters may begin to feel more comfortable around other dieters from their group because they can understand, support, and encourage each other. They can also reprimand, discipline, and become "accountability partners," a phrase often used in religious groups. Stinson describes this "surveillance" in her book.

> . . . in every case, a member talking to the leader or the group about an individual who is not present. Where a transgression or mistake is involved, the member brings it to the attention of the community, not the sinner. There is little direct effect on the erring member, but the message to the group is clear: your behavior is being watched and might be discussed even in your absence.[78]

A lot of religious and cult groups spend a great deal of time explaining things that are, essentially, inexplicable. In diet groups, this happens as well. When an enthusiastic dieter is not experiencing the expected results, group leaders and members come up with explanations to ensure blame is not placed on the dieter, and, more importantly, the program. A woman's monthly cycle, her consumption of sodium, and water retention are all explanations given for why weight loss is either inconsistent or insufficient.[79] These attitudes lead to reliance on practices that are "superstitious" and ritual-like in order to prevent these inexplicable blips in weight loss.

The Self-Help and Recovery Markets

During the late 1980s and throughout the 1990s, self-help books were huge sellers, and women were the predominant buyers. Books like Melody Beattie's *Codependent No More* and Thomas Nelson's *Love Hunger* sold millions as women strove for satisfaction, independence, and great bodies. While these books can be helpful tools, they are far from the best or only source of information or advice, and may just reinforce current societal structures.

In the first decade of the twenty-first century, the booming self-help and recovery publishing industry remains a good indicator of how women seek to solve their problems. Recent estimates suggest that women are responsible for as much as 85% of their total sales. Karen Casey's *Each Day a New Beginning: Daily Meditations for Women* has sold over 3 million copies since it was published in 1996. *He's Just Not That into You: The No Excuses Truth to Understanding Guys* by Greg Behrendt and Liz Tuccillo sold out in only 2 weeks after being featured on the Oprah Winfrey show in 2004.[80] Increasingly, media personalities are bridging the gap between TV and books. Dr. Phil, one of the most reliable voices on everything from weight loss to cheating husbands and pregnant teens, appeared weekly on Oprah before launching his own program in 2002. His "get real" strategy has helped him dominate both the TV and book industry, with four #1 *New York Times* best sellers.[81] In fact, Dr. Phil seems likely to become one of the best-selling authors in self-help history. His 2002 *Self Matters*, a guide to discovering one's "true self," sold more copies than any other nonfiction book. Over 9 million copies of his books have appeared in 30 languages.[82]

Recovery is a lucrative area in the self-help market. There are self-help books for almost every problem and social group imaginable. According to Peter Vegso, HCI Books publisher and president, "The market is huge: 76 million Americans, or 43% of the adult population, have been exposed to alcoholism in the family, and 20 million adults abuse, or are addicted to, substances."[83]

Shaye Areheart, publisher of Harmony Books and Shaye Areheart Books, is quoted to say that "If you really believe in the ability of people to help people, you can't help but believe that every copy you sell is a good thing."[84] One can assume that the millions of dollars her publishing house rakes in from self-help sales is also "a good thing." On first examination, the idea of "people helping people" does seem like a good thing. But what about "people making money from other people's problems?" When companies capitalize on our problems by providing us with diets and books that are often ineffective, is that still "a good thing?"

While an addiction or disease model lessens the burden of guilt and shame and may free people to work on change, it also has political significance.

According to feminist theorist Bette S.Tallen, "The reality of oppression is replaced with the metaphor of addiction." It places the problem's cause within a biological realm, away from outside social forces.[85] Issues such as poverty, lack of education and opportunity, and racial and gender inequality remain unexamined. More importantly, a disease-oriented addiction model, involving treatment by the health care system, results in profits for the medical-industrial complex. The addiction model, Tallen notes, suggests a solution that is personal ("Get treatment!") rather than political ("Smash patriarchy!"). It replaces the feminist view that the personal is political with the attitude of "therapism," that the "political is personal."[86] One of Bette Tallen's students told her that she had learned a lot from reading *Women Who Love Too Much* after her divorce from a man who had beaten her. Tallen suggested that "perhaps the best book to read would not be about women who love too much but about men who hit too much."[87]

The ideas that overweight is a disease and that overeating represents an addiction reinforce the "dis-ease" that American women feel about their bodies. The capitalist and patriarchal mirror held before them supports and maintains their obsession and insecurity. Who is watching what the corporations are doing? Can we rely on governmental oversight? Is there medical-industrial collusion when doctors are more than willing to partner with the weight-loss industries to promote the next "diet plan"? What is missing from the discussion so far is the voice of consumer advocacy. What nonbiased information can the average consumer obtain that is not tainted by the medical-industrial information complex? Where are Americans getting their information on dieting and weight loss? Who is advocating for children, the most vulnerable population?

We know that obesity rates within our culture are skewed toward the poor. We have seen how the food, diet, and recovery industries "feed" on individuals who do not have informational and nutritional alternatives within their families and communities. What we need is political advocacy, helping families and individuals to become more aware and educated about their options as consumers—and to demand better choices.

Notes

1. Caroline Knapp, *Appetites: Why Women Want* (New York: Counterpoint, 2003), 88–89.
2. Ilana Attie and J. Brooks-Gunn, "Weight Concerns as Chronic Stressors in Women," *Gender and Stress*, ed. Rosalind K. Barnett, Lois Biener, and Grace Baruch (New York: The Free Press, 1987), 218–252.

3. Katha Pollitt, "The Politically Correct Body," *Mother Jones*, 7, no. 7 (1982): 67. I do not want to disparage the positive benefits of exercising and the positive self-image that can come from feeling good about one's body. This positive image can spill over into other areas of one's life, enhancing, for example, one's self-esteem or job prospects.

4. See: Lawrence D. Cohn and Nancy E. Adler, "Female and Male Perceptions of Ideal Body Shapes: Distorted Views among Caucasian College Students," *Psychology of Women Quarterly*, 16, no.1 (1992): 69–79. See also: A. Fallon and P. Rozin, "Sex Differences in Perceptions of Desirable Body Shape," *Journal of Abnormal Psychology*, 94, no. 1 (1985): 102–105.

5. "Women Are More Critical of Their Own Bodies Than Those of Others," *Marketing to Women: Addressing Women and Women's Sensibilities*, 17, no. 1 (2004): 1–2.

6. "How to Look Like a Beauty," *Vogue*, September 1957.

7. "How to Slim a Chin," *Cosmopolitan*, June 22, 2005, http://magazines.ivillage.com/cosmopolitan/print/0,,289963,00.html

8. "Magazine Admits Airbrushing Winslet," *BBC News*, January 9, 2003, http://news.bbc.co.uk/1/hi/entertainment/showbiz/2643777.stm

9. "Miramax Slimmed Down Latifah in 'Chicago' Ad," *St. Petersburg Times*, April 5, 2003, http://www.sptimes.com/2003/04/05/Artsandentertainment/Sir_Mix_A_Lot_concert.shtml

10. Kate Betts, "The Man Who Makes the Pictures Perfect," *New York Times*, February 2, 2003, p. 1.

11. "CVS Pharmacy," http://www.cvs.com/CVSApp/cvs/gateway/cvsmain

12. "Macys", http://www.macys.com/catalog/syndicated/chanel/chanel.ogno?keyword=chanel

13. Neiman Marcus Online. "La Prairie: Skin Caviar Luxe Cream," Neiman Marcus 2005 http://www.neimanmarcus.com/store/catalog/prod.jhtml?itemId=prod7560077&parentId=cat4670733&materId=cat000378&index=3&cmCat=

14. B.F. Liebman, "Fated to be Fat?" *Nutrition Action Health Letter*, 14, no. 1 (Jan./Feb. 1987): 5.

15. Geraldine Sealey, "Whose Fault is Fat? Experts Weigh Holding Food Companies Responsible for Obesity," abcNEWS.com, http://abcnews.go.com/sections/us/DailyNews/obesityblame020122.html

16. Brett Silverstein, *Fed Up!* (Boston: South End Press, 1984): 4, 47, 110. Individuals may be affected in many different ways, from paying too much (in 1978, concentration within the industry led to the overcharging of consumers by $12-$14 billion (p. 47) to the ingestion of unhealthy substances.

17. "Weight Loss: U.S. Weight-Loss Product Retail Sales Increase Almost 90% over Past 5 Years," *Fitness and Wellness Business Week* February 18, 2004, http://www.lexisnexis.com

18. Jeremy Boyer, "Sales Go on Low-Carb Diet: The Food Industry Is Having to Adjust as More Consumers Buy into the Idea of Reducing Their Intake of Carbohydrates," *Times Union*, December 28, 2003, http://www.lexisnexis.com

19. "Diet/First Aid Sales Statistics," *Drug Store News*, 23, no. 7 (2001), p. 44, http://www.findarticles.com

20. Ibid.

21. Warren J. Belasco, "'Lite' Economics: Less Food, More Profit," *Radical History Review*, 28–30 (1984): 254–278; Hillel Schwartz, *Never Satisfied* (New York: Doubleday, 1986), 241.

22. Hillel Schwartz, *Never Satisfied* (New York: Doubleday, 1986), 270.

23. "Demand Performance; As the Low-Carb Phenomenon Plays out on the Public Stage, Mainstream Retailers Act in a Role That Promotes Choice and Education," *Supermarket New*, March 22, 2004, 33.

24. "FDA to Rule on Low-Carb Labeling," *Drug Store News*, 26, no. 7 (2004): 6–7.

25. *Prepared Foods*, "Cold Beverages Run Hot: New Beverages Lead the Way in Sales, as Product Introduction Declines for the First Time in Two Years, Setting the Stage for a Bump Due to Low-Carb Launches Next Year," 173, no. 5 (2004): 13.

26. "Low-Carb Products in Demand," *Mass Market Retailers*, 21, no. 9 (2004): 20.

27. Coca-Cola Company, "Coca-Cola," http://www.cocacola.com

28. PepsiCo, Inc., "Pepsi," http://www.pepsi.com

29. Jeff S. Volek and Eric C. Westman, "Very-Low-Carbohydrate Weight-Loss Diets Revisited," *Cleveland Clinic Journal of Medicine*, 69, no. 11 (2002): 849–862.

30. US Food and Drug Administration. [Food pyramid], accessed on November 19, 2005, from http://www.fda.gov/fdac/special/foodlabel/pyramid.html

31. "Atkins Physicians Council: Food Pyramid Recommendations Made to U.S. Congress," *FDA Law Weekly*, March 11, 2004, http://www.lexisnexis.com

32. She Knows Network. "Atkin's Food Pyramid," copyright: 2003–2005, accessed on November 19, 2005 from http://sheknows.com/about/look/4432.htm

33. "Atkins Physicians Council," March 11, 2004. (see n. 31)

34. U.S. Department of Health and Human Services, "Prevalence of Overweight and Obesity among Adults: United States, 1999–2002," www.cdc.gov/nchs/products/pubs/pubd/hestats/obese/obse99.htm#Table%201

35. Chris Hoyt, "Capitalizing on Corpulence," *Beverage Aisle*, 12, no. 11 (2003): 38–39, http://www.factiva.com

36. Russell Mitchell, Lois Therrien, and Gregory L. Miles, "ConAgra: Out of the Freezer," *Business Week*, no. 3166 (June 25, 1990): 24.

37. J. Dagnoli and J. Liesse, "Kraft, ConAgra Go Head-to-Head in Healthy Meals," *Advertising Age*, October 22, 1990, p. 59.

38. Kraftco, long the maker of various dairy products (including Kraft Macaroni and Cheese, Velveeta, Sealtest ice cream, creamy salad dressings, and the like), decided in 1989 to produce no-fat versions of many of its products, including Entenmann's desserts, cheese slices, dressings, and ice cream. Kraft's profit jumped 26% to $2.1 billion that year, partly due to its marketing of no-fat products. See: Lois Therrien, "Kraft Is Looking for Fat Growth from Fat-Free Foods." *Business Week*, March 26, 1990: 100–101. However, having no-fat versions of lots-of-fat products was only the beginning. Kraft also created Eating Right and

Budget Gourmet Light and Healthy frozen dinners. See: J. Dagnoli and J. Liesse, "Kraft, ConAgra Go Head-to-Head in Healthy Meals," *Advertising Age*, October 22, 1990: 59. Since Kraft was purchased by cigarette and (through Miller) beer giant Phillip Morris, the same people who profit from Eating Right and Entenmann's no-fat chocolate cake also profit from Jello, Kool-Aid, and the sugar-coated cereals which General Foods (now owned by Phillip Morris) creates. See: Brett Silverstein, *Fed Up!* (Boston: South End Press, 1984), 13.

39. Jim Hightower, *Eat Your Heart Out: Food Profiteering in America* (New York: Crown Publishers, 1975), 9.

40. Lois Therrien, "The Food Companies Haven't Finished Eating," *Business Week*, no. 3086 (January 9, 1989): 70. Therrien explains further: "In the past three years, for example, Borden Inc. has increased its share of the pasta market from 10 percent to 31 percent, largely by snapping up regional producers." Therrien further notes that in 1989, the 10 biggest food processors accounted for 35% of all U.S. food shipments, and the largest 20 companies widened their gross profits from 27% in 1982 to 35% in 1988. (January 9, 1989: 70).

41. Candie Sackuvich, "Cereal Competition Intensifies in Narrowing Market," *Milling and Baking News*, 79, no. 9 (April 2000): 32.

42. Phil Lempert, "Youth Must Be Served," *Progressive Grocer*, April 15, 2004, http://www.lexisnexis.com

43. Marion Nestle, *Food Politics* (Los Angeles: University of California Press, 2002), 188–191.

44. Channel One Network, "Channel One: About Us," http://.www.channelone .com/common/about

45. Ibid.

46. Nestle, *Food Politics,* 188–191. (See n. 43)

47. Kelly D. Brownell and Katherine Battle Horgen, *Food Fight* (New York: McGraw-Hill, 2004), 163.

48. Susan Linn, *Consuming Kids* (New York: New Press, 2004), 89–90.

49. Brownell and Horgen, *Food Fight,* 167. (See n. 47)

50. Morgan Spurlock, *Don't Eat This Book* (New York: G.P. Putnam's Sons, 2005), 95–96.

51. Ibid., 11.

52. Ibid., 14.

53. Margo Maine, *Body Wars: Making Peace with Women's Bodies* (Carlsbad, CA: Gurze Books, 2000), 45.

54. "Diet Industry Banks on Failure," *Irish Times*, July 28, 2003, http://www .lexisnexis.com

55. "Health Solutions: Diets and Interest in Healthy Eating Offer a New Platform around Which to Build Meal Solutions," *Business and Industry*, 53, no. 2 (2004): S5, http://www.lexisnexis.com

56. Ibid.

57. Adam Scheer, "Fad Diets Are Too Good to Be True," *Daily Nebraskan*, June 21, 2004, http://www.lexisnexis.com

58. Ibid.

59. Abbott Laboratories, "Lose Weight and Actually Keep it Off," http://www .meridia.net

60. Best-sellers compiled from http://www.amazon.com

61. Dermot McEvoy, "Something New, Something Old; Rachael Ray Cooks, Sudoku puzzles and tie-ins pack a wallop," *Publishers Weekly*, 253, no. 13 (2006): 30.

62. Ibid, 35.

63. Deralee Scanlon, *Diets That Work* (Chicago: Contemporary Books, 1991), 1.

64. Adam Gilden Tsai and Thomas A. Wadden, "Systematic Review: An Evaluation of Major Commercial Weight Loss Programs in the United States," *Annals of Internal Medicine*, 142, no. 1 (2005): 59.

65. PR Newswire Association, LLC, "Weight Watchers Announces Full-Year 2005 Results and Initiates Cash Dividend," (February 2006), http://www.lexisnexis.com

66. Julie Rawe, "Snacks Go Low Carb," *Time*, 162, no. 7 (2003): 46–48, http://search.epnet.com

67. Tsai and Wadden, *Annals of Internal Medicine*, 59–61. (See n. 64)

68. "Finance; Weight Control Company Reports Record First Quarter Revenues," *Life Science Weekly*, June 7, 2005, http://www.factiva.com

69. Annetta Miller, Karen Springen, Linda Buckley, and Elisa Williams, "Diets Incorporated," *Newsweek,* September 9, 1989, p. 60.

70. Tsai and Wadden, *Annals of Internal Medicine*, 59. (See n. 64)

71. Novartis Nutrition Corporation, *Optifast*, http://www.optifast.com

72. William Bennett and Joel Gurin, *The Dieter's Dilemma: Eating Less and Weighing More* (New York: Basic Books, 1982), 238.

73. General Nutrition Centers, http://www.gnc.com

74. Elisabeth Rosenthal, "Commercial Diets Lack Proof of Their Long Term Success," *New York Times,* November 24, 1992, pp. Al, C11.

75. *American Family Physician,* "Hypothalamic Set-Point System May Regulate Weight Loss," 29, no. 7 (1984): 269.

76. Atkins Nutritionals, Inc., *Getting Psyched to do Atkins*, http://atkins .com/Archive/2001/12/15-859588.html

77. Kandi Stinson, *Women and Dieting Culture: Inside a Commercial Weight Loss Group* (New Brunswick, NJ: Rutgers University Press, 2001), 122–136.

78. Ibid., 138.

79. Ibid., 142–143.

80. Judith Rosen, "Climbing Every Mountain; In This Ever-Expanding Area, Books Provide Assistance and Inspiration across a Broad Spectrum," *Publishers Weekly*, October 18, 2004, p. 36, 38.

81. Harpo Productions and Paramount Pictures Corporation, "Dr. Phil," http://www .Dr.Phil.com

82. Skip Hollandsworth, "Love Thy Self-Help," *Texas Monthly*, September 2003, http://www.lexisnexis.com

83. Rosen, *Publishers Weekly*. (See n. 80) p. 42.

84. Ibid.

85. Bette S. Tallen, "Twelve Step Programs: A Lesbian Feminist Critique," *NWSA Journal*, 2, no. 3 (1990): 396.

86. Tallen, *NWSA Journal*, 404–405. (See n. 85)
87. Tallen, *NWSA Journal*, 405. (See n. 85)

Bibliography

Abbott Laboratories. "Lose Weight and Actually Keep It Off." http://www.meridia.net

Amazon.com, Inc. Amazon.com. http://www.amazon.com

"Hypothalamic Set-Point System May Regulate Weight Loss." *American Family Physician*, 29, no. 7 (March 1984): 269.

"Atkins Physicians Council: Food Pyramid Recommendations Made to U.S. Congress." *FDA Law Weekly*, March 11, 2004. Accessed from http://www.lexisnexis.com

Atkins Nutritionals, Inc. "Getting Psyched to Do Atkins." http://atkins.com/Archive/2001/12/15-859588.html

Attie, I., & J. Brooks-Gunn. "Weight Concerns as Chronic Stressors in Women." *Gender and Stress*, ed. R.K. Barnett, L. Biener, & G. Baruch, pp. 218–252. New York: Free Press, 1987.

Belasco, W. J. "'Lite' Economics: Less Food, More Profit." *Radical History Review*, 28–30 (1984): 254–278.

Bennett, W., & J. Gurin. *The Dieter's Dilemma: Eating Less and Weighing More*. New York: Basic Books, 1982.

Betts, K. "The Man Who Makes the Pictures Perfect." *New York Times*, February 2, 2003, p. 1.

Boyer, J. "Sales Go on Low-Carb Diet: The Food Industry Is Having to Adjust as More Consumers Buy into the Idea of Reducing Their Intake of Carbohydrates." *Times Union*, December 28, 2003. http://www.lexisnexis.com.

Brownell, K.D., & K.B. Horgen. *Food Fight*. New York: McGraw-Hill, 2004.

Channel One Network. "Channel One: About Us." http://www.channelone.com/common/about.

Coca-Cola Company. "Coca-Cola." http://www.cocacola.com.

Cohn, L.D. & N.E. Adler. "Female and Male Perceptions of Ideal Body Shapes: Distorted Views among Caucasian College Students." *Psychology of Women Quarterly*, 16 (1992): 69–79.

"Cold Beverages Run Hot: New Beverages Lead the Way in Sales, as Product Introduction Declines for the First Time in Two Years, Setting the Stage for a Bump due to Low-Carb Launches Next Year." *Prepared Foods*, 173, no. 5 (2004): 13.

CVS.com. *CVS Pharmacy*. http://www.cvs.com/CVSApp/cvs/gateway/cvsmain

Dagnoli, J., & J. Liesse. "Kraft, ConAgra Go Head-to-Head in Healthy Meals." *Advertising Age*, October 22, 1990, p. 59.

"Demand Performance; As The Low-Carb Phenomenon Plays Out on the Public Stage, Mainstream Retailers Act in a Role That Promotes Choice and Education." *Supermarket News*, March 22, 2004, p. 33.

"Diet/First Aid Sales Statistics," *Drug Store News*, 23, no. 7 (2001). http://www.findarticles.com

"Diet Industry Banks on Failure." *Irish Times*, July 28, 2003. http://www.lexisnexis .com

Fallon A., & P. Rozin. "Sex Differences in Perceptions of Desirable Body Shape." *Journal of Abnormal Psychology,* 94, no. 1 (1985): 102–105.

"FDA to Rule on Low-Carb Labeling." *Drug Store News*, 26, no. 7 (2004): 6–7.

"Finance; Weight Control Company Reports Record First Quarter Revenues." *Life Science Weekly*, June 7, 2005. http://www.factiva.com

General Nutrition Centers, Inc. *GNC.com*. http://www.gnc.com

Harpo Productions and Paramount Pictures Corporation. "Dr. Phil." http://www .Dr.Phil.com

"Health Solutions: Diets and Interest in Healthy Eating Offer a New Platform around Which to Build Meal Solutions." *Business and Industry*, 53, no. 2 (2004): S5. http://www.lexisnexis.com

Hightower, J. *Eat Your Heart Out: Food Profiteering in America.* New York: Crown Publishers, 1975.

Hollandsworth, S. "Love Thy Self-Help." *Texas Monthly*, September 2003. http://www.lexisnexis.com

"How to Look Like a Beauty." *Vogue*, September 1957.

"How to Slim a Chin." *Cosmopolitan*, June 22, 2005. http://magazines.ivillage .com/cosmopolitan/print/0,,289963,00.html

Hoyt, C. "Capitalizing on Corpulence." *Beverage Aisle*, 12, no. 11 (2003): 38–39. http://www.factiva.com

Knapp, C. *Appetites: Why Women Want.* New York: Counterpoint, 2003.

"La Prairie: Skin Caviar Luxe Cream." Neiman Marcus Online 2005. http://www .neimanmarcus.com/store/catalog/prod.jhtml?itemId=prod7560077&parentId =cat4670733&masterId=cat000378&index=3&cmCat=

Lempert, P. "Youth must be served." *Progressive Grocer*, April 15, 2004. http://www .lexisnexis.com

Liebman, B.F. "Fated to Be Fat?" *Nutrition Action Health Letter*, 14 no. 1 (January/ February 1987): 1, 4–6.

Linn, S. *Consuming Kids.* New York: New Press, 2004.

"Low-Carb Products in Demand." *Mass Market Retailers,* 21, no. 9 (2004): 20.

Macys.com, Inc. *Macys* http://www.macys.com/catalog/syndicated/chanel/chanel .ognc?keyword=chanel

"Magazine Admits Airbrushing Winslet." *BBC News*, January 9, 2003. http://news .bbc.co.uk/1/hi/entertainment/showbiz/2643777.stm

Maine, M. *Body Wars: Making Peace with Women's Bodies.* Carlsbad, CA: Gurze Books, 2000.

McEvoy, D. "Something New, Something Old; Rachael Ray Cooks, Sudoku Puzzles and tie-ins pack a wallop." *Publishers Weekly*, 253, no. 13 (2006): 30–36.

Miller, Annetta, Karen Springer, Linda Buckley, and Elisa Williams. "Diets Incorporated." *Newsweek*, September 9, 1989: 60.

"Miramax Slimmed Down Latifah in 'Chicago' Ad." *St. Petersburg Times*, April 5, 2003. http://www.sptimes.com/2003/04/05/Artsandentertainment/Sir_Mix_A_Lot _concert.shtml

Mitchell, R., L. Therrien, & G.L. Miles. "ConAgra: Out of the Freezer." *Business Week*, no. 3166. June 25, 1990: 24–25.

Nestle, M. *Food Politics*. Los Angeles: University of California Press, 2002.

Novartis Nutrition Corporation. "Optifast." http://www.optifast.com

PepsiCo, Inc. "Pepsi." http://www.pepsi.com

Pollitt, K. "The Politically Correct Body." *Mother Jones*, 7, no. 7 (1982): 66–67.

PR Newswire Association, LLC. "Weight Watchers Announces Full-Year 2005 Results and Initiates Cash Dividend," February 2006. http://www.lexisnexis.com

Rawe, J. "Snacks Go Low Carb" [Electronic version]. *Time*, 162, no. 7 (2003): 46–48. http://search.epnet.com

Rosen, J. "Climbing Every Mountain; In this ever-expanding area, books provide assistance and inspiration across a broad spectrum." *Publishers Weekly*, 251, no. 42, (2004): 36–43.

Rosenthal, E. "Commercial Diets Lack Proof of Their Long Term Success." *New York Times*, November 24, 1992, pp. A1, C11.

Sackuvich, C. "Cereal Competition Intensifies in Narrowing Market." *Milling and Baking News*, 79 no. 9 (April 2000): 1, 32–38.

Scanlon, D. *Diets That Work*. Chicago: Contemporary Books, 1991.

Scheer, A. "Fad Diets Are Too Good to Be True." *Daily Nebraska*, June 21, 2004. http://www.lexisnexis.com

Schwartz, H. *Never Satisfied*. New York: Doubleday, 1986.

Sealey, G. "Whose Fault Is Fat? Experts Weigh Holding Food Companies Responsible for Obesity." *abcNEWS.com*. http://abcnews.go.com/sections/us/DailyNews/obesityblame020122.html

She Knows Network. "Atkins Food Pyramid," http://www.shcknows.com/about/look/4432.htm accessed on November 19, 2005.

Silverstein, B. *Fed Up!* Boston: South End Press, 1984.

Spurlock, M. *Don't Eat This Book*. New York: G.P. Putnam's Sons, 2005.

Stinson, K. *Women and Dieting Culture: Inside a Commercial Weight Loss Group*. New Brunswick: NJ: Rutgers University Press, 2001.

Tallen, B.S. "Twelve Step Programs: A Lesbian Feminist Critique." *NWSA Journal*, 2, no.3 (1990): 396–405.

Therrien, L. "The Food Companies Haven't Finished Eating." *Business Week*, no. 3086 (1989): 70.

Therrien, L. "Kraft is Looking for Fat Growth from Fat-Free Foods." *Business Week*, March 26, 1990: 100–101.

Tsai, A.G., & T.A. Wadden. "Systematic Review: An Evaluation of Major Commercial Weight Loss Programs in the United States." *Annals of Internal Medicine*, 142, no. 1 (2005): 56–66.

U.S. Department of Food and Drug Administration. "Food Pyramid." http://www.nalusda.gov/fnic/Fpyr/pyramid.gif

U.S. Department of Health and Human Services. "Prevalence of Overweight and Obesity among Adults: United States, 1999–2002." http://www.cdc.gov/nchs/products/pubs/pubd/hestats/obese/obse99.htm#Table%201

Volek, J.S., & E.C. Westman. "Very-Low-Carbohydrate Weight-Loss Diets Revisited." *Cleveland Clinic Journal of Medicine*, 69, no. 11 (2002): 849–862.

"Weight Loss: U.S. Weight-Loss Product Retail Sales Increase Almost 90% over Past 5 Years." *Fitness and Wellness Business Week*. February 18, 2004. http://www.lexisnexis.com

"Women Are More Critical of Their Own Bodies Than Those of Others." *Marketing to Women: Addressing Women and Women's Sensibilities*, 17, no. 1 (2004): 1–2.

FOUR

There's No Business Like the Body Business: Fitness and Cosmetic Surgery

Somewhere in the back of my brain there exists this certainty: The body is no more than a costume, and can be changed at will. That the changing of bodies, like costumes, would make me into a different character, a character who might, finally, be all right.

—Marya Hornbacher[1]

"I want you to watch the mirror like a hawk! Make sure you are squeezing your thighs tight the whole time! Now I want you to work on your abs. Pretend you're wearing a steel girdle, and your belly button is touching your spinal column. Squeeze!"

—Annette, fitness trainer

The Right Body: Sculpting with Exercise

The words in vogue at my fitness club are "tight" and "steel," as in "buns of steel." "Discipline," "strength," and "power" are also part of the vocabulary. "Muscle definition" is the term trainers use to urge both men and women to sculpt their bodies. To make the point, the club has changed the name of an aerobics and conditioning class to "Body Defined." Some of the women here think of body parts as fashion accessories. One works on the triceps so that she can show them off in a new strapless dress; another counts sit-ups in order to reveal her "abs of steel" in a bikini.

Our cultural mirrors have undergone a massive transition from the 1950s, when the ideal female body had soft curves. The illustrated pages of *Cosmopolitan* and *Vogue* reflect these changes over the past four decades. In the late 1950s, clothing was tailored to fit a tiny waistline, emphasizing the shoulders and hips; girdles helped achieve this look.

During the 1960s, fashion abandoned the hourglass shape for a more stick-like figure. The waistline disappeared. Girdles, still important aids to the slim figure, became lighter and more flexible. The real move toward slimness became very pronounced later in the decade, as the miniskirt shifted attention to the legs, shaped by pantyhose. Today, women are expected to be thin and firm with exercise and dieting. Liberated from the girdle, all a woman needs is the "control" provided by Flexees Shapewear.[2] The idea that "thin is in" has become pervasive throughout our culture. The magazine racks at your local grocery store hold a treasure trove of what "could" be attained if diet and exercise become a priority, and ripped abs, voluptuous breasts, and toned arms of the cover girls remind the consumer of "what could be." Consequently, lingerie stores and companies like Victoria's Secret and Maidenform offer women the supposed tools they need to shape and create the body that our culture mandates.

Marketing the Slender Amazon

The interest in physical fitness for both men and women has been growing since the 1970s. Exercise is now considered an essential part of a healthful life style.[3] The 1980s brought a new female ideal—the slender Amazon. The subcutaneous fat layer, which gives softness to the female physique, has been

FIGURE 4.1 The Secret Body Miracles of Victoria. *Simply travel to your nearest Victoria's Secret store & you too can have a "body by Victoria." Raise your breasts and your butt up high, slim your tummy, and add a cup size—all with the help of Victoria's Secret "miracle bra," "miracle suit," and "uplift" (buttocks) technology. (Victoria's Secret.)*

rejected in favor of large, hard muscles. *Time* magazine devoted a 1982 cover story to this, titled "New Ideal of Beauty."[4] Examples include actress/models like Jane Fonda, Cindy Crawford, and one of today's highest paid models, Gisele Bundchen. The 1990s and the first decade of the twenty-first century continued the trend, demanding that women pursue an even leaner, more toned physique.

Annette, the fitness trainer quoted earlier, commented:

> Women come to me and tell me they want their bodies changed. . . . They want everything smaller, tighter. They want "cuts," like in male bodybuilding, where you can see the muscle right under the skin, no fat anywhere, the very thing that's feminine. But it's hard for a woman to develop cuts. It requires extreme leanness and a good amount of testosterone, which most women just don't have much of in their bodies.

Early religious asceticism accepted persecutions and self-denial to achieve "expiation of sin, self-conquest, the intercession for divine graces and favors, and the imitation of Christ."[5] The fitness movement is a new form of asceticism, which "serves no higher moral aim but which, paradoxically, promises pleasure through self-denial."[6] Fitness fanatics follow specific painful rituals, often compulsively.[7] Annette mentioned clients who never miss their daily workouts, who pay careful attention to the "correct" costume, who insist on certain spots in class with the best mirror view. They worship certain aerobics instructors, or are attached to a particular fitness machine. "One club member with the flu literally crawled down her apartment stairs to come and try to use the Stairmaster. . . . People are in bondage—it's not something they do, the thing does them." These fanatics are a boon for the fitness industry.

Fitness Demographics and the Aging Market

Who comprises the fitness market? Fifty percent of gym-goers are over 40 years old.[8] Forty-eight percent of gym members are men and 52% are women.[9] Bally Total Fitness has reported that the average income of its members is $52,000 per year.[10]

A little over 20 years ago, the Census of Service Industries lumped "fitness clubs" together with sports and athletic clubs.[11] Today it is a distinct category. Similarly, the Census of Manufacturing has separated "home fitness equipment" from playground and gymnasium gear. Exercise as play; exercise as sport; exercise as weight loss technique—the same activity can have different meanings and intentions.

The U.S. Industrial Outlook 1993 indicates that "the exercise and fitness sector of the sporting goods industry has been the fastest growing since the end of the 1980's . . . exercising with equipment was the seventh most

FIGURE 4.2 Romancing the Body. *The ideal body has changed even in the last ten years. Both men and women are expected to be more muscular. The magazine ads have changed, too—the models are younger, and now men, in addition to women, are expected to wax. A hairy chest is no longer sexy—though, as these poses attest, sex still sells. (Nautilus, Inc.)*

popular activity in terms of participation."[12] In 2001, Americans spent \$5.9 billion on home gym equipment—a 7% increase from the total in 1999.[13] ICON Health and Fitness, the world's largest marketer and manufacturer of home fitness equipment,[14] includes NordicTrack, HealthRider, ProForm, Reebok, Weslo, Weider, Image, and iFIT.com.[15] The company, which has over 4,200 employees and 11 locations around the globe, recently reached the \$1 billion revenue mark in 2004.[16]

U.S. health club membership numbers grew 75% since 1997, when 22.5 million Americans were members.[17] In 2001, 58 million people attended health clubs, and annually, club memberships generate about \$12.2 billion.[18] Membership has continued to increase steadily: 2003 saw a nearly 8% growth over the previous year,[19] with \$14.1 billion in industry revenues.[20] According to the International Health, Raquet, and Sportsclub Association (IHRSA) and the Fitness Products Council of the Sporting Goods Manufacturers Association study, industry revenues were \$9.6 billion in 1998, and by 2010 they are estimated to reach \$20 billion.[21] With such a rapid increase in gym membership and annual revenue it is clear that the fitness industry has a vested interest in Americans believing they need to have a "fit" body. (The health club industry has financial interests in maintaining and expanding the Cult of Thinness as well.)

Exercise videos also have been a big-bucks market since Jane Fonda pioneered the genre in 1982. To date, Fonda's first exercise video is the biggest selling video of all time—17 million copies—in the United States[22] Kathy Smith and Denise Austin are bestsellers now, including their pregnancy workouts.[23] In 25 years, fitness "guru" Denise Austin has sold nearly 20 million exercise videos and DVDs.[24] Her last release is explicit: "Shrink your female fat zones: lose pounds and inches . . . Fast!"[25] In the spirit of expanding the market, many video companies offer "modular sections that can be completed in about a half-hour" since "consumers' schedules are usually tighter than their buttocks."[26] Again, a powerful marketing industry engages women in a losing battle against nature. It plays the same "game" as any other industry, using the same market and consumer analysis tools, pursuing greater market shares. Heavily marketed new products, like the NordicTrack Futura 2200 exercise chair[27] or Kathy Smith's latest "Timesaver Lift Weights to Lose Weight 2" video,[28] create big profits and drive the industry. While equipment salespeople, fitness club managers, and video instructors may be speaking the language of concern for one's personal health and well-being, the industry literature clearly speaks the language of business. As one marketing executive says, "It's clear we spend a lot of dollars on advertising. . . . It's one of the major reasons why our programs are so successful."[29] Annette said of the club where she works:

> The problem is that the people who own the clubs are part of the fitness cult themselves; they subscribe to a lot of the same behaviors as the members. So they're not necessarily going to be promoting moderation when they are part of this fanaticism. And it's money! If you have somebody coming in here and paying for four aerobics classes a day you are making money off that person, even if she can barely crawl out afterwards. But . . . you can't give people something they don't want.

However, what people want may change. A large segment of the American population, the baby boomer generation, is in fact getting older and fatter.[30] New data from the National Health and Nutrition Examination Survey show that today's American adults ages 20-74 are twice as likely to be obese as were adults in the late 1970s (31% of adults were obese in 1999–2000, versus 15% in 1976–1980).[31] Since 1980, the percentage of kids who are overweight in the United States has doubled.[32] The percentage of overweight adolescents has tripled.[33] Since the 1960s, the number of obese American 6-11-year-olds has increased more than twofold.[34] And it's not just in this country. According to the World Health Organization, "In 1995, there were an estimated 200 million obese adults worldwide and another 18 million children under five classified as overweight. As of 2000, the number of obese adults has increased to over 300 million."[35] In Thailand, for example, the percentage of obese 5-12-year-olds grew from 12.2% to 15.6% in just 2 years.[36]

There is a huge gap between the reality of our own bodies and the images to which we aspire, yet we continue to strive for the image. And business gladly serves us as long as it is profitable. There may be a limit to how much longer the boomer market will support this game as they live with aging bodies.[37] We will see how the fitness industry responds.

The Right Face and Body: Sculpting with Surgery

A fundamental change is taking place in American medicine, as hospital chains and physician groups are corporate-owned, creating a "medical-industrial complex."[38] The increase in for-profit hospital chains claiming a growing share of the medical market is part of the cause of change.[39] In many ways the medical establishment has become a capitalist production system, subject to "a contradiction between the pursuit of health and the pursuit of profit."[40]

The medical industry needs revenue for underused facilities, and very often the solution is to drum up some business geared to women's body insecurity. Says one analyst,

> Pick up a magazine that carries glossy ads, and you will see a full-color photograph of a wistful-looking woman in her thirties. . . . Her overall appearance lends a palpable persuasiveness to the copy that invites her to look carefully at her body—her falling buttocks, her flabby thighs, her sagging breasts, her aging face—and to do something about it. The ad is copyrighted by one of the large hospital corporations, Humana, Inc. The corporation, it would seem, is seeking more revenue from one of its underutilized operating rooms by playing, as ads have always played, on the weaknesses and insecurities of frail humanity. But this time it's not a cosmetic or a mouthwash that's being hawked—it's invasive surgery that, even under conditions of necessity, should not be lightly undertaken. But corporate practice calls for each branch of the "operation" (the appropriate word here) to earn its share of profits. Staff surgeons must cut; hospital beds must be filled. Besides, who can really hold a corporation responsible for what an individual freely chooses to do? The surgery, when it takes place, will in every way be voluntary.[41]

Plastic surgery has become a more than $8 billion a year industry and is increasingly considered part of the natural order of things for women.[42] Nearly 9 million surgical and minimally invasive cosmetic procedures were performed in 2003, an increase of 33% from the year before, according to statistics released by the American Society of Plastic Surgeons (ASPS).[43] In the last 10 years, the number of cosmetic procedures increased 192%.[44] The number of breast augmentations increased by 657% and the number of lipo-suctions increased by 412% from 1992.[45] Women represent the majority of cosmetic plastic surgery patients.[46] They account for 7.4 million procedures (86% of patients), while more than 1.2 million men (14% of patients) had cosmetic plastic surgery in 2003.[47] In fact, some research has shown such surgery is considered an "extension of a woman's regard for her appearance and therefore an expression of her essential femininity."[48]

Rhinoplasty, the ubiquitous "nose job," is one of the most popular plastic surgery procedures.[49] When I walked into a plastic surgeon's office to interview him, I overheard a conversation between a mother and the 18-year-old daughter she had brought in for a consultation.

> **MOTHER:** As your mother, I love you and I want you to be the best that you can be. I feel you'll benefit from having your nose done. But it's clear to me that you don't want it.

> **DAUGHTER:** I want people to like me for the way I am! If I have to do this to catch a future husband, then I'll do it, but I think they should like me the way I am.

Although the mother had mixed emotions about the operation, I felt the pressure she was placing on her daughter to consider this type of surgery as "self-improvement" would win out, with her daughter ultimately getting her nose altered.

Surgery as self-improvement is an increasing option, even a mandate, with an expanding market. As one recent survey conducted by the American Society for Aesthetic Plastic Surgery (ASAPS) pointed out, 22% of respondents with incomes under $25,000 indicated that they would consider cosmetic surgery.[50] Compared with the 35% of respondents with incomes above $75,000 who would consider surgery, the percentage of low-income respondents contemplating surgery seems puzzlingly high.[51] Similarly, the ASAPS annual survey of physicians found that the average recipients of Botox injections are working mothers ages 40-55[52] and are "more likely to have annual household incomes of less than $50,000 to $100,000 (44 percent) than to have annual incomes of more than $150,000 (36 percent)," said Leroy Young, M.D., Chair of ASAPS Non-surgical Procedures Committee.[53]

New Trends in Cosmetic Surgery

As social pressure to have the "perfect body" increases, more people use cosmetic surgery to acquire the body and face they want. What used to be primarily a route to correct physical abnormalities is now an acceptable practice dictated by fashion and affordable to almost all consumers. Famous faces are held up as paragons of beauty, and surgeons report that it has become more common for patients to request "Julia Roberts's nose" or "Angelina Jolie's lips." MTV's show "I Want a Famous Face" hopped on the trend, and during its first season (March-April 2004) showcased six candidates eager to suffer the pain and expense of reconstructive surgeries to look like a celebrity. Breast augmentation, rhinoplasty, chin and cheek implants, porcelain veneers . . . all are valid means to get the desired face.

The ASAPS claims the MTV show "sends the wrong message."[54] "Having plastic surgery because you want to look like someone else is the wrong way to start out," says ASAPS President Robert W. Bernard, MD.[55] "Plastic surgery was never intended to change who you are, and to believe that surgery can achieve that will only lead to disappointment. . . . In most cases, such requests are simply not possible to fulfill, but more important they are indications of unrealistic attitudes toward cosmetic surgery."[56] The influence that programs like "I Want a Famous Face" can have on millions of adolescents is further cause for alarm.

Banishing Fat and Wrinkles—By the Knife

Another plastic surgeon commented on the high profits in trimming fat and removing wrinkles:

> Plastic surgery is now not only for the upper class but the middle class as well and within reach of even the lower middle class. In New York they now have a chain of clinics which specialize in cosmetic surgery marketed to the masses— assembly line cosmetic surgery. Those who own the operation are not necessarily the doctors. Some surgeons feel pressured to drop their standards because they are economically driven by competitive forces. For example, in Massachusetts an M.D. is licensed to perform any type of plastic surgery he or she wants. If they do not want to spend the money opening up a surgery clinic all they need to do is to team up with an M.B.A. who buys a clinic and says to the doctor, "OK, get to work and start doing suction lipectomies . . . as many as you can." There is no law that says he cannot. He hires an M.D. with no training and says, "We'll show you a movie on how to do it. I'll pay you $500 per person, and I'll charge $1,000. More certified plastic surgeons are charging $2,000. I'll undercut them by half." So they have stolen the soul of medicine.

According to the ASPS, the top five surgical cosmetic procedures for women in 2004 were liposuction (292,402), breast augmentation (264,041), eyelid surgery (200,667), nose reshaping (195,504), and facelift (103,994).[57] The 35-50 age group underwent 38% of all cosmetic plastic surgeries, with 668,402 procedures.[58] The body-fat removal procedure known as liposuction was the most popular,[59] with 324,891 procedures (a 15% increase from 2002).

Guaranteed Financing for Your Cosmetic Surgery Regardless of Your Past Credit History

Breastloans.com manages a group of **Board Certified Plastic Surgeons** who guarantee they **Will Finance** all or part of your plastic surgery procedure regardless of your past credit.

You will be given a **Free Consultation** with a board certified plastic surgeon in you area. That's a $200 value absolutely free.

* Free Consultation

* Board Certified Plastic Surgeons

The Best Loan Is At BreastLoans.com It's Just One Click Away.

Don't Waste Any Time. Visit BreastLoans.com Right Now.

breastloans.com

FIGURE 4.3 Get Loan = New Breasts. *Breastloans.com: New Breasts, "Just one click away."*

The national average physician fee was $2,704, for a total national expenditure of over $1 billion.[60]

This recent advertisement for plastic surgery notes that breast surgeons will "guarantee they will finance all or part of your plastic surgery procedure regardless of your past credit."

Breast augmentation was the second most popular procedure in the United State in 2004,[61] affecting more than a quarter-million women.[62] Approximately 60,000 of these were reconstructive surgeries—the remaining were performed on healthy women who wanted to change their breast size.[63] Ironically, women who strive for ultra-lean figures often find their breast fat disappears. Increasingly, the "right" female body is an amalgam of the impossible, demanding flat stomachs, thin thighs and boyish hips, yet large breasts.

In 2004, American women spent over $1 billion on breast enlargement,[64] a seemingly endless market served by eager surgeons. Dr. Adriane Fugh-Berman, medical advisor to the National Women's Health Network, wrote, "In the early 1980's the American Society of Plastic and Reconstructive

Surgeons reached a new low when it suggested that small breasts be considered a disease—they named it 'micromastia.' "[65] Previously it seemed that the cure for this "disease" had backfired. A class-action lawsuit brought by women claiming their medical problems were caused by their silicone implants resulted in a $2.3 billion settlement by Dow Corning in 2004.[66] To date, an estimated 240,000 people are awaiting payment from this settlement.[67] The companies involved insisted that the implants were safe despite the wide range of immune-related problems reported by the women.[68] Recently, however, the Food and Drug Administration has considered lifting its 13-year ban on silicone-gel breast implants.[69] The Mentor Corporation, creator of new and "improved" silicone implants, has persuaded the FDA that its new product is "reasonably safe."[70] These new implants can only be sold under certain conditions specified by the FDA, one of which requires that Mentor must warn patients that they "should get an MRI scan every five years after implant insertion and every two years after that."[71] According to Mentor's own research trials, 1.4% of the implants they inserted broke within a time period of 3 years.[72] How often the implants break within a 10-year time period, however, is still unknown.[73]

Though relatively recent, liposuction and implant technologies are simple and speedy to execute. As one surgeon I interviewed said:

> In the past 20 years the technological advancements in plastic surgery have allowed people to alter any part of their body within a few hours, and to literally buy a beautiful face or body. Liposuction, for example, allows you to accomplish something that no human being could ever do before: to choose where to lose weight. Instead of going to a health club and working out for 1 year, and still not being satisfied, you can point to a place and say, "Doctor, I want to get rid of this specifically." We've never had that luxury of choice before. You can pretty much dictate a type of body that you want, though there still are certain shapes that are intrinsic to a person and cannot be created.

There are even more drastic weight loss surgeries. Those considered morbidly obese (160-225% above ideal body weight) can choose "stomach stapling." In this procedure, four rows of stainless steel staples across the upper stomach create a small "pouch" to which a portion of the small intestine is attached.[74] Reduced stomach size means less food ingested—and therefore, weight loss.

According to the American Society for Bariatric Surgery, 145,000 weight-reducing procedures were performed in 2004, each procedure costing an average of $25,000, or more than $3.5 billion charged to patients and their insurance companies.[75] Complications, however, can inflate a patient's expenses to $100,000 or more.[76] According to a recent study, the mortality rate for gastric bypass (the most common type of bariatric surgery) was 1 in 200[77]—higher than the rate for coronary angioplasty.[78]

I interviewed one woman who had her stomach stapled as a last resort, believing it would change her life when nothing else had worked.

Janet's Story

When Janet went to nursing school she weighed about 185 pounds.

> I was much heavier than everybody else. But the wonderful thing about nursing school was that these were all people like me. They wanted to be nurses and take care of people. Those values were important as a group. That was really the only time in my whole life I felt comfortable in a group, until much later

After nursing school she went to New York City and met Harry.

> He was tall and big, really interesting and bright. He didn't seem to care that I was heavier. I was head over heels in love for the first time in my life. The first time I went to visit Harry's family, he was scared to death. He said, "My mother is going to hate you." When I got to the door she looked at me with horror. She said to him, "This is what you bring home to me? This is what you're going to marry?" But we got married. Harry's mother wore black with a veil over her face and cried for the whole ceremony.

After they moved out of the city, Harry started drinking heavily and verbally abusing Janet. They were on the verge of breaking up when Janet discovered that she was pregnant. She felt that a baby could "fix things" between them. After their son was born, Janet tipped the scales at 270 pounds.

> At that time everybody was doing these stomach stapling operations, and the surgeon who was doing these surgeries had been a dialysis surgeon in a hospital I was working in. I went to see him and I said: "I'm out of control. I just keep eating. And I just can't do anything." And my blood pressure was way up. So, I put it in terms of really needing to save my life. And I was still trying to save my marriage

Janet's husband had sworn that "If I lost weight everything would be fine. So I had the surgery."

Janet lost 100 pounds in 9 months.

> I looked like a million bucks. On top of the world. And actually, my head was in a better space as far as my husband was concerned, because it was like, "Shape up or I'm out of here." You know, I didn't feel so desperate. Everybody thought I was just wonderful. I had a wonderful baby and I was taking care of my husband like I was supposed to, and I was going to school—I was managing it all.

I asked Janet about the effects from her surgery.

> The surgery was painful, though that goes away. But food became a real problem. I couldn't eat much—I would throw up. I would get pale and shaky, and I would sweat and I would have horrible cramps, and the food would go just right through me. I would have diarrhea for hours. It's kind of like surgical binging and purging, and I hated it. Also, I couldn't eat anything I liked, like apples, or anything that had any bulk to it. I couldn't eat protein. But what I could eat was candy, and potato chips and all this junk that makes you fat in the first place.[79]

Little by little she stretched her stomach out. And Janet realized that nothing in her life was really different.

> Nothing changed. When I was thin, sex was no better, nor more often, nor did my husband like me any better. I was still stressed out about my marriage and I just ate. I gained back 100 pounds.

Finally, Janet left her husband. Then a terrifying medical crisis, in which her stapled stomach developed an abscess, almost killed her. Janet had to have her surgery reversed. After a long recovery, she decided to accept her body on its own terms. Her weight stabilized, and she entered a second, satisfying marriage with a man who loves her the way she is. Today Janet has a Ph.D. and a successful academic career.

Janet's painful route to self-acceptance meant rejecting the cultural norms she had grown up with. She had to decide for herself what her personal shape should be. If we take a look at the everyday world of girls as they grow up and begin to develop a sense of body image, we will see how family and friends echo cultural values and attitudes. As the "nose job" plastic surgeon consulted by the mother/daughter duo told me, "If the daughter's friends and future husband do not recognize her qualities, and if a nose job does what it takes, she will do it. But it is mainly because of pressures imposed from without, coming through the mouthpiece of a mother, or any other force."

If we examine some of these forces at work within the family, peer group, and educational environment, we may understand how women become a "certain body."

Notes

1. Marya Hornbacher, *Wasted* (New York: HarperCollins, 1998), 31.
2. Maidenform, Inc., http://www.maidenform.com
3. A.G. Britton, "Thin Is Out, Fit Is In," *American Health*, July 1988, 66–71; T.F. Cash, B.A. Winstead, and L.H. Janda, "The Great American Shape-up," *Psychology Today,* 20, no. 4 (1986): 30–36.
4. R. Corliss, "Sexes: The New Ideal of Beauty," *Time*, August 1982, pp. 72–73.

5. Anthony Synnott, *The Body Social: Symbolism, Self and Society* (New York: Routledge, 1993), 16.
6. Richard A. Gordon, *Anorexia and Bulimia: Anatomy of a Social Epidemic* (Cambridge: Basil Blackwell, 1990), 96. Some researchers note how as a society Americans are obsessed with health, wellness, as well as fitness, and that they equate these things with "personal salvation." Getting fit and staying healthy, these authors suggest, is becoming a moral imperative within our society, and this imperative is used by groups and agencies to justify attempts to control those who do not measure up. They suggest there is a growing "health fascism" which exercises "increasing vigilance and control over what people put into their bodies and what they put their bodies into" (259). See: Charles Edgley and Dennis Brissett, "Health Nazis and the Cult of the Perfect Body: Some Polemical Observations," *Symbolic Interaction*, 13, no. 2 (1990): 257–259.
7. Some research suggests that "compulsive exercise" is becoming a clinical issue: See: S. Wichmann and D.R. Martin, "Exercise Excess: Treating Patients Addicted to Fitness," *The Physician and Sports Medicine*, 20, no. 5 (1992): 193–200.
8. Michael J. Weiss, "Chasing Youth," *American Demographics*, 24, no. 9 (2002): 37.
9. Pamela Paul, "Locker Room Advertising," *Advertising Age*, 24, no. 11 (2002): 29.
10. Ibid., 28.
11. U.S. Department of Commerce, *Census of Service Industries*, 1982.
12. U.S. Department of Commerce, *U.S. Industrial Outlook*, 1993.
13. Weiss, *American Demographics*, 37.
14. PR Newswire Association, LLC, "Leading Home Fitness Equipment Manufacturer Selects UCN™ to Reduce Customer Service Costs" (May 2005), http://www.lexisnexis.com
15. Ibid.
16. Ibid.
17. International Health, Racquet and Sportsclub Association, "IHRSA," http://cms.ihrsa.org
18. Paul, *Advertising Age*, 28. (See n. 9)
19. International Health, Racquet and Sportsclub Association, "IHRSA," http://cms .ihrsa.org
20. Ibid.
21. Ibid.
22. Geoffrey Wansell, "Frankly Fonda," *Daily Mail*, April 7, 2005, http://www .lexisnexis.com, p. 38.
23. Amazon.com, Inc, http://www.amazon.com
24. Waterfront Media, Inc., "About Denise," http://www.deniseaustin.com/free/aboutdenise.asp
25. Ibid.
26. Catherine Applefield, "Keeping Up with All the Fondas," *Billboard*, November 1991, p. 56.
27. ICON Health and Fitness, "NordicTrack", http://www.nordictrack.com
28. Kathy Smith Lifestyles, LLC, http://www.kathysmith.com.

29. "Exercise Video: Toned Up and Taking Off—Again," *Video Marketing News*, 13, no. 19 (1994): 58.
30. Chip Walker, "Fat and Happy," *American Demographics,* 15, no. 1 (1993): 52–57.
31. U.S. Department of Health and Human Services, "Health, United States, 2004 with Chartbook on Trends in the Health of Americans" (Hyattsville, MD: U.S. Government Printing Office, 2004).
32. World Health Organization, http://www.who.int.
33. Ibid.
34. Ibid.
35. Ibid.
36. Ibid.
37. Walker, *American Demographics*, 52–57. (See n. 30)
38. See: Stanley Wohl, *Medical Industrial Complex* (New York: Harmony Books, 1984), 18. Wohl notes: "Originally the term MIC (Medical Industrial complex) was coined to describe the loose influential alliance of drug companies and medical associations. It was first appropriated for use in the present sense in 1980 by Dr. Arnold S. Relman, editor of the *New England Journal of Medicine.*"
39. See: Douglas Shenson, "Will 'M.D.' Mean 'More Dollars'?" *New York Times*, May 23, 1985, p. 27.
40. Donald W. Light, "Corporate Medicine for Profit," *Scientific American* 255, no. 6 (1986): 38.
41. Stanley Wohl, *The Medical Industrial Complex* (New York: Harmony Books, 1984), 3.
42. American Society of Plastic Surgeons, http://www.plasticsurgery.org
43. Ibid.
44. Ibid.
45. Ibid.
46. Ibid.
47. Ibid.
48. Diana Dull, *Before and Afters: Television's Treatment of the Boom in Cosmetic Surgery,* paper presented at the 84th annual meeting of the American Sociological Association, San Francisco, CA, August 9–13, 1989.
49. American Society of Plastic Surgeons, http://www.plasticsurgery.org
50. American Society for Aesthetic Plastic Surgery, http://www.surgery.org
51. Ibid.
52. U.S. Newswire, "U.S. Newswire Medialink Worldwide," http://www.usnewswire.com
53. Ibid.
54. American Society for Aesthetic Plastic Surgery, http://www.surgery.org
55. Ibid.
56. Ibid.
57. American Society of Plastic Surgeons, http://www.plasticsurgery.org
58. Ibid.
59. Ibid.

60. American Society for Aesthetic Plastic Surgery, http://www.surgery.org
61. Ibid.
62. American Society of Plastic Surgeons, http://www.plasticsurgery.org
63. Ibid.
64. American Society for Aesthetic Plastic Surgery, http://www.surgery.org
65. Adriane Fugh-Berman, "Training Doctors to Care for Women," *Technology Review,* 97, no. 2 (1994): 35.
66. Dale Lezon, "Breast Implant Claims to Proceed; Dow Corning to Begin Paying Off Settlements," *Houston Chronicle,* June 3, 2004, http://www.chron.com, p. A1.
67. Ibid.
68. See: Lisa Billowitz, "Breast Implants: In the Aftermath of Corporate Greed," *Sojourner,* 17, August (1992): 12; Gina Kolata, "Details of Implant Settlement Announced by Federal Judge," *New York Times,* April 5, 1994, p. A1; Gina Kolata, "3 Companies Near Landmark Accord on Breast Implant Lawsuits," *New York Times,* March 24, 1994, p. B10.
69. Lauran Neergaard, "FDA Panel Backs Lifting Breast Implant Ban," Associated Press Online, April 13, 2005, http://www.lexisnexis.com
70. Ibid.
71. Ibid.
72. Ibid.
73. Ibid.
74. Armour Forse and George L. Blackburn, *Morbid Obesity: Weighing Treatment Options,* Unpublished manuscript, Department of Surgery, New England Deaconess Hospital, Harvard Medical School, Boston, 1989.
75. Milt Freudenheim, "Insurers Balk at Bariatric Operations, Citing Cost and Risks," *New York Times,* May 27, 2005, http://www.lexisnexis.com, p. C1
76. Ibid.
77. Ibid.
78. Ibid.
79. Esther Rothblum notes that the side effects of stomach stapling were stated as follows: "leakage of stomach fluid into the abdomen, ventral hernia, potassium deficiency, urinary tract infection, anemia, vitamin deficiency, osteoporosis due to lack of calcium, diarrhea, constipation, vomiting, malnutrition, stomach cancer and death." Esther D. Rothblum, "Women and Weight: Fad and Fiction," *Journal of Psychology,* 124, no.1 (1990): 19.

Bibliography

Amazon.com, Inc. *Amazon.com.* http://www.amazon.com.
American Society for Aesthetic Plastic Surgery. "American Society for Aesthetic Plastic Surgery." http://www.surgery.org
American Society of Plastic Surgeons. "American Society of Plastic Surgeons." http://www.plasticsurgery.org

Applefield, C. "Keeping Up with All the Fondas." *Billboard*, November 1991, p. 56.

Billowitz, L. "Breast Implants: In the Aftermath of Corporate Greed." *Sojourner,* 17 (August 1992): 12.

Britton, A.G. "Thin Is Out, Fit Is In." *American Health*, July 1988, pp. 66–71.

Cash, T.F., B.A. Winstead, & L.H. Janda. "The Great American Shape-up." *Psychology Today,* 20, no. 4 (1986): 30–36.

Corliss, R. "Sexes: The New Ideal of Beauty." *Time*, August 1982, pp. 72–73.

Dull, D. *Before and Afters: Television's Treatment of the Boom in Cosmetic Surgery.* Paper presented at the 84th annual meeting of the American Sociological Association, San Francisco, CA, August 9–13, 1989.

Edgley, C., & D. Brissett. "Health Nazis and the Cult of the Perfect Body: Some Polemical Observations." *Symbolic Interaction*, 13, no. 2 (1990): 257–279.

"Exercise Video: Toned Up and Taking Off—Again." *Video Marketing News*, 13, no. 19 (1994): 58.

Forse, A., & G.L. Blackburn. *Morbid Obesity: Weighing Treatment Options.* Unpublished paper, Department of Surgery, New England Deaconess Hospital, Harvard Medical School, Boston, 1989.

Freudenheim, M. "Insurers Balk at Bariatric Operations, Citing Cost and Risks." *New York Times*, May 27, 2005. http://www.lexisnexis.com, p. C1.

Fugh-Berman, A. "Training Doctors to Care for Women." *Technology Review,* 97, no. 2 (1994): 34–40.

Gordon, R.A. *Anorexia and Bulimia: Anatomy of a Social Epidemic.* Cambridge: Basil Blackwell, 1990.

Hornbacher, M. *Wasted.* New York: HarperCollins, 1998.

ICON Health and Fitness. "NordicTrack." Accessed from http://www.nordictrack.com

International Health, Racquet and Sportsclub Association. "IHRSA." http://cms.ihrsa.org.

Kathy Smith Lifestyles, LLC. "KathySmith.com" http://www.kathysmith.com

Kolata, G. "Details of Implant Settlement Announced by Federal Judge." *New York Times*, April 5, 1994, p. A1.

Kolata, G. "3 Companies Near Landmark Accord on Breast Implant Lawsuits." *New York Times*, March 24, 1994, p. B10.

Lezon, D. "Breast Implant Claims to Proceed; Dow Corning to Begin Paying Off Settlements." *Houston Chronicle*, June 3, 2004. http://www.chron.com, p. A1.

Light, D.W. "Corporate Medicine for Profit." *Scientific American*, 255, no. 6 (1986): 38–45.

Neergaard, L. "FDA Panel Backs Lifting Breast Implant Ban." Associated Press Online, April 13, 2005. http://www.lexisnexis.com.

Paul, P. "Locker Room Advertising." *Advertising Age*, 24, no. 11 (2002): 28–30.

PR Newswire Association, LLC. "Leading Home Fitness Equipment Manufacturer Selects UCN™ to Reduce Customer Service Costs," May 2005. http://www.lexisnexis.com

Rothblum, E.D. "Women and Weight: Fad and Fiction." *Journal of Psychology,* 124, no. 1 (1990): 5–24.

Shenson, D. "Will 'M.D.' Mean 'More Dollars'?" *New York Times*, May 23, 1985, p. 27.

Synnott, A. *The Body Social: Symbolism, Self and Society.* New York: Routledge, 1993.

U.S. Department of Commerce. *Census of Service Industries.* Washington, DC: U.S. Government Printing Office, 1982.

U.S. Department of Commerce. *U.S. Industrial Outlook.* Washington, DC: U.S. Government Printing Office, 1993.

U.S. Department of Health and Human Services. *Health, United States, 2004 with Chartbook on Trends in the Health of Americans.* Hyattsville, MD: U.S. Government Printing Office, 2004.

U.S. Newswire. "U.S. Newswire Medialink Worldwide." http://www.usnewswire.com

Walker, C. "Fat and Happy." *American Demographics*, 15, no. 1 (1993): 52–57.

Wansell, G. "Frankly Fonda." *Daily Mail*, April 7, 2005. http://www.lexisnexis.com

Waterfront Media, Inc. "About Denise." http://www.deniseaustin.com/free /aboutdenise.asp

Weiss, M.J. "Chasing Youth." *American Demographics*, 24, no. 9 (2002): 35–41.

Wichmann, S., & D.R. Martin. "Exercise Excess: Treating Patients Addicted to Fitness." *Physician and Sports Medicine*, 20, no. 5 (1992): 193–200.

Wohl, S. *The Medical Industrial Complex.* New York: Harmony Books, 1984.

World Health Organization. "World Health Organization." http://www.who.int

FIVE

Becoming a Certain Body

I don't care if it hurts
I want to have control
I want a perfect body
I want a perfect soul

—Radiohead[1]

My parents were always complimenting me on how I looked.
My father would say, "You look good, you lost weight." He
also commented on other women, more than me—always
commenting on pretty young girls. So I knew it was very
important that I looked good too. When I'd dress up, I
wanted him to see that I could be just as pretty as all those
women he was commenting on.

—Jane, college sophomore

As members of our society, young women have to learn how "to be a body."[2] For the most part, what a woman observes in the mirror is what she uses to measure her worth as a human being.[3] We have just seen how the food, diet, and fitness industries, aided by the media, have systematically convinced women that independence means self-improvement, self-control, and responsibility for achieving the ultra-slender body ideal. But the family, school, and peer group also have a role in reflecting and frequently amplifying societal norms. These social rewards and punishments urge women's bodies toward thinness, creating vast differences in how men and women feel about their bodies.

Sara Shandler,[4] author of *Ophelia Speaks* (1999), observes other people's bodies as a point of reference from which she comes to see and evaluate her own, a phenomenon all too common for many young girls and women.

> I do not have a cute nose, perfect skin, long legs, a flat stomach, or long eye-lashes. My awareness of these facts makes my body a backdrop for my every-day life. My stomach, back, skin, knees, hair are always in my peripheral vision.

FIGURE 5.1 Hollywood: Objects of Desire Collage.

Never my sole focus (I'm too healthy for that!), but always just tickling at my consciousness. I sometimes catch myself comparing my body to those of actresses, models, women walking down the street. Then I remind myself: Healthy, happy, normal girls don't notice, don't envy other women's small frames or sunken cheeks. They don't find pride in the comment, "Wow. Your collar bones really stick out." They don't feel guilty for not being as thin, or as muscular, as the star in the magazine clipping. Oh, they don't do they?[5]

In *Ophelia Speaks*, Shandler comments on stories and essays girls have submitted to her about growing up female. She has her own personal narratives to share, and while she can intellectualize and understand these sociocultural pressures on females, such awareness does not free her from these pressures.

Seeing the Self

Growing up in American society, most of us are taught, of course, to value what our society values—we learn to see ourselves as others see us. Self-image develops through social interaction. According to noted social psychologist

George Herbert Mead, "The self has a character which is different from that of the physiological organism, with a development all its own.[6] The self is not even present at birth but arises later in the process of social experience and activity."[7]

Mead adds that we experience ourselves as both subjects and objects, "as such, not directly, but only indirectly, from the particular standpoints of other individual members of the same group or from the generalized standpoint of the social group as a whole to which he belongs."[8] Sociologist Charles Horton Cooley refers to this as the "looking-glass" self.[9] Our family, friends, and significant others are the mirrors which reflect us. What they value in us provides the basic building blocks of selfhood—ultimately, there is a significant relationship between one's social interactions and one's personal psychology. That there must be a relationship between an individual with an eating disorder and the society in which she lives is a major premise of this book.

Unlike personality, tastes, and social values, our physical appearance is always visible to others. It is a critical factor in the development of self-concept for women, especially during adolescence and young adulthood. And weight is an important aspect of appearance, affecting young women's sense of social and psychological well-being.[10] Many women experience even a few extra pounds as a major issue in their lives; they tend to weigh themselves frequently and report seeking medical help for weight problems more often than men. Although physical appearance is important for men, their traditional socialization stresses the importance of achievement (the mind) as a primary determinant of self-image and self-esteem—as opposed to their bodies.

Women's bodily focus develops from discussions with friends, interactions with family and social groups, and messages they receive from outside this intimate circle. It is reinforced by the everyday practices that make the body central to their identity as a female—from clothing, hairstyle, and makeup, to speech, walk, and gesture. The Cult of Thinness becomes a powerful lure as society decides which is the "right" and the "wrong" body, and treats women accordingly.[11] Reality TV shows, such as "Extreme Makeover" and "Doctor 90210" love showing "right" and "wrong" bodies. Diet advertisements also frequently depict the same body dichotomy in "before" and "after" photos. According to these advertisements, all we have to do is buy and follow a particular diet, and we, too, can make our "wrong" bodies "right." Makeovers, or the transformation of "wrong/bad" to "right/good," emphasize socially valued female attributes, such as youth, thinness, and sexual attractiveness.

The Good, the Bad, and the Ugly

As a culture, we associate beauty with the good, and ugliness with the bad. Attractive people are "viewed as being happier, more successful, smarter, more interesting, warmer, more poised, and more sociable".[12] Research suggests that the social consequences of looking good begin as early as infancy.[13] As they enter school, less attractive youngsters are likely to be blamed and punished more often than attractive children.[14] For example, one study concluded that adults not only ascribe negative traits to unattractive children, they are also reluctant to ascribe such traits to attractive ones. Participants in this study were given written descriptions of supposed behavioral transgressions with photos of either attractive or unattractive kids attached, as judged previous by a separate group of adults. Their evaluations confirmed the researcher's hypothesis:

> An attractive child who commits a harmful act will be perceived as less likely to exhibit chronically antisocial behavior than an unattractive child, primarily when the offense is severe. Thus, adults evaluating an attractive child . . . perceive him as less likely to have committed a similar transgression in the past and less likely to commit one in the future than an unattractive child.[15]

Moreover, the youngsters themselves do not want to be associated with unattractive, namely, "fat," peers. Goldberg (2000), a *New York Times* columnist, reports the following:

> Studies indicate that opinions about fat people turn negative in childhood and stay negative: As early as nursery school, they have found children prefer drawings of peers in wheelchairs, on crutches, or with facial disfigurements, to those of fat children. [In addition,] a National Education Association position paper says that "for fat students, the school experience is one of ongoing prejudice, unnoticed discrimination, and almost constant harassment" . . . a 1988 study found that students would rather marry an embezzler, a cocaine user, a shoplifter, or a blind person than an obese person.[16]

Similar attitudes apparently exist in correlating attractiveness and academic performance. In another study, 400 fifth-grade teachers examined report cards with pictures of either attractive or unattractive children. The teachers were asked to evaluate the students' IQ and academic potential. The researchers noted, "We predicted that the child's appearance would influence the teacher's evaluation of the child's intellectual potential, despite the fact that the report cards were identical in content. It did. The teachers assumed that the attractive girl or boy had a higher IQ, would go to college, and that his parents were more interested in his education."[17] Sadly, teachers' attitudes often become self-fulfilling prophecies for some students. Goldberg points out how ". . . studies have shown that fat students are less likely to go to college and that their parents are less likely to pay for it; once there, they face still more hostile attitudes from their fellow students."[18]

Furthermore, while it is evident that the social consequences of attractiveness (or lack thereof) may begin in infancy, they often continue through adulthood. Job discrimination based on appearance accompanies the socially ascribed "gender-ness" in occupations and highlights how social rules about desired appearance can affect one's ability to acquire and maintain a number of jobs.

An overview of research studies on discrimination and body image notes that slightly obese white women tend to earn 5.9% less than their thinner counterparts and that as women get heavier, they earn less, such that as women's weight increases into the morbidly obese category, they earn, on the average, a 24.1% lower pay rate. Males, on the other hand received lower pay only at the very mobidly obese category.[19]

In a similar vein of prejudice, recent lawsuits targeting United Airlines, Atlantic City's Borgata Hotel Casino & Spa, (discussed in chapter 1), and clothing juggernaut Abercrombie & Fitch call attention to "appearance discrimination."

United Airlines

According to Laura Scott (2000) of law firm Parsons Behle and Latimer,

> United States Airlines discriminated against female flight attendants from 1989 to 1994 by requiring them to stay thinner than their male counterparts, the Ninth Circuit of Appeals recently ruled. Some female attendants lost pay when they were suspended or dismissed for being overweight. Others may have suffered emotionally and physically as they struggled to stay within the stricter weight standards imposed on women.[20]

United used "stricter standards for women than men," employing weight standards for a "large frame" for men, while simultaneously employing weight standards for a "medium frame" for women.

> Under United's policy, men could generally weigh as much as large-framed men whether they were large framed or not, while women could generally not weigh more than medium framed women.[21]
>
> The Ninth Circuit found that the different "medium" and "large" body frame standards applied by United imposed "unequal burdens" on women. The standards were thus "facially discriminatory" in violation of Title VII.[22]

Abercrombie and Fitch.

Abercrombie & Fitch has been forced to settle numerous lawsuits charging that they engage in discriminatory hiring practices, based on the applicant's appearance. In a *CBS News* report, a respondent explained what the "Abercrombie & Fitch look" entailed, "It's dominated by Caucasian, football

FIGURE 5.2 Abcrombie Love. *Abercrombie does not just sell clothing, but also confers social status, attractiveness, and romance as well. (Abercrombie and Fitch.)*

looking, blonde-hair, blue-eyed males; skinny, tall. . . . . You don't see any African-Americans, Asian-Americans, and that's the image they're portraying and that they're looking for."[23] Another respondent answered, "They [a]re all tall, skinny white girls."[24]

The lawsuit revealed how not only body type—tall and thin—determined who worked at Abercrombie, but skin color and ethnicity as well. According to an interviewee for *CBS News*, "blacks, Asians, Latinos were sometimes hired by Abercrombie, but weren't given the opportunity to work in sales. 'The greeters and the people that worked in the in-season clothing, most of them [were] white, if not all of them. . . . The people that worked in the stock room, where nobody sees them, were mostly Asian-American, Filipino, Mexican, Latino.'"[25] For Abercrombie & Fitch, only "all-Americans" ("non-ethnic-looking" Americans), are considered attractive enough to sell their brand.

Body type has long been associated with temperament, and has given us stereotypes like jovial Santa Claus, or Shakespeare's lean and hungry Cassius. Various pseudoscientific attempts at inferring personality from physiology were in vogue well into the last century, including the analysis of body type. Attempts at a more scientific body-personality study date from the 1930s, the best known being the work of W.H. Sheldon. Sheldon adopted three body type categories: ectomorphic (lean, angular); mesomorphic (muscular); and endomorphic (rounded or plump). They were associated—tentatively by Sheldon, but more assertively in folklore—with cerebral, active, and sensuous personality types, respectively. It is easy to criticize this oversimplified approach. But researchers continue to investigate the body build and personality correlation, albeit in a more sophisticated manner. [26]

Some researchers emphasize the moral implications of obesity, a legacy of our Puritan heritage.[27] The overweight body signifies immoderation, greed, and the inability to control gratification, whereas slimness epitomizes the opposite, and is attributed to strong moral fiber. (So much for the validity of the Santa and Cassius types.)

This attitude is flatly expressed by three female college freshmen:

> How can people not even care how they look? It's just like they let themselves go to pot. (Not only) how they look to others and themselves, but what's going on inside of them? It's unhealthy. I'm determined to never, ever look like that.

> If I was at my ideal weight I'd feel really in control of my life. Even though I'm comfortable, I still feel that if I was perfect, I would be maybe 7 pounds less than I am. And I would feel a little more positive with myself, I think. More in control.

> I think being thin would just make me a better person. I just feel like I'd have more self-confidence and stuff.

Not surprisingly, weight-related aspects of appearance are more intertwined with self-concept in females than in males, and they are a major factor in how others view them.[28] The stakes are even higher for females because the relationship between attractiveness and higher social status is in fact stronger for girls than boys.[29] For example, a study on the social patterns of college undergraduates found that the more good-looking the female, the more her date liked her, regardless of other factors such as personality or intelligence.[30] Women who are overweight date less often and are less satisfied with their mate.[31] In a society where beauty and charm still strongly affect a woman's social, marital, and economic success, fat women risk downward social mobility. By the same token, a man can maintain or gain status by marrying a beautiful, thin woman.[32]

My interview subjects believed in the close connection between thinness, good looks and marriage:

Julia commented on how becoming thinner really made a difference in getting men to respond to her: "Last summer when I lost a lot of weight, men were much more receptive to me, and it's flattering. Because I've never experienced that before." And Elizabeth said, "When I lose weight, I have a wonderful feeling of power. It's like I am in control of my body."

Marya Hornbacher, best-selling eating disorder author of *Wasted: A Memoir of Anorexia and Bulimia* (1998) details how thinness can offer social mobility:

> The town I lived in operated on money. Money—class, really—and eating disorders share a direct relationship with each other. In our culture, thinness is associated with wealth, upward mobility, success. I may not even need to point out that these things are associated with self-control and discipline: the yuppification of body and soul, perfect people with high powered jobs and personal trainers, perfect-toothed smiles and happy-happy lives. Conversely, fat is associated with weakness, laziness, and poverty. Thinness has become "an ideal symbolizing self-discipline, control, sexual liberation, assertiveness, competitiveness, and affiliation with a higher socioeconomic class." . . . The "perfect body" becomes a public display of those means. The body as a costly bauble.[33]

In simplest terms, thinness becomes associated with "upper-class-ness" (regardless of the individual's actual economic status), while fatness becomes associated with the opposite. For so many women whose bodies are their primary identities, their ultimate "project,"[34] the Cult of Thinness promises them all the rewards of cultural acceptance.

Dissatisfied with Weight and Shape: A Survey of College Students

Given the premium on looking good, and the fear of its opposite, it is not surprising that I found a greater degree of dissatisfaction with body weight and shape among the women in my college student survey.[35] Their concerns with their bodies reflect large-scale trends found in other studies.[36] I discovered distinct gender differences in perception of body weight:

- Women overestimated their relative weights and thought their bodies were heavier than the medically desirable weights on the standard Metropolitan Life Insurance Co. chart. Men, on the other hand, judged their weights more accurately.

- When I asked my sample of students how much they wanted to gain or lose, the vast majority of women (95%) wanted to lose weight while the men were almost evenly split between wanting to lose and wanting to gain weight.

- More than three quarters of the females in my sample, but less than one third of the males, ever dieted.

- Even more startling is the difference between the proportion of men and women who said they dieted "most of the time"—37% of the women and only 15% of the men.

- I asked the question: "When you look in the mirror, which best describes your feelings: proud, content, neutral, anxious, depressed, or repulsed?" In my sample, 50% of the men were at least content with their body image, compared with only 37% of the women.

- Many women expressed anxiety about their bodies (28% of the women compared to 6% of the men). About 7% of the women felt depressed and repulsed by their bodies compared with 4% of the men.

Dissatisfied with Weight and Shape: A Survey of Teenage Girls

The August 2005 issue of *Teen People* (circulation 1.45 million) released the results of their first-ever body image survey, to which 1,553 teen girls ages 13-18 responded. Here are some of the results:

- "55% often feel confident about their bodies."

- ". . . 17% claim body confidence all the time, while 27% say they 'hardly ever' feel confident about their bodies."

- ". . . Models in magazines and women on TV and in films were equal factors in causing the greatest body insecurity."

- "While girls are influenced by what they see on TV and in magazines, of the people in their lives, parents are most likely to pressure girls to lose weight—not friends, boyfriends, or coaches. In fact, 1 in 3 teen girls has been urged by her parents to change her weight—mainly to lose weight."

- "The [cosmetic surgery] procedure most teen girls (49%) would contemplate is liposuction."

- ". . . 53% of girls believe that they weigh too much."

- "51% of black girls claim total body satisfaction, as compared to 31% of white girls and 30% of Hispanic girls"

- "While most white girls (56%) feel that their friends have better bodies than they do, only 41% of black girls feel that way."

How Much Should I Weigh?

There is no single definition of the ideal body for every woman and not everyone pursues their ideal with the same intensity. In my interviews, some women expressed ambivalence about their ideal, or even found ways to rebel against the Cult of Thinness. But in general, women say they want to be thin, and they have a very definite weight in mind. Where do they get this number? While pondering this question, I decided to go to a local diet center on initiation night. When I entered and filled out a registration form, I immediately got weighed. My weight counselor consulted a weight chart and told me that I needed to lose 10 pounds. I am 5' 6", and at that time, in the mid-1990s, I weighed 130 pounds.[37] When I asked her how she decided on this amount, and where her chart came from, she said she did not know. I asked if I could see the chart, perhaps take a copy, but she said she would have to ask for permission.[38,39]

Charting Weights

The weight charts that appear in many women's magazines and elsewhere are important definers of desirable or "ideal" weight—another mirror promoting weight obsession.

To find your "ideal" weight on a weight chart, you must identify your height and frame as small, medium, or large to get a suggested ideal weight range. I chose a chart from one of the largest weight-loss organizations in the United States.

Then I compared this chart to the one my physician uses, the Metropolitan Life Insurance Company's 1983 height and weight chart for men and women. They are the weights for a given frame and height for which mortality rates are lowest,[40] based on medical-actuarial studies of insured men and women.[41] According to the medical chart, and my doctor, my weight was within the "normal" range for my height.

I compared the two sets of charts for men and for women. I termed the diet center chart the "cultural" model of ideal weight and called the Metropolitan Life Insurance's chart the "medical" model of ideal weight. These two charts appear in Figure 5.3 (for men) and Figure 5.4 (for women). When we compare these two figures they reveal a large gap between the two charts for women.

On the average, the difference between the two charts for men is about 5 pounds, whereas the difference is close to 20 pounds for women.[42] This difference represents, in pounds, our culture's pressures on women to be thin.

I wondered if women really *wanted* to be at a "culturally desirable" weight. So I asked the students in my sample: "How much weight would you like to lose or gain at this time?" Each response was added to, or subtracted from, the student's actual reported weight in order to determine desired weight. I

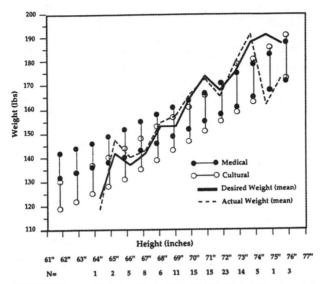

FIGURE 5.3 Range of Actual and Desired Body Weight of Male College Sample Compared to Cultural and Medical Standards.

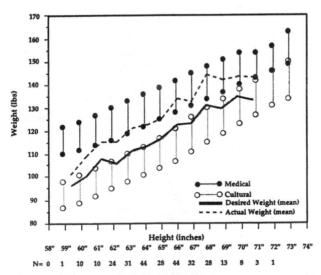

FIGURE 5.4 Range of Actual and Desired Body Weight of Female College Sample Compared to Cultural and Medical Standards.

plotted the students' desired weights and actual weights and compared them to the cultural and medical chart (see Figures 5.3 and 5.4).

The graph illustrates clearly how women's average desired weight gravitates toward the cultural model of ideal weight, rather than toward the medical model. For men, the deviation between actual and desired weight was minimal. On the average, there was approximately a 1 pound difference for men between their actual and desired mean weight compared to a 10 pound difference for women.

For some height categories the men's mean desired weight was *heavier* than their mean actual weight. This is not surprising. Men are taught that being big is one way of being powerful, and they often confuse weight with build and may avoid dieting because they believe that it will reduce their strength and virility.

In the meantime, the average American female has become heavier, finding it impossible to meet these stringent and increasingly elusive cultural weight norms.[43] Ironically, dieting can cause weight gain; we know that especially restrictive diets may disrupt metabolism, create feelings of deprivation, and trigger overeating. Many dieters have great difficulty breaking this cycle. As we noted in chapter 3, within a culture obsessed with thinness, Americans are becoming increasingly obese.

The following memoir shows how our culture rewards and punishes women as they spend a lifetime becoming a "certain body."

Growing Up Fat: The Story of Renée

When I interviewed Renée, who was a graduate student, in her late 30s. An attractive woman with a great sense of humor, she was 5' 6" and weighs approximately 160 pounds. She was eager to tell her story, hoping that younger women might benefit from her experience.

Renée's young parents fled Europe during World War II, and she was born in the United States. In her first memories concerning her body image she recalls being a normal-sized 4- and 5-year-old:

> I had big bones, but I was not fat. But growing up I got very mixed messages from my mother and my grandmother. They would say, "You need to thin out, you know. Hopefully, when you grow taller, you'll be a little thinner." And then of course, my mother and grandmother would play it off on one another, doing their own mother-daughter thing. If my mother was on my side, my grandmother would say I needed to go on a diet. If my grandmother was on my side, my mother would say that I needed to diet. But no support ever.

Renée remembered the first time she felt bad about her weight:

> I was in the sixth grade, and you know how girls are in the sixth grade. It's just
> a hard time, and everybody is very cliquey, and I never could figure that out. I
> was walking past some girls on my way to the bathroom, and they started
> singing the theme song to the TV show *Rawhide*—about cowboys herding
> cows—"Rollin', rollin', rollin', keep those dogies rollin'." I pretended I didn't
> hear it, put my head up, and just walked right past them into the bathroom. I
> remember feeling horrible about that.

She also recalled a high school dance:

> My grandmother came to my friend's house to see us go to the dance. My friend
> Jill was blond and tiny, and she had on a white dress with roses. And I had on a
> royal blue satin dress, that of course you had to buy in the women's department,
> so it was a much older-looking dress. My grandmother had difficulties with
> English and she said, "Oh, Jill, you look like a flower" in her heavy accent. And
> looking for something nice to say about me, she said, "Oh Renée, you look like
> a tree," thinking of it as a compliment.

Renée paid a high price for her perceived unattractiveness, not just in terms
of her emotional and social well-being, but in her educational life too. The
unconscious favoritism shown to attractive school children, mentioned earlier,
may ensure their higher degree of academic success. Renée fulfilled those
expectations. Ambivalent about drawing attention to herself, when she got to
high school her grades dropped. She was told, and she felt, that she was "dumb."

> The teachers kept saying to me, "If you would pay attention, if you would con-
> centrate, if you would do your homework, if you would try harder, you could
> have straight A's." And I never believed them. Because it was too scary to think
> about being outstanding. But I also kept getting mixed messages. The guidance
> counselor told me when I was a junior that I could not go to college because I
> was not smart enough. The same year I was a National Merit Scholar because
> I scored so high on the test. But then they said the test was a fluke. "You test
> well, but you're not really smart." That's what I was told and I believed it.

She struggled with her growing anger at how she was treated, and she
looked for acceptable ways to develop herself, trying to compensate for her
bad feelings about being overweight by being "everybody's buddy."

> I was also the mediator. It's always been my role. I never had any dates in high
> school, but I hung out with the guys, you know, I was always their friend. I knew
> that I was never going to be a cheerleader, and no one was going to say, "Wow,
> isn't she beautiful." What they were going to say is, "Gee, she's a really nice
> person. I really like her." And that became what was important to me, that I was
> a nice person, and that I was a good person.

In many ways Renée rejected a traditionally feminine role: "In terms of all the games and the complexities of being a girl, I never bought into that. It didn't make any sense to me." She remembered wanting to be a boy for a long time.

When I was in 5th and 6th grade, I played Little League baseball because there was a new coach in town, and nobody told him that I was a girl. The boys all knew that I was a girl, but I cut my hair really short and I wore clothes so that I didn't look like a girl. And I was the star catcher.

Boys weren't terribly complex. You knew what they were thinking because they were pretty much head to mouth—You knew where you stood. And also, since I wasn't date material, they didn't care if I was fat. I was OK.

She described how she tried to negotiate a gender role identity for herself that was a mixture of what was culturally expected of boys and girls.

The male side of me became very developed, because my bravado fit in with being a boy. You know, like "If you don't like the way I look, then don't look." That was very boy-like. But I was very nurturing, very caring and very sensitive, which are girl characteristics.

Eventually, Renée was able to develop a self-identity and self-esteem outside of society's expectations. She ignored her guidance counselor's advice, went to college, and discovered that she could excel academically. In fact, she has completed her doctorate in the health field. She found that she had her own kind of femininity and attractiveness, and is now happily married.

But the emotional pain of her journey shows how, even for average-looking women, it is difficult to grow up in a culture of such high standards and expectations of appearance. For those who are overweight, it is an especially punishing experience.

Notes

1. Yorke, Thom. "Creep" [Recorded by Radiohead] on *Pablo Honey*, [CD]. Hollywood, CA: Capitol, 1993.
2. Anthropologist Mary Douglas was one of the first social scientists to point out the implications of the social meanings of the body: "The social body constrains the way the physical body is perceived. The physical experience of the body, always modified by the social categories through which it is known, sustains a particular view of society." Mary Douglas, *Natural Symbols: Explorations in Cosmology* (2nd ed.), (London: Barrie and Jenkins, 1973), 93.
3. R.M. Lerner, S.A. Karabenick, and J.L. Stuart, "Relations among Physical Attractiveness, Body Attitudes and Self-Concept in Male and Female College Students," *Journal of Psychology*, 85, 1st half (1973): 119–129. P. Rozin and A.E.

Fallon, "Body Image, Attitudes to Weight and Misperceptions of Figure Preferences of the Opposite Sex: A Comparison of Men and Women in Two Generations," *Journal of Abnormal Psychology*, 97, no. 3 (1988): 342–345. Linda A. Jackson, *Physical Appearance and Gender: Sociobiological and Sociocultural Perspectives* (Albany: State University of New York Press, 1992).

4. Sara Shandler, author of *Ophelia Speaks*, states how she wrote this book in response to Mary Pipher's (1994) book, *Reviving Ophelia*. Shandler details how Pipher's book (though a great contribution), left her "unsettled," in that she felt Pipher was speaking for her, whereas Shandler wanted "to speak for [her]self." Shandler writes, ". . . *Reviving Ophelia* had been a gift for us, but it had also sold us short. If Ophelia is to be revived then it must be done by the collective voice and actions of Ophelias everywhere" (xiii). Consequently, Shandler's desire to speak for herself and to have the voices of other girls be heard cast the idea for her book *Ophelia Speaks* (1999), which is a compilation of personal writings from girls, ages 12-18, who write about "our experiences of being young and female" (283). See: Sara Shandler, *Ophelia Speaks: Adolescent Girls Write about Their Search for Self* (New York: Harper Perennial, 1999).

5. Ibid. 3–4.

6. "Mead provides a profoundly social, although not socially deterministic, view of the self. The self is profoundly social not only in the sense that it arises in social experience, but also in the sense that it is a social process—a continuous inner conversation between an 'I' and a 'me.'" See: George Herbert Mead, "The Self as Social Structure," *Inside Social Life: Readings in Sociological Psychology and Microsociology*, ed. Spencer E. Cahill (Los Angeles, CA: Roxbury Publishing, 1998), 21.

7. George Herbert Mead, *Mind, Self and Society* (Chicago: University of Chicago Press, 1934), 135.

8. Mead. *Mind, Self and Society*, (see n. 7).

9. Charles Horton Cooley, *Social Organization* (New York: Schocken Books, 1909/ 1962). Charles Horton Cooley, "The Self as Sentiment and Reflection," in *Inside Social Life: Readings in Sociological Psychology and Microsociology*, ed. Spencer E. Cahill, (Los Angeles, CA: Roxbury Publishing, 1998), 16. Cahill writes,

> For Cooley, the human self also rests on individuals' emotional responsiveness to one another. . . . The individual not only appropriates people and material objects by claiming them as "mine," but he or she also appropriates images of himself or herself reflected in others' treatment of him or her. This is what is commonly known as Cooley's theory of "the looking glass self." Cooley suggests that the individual can only reflect upon and form images of himself or herself through the imaginary adoption of someone else's perspective. The individual imagines how that person must be judging his or her appearance and behavior, and consequently feels either pride or shame. Such socially reflected images inform the individual of who and what she or he is, and the consequent feelings of pride and shame provide the grounds for her or his sense of self-worth or esteem. (16)

10. G.R. Adams, "Physical Attractiveness Research: Toward a developmental social psychology of beauty." *Human Development*, 20, no. 4 (1977): 217–239. Marcia Millman, *Such a Pretty Face* (New York: Berkeley Books, 1980); J. Rodin, L. Silberstein, and R. Striegel-Moore, "Women and Weight: A Normative Discontent," in *Psychology and Gender: Nebraska Symposium on Motivation*, ed. T.B. Sonderegger (Lincoln: University of Nebraska Press, 1985), 267–307; R.G. Simmons and F. Rosenberg, "Sex, Sex Roles, and Self-Image," *Journal of Youth and Adolescence*, 4, no. 3 (1975): 229–258.

11. This is not to imply that women passively adapt to the dictates of patriarchal/capitalist mirrors of beauty. They also act according to their consciousness and will. However, there are strong rewards and punishments that women experience in the process of growing up which serve to provide women with a "pseudo-choice." They choose to conform and their actions combine over space and time to re-create or reproduce the beauty standards of patriarchy and capitalism.

12. Thomas F. Cash, "The Psychology of Physical Appearance: Aesthetics, Attributes and Images," in *Body Images Development, Deviance and Change*, ed. Thomas F. Cash and Thomas Pruzinsky (New York: Guilford Press, 1990), 53. See also: K.K. Dion, E. Berscheid, and E. Walster, "What Is Beautiful Is Good," *Journal of Personality and Social Psychology*, 24, no. 3 (1972): 285–290. For a review of the literature on this topic, see: E. Hatfield and S. Sprecher, *Mirror, Mirror: The Importance of Looks in Everyday Life* (Albany: State University of New York Press, 1986).

13. For example, research on infants notes that the perception of cuteness is related to the degree to which maternal bonding takes place. See: G.H. Elder, Jr., T.V. Nguyen, and A. Caspi, "Linking Family Hardship to Children's Lives," *Child Development*, 56, no. 2 (1985): 361–375.

14. Thomas F. Cash, "The Psychology of Physical Appearance: Aesthetics, Attributes, and Images," in *Body Images: Development, Deviance, and Change*, ed. Thomas F. Cash and Thomas Pruzinsky (New York: Guilford Press, 1990), 34; L. Berkowitz and A. Frodi, "Reactions to a Child's Mistakes as Affected by His/her Looks and Speech," *Social Psychology Quarterly*, 42, no. 4 (1979): 420–425; K.K. Dion, "Physical Attractiveness and Evaluation of Children's Transgressions," *Journal of Personality and Social Psychology*, 24, no. 2 (1972): 207–213; K.K. Dion, "Children's Physical Attractiveness and Sex as Determinants of Adult Punitiveness," *Developmental Psychology*, 10, no. 5 (1974): 772–778; V. McCabe, "Facial Proportions, Perceived Age, and Caregiving," in *Social and Applied Aspects of Perceiving Faces*, ed. T.R. Alley (Hillsdale, NJ: Erlbaum, 1988), 89–95.

15. K.K. Dion, "Physical Attractiveness and Evaluation of Children's Transgressions," *Journal of Personality and Social Psychology*, 24, no. 2 (1972): 211–212.

16. Carey Goldberg, "Discrimination against Obesity Is Widespread," *Post and Courier*, November 5, 2000, accessed July 3, 2005 from http://www.musc.edu/psychiatry/slater/weight1.htm

17. E. Berscheid and E. Walster, "Beauty and the Beast," *Psychology Today*, 5, (March 1972): 42–6.

18. Carey Goldberg, "Discrimination against Obesity Is Widespread" (See n. 16); M. Roehling, "Weight-Based Discrimination in Employment: Psychological and Legal Aspects," *Personnel Psychology,* 52, no. 4 (1999): 969–1016.

19. M. Roehling, "Weight-Based Discrimination in Employment." (See n. 18)

20. Laura S. Scott, "Weight Standards May Constitute Sex Discrimination," *Parsons Behle, and Latimer,* 2000. http://library.findlaw.com/2000/Sep/1/132878.html

21. In 1992, plaintiffs, a group of thirteen current and former female United Flight attendants, filed a class action challenging these weight requirements. In the case, *Leslie Frank, et al. v. United Airlines, Inc.*, plaintiffs contend that United's weight policy discriminated against women in the violation of Title VII of the Civil Rights Act of 1964 ("Title VII"). [Law firm] Lieff Cabraser serves as co-counsel for plaintiffs.

    See: United Airlines, "United Airlines Gender Discrimination Class Action," July 1, 2005, http://www.lieffcabraser.com/united_airlines.htm

22. Inquiries of gender discrimination against males in certain occupations have also garnered public attention. For instance, the question of discriminatory hiring practices, based on appearance and gender, was examined in 1996,

    when Hooters was the subject of a four-year sexual discrimination investigation by the Equal Opportunity Commission and also the defendant in a private class action lawsuit for refusing to hire male waiters. Hooters claimed its revealingly clad women are part of its product, making female sexuality a bona fida occupational qualification. Eventually the EEOC backed off, but Hooters ended up paying a $3.75 million settlement to make the lawsuit go away.

    See: Victor Kisch, "When Appearance Isn't Just Personal," *Portland Business Journal,* June 29, 2005, http://portland.bizjournals.com/portland/stories/2005/06/13

23. "The Look of Abercrombie & Fitch," *CBS News,* November 24, 2004, http://www.cbsnews.com/stories/2003/12/05/60minutes. 06/29/2005

24. AF Justice "*Daily Orange* (Syracuse University Newspaper), 'Minority Groups Sue Abercrombie for $40 Million,'" Abercrombie and Fitch Class Action Lawsuit Media Center, January 27, 2005, accessed June 29, 2005 from http://afjustice.com/media.htm

25. See: AF Justice.com. 2003–2005. Lieff Cabraser Heimann & Bernstein. LLP. Accessed on May 23, 2006.

26. W.H. Sheldon, *The Varieties of Human Physique: An Introduction to Constitutional Psychology,* (New York: Harper & Row, 1940). While the relationship between body type and personality characteristics was not empirically supported in subsequent research studies for given individuals, there is some evidence that others believe that this relationship is true, even when there is not empirical proof. For a review of this research see: Linda A. Jackson, *Physical Appearance and Gender: Sociobiological and Sociocultural Perspectives.* (Albany: State University of New York Press, 1992), 156–158.

27. Rita Freedman, *Beauty Bound* (Lexington, MA: D.C. Heath, 1986). One newspaper reporter commented on the coming of the "New Puritans," and noted that

> New Puritans are not merely concerned with developing clearer complexions or trimmer thighs. They pursue self-denial as an end in itself, out of an almost mystical belief in the purity it confers. They work hard and play harder—if your idea of play is Olympic competition. . . . But while the benefits of moderate exercise and the value of a high-fiber, low-cholesterol diet are enshrined in the canons of medicine and the annual reports of the publishing world, and while it is probably a good idea to use a little caution in choosing a sex partner, the New Puritanism goes well beyond the minimum daily requirements for sound minds in sound bodies. (26)

See: Dinitia Smith, "The New Puritans: Deprivation Chic," *New York Magazine,* June 11, 1984, pp. 24–29.

28. G.R. Adams, "Physical Attractiveness Research," *Human Development,* 20, no. 4 (1977): 217–239; R.M. Lerner and S.A. Karabenick, "Physical Attractiveness, Body Attitudes, and Self-Concept in Late Adolescents," *Journal of Youth and Adolescence,* 3, no. 4 (1974): 307–316; R.G. Simmons and F. Rosenberg, "Sex, Sex Roles, and Self-Image," *Journal of Youth and Adolescence* 4, no. 3 (1975): 229–258.

29. B.E. Vaughn and J.H. Langolis, "Physical Attractiveness as a Correlate of Peer Status and Social Competence in Pre-school Children," *Developmental Psychology* 19, no. 4 (1983): 561–567.

30. See: E. Berscheid and E. Walster, "Beauty and the Beast," *Psychology Today,* 45 October, 1972, pp. 42–46. For an excellent review of this literature, see: J. Rodin, L. Silberstein, and R. Streigel-Moore, "Women and Weight: A Normative Discontent," in *Psychology and Gender: Nebraska Symposium on Motivation,* ed. T.B. Sonderegger (Lincoln: University of Nebraska Press, 1985), 267–307.

31. M. Tiggemann and E.D. Rothblum, "Gender Differences in Social Consequences of Perceived Overweight in the United States and Australia," *Sex Roles,* 18, no. 1/2 (1988): 75–86; J. Blake and M.L. Lauer, "The Consequences of Being Overweight: A Controlled Study of Gender Differences," *Sex Roles,* 17, no. 1/2 (1986): 31–47.

32. D. Bar-Tal and L. Saxe, "Physical Attractiveness and Its Relationship to Sex-Role Stereotyping," *Sex Roles,* 2, no. 2 (1976): 123–133; P.W. Blumstein and P. Schwartz, *American Couples* (New York: Morrow, 1983).

33. Marya Hornbacher, *Wasted: A Memoir of Anorexia and Bulimia* (New York: HarperCollins, 1998), p. 46.

34. See: Joan Jacobs Brumberg, *The Body Project: An Intimate History of American Girls* (New York: Vintage Books, 1997), 97. "The body is a consuming project for contemporary girls because it provides an important means of self-definition, a way to visibly announce who you are to the world" (97).

35. Questionnaires were distributed to 960 sophomores at a private New England college, and 395 questionnaires were returned and analyzed. The resulting response rate was 41%, and the sample consisted of 71% females and 29% males.

36. Our research is confirmed by numerous studies of gender differences in perceived weight. See: S. Gray, "Social Aspects of Body Image: Perceptions of Normality of Weight and Affect on College Undergraduates," *Perceptual and Motor Skills,* 10 (1977): 1035–1090; A. Fallon and P. Rozin, "Sex Differences in Perceptions of Desirable Body Shape," *Journal of Abnormal Psychology,* 94, no. 1 (1985): 102–105; P. Rozin and A. Fallon, "Body Image, Attitudes to Weight and Misperceptions of Figure Preference of the Opposite Sex: A Comparison of Men and Women in Two Generations," *Journal of Abnormal Psychology,* 97, no. 3 (1988): 342–345; Linda A. Jackson, *Physical Appearance and Gender: Sociobiological and Sociocultural Perspectives,* (Albany: State University of New York Press, 1992).

37. A weight of 130 pounds for 66 inches is considered to be ideal for a *small body frame* according to the 1983 Metropolitan Height and Weight Chart. See: Steven B. Halls, "About the 'Metropolitan Life' Tables of Height and Weight," *Met Life Ideal Height Weight Table References,* 2003, http://www.halls.md/ideal-weight/met.htm. Furthermore, according to charts including U.S. National Center for Health Statistics, North American Association for the Study of Obesity, and the U.S. Army, a weight of 130 pounds for a height of 66 inches is actually considered to be *less than* the ideal weight. See: Nutribase, "Recommended Body Weights and Percent Body Fat Contents for Women," http://www.nutribase.com/fwchartf.shtml

38. The Body Mass Index (BMI), is another commonly used tool to determine ideal weight for height. According to the National Heart Lung and Blood Institute (NHLBI), the normal BMI weight range is from 18.5-24.9. Consequently, in order to be considered overweight according to the BMI, a person of 5' 6" would have to weigh 155 pounds, 25 pounds more than the weight of 130, which the diet center declared was 10 pounds overweight. According to the BMI, a weight of 130 pounds for a person of 66 inches equals a BMI of 21, clearly on the lower side of the weight continuum considered to be within a "normal," or optimum, weight range. See: Whathealth, "Body Mass Index Chart-Inches/Pounds- (BMI:19–35)," http://www.whathealth.com/bmi/chart-imperial.html (Interactive BMI chart, copyright 2003–2005, WhatHealth.com; Adapted from: National Heart Lung and Blood Institute [NHLBI]).

39. Also see: Steven B. Halls, "About the 'Medical Recommendation' of Ideal Weight,": http://www.halls.md/ideal-weight/medical.htm

> The medical profession likes simplicity. Researchers have tested if being overweight causes health risks, using a body mass index (BMI) of 25/kg/m2 as the definition of overweight. . . . Numerous studies have confirmed that having a body mass index over 25kg/m2 is associated with increased risk of disease (like diabetes, high blood pressure, heart attacks, etc) and a risk of shortened lifespan. It is important to point out that this simple definition of "overweight" by medical researchers, is not representative of how people regard each other, nor is it how a doctor would judge

an individual patient, nor is it used by most nutritionists. Furthermore, the BMI of 25 kg/m2 definition of overweight is a 'unisex' threshold, that suits neither men or women particularly well. Nevertheless, a BMI of 25-29.9 is defined as 'overweight' by some important institutions.

40. W. James Hannan, Robert M. Wrate, Steven J. Cowen, and Christopher P.L. Freeman, "Body Mass Index as an Estimate of Body Fat," *International Journal of Eating Disorders*, 18, no. 1 (1995): 91–97.

41. Experts have criticized the validity of these tables for several reasons:
    1) Insured people tend to be healthier than uninsured people.
    2) Frame size was never consistently measured.
    3) The people who were included were predominantly white and middle-class.
    4) Some persons were actually weighed, some were not.
    5) Some wore shoes and/or clothing, some did not.
    6) The tables do not consider percentage of body fat distribution, which are now known to be important factors in longevity.

    Excerpted from Nutribase.com. 2005, "Recommended Body Weights and Percent Body Fat Contents for Women."

42. An elaborate analytical procedure involving students' self-reported weight and height and stated desired weights were used to determine the weight model ("cultural" or "medical") students were following. A medium-size body frame was assumed in our calculations.

43. L.K.G. Hsu, "Classification and Diagnosis of the Eating Disorders," *The Eating Disorders: Medical and Psychological Basis of Diagnosis and Treatment*, ed. B.J. Blinder, B.F. Chaitin, and R.S. Goldstein, (New York: PMA Publishing, 1988), 235–238.

Bibliography

Adams, G.R. "Physical Attractiveness Research." *Human Development*, 20, no. 4 (1977): 217–239.

AF Justice. "Daily Orange (Syracuse University Newspaper), "Minority Groups Sue Abcrcrombie for $40 Million." Abercrombie and Fitch Class Action Lawsuit Media Center, January 27, 2005. http://afjustice.com/media.htm (accessed June 29, 2005).

Bar-Tal, D., & L. Saxe. "Physical Attractiveness and Its Relationship to Sex-Role Stereotyping." *Sex Roles*, 2, no. 2 (1976): 123–133.

Berkowitz, L., & A. Frodi. "Reactions to a Child's Mistakes as Affected by His/Her Looks and Speech." *Social Psychology Quarterly*, 42, no. 4 (1979): 420–425.

Berscheid, E., & E. Walster. "Beauty and the Beast." *Psychology Today*, 5, 1972, p. 45.

Blumstein, P.W., & P. Schwartz. *American Couples*. New York: Morrow, 1983.

Brumberg, J.J. *The Body Project: An Intimate History of American Girls*. New York: Vintage Books, 1997.

Cash, T.F. "The Psychology of Physical Appearance: Aesthetics, Attributes and Images." In *Body Images Development, Deviance and Change*, ed. T.F. Cash & T. Pruzinsky, p. 57–79. New York: Guilford Press, 1990.

CBS News. "The Look of Abercrombie & Fitch." *CBS News*, November 24, 2004. http://www.cbsnews.com/stories/2003/12/05/60minutes (accessed June 29, 2005).

Cooley, C.H. "The Self as Sentiment and Reflection." In *Inside Social Life: Readings in Sociological Psychology and Microsociology*, p. 16–20, ed. S.E. Cahill. Los Angeles: Roxbury Publishing, 1998.

Cooley, C.H. *Social Organization*. New York: Schocken Books, 1909, 1962.

Curran, J. "Servers File Discrimination Complaints over Casino Weight Limits," April 27, 2005. http://www.philyburbs.com (accessed June 29, 2005).

Dion, K.K. "Children's Physical Attractiveness and Sex as Determinants of Adult Punitiveness." *Developmental Psychology*, 10, no. 5 (1974): 772–778.

Dion, K.K. "Physical Attractiveness and Evaluation of Children's Transgressions." *Journal of Personality and Social Psychology*, 24, no. 2 (1972): 207–213.

Dion, K.K., E. Berscheid, & E. Walster. "What Is Beautiful Is Good." *Journal of Personality and Social Psychology,* 24, no. 3 (1972): 285–290.

Douglas, M. *Natural Symbols: Explorations in Cosmology* (2nd ed.). London: Barrie & Jenkins, 1970, 1973.

Elder, G.H., Jr., T.V. Nguyen, & A. Caspi. "Linking Family Hardship to Children's Lives." *Child Development*, 56, no. 2 (1985): 361–375.

Fallon, A., & P. Rozin. "Sex Differences in Perceptions of Desirable Body Shape." *Journal of Abnormal Psychology*, 94, no. 1 (1985): 102–105.

Freedman, R. *Beauty Bound*. Lexington, MA: D.C.: Heath, 1986.

Goffman, E. *The Presentation of Self in Everyday Life*. New York: Anchor Books, 1959.

Goldberg, C. "Discrimination against Obesity is Widespread." *The Post and Courier*, November 5, 2000 http://www.musc.edu/psychiatry/slater/weight1.htm (accessed July 3, 2005).

Gray, S. "Social Aspects of Body Image: Perceptions of Normality of Weight and Affect on College Undergraduates." *Perceptual and Motor Skills*, 45, no. 3, pt. 2. (1977): 1035–1040.

Halls, S.B. "About the 'Medical Recommendation' of Ideal Weight." http://www.halls.md/ideal-weight/medical.htm

Halls, S.B. "About the 'Metropolitan Life' tables of height and weight." *Met Life Ideal Height Weight Table References*, 2003. Accessed from http://www.halls.md/ideal-weight/met.htm

Hannan, J.W., R.M. Wrate, S.J. Cowen, and C.P.L. Freeman, "Body Mass Index as an Estimate of Body Fat." *International Journal of Eating Disorders* 18, no. 1 (1995): 91–97.

Hatfield, E., & S. Sprecher. *Mirror, Mirror: The Importance of Looks in Everyday Life*. Albany: State University of New York Press, 1986.

Hesse-Biber, S., Leavy, P., Quinn, C.E., & Zoino, J. "The Mass Marketing of Disordered Eating and Eating Disorders: The Social Psychology of Women, Thinness, and Culture." *Women's Studies International Forum,* 29, no. 2 (2006): 96–114.

Hornbacher, M. *Wasted: A Memoir of Anorexia and Bulimia.* New York: HarperCollins, 1998.

Hsu, L.K.G. "Classification and Diagnosis of the Eating Disorders." *The Eating Disorders: Medical and Psychological Basis of Diagnosis and Treatment,* ed. B.J. Blinder, B.F. Chaitin, & R.S. Goldstein, p. 235–238. New York: PMA Publishing, 1988.

Jackson, L.A. *Physical Appearance and Gender: Sociobiological and Sociocultural Perspectives.* Albany: State University of New York Press, 1992.

Kisch, V. "When Appearance Isn't Just Personal." *Portland Business Journal,* June 13, 2005. http://portland.bizjournals.com/portland/stories/2005/06/13. Accessed June 29, 2005.

Lerner, R.M., & S.A. Karabenick. "Physical Attractiveness, Body Attitudes, and Self-Concept in Late Adolescents." *Journal of Youth and Adolescence,* 3, no. 4 (1974): 307–316.

Lerner, R.M., S.A. Karabenick, & J.L. Stuart. "Relations among Physical Attractiveness, Body Attitudes and Self-Concept in Male and Female College Students." *Journal of Psychology,* 85, no. 1 (1973): 85, 119–129.

McCabe, V. "Facial Proportions, Perceived Age, and Caregiving." *Social and Applied Aspects of Perceiving Faces,* ed. T.R. Alley, pp. 89–95. Hillsdale, NJ: Erlbaum, 1988.

Mead, G.H. *Mind, Self and Society.* Chicago: University of Chicago Press, 1934.

Mead, G.H. "The Self as Social Structure." In *Inside Social Life: Readings in Sociological Psychology and Microsociology,* ed. S.E. Cahill. Los Angeles: Roxbury Publishing, 1998.

Milford, M. "If You Don't Fit In—Watch Out." *News Journal,* June 29, 2005. Accessed from www.delewareonline.com

Millman, M. *Such a Pretty Face.* New York: Berkeley Books, 1980.

Nutribase, "Recommended Body Weights and Percent Body Fat Contents for Women." http://www.nutribase.com/fwchartf.shtml

Parmley, S. "Suit over Casino's Weight Rule Could Have Wide-Ranging Repercussions." May 22, 2005. *The Philadelphia Inquirer/Knight Ridder/Tribune Business.* Accessed from www.hotel-online.com/News/2005_May_22/k.PHC.1117031048.html

Perrin, S. "How Executives Get Jobs," *Fortune,* August 1953, p. 182.

Richardson, S.A., N. Goodman, A.H. Hastorf, & S.M. Dornbusch. "Cultural Uniformity in Reaction to Physical Disabilities." *American Sociological Review,* 26, no. 2 (1961): 241–247.

Rodin, J., L. Silberstein, & R. Striegel-Moore. "Women and Weight: A Normative Discontent." In *Psychology and Gender: Nebraska Symposium on Motivation,* ed. T.B. Sonderegger, pp. 267–307. Lincoln: University of Nebraska Press, 1985.

Roehling, M., "Weight-Based Discrimination in Employment: Psychological and Legal Aspects." *Personnel Psychology,* 52, no. 4 (1999):969–1016.

Rozin, P., & A.E. Fallon. "Body Image, Attitudes to Weight and Misperceptions of Figure Preferences of the Opposite Sex: A Comparison of Men and Women in Two Generations." *Journal of Abnormal Psychology,* 97, no. 3 (1988): 342–345.

Scott, L.S. "Weight Standards May Constitute Sex Discrimination." *Parsons, Behle, & Latimer,* 2000. http://library.findlaw.com/2000/Sep/1/132878.html. 7/1/2005

Shandler, S. *Ophelia Speaks: Adolescent Girls Write about Their Search for Self.* New York: HarperPerennial, 1999.

Sheldon, W.H. *The Varieties of Human Physique: An Introduction to Constitutional Psychology.* New York: Harper & Row, 1940.

Simmons, R.G., & F. Rosenberg. "Sex, Sex Roles, and Self-Image." *Journal of Youth and Adolescence,* 4, no. 3 (1975): 229–258.

Smith, D. "The New Puritans: Deprivation Chic." *New York Magazine,* June 11, 1984, pp. 24–29.

Stake, J., & M.L. Lauer. "The Consequences of Being Overweight: A Controlled Study of Gender Differences." *Sex Roles,* 17, no. 1-2 (1986): 31–47.

Teen People. "Teen People Releases Results of Its First Body Image Survey in the August 2005 Issue, on Stands July 1," [Electronic version]. http://biz.yahoo.com/prnews/050630/nyth132.html?.v=14&printer=1. New York, June 30/ PRNewswire/06/30/2005

Tiggemann, M., & E.D. Rothblum. "Gender Differences in Social Consequences of Perceived Overweight in the United States and Australia." *Sex Roles,* 18, no. 1–2 (1988): 75–86.

United Airlines. "United Airlines Gender Discrimination Class Action." July 1, 2005. http://www.lieffcabraser.com/united_airlines.htm Retrieved 07/01/2005.

Vaughn B.E., & J.H. Langolis. "Physical Attractiveness as a Correlate of Peer Status and Social Competence in Pre-school Children." *Developmental Psychology,* 19, no. 4 (1983): 561–567.

Whathealth. "Body Mass Index Chart—Inches/Pounds— (BMI:19–35)." http://www.whathealth.com/bmi/chart-imperial.html

Yorke, T. "Creep" [recorded by Radiohead]. On *Pablo Honey* [CD]. Hollywood, CA: Capitol, 1993.

SIX

Joining the Cult of Thinness

I was raised by a domineering mother and a strong father
who didn't give me very much personal space to develop, so
I was really used to being told what to do . . . surrender-
ing myself to other people's will, desire, and wants . . .
really setting myself aside.

—Anna, former religious cult member

I see commercials with these bodies and I want to look like
that. I have this collage in my room of just beautiful bodies,
beautiful women. And at the bottom it says "THIN
PROMISES" in really big letters. I have it up on my mirror
so I look at it every morning, just to pump me up a little bit,
motivate me, dedicate me.

—Elena, college sophomore

The college-age women I interviewed related their struggles, rewards, and dis-
appointments as they learned the culturally accepted ways of "being a body."
Their body watching and food monitoring practices are powerful anchors to
membership in the Cult of Thinness.

For Elena, the pursuit of thinness has become almost a religion. Media
images—paragons of female beauty—are the "totems" that she worships, the
inspiration for her quest. Her mirror is an altar, where she examines herself and
fervently prays that she will be able to attain her ideal through practicing dieting and exercising rituals. Her daily mantra, "Thin Promises," keeps her dedi-
cated and focused on a physical self that must be continually improved. Body
monitoring—scrutinizing the mirror for one's physical flaws, or examining
"the competition" for comparisons and defects—requires treating the body
as an object, maintaining the mind/body split. Body measuring and food-
watching rituals keep women like Elena "pumped up" and faithful to the Cult.
In some cases, these rituals are painful reminders of one's shortcomings, sins,
and failures, threatening eternal damnation. Rituals require time and energy,
even a reorganization of daily life, not unlike the practices Anna followed in
her religious cult. "We would get up at 4 A.M. to meditate and do yoga for 2½

FIGURE 6.1 Ultimate Transformations Collage.

hours every morning," she told me. "It was hard." Guilt and craving for atonement may prompt people to turn to their own internal dictators. Cult of Thinness followers take self-surveillance and self-punishment into their own hands once they learn the rules.

Body evaluations and fixations with clothing sizes and numbers on a scale are some quantitative aspects that Cult of Thinness members also share. These practices become normative, spilling over into a growing segment of women's and girls' everyday practices.

Many Ways to Measure Up: Mirrors, Clothing, Photographs, and Scales

Evaluating the body can be precisely quantitative—the scale's number, the size of the mirror's image, or the waistband's extra inch. There are also more subtle indications —the admiring or critical glances and remarks from friends, relatives, or boyfriends.[1] Do we measure up to others in our circle of friends and relations? In *Self* magazine's "Compare and Compare Alike: When Does

Playing the Rating Game Become a Losing Proposition?"[2] Elizabeth Devita-Raeburn, a science and health writer, weighs in on her "obsession with measuring up." She describes her experience in yoga class, the purpose of which is to "focus on [her]self and how [her] body feels." Yet she finds herself feeling fierce competition. She cannot help but compare her yoga poses and her body to the poses and bodies of those around her.

> So I look, albeit furtively, not only at poses, but at body parts—thighs, biceps, butts. My gaze fixes on a woman with sinewy arms. Mine are doughy in comparison. I feel bad. Later, in the locker room, I notice a swatch of cellulite on the back of her thighs. I feel better. I don't know exactly when I developed this penchant for comparing myself to others, but I became aware of it when I started taking yoga classes. . . . I realized I did it all the time.[3]

Society presents more global comparisons. Women may judge themselves by advertising's perfect images or compare themselves to high-profile women in acting, modeling, ballet, or gymnastics. Many of the women I interviewed looked into the mirror and believed they didn't measure up to the societal expectations of the correct body image. "Not measuring up" sometimes led to strong feelings of self-hatred.

Cathleen reacted to these feelings by going on an extreme diet that led to anorexia: "I will never be satisfied with what's in the mirror. When I see other women I want to be better, thinner, than them. I would rather be anorexic than not."

Other women look in the mirror and enter the purgatory of self-blame for not being able to control their appetites. Lisa said,

> I think the real problem is my whole self image—the way I see myself—never being able to achieve the goal of looking like those women body builders or being able to control myself. I feel so weak—"there you go again giving into your eating problem." I'm just so powerless. I feel awful about myself, pretty much hate myself if I don't look a certain way. When I'm home and I'm gaining all that weight, I feel like shit. I avoid mirrors.

All of the women I talked with used the fit of their clothes as a way to watch their bodies, as well as a reward to maintain or to improve their shape.[4] When the clothing was loose, it was a time for celebration; when the fit felt tight, it was a source of emotional pain. Judy noted that when her pants are too tight, "I snap at everyone and I'm cranky and miserable. And when my clothes fit right and I walk down the street I feel great. It's like a high." Many defined explicit measurements and swore to stay within certain sizes: "You know there are limits," said Angela. "I don't want to go above size 10 or whatever—I'd like to stay at my size 8." As one woman put it, "You've got to find yourself some incentive clothes."

Photographs provide another important body measuring yardstick. Women examine these pictures in excruciating detail and evaluate their body shape over months and years. Several students I interviewed frequently compared their pictures from high school with their current college pictures. Rita commented:

> When I picture the body that I want, I picture myself during my freshman year in high school. I have a picture at home. It was of me standing there in a move from a cheerleading routine. You could see the bones. I wasn't anorexic looking, I was just tight. I was thin, but everything was in place.

Scales exert another kind of tyranny.

In Michelle's Words

> I can't remember a time when my whole life didn't revolve around my weight. My mood is based on what my scale says every morning. . . . I decide what I'll eat today depending on that stupid scale. . . . I pull it out several times a day to see what it says. Several times a day getting undressed and then criticizing myself for weighing too much. I don't think I'll ever be happy. . . . It's always '10 pounds.' I'll be happy if I can just lose '10 pounds!' That was over 40 pounds ago. I still haven't figured out how to be satisfied. My hands shake all the time. Every-time I stand up I feel like I'm going to pass-out. My hands and feet are always cold. I would love to break every mirror in my house, but i know it wouldn't help. I see people at the store and think, how did she get so small? . . . Then I see people who in my eyes are overweight and I start to get nervous. I don't think I could handle it if I ever returned to that size. I lay awake at night thinking of what I ate that day and hope i didn't gain a pound. I am anxious as soon as i wake in the morning because I know I have to face the scale.
>
> My son is 3 and my daughter is 2. I try to hide this all from them and especially my husband. I pray that my daughter will never feel this way. And that she'll never have to know what it's like to face my day. . .
>
> —*Michelle, an excerpt from an eating disorder recovery website*[5]

Michelle's obsession is not rare. According to David M. Garner, Ph.D., clinical psychologist with the Central Behavioral Healthcare Eating Disorder Program in Toledo, Ohio, as quoted in Michelle Stacey's "Bodysense"

> The way many women use scales is grossly destructive. The scale is a cruel purveyor of personal worth for the day. If you wanted to come up with a plot to take an entire gender and render them less effective, you'd put them on a diet and have them buy a scale. The human energy wasted by women thinking about these numbers is enormous.[6]

The scale is the totem of all totems, which "Members swear total allegiance to [as] an all-powerful leader whom they believe to be the Messiah."[7] Encountered at gyms, fitness clubs, diet centers, and at home, it carries its own prescribed daily ritual. Most women disrobe before going on the scale, stripping themselves of jewelry or hair clips in the hope that they will "measure up." My college student interviewees were no exception.

> The big thing at my house is getting on the scale every day. My mother will ask "What do you weigh?" and it's a big thing. We weigh ourselves separately, but the question always comes up during the day.
>
> *—Joan*

> I gained weight and I didn't feel good about myself. I gained 4 pounds. Doesn't that sound stupid? I say that to myself, but when you see it on a scale, it's like death. It's like someone scraping their nails on a chalkboard. It's like you can't go up there.
>
> *—Marina*

> I panic when I get above 120. When I get on the scale . . . I just get really nervous. A lot of times I'll go out and exercise right then. I tell myself a lot I'm not going to eat for the rest of the day but I always end up eating.
>
> *—Miriam*

On an eating disorder recovery website, a woman describes her daily struggle with a demonically personified scale:

> The scale is something I hate, but also something I need. It controls me. What I eat depends on it. It screams at me, "You need to lose more weight!" I obey this command. I am hungry—always, but at least I'm making the scale happy. The scale controls me. Today I am a different person then [*sic*] I was yesterday. My smile slowly fades and is being replaced by tears. The hurt inside me is immeasurable. Maybe when I lose 5 more pounds, and the scale is finally happy, I will be to [*sic*] I am beautiful, I am thin, I am happy. Then I step on the scale. This once happy girl has been transformed into an ugly monster of a person. Moments earlier I was laughing. Now the tears flood out like a stream. Why am I crying? Because the scale has punished me for eating. The scale screams at me that I'm no good. I'm a failure and need to be punished. I'm sick of being punished. The scale will never be happy . . . and neither will I.[8]

For those women, a mere number on a scale, with its verdict of "saint" or "sinner," determines self-worth, emotional state, and even "what to do next." The scale is a judge, who tells Miriam (like so many others) whether she needs to exercise immediately—or find some alternate means for atonement. The scale is a vengeful god, controlling and punishing when the numbers are not right. The scale is a punitive commander who must be obeyed—yet is never satisfied. The website narrator describes how she hates being ruled by the scale and punished for not measuring up—but she also acknowledges that she *needs* the scale and she *needs* the punishment; the scale is her identity, good or bad.

Measuring Up to the "Pros": Celebrity Gurus

With increasing exposure to entertainment media, celebrity adulation has reached an all-time high, creating a cultural craving for information on celebrities' economic privileges, relationships, and, very often, bodies. For women in the media or entertainment industry, and celebrity women in general, the body's form becomes more important than function. We are not interested in how fast Jennifer Aniston runs a 10K race; instead, we want to know how we can get her abs (preferably without having to exercise at all). We are not interested in Paris Hilton's nutrition regimen; we want to know how we can have tall willowy figures. We flock to tabloids telling us what Lindsay Lohan really eats in a day to lose so much weight so quickly. And if Nicole Richie can swear off carbs, we can too.

What about the other ways celebrities obtain their "perfect" bodies, such as diet pills, personal trainers and chefs, diet coaches, and cosmetic surgery? It makes us feel better to tell ourselves that if we had these privileges, this special celebrity access, we too could look perfect. When the satisfaction of celebrity watching fades, we are left with the sins of our "weak," "immoral," "imperfect" bodies. Still, we look to the "pros" for sacramental inspiration and the salvation of the latest diet they are touting. When we hear "The Zone Diet," we think of Jennifer Aniston, Renée Zellweger, or Cindy Crawford. "Atkins" brings to mind Sarah Jessica Parker or Geri Halliwell. Bill and Hillary Clinton are "South Beach"; Sarah Ferguson is "Weight Watchers"; Whoopie Goldberg is "Slimfast"; Kirstie Alley is "Jenny Craig."

But not every diet pro is sublimely glamorous—the ridiculous catches our attention, too. With Snack Packs, Nabisco introduces the Snack Fairy, an improbable guy in a "fetching pink tutu and magic wand . . . to help you make sensible choices in snacking." "Let's be frank," he confides, "what the world needs now is love and 100 Calorie Snack Packs from Nabisco. Snack happy—not just an advertising slogan, but a mantra to live by." What a relief to know we can find sweet love and sensible eating with Snack Packs delivered by a guy in a tutu.

Good/Bad, Right/Wrong, Sin/Atonement

Certain body-conscious endeavors calling for the "right" body create other subcults. For most of Cindy's life, gymnastic aspirations meant constant attention to body work. Cindy is now a college junior. During high school, years of rigid discipline and practice backlashed into an eating disorder,

> In gymnastics, they made us so weight conscious. Every single day we weighed in. Once, the day before an important competition, one of my friends weighed

FIGURE 6.2 Snack Happy Fairy: The Guru in a Tutu, Nabisco.

in over by 5 pounds. The coach told her that if she didn't lose the weight by the next morning, she couldn't compete. She did everything she could. She put on a [sweat]suit and ran all night. She had beautiful long hair but she just chopped it all off. Whenever there was a weigh-in, if you walked into the bathroom there was someone puking or on Ex-Lax.

Cindy started gymnastics at 5 A.M., practicing for 4 hours a day, 6 days a week, with weekend competitions. The obsessive focus destroyed her pleasure in the sport, but not before it had also stunted her physical growth.

My father is over 6 feet. My mother is 5′9″ and my sister is also tall. I was supposed to be tall too—I wear a size 8½ shoe. But my doctor said the hard training stunted my growth. I am only 5′3″.

During her years as a gymnast, however, Cindy ate what she wanted.

Typically, I would get home from school and have dinner about 3:30 P.M. by myself. Then I'd go to the gym. So I never really ate with my family. On weekends we tried to get together on Sundays and sit down and eat. If I hadn't been in that kind of active sport, burning everything up so fast, I think my body would have been like a normal person. I was the good girl and I stayed in gymnastics for 2 years longer than I wanted because my parents wanted me to. I started to burn out. My freshman year of high school was my peak.

Around sophomore year, her coach started to monitor her food.

My coach was saying "You have to lose weight before you compete." When my mother found out she would just oversee it herself, "You can't have this, you can't have that." I'd find a way to binge. I'd go into my room with a bag of cookies and I'd shove them all in my mouth. She never knew. This was a big problem for me because I am a binger. I'll binge and then I'll starve myself the next day. I've been through it all: the bulimic stage; the Ex-Lax; binging and starving. When I was really thin, my junior year of high school, I looked good. I got compliments from everyone. [9]

Whether they have a full-blown eating disorder or merely fall somewhere on the spectrum, many people share aspects of Cindy's struggle with binging and starving. They may overeat and then fast, follow a "bad" eating day with a "good" day of "safe" foods, eat only after strenuous exercise, or endure exercise after eating. Even school children learn about food calories and the energy expenditure of exercise. In our food-oriented, perfect-body culture, it can be a short step to a calories in/calories out, binge/purge, sin/atonement mentality.

 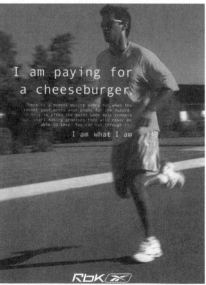

FIGURE 6.3 Aerobic Atonement: Running for Skinny Jeans & Paying for a Cheeseburger, Reebok.

Family and Peer Pressure

. . . I know I'm going to slap my mother one of these days
For telling me to eat less,
And giving me the look.
I know she is ashamed that I'm not as thin as she was in high school.
I can't even wear her vintage cardigans,
I can't even fit into her wedding shift.
She says it's about health . . . maybe it is.
But when her eyes are sorrowful as I walk into the kitchen,
Maybe not even eating,
And the corners of her lips curl inward with implication,
I scream at her, shout, "Leave me the fuck alone!"
And she just looks at me like she always does,
And that just makes me want to stuff myself.
If my own mother can't accept me with my body,
Who am I to love myself?
Mother knows best.
I'm letting her down.
I know if I were my mother I'd be ashamed of me . . .[10]

Parents, siblings, peers, and even family doctors and diet clubs are important body watching guides and gurus. What their parents thought of them had
quite an impact on how the women I interviewed perceived themselves.

My mother wanted me to have everything she never had, like a college education. But she was critical of my body. If she didn't like what I was wearing she'd
tell me right off the bat, "Don't you know how to dress?" Last year she called
me a moose, and that hurt. Sometimes I think I need that, so that I do something
about my weight . . . When I go home she's like a hawk. She's on my
back. She's like on my shoulder. "Don't eat that. Don't eat that. Put that down.
You don't want that. . . ." When I look fine, my mother says nothing about my
body, not even a compliment. But when I start gaining weight, the criticism
begins.

—*Dana*

My mother thought I was fat. I was 11 years old at the time. She took me to her
weight doctor. She put me on extensive diets and I didn't like that. She gave me
these amino tablets and she'd search around and make sure I didn't take cookies with me to school. She watched me. . . .

—*Cathleen*

When I was smaller it was overlooked. But then as I got into grammar school I
became heavier. From that point my mother was always concerned. She'd say,
"Couldn't you go on a diet?" And she tried her best to be nice about it, but when

you're heavy you don't care to hear it from anybody. I joined a diet club when I was in high school because my mother said I had to. I was practically dragged to this place, totally against my will. I was so embarrassed. But I looked at everyone else who was there, and thought, "Well at least someone's bigger than me."

—Andrea

Peer attitudes also have an impact, especially during the transition from elementary to middle school.

Because I was taller than all the guys in middle school, this one kid used to call me "Amazon." When I look back, it was because of my height, but I thought it was because I was fat. I really was never overweight as a kid, just the tallest. But then, when I went into seventh grade, I had this incredible will power. I just didn't eat.

—June

Mirror, Mirror

Snow White's stepmother, the Queen, prided herself on being the fairest in the land. She consulted her magic talking mirror for reassurance every day. But when Snow White grew up to be more beautiful, as confirmed by the mirror, the wicked Queen ordered her killed. In the end, of course, Snow White was rescued and the cruel, jealous Queen met a grisly end.

Like the stepmother, many women perceive others as more attractive than themselves and feel envy, rage, and even violence toward one another. For instance, it was not that long ago that Pantene Shampoo advertisements begged, "Don't hate me because I'm beautiful." Good-looking women, regardless of their other attributes, are just more competition for the few Princes out there. My interview subjects constantly compared themselves to their sisters, mothers, and girlfriends. When they felt they did not measure up to the competition, their anger and resentment rivaled the wicked Queen's. Sometimes it turned inward, to self-hatred and despair.

I think I am not attractive. I hate my skin and I hate my body. I'm small-chested, and have big hips and cellulite on the back of my thighs. It's disgusting. I see girls in my classes and I think they are very pretty. They've got gorgeous long hair, blue eyes. I tried to change myself in addition to my weight. I've tried to comb my hair long, and it doesn't look good. I've changed the color of my hair. Nothing is right. I don't like my nose, I don't like my face and I hate my double chin.

—Cory

Beauty pageants offer plenty of opportunity for competition and envy. While giving a passing nod to talent contests and oral interviews, pageants still focus on the ritual lineup of bodies in swimsuits and gowns. One student experienced that competitive jostling.

Last year I won the local competition and I went on to compete in the state competition. My agent said I had a chance. As soon as I got to the contest, I realized that girls just enter year after year until they win. And I was one of the few people who was there for the first time. The girls were so bitchy and so catty and not friendly at all. A big part of winning is showmanship. It's how you approach the judges.

—*Kathy*

Some women find the transition to college involves heightened and competitive beauty expectations.

I feel the competition here to look good. I mean you've got some incredibly good-looking women that go to this school. They call it "the beautiful school." I never felt like I had to compete until I came here and people put all this pressure on you.

—*Molly*

Male attention is another indication of a woman's culturally correct body—whether she gets a date or merely a nice remark about her appearance.

Now, looking back at pictures, I looked fine, I was never even overweight. But at that time I thought, "Oh I'm horrible and that must be the reason I don't have a boyfriend."

—*Virginia*

The host called me over last night, and he said, "You know the waiter thinks you're very attractive. Is there a chance you'd say yes if he asked you out?" So if he calls I will go out with him. It really made me feel good last night because I was out with five other very pretty girls, and he picked me, thought I was attractive. It's usually my roommate that gets the guys.

— *Judy*

Sometimes the competition for male attention can even cause confrontation and threat.

I was at a bar hanging out, and my roommate called me over to introduce me to a couple of her friends. I didn't look good, I had a bandana in my hair. My makeup was all over the place. So I was talking to these guys, and this girl comes over and nudges me. She was made-up, her hair beautiful. She said, "Excuse me, but are you with this party? Cause if you're not, would you mind moving?" I completely lost it. The next thing I knew, I was in this girl's face and said, "Who the hell do you think you are?" And my roommate just pulled me out of the bar because there was going to be trouble.

—*Mary*

Dangerous Comparison, Deadly Competition

The competition packs an extra punch when it is close to home, among mothers, daughters, siblings, and peers. In a recent Weight Watchers (2005) diet aid commercial, a mother rejoices that she has lost so much weight she can fit into her daughter's clothes. Robin, the woman in the commercial, enthusiastically recalls one of her "most memorable moments"—"the first time I could share my 13-year-old daughter's clothes!"[11] A young girl watching this with me said flatly, "I would hate her for that."

> My mother was a model. She was always Little Miss Beauty Queen. And there was pressure for me to follow in her footsteps. But my mother was jealous of me. I could feel that tension between us. She would often say, "Well you look a little scruffy today."
>
> —*Lucy*

> When I was in high school my mom was skinnier than I, and I was incredibly jealous. It drove me crazy. I didn't want guys I liked to meet her. On the beach she'd wear bikinis, and I hated it. My father used to say my sister had all the style. She could wear anything because she was so thin. I always got A's in school, and I was in Honor Society, whereas my sister did badly. But that was the least of my concern, getting A's. I wanted to be thin. I would just look at my sister, and think, "If I could only be thin like her."
>
> —*Irene*

Fear of the infamous "freshman 15" weight gain is not limited to college—it has percolated down to a similar environment in boarding schools. Peer competition intensifies in a closed community like a boarding school, where girls practice body and food watching rituals with great concentration and sometimes deadly results.

Maria's Story

> The first year there, when I was 15, I didn't have any problem with my eating. The second year, Sandra came along. Sandra is German and very pretty. She and I became good friends. We had both been friends with Claire, who had steadily become anorexic at school, then died that summer. It really didn't hit Sandra and me. We had gone on a diet the previous year and continued this at school the next year. First we started purging (vomiting). We'd actually gotten this idea from Claire. I was bulimic for 6 months. It was horrible. My housemaster noticed, and sent me to the doctor. I had a lot of chest pains at the time—I had just destroyed the lining of my stomach. They gave me this awful white liquid. Then the following year, as seniors, Sandra and I started with this vicious competition about losing weight. I ate only carrots and this low-fat cream with diet crackers. I started losing weight and Sandra was losing weight faster, because she was thinner than I was to begin with, and taller. So everyone was yelling at me, "Why are you letting Sandra do this to you?"

At this boarding school appearance is everything. Everyone there was gorgeous. Everyone also definitely tried to be skinny. The girl next door to me was anorexic. She used diuretics. Another friend upstairs was also anorexic and she had to go to the hospital because she had used laxatives for so long her body would no longer function normally. Last year when I went back for a reunion I found out that another good friend of mine, Carla, had died of an eating disorder.

At this school, if you had dinner at the table and ate the entire meal, you were considered a pig, and you were going to be talked about. The biggest thing was to just run around with the salad bowl and ask if anyone had any extra salad.

—Maria

Like the jealousy and competition that fueled Maria and Sandra's eating disorders, envious comparisons are a recurrent element in the Cult of Thinness and echo themes in spiritual cults like the one to which Anna belonged. Anna described her cult's dependence on comparison in the following way: "My guru said I should go . . . to yoga class. I would do this for 6 months. Kundilini is very strenuous. . . . Everybody watched to see who showed up, who stayed awake, who practiced correctly. People felt guilty and did self-penance if they didn't follow the practice."

Some aspects of boarding school life, as well as the semi-enclosed environment of college life, discussed in the next chapter, share the aspects of a "secret society"—one of the primary characteristics of a cult. Those who suffer from clinical eating disorders are beginning to take on aspects of spiritual cults as well.

Pro-Ana Subculture

They are a sign of membership in a world of underground Web sites that connect people who share a dangerous passion. . . . Red bracelets represent anorexia, purple is for bulimia. . . . The Web sites don't discourage eating disorders. They encourage the behavior of people who want to keep starving themselves. . . . The lingo includes nicknames like Ana and Mia. . . . Ana is for anorexia and Mia is for bulimics.[12]

"They are encouraging people to be ill, and it's like a secret cult, a secret society." Word spreads around and people have a lingo now," said Lynne Grege, of the National Eating Disorders Association. [13]

"They strive to be perfect. Thin, thinner, thinnest . . . To mark membership in this anonymous community, they wear red bracelets."[14]

Pro-anorexia websites provide information about eating disorders, particularly anorexia nervosa, and a forum for sharing personal experiences.[15] Karen Dias's research into the subculture of pro-ana websites finds that cyberspace is often a respite for those women and girls who struggle with their disorder and want to get away from the "surveillance and regulatory mechanisms of control in the public sphere." She notes: "My intent, by putting women's narratives at the center of my research is to listen and to take seriously their voices; voices which are subversive because they exist."[16] In this respect, pro-anorexia sites are one of the few arenas where eating-disordered individuals gain the opportunity to correspond with similar individuals who can "offer nonjudgmental support."[17] Some "pro-ana" factions maintain that anorexia is not a disease, but a lifestyle, while other factions recognize anorexia as a disease, but support it as inextricably linked to their life and well-being. Some wear colored bracelets that silently identify their membership and commitment to their eating-disordered life style.

These secret signs are mostly detected, understood, and appreciated by those people who have been eating disordered themselves. One recovery website names the phenomenon "EDU," or "Eating Disorder Underground."[18]

A girl on the website writes, "I see us out there, people with eating disorders. I recognize them, not all, (of course) and maybe I'm not always right, but sometimes I am. We are a secret society, it's been said . . . and I know we see each other, recognize one another out in the world, see our own behavior (either current behavior or past behavior) in a stranger and we just know."

A secret society creates and supports "isolation from the outside world," "shrouded in secrecy"—also distinguishing characteristics of a cult. Another girl, a bulimic who describes herself as a "veteran and re-enlisted sufferer," notes the ritualistic routines that only those who practice them can recognize.

> . . . Still, my suspicions weren't confirmed until she opened her purse and brought out The Kit. A clear Baggie containing travel toothbrush, toothpaste, Scope, Certs, lipstick, and hand lotion. I watched her in the mirror as she preformed the cleansing part of the ritual, so familiar to me. She finished, measured her small waist (23 inches? 22?) with her hands and smiled (grimaced) at her reflection before striding out of the restroom. The entire time I watched her, I was torn between the feelings of déjà vu and longing for this covert ritual, and the silent sorority with the woman, and wishing I could say something to help her conquer the damaging and disgusting behavior. I went home, however, with renewed conviction: to halt my overeating and be thin again. I knew how.[19]

Food Watching Rituals

Food watching goes hand in hand with body watching. It is often practiced on a daily basis, either alone or with the help of another individual (usually a family member) or with a group such as a diet club. Food watching ranges from calorie counting, to full scale dieting, to the behavioral symptoms of anorexia or bulimia. And there's one-upmanship involved, as Hornbacher tells it,

The bragging was the worst. I hear this in schools all over the country, in cafés and restaurants, in bars, on the Internet, for Pete's sake, on buses, on sidewalks: Women yammering about how little they eat. Oh, I'm starving, I haven't eaten all day, I think I'll have a great big piece of lettuce, I'm not hungry, I don't like to eat in the morning (in the afternoon, in the evening, on Tuesdays, when my nails aren't painted, when my shin hurts, when it's raining, when it's sunny, on national holidays, after or before 2 A.M.). . . . Food makes us queasy, food makes us itchy, food is too messy, all I really like to eat is celery. To hear women tell it, we're ethereal beings who eat with the greatest distaste, scraping scraps of food between our teeth with our upper lips curled.[20]

Almost all women in my sample of college students had been on what they termed "a diet" during their teenage years. They consider dieting normal behavior. For example:

I would do just normal dieting and then exercising, nothing crazy, but just cutting down, maybe more than I should. I'd just eat very little from each food group, and exercise a lot. I was always hungry.

—*Jenna*

I never went to Weight Watchers or anything. I went on a diet a couple of times. You know, no junk, nothing between meals, don't eat after supper, that kind of thing. I would eat three times a day but small amounts. And sometimes like at night, the room would start to spin a little bit, and then I'd have to get some whole milk or something to put in my stomach.

—*Sylvia*

Georgia went on a fast after her boyfriend made a comment about her weight.

I was so hurt at the time, so mad at him. What I did was just not eat anything. I went to aerobics every night. And of course there was nothing else in my life. I had my schoolwork, but I had no other interests. I'd go out on weekends with my friends, but I didn't even want to do that much because that was always sitting around food. It was great while I looked good and I got all the compliments, but I don't think it was worth all the anguish and deprivation I went through. And I hadn't changed my eating problems, I had just suppressed them for 8 weeks. I lost 30 pounds. I was exhausted when I got home from school. Once I started eating, I gained the weight back again.

Parents, friends, and diet organizations can also be involved in "helping" women food watch.

My mother was very critical of my appearance. I was always the fat one and she was the thin one. She would say that I have the fattest thighs in the world, and that I'd better watch what I'm eating. She would always make sarcastic remarks. She would say, "If you want to diet, I'll help you. I'll make special meals for you. I'll do anything I can for you." She was good in that aspect, but in the back of my mind I knew she was always going to say something when I picked up that Twinkie.

—Judy

Good Food, Bad Food, and Disciplined Eating

Food watching rigidly divides food into "good" and "bad" categories. "Good" foods are nutritionally sound and/or low in calories. "Bad" foods are the ones that tempt you to overeat and gain weight. They include sweets, refined carbohydrates, and anything with the "F-word," fat. With today's carbohydrate hysteria, a bad day for many people means succumbing to a dinner roll, a cracker, or a potato chip, similar to the fat fear and demand for fat-free foods in the early to mid-1990s.

My student subjects knew the pattern well.

When I'm trying to eat well, I'll have my carbohydrate in the morning. And for lunch I'll probably have a salad. Then for dinner I'll have a nice piece of fish

FIGURE 6.4 Devil and Angel *"Pure Protein" bars permit us to seemingly transcend the good/bad food dichotomy as we surrender to our temptations to eat what tastes sinful, yet we are rewarded by the "pure" and "good" that allows us to "look great." (Worldwide Sport Nutritional Supplements, Inc.)*

with vegetables and a salad. When I want to eat well, I can. But I have bad eating days. That's when I have a bagel with eggs and a banana. For lunch I'll eat something fried, or a sandwich. Then have a big bag of chips and then will come dinner. A potato and meat with a huge salad with everything on it including dressing. And then going to the sweets and treats and getting six chocolate chip cookies and going home and having late night snacks, like nachos with cheese or another huge sandwich. That's bad eating.

—*Emily*

I had to sneak forbidden food in our house. I would wait until everyone was in the bedroom watching TV and then I'd go into the kitchen, maybe steal a piece of pie. If we were having a main meal you could have a second helping of meat or some more vegetables, but don't go for that second piece of pie. She would make mine really small. My mother was always watching me.

—*Marisa*

If I put a piece of cheese in my mouth I feel awful. I feel fat, I mean enormous. I've totally messed up. I'm ruining my body. I'm going to be 2 pounds heavier tomorrow because I ate this cheese. And this is going through my mind, and it's becoming this big drama.

—*Hillary*

Restricting food intake requires highly disciplined eating. Counting calories is an important ritual in maintaining this discipline—never transgressing the limit, following the scriptures of the calorie counter bible. The women in my sample who went off their diets by eating forbidden foods felt as if they had broken the rules or had fallen from grace. They had to confess the sin, even publicly, and make plans to atone. "I was so bad yesterday I can't eat a thing today," or "I'm not eating again until I can fit into my jeans." This kind of eating verges on the disorderly, as we see in the next chapter.

Notes

1. Foucault's analysis of power at micro-levels in society may set a useful context in which to grasp how much of a role both self-surveillance and social surveillance come to play in body monitoring and measuring up within a cult of thinness. Turner (1997) comments in his essay, "From Governmentality to Risk: Some Reflections on Foucault's Contribution to Medical Sociology": ". . . Foucault saw power as a relationship which was localized, dispersed, diffused, and typically distinguished through the social system, operating at a micro, local, and covert level through sets of specific practices" (xi-xii). For Foucault, power is embodied in "day-to-day practices" and "mundane arrangements"; power is "like a color dye diffused through the entire social structure and is embedded in daily practices" (xii). Turner adds, "This view of power is very closely associated with Foucault's fascination with discipline, namely that power exists through the disciplinary

practices which produce particular individuals, institutions and cultural arrangements" (xii). Next, Turner writes, "Foucault provided a description of what one
might call 'the institutions of normative coercion,' such as the law, religion, and
medicine (Turner 1992). These institutions are coercive in the sense that they discipline individuals and exercise forms of surveillance over everyday life in such a
way that actions are both produced and constrained by them" (xiv). These institutions are "readily accepted as legitimate and normative at the everyday level"
(xiv). Furthermore, "these institutions of normative coercion exercise a moral
authority over the individual by explaining individual 'problems' and providing
solutions for them. In this sense, we could say that medicine and religion exercise
a hegemonic authority because their coercive character is often disguised and
masked by their normative involvement in the troubles and problems of individuals. They are coercive, normative and also voluntary" (xiv). This passage helps us
better understand the powers and controls that are at work in cults (cults of thinness, pro-anorexic cults, etc.), in the individuals themselves, and in their daily
lives from a micro and meso perspective. Capitalism and patriarchy are two examples of macro institutions that we bring into our macro and meso lives via the
beauty and diet industries. See: Bryan S. Turner, "From Governmentality to Risk:
Some Reflections on Foucault's Contribution to Medical Sociology," in *Foucault,
Health, and Medicine*, ed. Alan Petersen and Robin Bunton (New York:
Routledge, 1997), p. ix–xxii.

2. Elizabeth Devita-Raeburn, "Compare and Compare Alike: When Does Playing the
   Rating Game Become a Losing Proposition?" *Self*, September 2004, pp. 160–163.

3. "Social Comparison Theory" can be employed as the theoretical backdrop to best
   understand this social phenomenon. Hesse-Biber et al. (2006) write the following:

   > Social comparison theory, originally developed by Festinger (1954) claims
   > that: 1) individuals want to improve themselves, 2) individuals compare
   > themselves to others, and 3) whenever possible individuals compare them-
   > selves to those with whom they are similar (Morrison et al., 2004: 573).
   > This theory has been revised and research now indicates that individuals
   > may compare themselves to those with whom they are dissimilar (Martin &
   > Kennedy, 1993; Morrison et al., 2004) and comparisons may involve phys-
   > ical appearance and eating habits (Morrison, 2004; Wheeler & Miyake,
   > 1992). The consequences of this social comparative process depends on
   > whether the individual is comparing herself to someone she perceives to be
   > better or worse than her on the relevant dimension and whether the com-
   > parison is "universalistic" (such as media images) or "particularistic" (such
   > as intimate person) (Morrison et al., 2004: 574). In sum, social comparisons
   > made regarding physical appearance are usually upward (Morrison et al.,
   > 2004; Wheeler and Miyake, 1992). Further, these upward comparisons usu-
   > ally cause decreased or negative self-perception of attractiveness (Morrison
   > et al., 2004) and comparison to universal markers (such as media images)
   > create more pressure to conform to idealized standards (Irving, 1990;
   > Morrison et al., 2004).

See: Hesse-Biber, Leavy, Quinn & Zoino, "The Mass Marketing of Disordered Eating and Eating Disorders: The Social Psychology of Women, Thinness and Culture," (in press), *Women's Studies International Forum, 2006.*

4. See: Joan Jacobs Brumberg, *The Body Project: An Intimate History of American Girls* (New York: Random House, 1997), 128. "Because the body is a proxy for the self, selecting clothes for it is always of vital concern. American girls typically evaluate the success or failure of their personal body project in the dressing rooms at the local mall or department store. At this stage in life, what a girl wears and how she looks in it determine her level of self-acceptance, as well as her relations with her peers" (128).

5. Lisa Arndt, *The Anorexic Web*, http://www.anorexicweb.com

6. See: Michelle Stacey, "Bodysense," *Elle*, May 1999, 226. In addition to her contributions to *Elle*, Stacey frequently contributes to *Shape* magazine and the *New Yorker*, and was also the former editor at *Mademoiselle*, and author of *Consumed: Why Americans Hate, Love, and Fear Food* (1994).

7. J. Gordon Melton, *Encyclopedic Handbook of Cults in America* (Rev. and updated ed.). (New York: Garland Publishing, 1992), 6.

8. Lisa Arndt, *The Anorexic Web*, http://www.anorexicweb.com.

9. As long as looking good is emphasized as a goal of physical activity for women, then self-esteem will continue to be wrapped up in how well we personify the culturally ideal body. . . . Thus, we need to address the social bias in favor of females who most closely match the cultural ideal female body shape (Shisslak and Crago: 1994; Stein-Adair: 1994). This bias in favor of stereotypic femininity and beauty often leads to obsession with thinness and body shape. Therefore, coaches, exercise leaders, and administrators should minimize discussion of weight and specific body shapes and instead focus on being healthy and improving fitness levels and athletic skills. They also should discourage comparisons among women with different body shapes. Concerns about body image need to be addressed as a social issue, not an individual problem (Shisslak and Crago: 1994; Stein-Adair: 1994). . . . Though seemingly lofty goals, change can begin in individual sport and exercise settings that will eventually lead to broader social change. (21)

See: Vikki Krane and others, "Body Image Concerns in Female Exercisers and Athletes. A Feminist Cultural Studies Perspective," *Women and Sport and Physical Activity Journal*, 10, no. 1 (2001): 17.

10. Charlotte Cooper, "Mirrors," in *Ophelia Speaks: Adolescent Girls Write about their Search for Self*, ed. Sara Shandler (New York: HarperCollins, 1999), 8.

11. See: Weight Watchers, www.weightwatchers.ca "Online Achiever Stories" under "Success Stories."

12. "Bracelets Reveal Secret Society of Eating Disorders: Parents Should Recognize Warning Signs," NBC51.com, February 15, 2005, http://www.nbc5i.com/print41942951detail.html

13. Ibid.

14. *Blue Dragonfly*, "Some Anorexics Don't Want to Recover," *Knight Ridder Newspapers*, October 14, 2002, http://www.bluedragonfly.org/notorecovery.html
15. See: Karen Dias, "The Ana-Sanctuary: Women's Pro-Anorexia Narratives in Cyberspace," *Journal of International Women's Studies,* 4, no. 2. (2002): 31–45.
16. See: Karen Dias, n. 15. Dias declares the following:

> I explore the narratives of women who create and visit pro-anorexia or pro-ana websites in order to listen to these women's experiences of anorexia and rationale for inhabiting these spaces. Taking seriously the voices of these women can be viewed as a transgressive act, in contrast to hegemonic biomedical and psychiatric discourses of anorexia that portray women with eating disorders as "irrational" and "in denial" of their behavior, and pathologize and medicalize their experiences. Through their narratives we see how dominant cultural scripts about their bodies are reproduced, negotiated, and/or resisted. We can also observe women's engagement in the interpretation of their own experiences. The transient and fluid nature of pro-ana websites (in response to the backlash they receive) also illustrates the resilience of women who seek them out and (re-)create them. Just as the body is a site of struggle (and resistance), so too there are struggles over where and how women's stories of the body can be told.

17. Ibid.
18. Lisa Arndt, *The Anorexic Web*, http://www.anorexicweb.com.
19. Ibid.
20. Marya Hornbacher, *Wasted: A Memoir of Anorexia and Bulimia* (New York: HarperCollines, 1998), 117–118.

Bibliography

Arndt, L. "The Anorexic Web." http://www.anorexicweb.com
Blue Dragonfly. "Some Anorexics Don't Want to Recover." *Knight Ridder Newspapers*, October 14, 2002. http://www.bluedragonfly.org/notorecovery.html
"Bracelets Reveal Secret Society of Eating Disorders: Parents Should Recognize Warning Signs." NBC51.com, February 15, 2005. Accessed from http://www.nbc4.com/health/4194295/detail.html
Brumberg, J.J. *The Body Project: An Intimate History of American Girls.* New York: Random House, 1997.
Cooper, C. "Mirrors." In *Ophelia Speaks: Adolescent Girls Write about Their Search for Self*, ed. S. Shandler. New York: HarperCollins, 1999.
Devita-Raeburn, E. "Compare and Compare Alike: When Does Playing the Rating Game Become a Losing Proposition?" *Self*, September 2004, pp. 160–163.
Dias, K. *The Ana-Sanctuary: Women's Pro-Ana Narratives in Cyberspace. Journal of International Women's Studies,* 4, no 2 (2003): 31–45.

Hesse-Biber, S., P. Leavy, C.E. Quinn, & J.H. Zoino. *The Mass Marketing of Disordered Eating and Eating Disorders: The Social Psychology of Women, Thinness and Culture, Women's Studies International forum,* 2006. (in press).

Hornbacher, M. *Wasted: A Memoir of Anorexia and Bulimia.* New York: HarperCollins, 1998.

Krane, V., J. Waldron, J. Michalenok, & J. Stiles-Shipley. "Body Image Concerns in Female Exercisers and Athletes: A Feminist Cultural Studies Perspective." *Women in Sport and Physical Activity Journal,* 10, no. 1 (2001): 17.

Melton, J.G. *Encyclopedic Handbook of Cults in America,* (rev. and updated ed.). New York: Garland Publishing, 1992.

Stacey, M. "Bodysense." *Elle,* May 1999, 226.

Turner, B.S. "From Governmentality to Risk: Some Reflections on Foucault's Contribution to Medical Sociology." In *Foucault, Health, and Medicine,* ed. A. Petersen & R. Bunton, p. ix–xxii. New York: Routledge, 1997.

Weight Watchers International. "Online Achiever Stories" under "Success Stories." www.weightwatchers.ca

How Young Women Experience Being a Body in Their Families, Peer Groups, and School Environments

It's Your Duty to Be Beautiful

Keep young and beautiful.
It's your duty to be beautiful.
Keep young and beautiful,
If you want to be loved.

Don't fail to do your stuff
With a little powder and a puff.
Keep young and beautiful,
If you want to be loved.

If you're wise, exercise all the fat off.
Take it off over here, over there.
When you're seen anywhere with your hat off,
Wear a marcelled wave in your hair.

Take care of all those charms,
And you'll always be in someone's arms.
Keep young and beautiful,
If you want to be loved.[1]

The words of a popular song echo a powerful message in our culture—that only the beautiful and thin are valued and loved. Reiterated by families, peers, and the school environment, this notion is taken seriously by many young women. So seriously, in fact, that anorexia nervosa (starvation dieting, severe weight loss, obsession with food) and bulimia (compulsive binge eating, followed by purging through self-induced vomiting or laxatives) occur 10 times more frequently in women than in men.[2] These syndromes usually develop during adolescence[3] and, until recently, were more prevalent among upper- and middle-class women.[4]

These behaviors carry long-term physical risks, including the destruction of tooth enamel by stomach acid, malnutrition, organ damage, and even death. One in every 100 females between 10 and 20 suffers from anorexia nervosa.[5] Anorexia is one of the few psychiatric disorders with a significant mortality rate. The American Anorexia/Bulimia Association estimates that 10% of those diagnosed with anorexia may die.[6] Those who do not die may face chronic conditions. According to the National Association of Anorexia Nervosa and Associated Disorders, recovery statistics range from 25% to 35%, and as with 12-step program diagnoses, a victim may remain "a recovering anorexic for life." Relapses are common, however, as are continued dangerous food and weight preoccupations.[7] Bulimia is thought to be 4-5 times more common than anorexia, but is more difficult to detect, since bulimics are usually secretive about their gorge-and-purge episodes. There is often nothing about their external appearance to alert anyone to the presence of the disorder, so the condition goes undiagnosed unless they seek help themselves. "Although many people struggle in secret, estimates suggest that between 1 and 3% of adolescent and college-age women in the U.S. are bulimic; between 10 and 20% of bulimic patients are male."[8] The number of women dying from bulimia is hard to estimate, but bulimia can have serious medical consequences, like gastrointestinal damage. Then there is the emotional toll—despair, self-loathing, guilt, depression, low self-esteem, and an inability to conduct normal relationships.

In the past couple of decades, eating disorders have emerged from the realm of scholarly journals to public prominence. As is often the case, celebrity afflictions have helped pave the way for a greater focus on this widespread problem. The starvation-related death of singer Karen Carpenter, and the bulimic confessions of Jane Fonda and Princess Diana received copious coverage and created a climate of acceptance, even as a type of fashion trend, some experts have observed.[9] More recently, actresses Tracy Gold,[10] Jaime-Lynn Sigler,[11] Mary-Kate Olsen, and singer/songwriter Alanis Morissette[12] have personalized eating disorders for younger generations. Thanks to the celebrity press, eating disorders receive more attention today than ever before.

Numerous psychological theorists believe that some kind of "overwhelming despair" often precedes the "quick fix" solution mentality of weight loss.[13] For example, eating disorders specialist Sylvia Brody cites "physical, emotional, and social deprivations" as predictors of an eating disorder.[14] Psychiatrist Hilde Bruch believes that an eating disorder begins with low self-esteem, self-condemnation, and self-doubt; anorexia is a way of "bringing order to one's universe"[15] and can also serve as "an escape from [an] over-whelming situation."[16] Susie Orbach, a prominent eating disorders therapist and author of *Fat Is a Feminist Issue*, contends, "Anorexia is most particularly a defense against dependency needs; it is a statement about how unneedy the woman has had to be from early on in life . . . She feels a strength, for she has become someone with no needs and no appetites. . . . *The anorectic woman has absorbed from early on, but in quadraphonic sound, the very same message that all girls take in their passage towards femininity.*" (emphasis added).[17]

Culturally Induced Eating Disorders: The Cultural Link

Chapter 5 describes the differences between the cultural and medical models of ideal weight. I was not surprised that 77% of the college women in my sample chose the cultural model as their desired image and only 23% saw the medical model as "ideal."

But I wanted to know if the cultural demand for slenderness might make these young women more vulnerable to eating problems. To check my suspicions I administered the Eating Attitudes Test,[18] a standard measure of eating

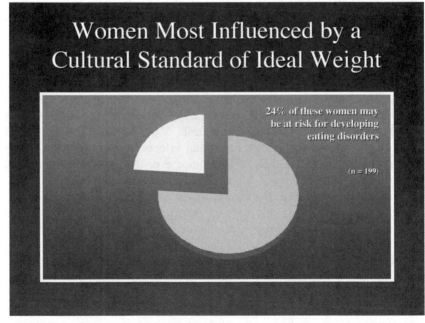

FIGURE 7.1 Women Most Influenced by a Cultural Standard. (*Hesse-Biber,* Am I Thin Enough Yet?, *1996, p. 82.*)

disorders, to the women I interviewed. The results were unequivocal. Of the women who followed the cultural ideal, *24% scored in the abnormal range*, compared to only 8% of the medical model followers (see Figures 7.1 and 7.2).

In addition, almost half of the cultural ideal followers (47%), compared to only about one fourth of the medical followers (26%), reported significant-to-extreme concern about their body weight. Thirty-four percent said they felt anxious, depressed, or repulsed by their bodies, compared with only 25% of medical model followers. The link was clear: *Those women who subscribed to the cultural definition of body image were more at risk for developing eating difficulties.*[19]

If we were to rely only on traditional psychology to explain the current near-epidemic increase in eating disorders among college women, we would assume an increase in the underlying mental and emotional features that produce such symptoms.[20] *There is a big difference, however, between disorderly eating patterns I found among the majority of students I interviewed and clinically defined eating disorders.* Disorderly eating and obsession with food is a widely accepted way to deal with weight and body image issues in a culture where thinness "symbolizes beauty, attractiveness, fashionability, health,

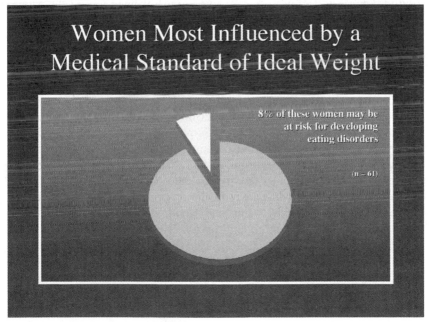

FIGURE 7.2 Women Most Influenced by a Medical Standard. (*Hesse-Biber, Am I Thin Enough Yet?, 1996, p. 82.*)

achievement, and control."[21] *It is normative behavior for women who are part of the Cult of Thinness,* those who are socialized to apologize for their appetites. Best-selling author and therapist Kim Chernin adds, "Women today, because they cannot bring their natural body into culture without shame and apology, are driven to attack and destroy that body. . . . Women today seem to be practicing genocide against themselves, waging a violent war against the female body precisely because there are no indications that the female body has been invited to enter culture."[22] Commenting on our cultural fear of fat, a leading eating disorders therapist, Nancy J. Kolodny, writes, "The flip side of glorifying thinness is degrading fat, which results in a cultural phenomenon called 'weight prejudice.' . . . Over 50% of females ages 18-25 'would prefer to be run over by a truck than be fat,' and two-thirds of those surveyed 'would rather be mean or stupid' than fat!"[23]

Strategies for weight reduction have unintended consequences. Dieters know severe food restriction over time may trigger an uncontrollable binge. Women who tamper with their body's natural metabolism through dieting, bingeing, and purging may find they gain weight on fewer calories.[24] Excessive exercise can lead to injury or burnout, or even halt menstruation. All of this fosters constant weight and body image preoccupation and may lead to depression and in its wake serve to push women toward the eating-disordered end of the continuum, resulting in full-blown eating disorders *with* their accompanying psychopathologies.[25]

Some of the young women I talked with demonstrated anorectic and bulimic behavior—they engaged in calorie restriction, chronic dieting, binge-ing and purging, diuretics or laxatives, or extreme exercise to control their weight. However, they did *not* exhibit the full constellation of psychological traits usually associated with an eating disorder, such as maturity fears, inter-personal distrust, and perfectionism.[26] Some researchers refer to this pattern as "imitative anorexia," "subclinical eating disorders," or "weight preoccu-pation."[27] I refer to it as *culturally induced* eating—a pattern of eating-disordered symptoms in otherwise psychologically "normal" women.

This group of women appears to be driven in large part by the social and economic rewards of looking "right" and "good," notions driven by capitalism and patriarchal systems of profit and control. They are the primary motivators of a culturally induced eating disorder. This is not to say that placing extreme pressures on the body will not disrupt their physiological or psychological well-being, or that manipulating food intake cannot assuage psychological stress or trauma after the disorder develops. But if psychological struggles have not driven the individual to clinical manifestation of anorexia or bulimia, then there are different agents at work.

The Eating and Body-Image Disorders Continuum

> *Eating disorders linger so long undetected, eroding the body in silence, and then they strike. The secret is out. You're dying.*
>
> —Marya Hornbacher, from her memoir Wasted[28]

> *Now even at work I wear things that are more contemporary. I never used to tuck in my shirt, and everything had an elastic waist. Now I wear much more tailored clothes. Everything has slim lines as opposed to a gathered waist, and I tuck in my shirt, no problem. It feels like a different world.*
>
> —Robin, from Weight Watchers[29]

The college women and young girls who shared their stories with me reside along a "continuum" of eating and body image disturbance. At the one end are those few young women I interviewed who exhibit minimal distress in dealing with their food intake, weight, and body image. At the other end of this scale reside those who struggle mightily with these issues and in fact manifest full-blown clinical eating disorders; this group is also small. It turned out that the vast majority of college-age women and young girls I talked with lie in between the two poles of this continuum—that part I call "The Cult of Thinness." During their college careers and postcollege years, some women may move up and down this continuum, while others remain at the more eating-disordered end.

In this chapter you will meet women who reside along this continuum for whom the Cult of Thinness becomes a normative life style. We will meet Suzannah, who spends a great deal of her college life starving, bingeing, and purging, but manifests none of the clinical psychological symptoms of an eating disorder. Kim, another student you will meet, meanwhile remains fixed at the eating-disordered end of the continuum, making little movement toward a healthier life style. Although the experiences of these two young women differ, they are, in fact, equally damaging.

Much of the self-help literature on eating disorders and treatment protocols ignores this large middle group, and there remains a lack of understanding of the role that the environment—especially the micro and macro environment of women's lives—plays in the genesis of their position along the "Cult of Thinness" continuum. It is these micro environmental factors that we take up in this chapter—those factors in our immediate family, peer group, and school environment—that often echo the wider societal cultural pressures on women to "be a slender body." Factors that mitigate against these cultural messages among these groups and that serve to promote a healthier outlook on food and body image issues as well are discussed in this chapter.

The Cultural Link: Family, Peer Group, and the College Environment

Biological and psychological factors are important in understanding the development of "clinical" eating disorders. Yet, argued in the previous chapters, this group of "clinical" cases of eating disorders is small and, in fact, may become stable over time and to a greater extent, independent of a particular cultural context.[30] Instead, I focus on how young women experience today's cultural expectations on women to be ultra-slender. This chapter takes up the range of multidimensional factors that may trigger a move up or down the body image/eating disorders continuum by focusing on those groups who often are the cultural brokers of these messages—families, peer groups, and school environments.

EATING DISORDERS AND DISORDERLY EATING: WHAT'S THE DIFFERENCE?

There were indeed women in my research sample who *would be* classified with an eating disorder. Frequently they were women who had a history of sexual abuse, severe family dysfunction, or physical abuse. Eating (or not eating) was their empowering tool for coping. They saw controlling their bodies as a culturally approved substitute for controlling their economic, political, and social lives. Bodies often hold feelings too painful to hold in consciously.[31] For example, rejecting food may send a powerful message of a problematic family. At the same time, overeating may be a safe way to soothe emotional pain.[32]

Linda, one of my bulimic interview subjects, told me:

> When I do have a problem, I know what I'm doing with the food. It's nurturance, and I understand that, at the time, and that's when I give in to it. You know, you can't fight your battles on every front all the time. I realize I'm giving in to this bulimia, but if that is what I need right now to take care of me, that's all right.

Despite their cruelly limiting consequences, anorexia and bulimia are effective survival strategies for some women. For women with clinical bulimia, the primary motivation for purging may be to vent the anger and frustration of abuse or mistreatment, rather than weight loss. *Body control or psychological pain management is not what motivates culturally induced eating disorders.*

Kim, an anorectic, expressed this difference.

I think my issue was wanting to control my life. There were a lot of family issues and personal issues that were going on in my life freshman year of high school and I just started with a diet. I suddenly decided I wouldn't eat more than 300 calories. My parents had gotten separated freshman year, my dad remarried that summer and my mom had gotten cancer. There was a tremendous amount of anger, pain that I didn't deal with. I have two brothers and a sister, and everyone took a different route to deal with all of these things that were happening— trauma, basically. And I was always an internal person. My sister is quicker and lets out anger, and I didn't do that as much. So I just sort of went into my own little world. And then that world became totally about eating and weight.

Kim's coping mechanism co-opted the culture's "look thin, be self-controlled" mandate and used it for her emotional survival. Best-selling author Caroline Knapp echoes this experience in *Appetites: Why Women Want*:

At a time when I felt adrift and confused and deeply unsure of myself, starving gave me a goal, a way to stand out and exert control, something I could be good at . . . I could not express what I'd been feeling with words, but I could wear it. The inner life —hunger, confusion, longings unnamed and unmet, the whole overwhelming gamut—as a sculpture in bone.[33]

But unlike Kim and Linda, the majority of women in my sample used disorderly eating primarily for socially correct thinness. I interviewed Suzanna a year after she graduated from college. She traced the beginnings of her body image problems to her junior year, when she and two roommates effectively joined the Cult of Thinness:

For the first 2 years of college there was really no problem. Eating was sort of the thing, "Let's go to dinner with these people" and "I'll meet you for lunch" and so on. In fact, I maintained my three meals a day routine.

Then things changed drastically.

I always had a good self-image until I roomed with a group of girls who are my closest friends, and super weight conscious. Now that I can look back on it I really can see how out of whack it was. They sort of became my family and . . . their weight was the thing. . . . One of them looked very skinny to me. She was like 5′8″ and had a beautiful shape, very thin. She did not eat—I think she lived on cigarettes and soda. She was really bad. There were days, there were weeks where she wouldn't eat solid food. Her cousin, another roommate, also had very strange eating patterns. She was a little overweight because she would eat in hiding. She would try to be like her cousin all day long and not eat. But you'd always hear her eating something in the middle of the night. . . . Junior and senior year I really went crazy living with them. I would go on diets with them. . . . liquid diets for days. I remember. I was in the library and I felt dizzy. They both made me feel very heavy. To this day, I'll never be skinny enough. Whenever I saw them they would say "you have 5 or 10 to go." And it bothers me because I'm so used to their mind-set. . . . The weeks I wouldn't eat they would remark, "Oh, Suzanna you are doing great and you look good." And they were so happy because I guess the more the merrier.

I would return home during college breaks, eating just oranges and Diet Coke. And my parent's didn't like that at all. They were paying all this money for a food plan and they would say "go eat" and "don't skip meals." So back there my logical sense would come through—then I'd be on campus and I'd decide I needed lunch and I would go eat by myself. And I'd feel very good about it. And I just wouldn't tell my roommates because they really had problems with it. . . . There were times I would get mad at them. During my senior year we had an apartment. I would have a really good time cooking for myself and my other roommates. And the cousins would pick at it and that would get me very angry, I guess they did that because they felt they weren't really eating.

I did have a third roommate named Sonia, who would be the only one to occasionally eat with me. Sounds so horrible. But she had a stronger personality than I did because she would tell these two cousins to their face that they were crazy! And I would just try to be the middle person and respect how they felt and say okay.

After I left school it took me awhile to get back into my old eating patterns. Now I think I'm eating just as normally as I did in high school. Working every day and I really need my breakfast, lunch, and supper. I'll go through my times and try to cut down a little bit but it's definitely healthier. College was a different swing.

The disordered eating Suzanna fell into, influenced by her roommates' values, is distinctly different from an eating disorder. She avoided the slippery slope of thinness-at-any-cost obsession, and once she left that social environment she returned to "normal" eating. Suzanna was lucky her Cult of Thinness membership was only brief. Others are not so fortunate.

The Family and the Thinness Message: Mothers, Fathers, and Siblings

Children learn who they are by studying the adults around them, and the family is a child's first interpreter of the larger world. Some families repeat the cultural values of thinness, while others modify the message.[34] Women raised in families who are hypercritical of their daughters' weight place them at greater risk of experiencing disordered eating patterns.[35] Furthermore, teasing about weight and body image during early childhood can lead to a detrimental impact on young girls' body images in later life.[36] Barbara's case is an extreme example of how parents amplify the message that to be beautiful is to be loved. This message dominated her life, fostering a full-blown eating disorder.

Barbara's Story

Barbara was 20 when I interviewed her for this book. She appeared to be a happy, average-weight, well-adjusted college coed, but I had had a 2-year ongoing dialogue with her about weight, body image, and her chronic anorexia and bulimia. Her hidden history of anorexia started in seventh grade; her bulimia began in the ninth grade and continued throughout high school and college.

Barbara's parents had serious marital problems. Her father, toward whom she felt a great deal of ambivalence, had very high standards of feminine beauty. Her own sense of femininity developed as she observed how difficult it was for her mother to live up to her father's expectations. Clinical psychologist Margo Maine writes, "A girl develops beliefs about feminine behavior by watching her father interact with women. She observes the traits he values, the behavior that evokes his support or his disdain, and the way he treats them. A father's treatment of his wife especially influences the adolescent daughter in her struggle to determine the ways in which she should be similar to, or different from, her mother."[37]

> For my father, a woman has to look perfect. She has no brains. My mother has to go to my dad's functions and she has to just sit there with a smile on her face and look great. My father loves it that his wife looks so much younger than everybody else. I don't think they were ever friends. They were just kind of physically attracted to each other. She does everything to please my father. She would go on a diet for my father. She colors her hair for my father. She lies out in the sun all summer—she wants to be as tan as she can for him. . . . And, my father would get in fights because her toenails weren't painted and she was wearing open-toed shoes!

Barbara did not escape her father's criticism of her own body. As a preadolescent she was taller than the other girls in her class, and this made her feel "big."[38]

> When I was little my dad always used to make fun of me. I was never fat, just tall, but he used to pinch my stomach and say, "Barbie, you got a little rubber tire in there."

So Barbara stopped eating in the seventh grade.

I lost so much weight they were going to send me to a hospital, because I refused to eat. I wanted to be thin and I loved it. I ate the minimum, a little bowl of cereal for breakfast. I remember my father forcing me to eat a bowl of ice cream. I was crying and he said, "You're going to eat this, you know," which was funny because he's the one who used to call me fat. I used to lie down every night on my bed to see how my hip bones stick out.

When my father said, "You're even skinnier than your sister," I was so happy. It was like an accomplishment; finally for once in my life I was thinner than my sister. I remember going shopping with her to get jeans. I tried on size zero and they fell off. It was the best feeling I'd ever had in my entire life. I went back to school weighing under 90 pounds and I was about 5'6". I loved competitive sports, so when I couldn't play tennis anymore because I was fainting, I started eating. I could eat and get on the scale and I wouldn't even gain any weight because I was playing so much tennis. My eating was normal during that period, the eighth grade. But I wouldn't eat in front of anyone.

Then Barbara started bingeing and vomiting.

It was awful. It was the worst feeling. You know you are about to throw up but you have to get the last bite in. My bingeing would only happen when I was alone, before my parents came home.

I still binge and I always do the exact same thing. I put on my backpack and go to the local food store. I don't want to talk to anybody. I always get cookies, cake, and ice cream because it is easy to throw up. Once I stole from the cafeteria because I was too embarrassed to buy it. The minute I get back to my room, I lock the door. I can't throw up in my bathroom because other girls will hear, so I turn on the music and throw up in a garbage bag. It's so gross. After I throw up I feel awful—it can be so exhausting all you do is fall asleep.

For Barbara, there was no escaping the pressure to be thin and attractive, "because that's what my father thinks and likes. I guess I want to live up to his standard." Yet she knew how devastating this had been for her mother and how rocky a relationship her parents had.

I always said to my mom that I'd never want to marry someone like Dad. I don't want what happened to my mom to happen to me. He just wants my mother to look young for the rest of her life. He doesn't want her to go gray. My mother's going through menopause and she just cries all the time. And my dad is like, "You're so old." And my mother is just devastated. And I mean, she has to wear bikinis. She always has to wear full face makeup on the beach, because you can't show like any blemishes, or anything. You have to look perfect.

I get angry, but then again, it's the way I've always been brought up. I was always angry at my mom for never saying anything. She was always such a wimp.

My dad has never seen divorce as an alternative. He thinks if you get married, it's for life. I know inside he loves my mother more than anybody. It's weird. He can't show it, but I know he does. When I was growing up I remember always listening to them fight. When my mother would be crying, I would say, "Why don't you just leave him?" and my mother's reason was "I like my financial life style. I like going to Europe every year. I like having a summer house. I like having my summers off. If I get divorced I can't have any of that."

Barbara's response to these pressures was a full-blown clinical eating disorder, accompanied by classic psychological symptoms like maturity fears. Afraid of growing up and facing what her mother experienced as an adult married woman, Barbara used compulsive eating to numb her anxiety and anger and purging to relieve her dread of being fat and unloved.

Just as every family's story is unique, there is no single factor that would explain how families induct their daughters into the Cult of Thinness. Some parents go out of their way to *avoid* emphasizing body image issues with their daughters. However, the college women I interviewed were quick to point out the little ways their families passed on the cultural message.

Mom's Influence

Mothers are crucial brokers of cultural norms. Some research studies note how a mother's attitudes about her own body image and eating behavior influence her daughter. Eating disorders expert Caroline Knapp writes, "Every generation measures itself against the one before; every daughter's experience of hunger will be shaped to some extent by that of her mother. What she had or did not have, how much it cost her, how much she herself wants or can allow herself to want in contrast."[39]

Cathleen, a sophomore I interviewed, notes that her own mother was careful about her weight and was constantly on a diet. She took Cathleen to the doctor when she was not getting rid of her baby fat. Her mother put a high premium on looking good for herself and her daughter. Cathleen notes:

> You know, my mother thought I was fat. I was 11 years old at the time. She put me on extensive diets, and I didn't like that. She gave me these amino tablets and she'd search around and make sure I didn't take cookies with me to school. She watched me. She took me to her weight doctor. My mother said: "Well you know you've got to get rid of that baby fat." I actually remember the moment when I got shame. I guess you call it that. I was undressing and all of a sudden, I jumped away from the window. I was 11 when I suddenly realized I should cover myself up.

Knapp asserts: "A mother who is tormented by diet and weight, who appears preoccupied with her appearance and disgusted by her own body, cannot easily teach her daughter to take delight in food, to feel carefree about weight or joyful about the female form."[40] A mother who is obsessed with being thin and who diets regularly is considered one of the eating-disorder risk factors for an adolescent girl.[41] In addition, if a mother struggled with a weight problem herself, psychotherapist Susie Orbach writes,

> she may revisit this problem on her adolescent daughter by becoming watchful of what she eats and preoccupied with her changing body contours. She does this with the best of intentions, but her observations are frequently experienced as intrusive. . . . At the same time that mothers transmit caution and limitation, where the physical expression of their daughter is concerned, they are consciously and unconsciously monitoring and shaping another important aspect of their daughter's physicality—their appetites.[42]

Betty's Story

Betty mimicked her mother's attitudes about weight and eating issues by being very conscious of her body image and becoming bulimic in college.

> My mom considers herself overweight. She always dieted, trying all those new, different diets, and I'd go on them with her. She'll fluctuate, losing some but then she'll gain it back. I have this little chart that I try to follow. It has your height and your build, if you're medium or small boned. It has how many calories are in anything you eat. My mom put it in my stocking at Christmas.

The message Betty's mother was sending—stay thin—was different from the message she received from her grandfather.

> My brothers and father liked to eat. We always had a lot of food on the table and my grandfather would reward us for cleaning our plates. Even now I feel like I have to eat everything on my plate, even if I'm not hungry.

When she was a college freshman she gained enough weight for her father to remark that she was getting a "little chubby." Conscious of the extra weight she put on, Betty knew she needed to do something. Her bulimia started during her sophomore year, after a Christmas party.

> I had been drinking at the party and I just ate out of control. I couldn't believe that I had eaten all that stuff. It was cookies mainly. I never thought I could throw up, and then I tried and it worked. I tried so hard to keep my weight down and I was 115 and that's where I wanted to stay. And then I'd creep back up. To get all the food out of my stomach, especially that high calorie food, I threw up.

I didn't have time to join a fitness club and I tried to run, but I didn't feel like I was exercising enough. I could just feel myself gaining weight and that made me nervous and I felt like if I didn't have time to exercise, then throwing up was the answer. I tried dieting and I wouldn't eat for awhile, and then I would eat a lot. I can't go a whole day without eating. I think that's a major reason why I throw up too. Because I like to eat.

Trapped by conflicting messages, "be thin" and "clean your plate," Betty's response was bulimia. To atone for the sin of overeating, purging seemed easier than exercise and fasting. The conflicting "eat/be thin" message is not new. It is everywhere, and, obviously, while only a few respond as Betty did, many women suffer in one way or another. As we have seen in Chapter 3, the diet food industry has been quick to capitalize on a solution. Diet foods can represent both sin and atonement—one-stop shopping for guilt-free pleasure.

Mother as Enforcer

Some mothers acted as "enforcers" of wider cultural norms of weight and body image. Sometimes the daughters I talked with complained that their mothers were overzealous in efforts to keep the daughters' bodies in line; others commented that even though they were upset at their mothers' tactics and what seemed at the time as unrelenting pressure on them "to behave their bodies," they noticed their body weight begin to drop under Mom's careful supervision, and this was a source of joy for them. Dana and her mom Joan depict this type of mother-daughter body work.

Dana notes how difficult it has been to take Joan's critical comments concerning her body image, but how much she also appreciates her nudging:

Last year my mom called me a moose, and that hurt. Sometimes I think I need something like that, or somebody like that to just make me aware, so that I do something about it. A lot of times I'll be just like, you know. Now I can see all her pushing, it's gotten me where I am. I am looking for the honest answer in terms of whether or not she thinks I am fat, and I'm always hoping she'll say, "No, you look good!" You know? But she doesn't. And then she'll tell me the bad news, and then I'll get upset, and she'll be like, "Well then why did you ask me if you didn't want to know the truth, no? I'm not going to lie to you!". . . I think sometimes I want her to lie just a little. She's just honest, you know? I mean, she says it like it is, "No!" Just boom! "You look fat. You look like a moose!" The next thing I know I starve myself. When I go home she's like a hawk. She's on my back. She's like on my shoulder. "Don't eat that. Don't eat that. Put that down. You don't want that." I remember I went home a couple of weeks ago and I went for a piece of bread at a restaurant and she goes (slap!), and I was like . . . . Guess I'm not going to have any bread. On the other hand,

> I guess I just need that push, I think. And I mean, I know whenever I go home I always come back thinner. No matter if it's a weekend and I come back 2 or 3 pounds thinner, I always come back thinner. Because my mother's telling me, This is what you should eat; this is what you should do. Get exercise every day, every morning. And I do it. And I start to feel better.

Dana's good feelings about her weight loss are ephemeral as soon as she gets out of target range of her mother's surveillance.

> I was talking with my mom on the phone the other day. She said, "How's your weight going?" Every time I talk to her, "How's your weight going? How do you look?" And finally I just said to her, "Mom," and I always color it, and I say, "Oh, it's fine; I'm the same, you know." This time I'm like, just, "Mom, I don't know what it is. I think it's just the atmosphere, but as soon as I get back here, no matter how hard I set my mind that I'm going to do what you tell me to do at home, I go right back into the old routine!" That's why I always lie to her. I'm not the same weight and I always come back home heavier, and she sees it. As soon as I come back to school it's like boom, I'm back to smoking. I'm back to drinking. I'm back to eating. . . .

Mothers can also serve to *modulate* cultural norms of thinness and alleviate some of the pressures young girls may feel. Joanna, who is not overweight, described her mother's attitude:

> All she wants is that I'm happy. I can weigh 500 pounds as long as I'm happy. Her focus was always on my health, not so much with my appearance. So her comments were more toward that positive support. Very rarely do I remember her giving anything like negative comments about how I looked. It was encouraging. My mother would stay stuff like "You have a beautiful face, you have beautiful hands." She would focus on individual qualities about me.

Father's Influence

For the most part, the fathers of the women in my study were silent about their daughters' body image. Barbara's father, as we noted earlier, was unusual. So was Mara's—her father wanted her to be thin and have perfect grades:

Mara's Story: Not Daddy's Little Girl

> He always looked at us as showpieces. That's how he thought other people saw us. . . . I was three years old when my dad started calling me fat. He used to sing me a song, "I don't want her, you can have her, she's too fat for me," and I used to cry every time. It was terrible. He was repulsed by my weight, just as he was by my mother's. He never really, like, talked about it. He always used to say I had no style. My sister always had all the style. She has real expensive taste,

dresses wonderfully, has a real flair with clothes. I'll admit I think she dresses really great. But that is what she is concerned about. Where my Dad is concerned, I never dress right, but he always was like, you've got a pretty face. I remember that so well. But it's weird, he used to always call me Princess Mara. And I guess, like he thought that was being nice, where my sister took it like, he likes her more than me. But I took it as if I always have to live up to this standard of being the best. And he commented on other women, more than me. If there was a waitress, he'd say "Boy she is beautiful." Always commenting on pretty young girls. So I knew it was very important for him that I look good, too. So when I'd dress up, I wanted him to see that I could be just as pretty as all those women he was commenting on. And I could tell that he was proud of me for that. He would say "You look good." I knew . . . he didn't comment on a lot of details. He wouldn't make it a huge deal. But I just knew. I could be wearing my hair totally differently and he'd never notice it. But if I looked good, he'd comment.

Supportive Dads

Jessica's father was more typical:

> I can't recall my father saying much about my appearance. Like if I put a skirt on he'd say: "Oh, you *do* have legs," and he joked about it. Never anything negative.

Helen's father was also quiet. On special occasions he might say a word or two:

> It was one of those things where if you bought a new dress for a prom, and you tried it on for him, he'd say, "Oh, that looks great" or "very nice" or whatever. But as far as day to day, he'd never say anything. To tell you the truth I don't think he would even know what to say because that's not the type of question that he'd answer. He'd think, "What kind of a question is that, 'How do I look?'" He was the same as my mom. He always thought I was fine. There were times you go through high school you go thinking you look horrible and your legs are too fat and things like that. Every time I went out I would, if I felt like I didn't look right, he would say don't even worry about it, you look fine and don't even think about it, don't let it get in the way of having a good time and things like that. There was a time, I don't know when it was, it was in high school. I think I was the heaviest I ever was and I was maybe depressed or something. I remember at Christmas time eating a whole lot and just gaining more weight. And everyone was on my case in the family. My sisters mainly, not my parents. My dad didn't see it. He's like, "You look the same" and obviously I was heavier and he didn't even see it. Didn't even comment on it. And then I

remember once this year at college I was thinner and it took him about 2 weeks to notice it. He says, "You do look OK," but it was not a big change.

Siblings' Influence

The role of siblings' influence in the development of an eating disorder or disordered eating has not been given much attention by researchers. An early study of the role that siblings may play in the development of an eating disorder comes from a research project that examined 50 women with eating disorders and looked, in particular, at their relationships with their sisters. Eating-disordered women tended to have sisters closest to them in age with whom they often developed a distant, conflictual, and rivialrous relationship.[43] One research group studied "sister pairs," with one sister who had anorexia and another who was a normal eater. The sister who was diagnosed as anorectic perceived her mother to be more controlling, expressed conflict and jealously toward her nonanorectic sister, and in fact had fewer friends and boyfriends than her non-eating disordered sister.[44]

Judith's older sister made fun of her weight:

My older sister teased me because I was larger than all my siblings. I was 3 or 4 inches taller than even my older sister. And I think I was also bigger. I started developing earlier. She used to say "You're a fatso." It used to get me mad, but then when I looked at myself, I would think "But, I'm not fat!"

Jenna notes,

My sister who is closest to me in age but a little bit younger, was always in the best shape, very athletic. She would just constantly call me fat because I was bigger than her. And so that was a big point with her. If there was ever a bad time that was always something she could, you know, bring up because she never had any sort of problem in that way at all.

Angela notes that when she was in high school she began to care about what her older brothers thought of her body.

When I was in high school, I got really shy. I started to look at them as boys and not as my brothers. I was very self-conscious around boys and I turned it on them. I became really shy. And they would always criticize me. And I'd take it to heart and try to change and be like they said. They'd say you shouldn't eat that or act that way and I'd try and change. I was heavier toward the end of high school. And my brothers would mention it to my mother and she would say, "Doug thinks you're getting fat" and then she'd say maybe you should stop eating so much. I pretended that it didn't bother me, that I didn't feel he was right. But I did feel that way. I tried to lose it.

Sometimes the teasing about body image heats up around the household, and siblings' comments can sting. Jenna notes that as a child her siblings' teasing about her weight became difficult for her to handle.

My brothers and sisters would go around me and make a pig noise. At the time it really hurt my feelings because I'm a very sensitive person. And then my parents really didn't . . . I think to this day I really was upset that they never really said, "Jenna may be heavy but she's a person, she's your sister. Don't talk to her like that." They never said that to me. I think I resent that to this day.

The College Environment: Breeding Ground for Food and Weight Obsession.

My grandmother is always telling me that I should eat and be strong and healthy, but when I do, she tells me to watch what I eat or I'll never find a husband.

—Davidson College, '98

I feel trapped between two worlds because I believe that what is African is really beautiful, and I don't want to look like a white model . . . but I do still think that being thin looks good.

—Spelman College, '96

I got to college and I never saw so many beautiful girls in my life. . . . I never had a problem with my looks, but suddenly there were all these tall, thin, blond girls with perfect figures everywhere I looked, and I totally felt short, fat, and ugly

—UCLA, '96

Because I'm tall and black, people didn't think it was odd that I was so thin, and they never suspected that I was anorectic.

—University of Connecticut, '92

I know so many women who fit the stereotypical eating disorder stat—middle class, overachiever, attractive—that when my Asian roommate was starving herself it took me awhile to recognize it as anorexia because I thought her eating patterns were cultural.

—University of Michigan, '96[45]

Nearly all of the women I studied felt college life had a profound impact on their body image and eating patterns. They are not alone: Colleges and universities across the country are reporting dramatic increases in eating disorders. Several studies on anorexia nervosa in college populations report that it affects between 6% and 25% of female students.[46] Bulimia ranges between 1% and 19%,[47] and between 23% to nearly 85% engage in binge eating.[48] Although the disorders are listed as separate, the symptoms overlap. While self-starvation is specific to anorexia, obsessive concern with weight and reliance on extreme diet measures is common to both, and bulimic episodes are common among anorectics. "Bulimarexia" describes the mix of symptoms.[49] "Researchers have suggested as many as 19% of college coeds have one form of eating disorder or another"[50] and "Subclinical forms of eating pathology [are] generally estimated to be five times more common than the full blown syndromes."[51]

There are several reasons why the college environment may be a breeding ground for weight obsession and the development of culturally induced eating problems.[52] First, college campuses are middle- and upper-middle-class enclaves—a group that places a high premium on thinness in women.[53] With the spread of mass media, especially television and magazine advertising, the Cult of Thinness as a prominent cultural message has reached across the class/race spectrum. As more and more women from working class or ethnic backgrounds populate a wide range of colleges and universities, they become increasingly vulnerable to this message. As we see in Chapter 8, "New Recruits" the Cult of Thinness has spread far beyond the stereotypical eating-disordered cohort of upper-middle-class, white, heterosexual, American adolescent girls.

Second, college life provides an enclosed environment, and this tends to amplify sociocultural pressures.[54] Disorderly eating can spread through imitation, competition, or solidarity. Some researchers note that bulimia is an "acquired pattern of behavior," or suggest that there is a "social contagion" phenomenon that occurs in such an environment.[55] In her book, *The Beginner's Guide to Eating Disorder Recovery*, social worker and eating disorders specialist, Nancy Kolodny, notes that a type of desensitiz[ation] to the problem of bulimia and anorexia may occur when students are in such a semi-enclosed environment. Kolodny contends, "When people are in close contact socially and emotionally, they can learn the rationale and techniques of binging and purging from one another."[56] Another important factor is the importance of an attractive physical appearance in dating. Students who live in close quarters, such as dorms or sororities, often feel pressured to live up to group standards of beauty even if it means engaging in eating disordered behavior.[57] It follows that schools that emphasize the dating scene may also have higher rates of bulimia.[58]

A recent study of female college students followed a group of 23 women at two universities, one predominantly white and the other historically and predominantly black. Over time, these women "shifted more and more of their interests and energy away from college work and toward the peer group, with its emphasis on romance." The authors of the study concluded that the peer group culture was of primary importance to college-age women. This culture centered around how to meet and attract the opposite sex—what the researchers term getting a grade on the "sexual auction block." How attractive a woman could be to men depended on looking good and maintaining a thin body. *This was the primary determination of her status within a peer group.* Academic studies were not highly valued by peer group culture and did not play an important role in the day-to-day college life of these women.[59]

College Eating, the "Freshman 15," and the Vicious Cycle

The stress and strain of college, from academics to social life, magnifies female students' problems with weight because women often use food as a means of calming or coping. Weight gained during college is especially detrimental in a climate already primed to value thinness. Extra pounds lead to efforts to lose, which trigger a new round of disorderly eating. This becomes a vicious cycle: stress leading to overeating, leading to weight gain, leading to restricted eating or over-exercising, leading to more stress if the diet or exercise does not work. Even if it does work, just worrying about how to keep the weight off can trigger more eating, more weight gain, and so on.

The transition from high school to college is a common time of weight gain for women students, and the time they report they began to diet or binge eat.[60] The "freshman 15," the 15 pounds a freshman is expected to gain the first year, is a cultural prescription in league with the "pig out" and the "frat barf."[61] In my sample, students reported weight gains of 15 or more pounds. Some students reported a smaller weight gain, and only a few said they lost weight.[62]

Merely being away from home affects the regularity of student eating patterns. Without parents to organize meals and supervise nutritional intake, they find themselves too busy to eat, or eating more than usual. Charlotte said:

> You kind of forget about eating and then all of a sudden you gorge yourself. At home you just realize, okay, I'm gonna have breakfast, lunch, and dinner. So you really don't think about food. In college I have classes on this day so I can't eat until this time. It's just different because you're used to a set pattern at home and Mom usually cooks it but here you have to get it yourself so it's very erratic. I definitely overeat.

The scheduling of cafeteria meals at college often conflicts with students' preferred eating times. Students often skipped breakfast, and some had "double dinners."

At home, we didn't eat until 6 or 6:30. If you're eating dinner early and you're still up at 11, you're hungry. That's why we would order out a lot. And my roommate ate junk food. I was never a big potato chip eater or any of that kind of stuff, but she was, and having food around meant I would eat it. I gained weight quickly.

—Julianna

I think actually freshman year everyone I knew gained weight. Probably at least 10 pounds. It's just like eating was the thing to do. It was a very social type thing. I can remember sending out for pizza at midnight a lot of times with a whole bunch of people and stuff; things that you wouldn't usually do.

—Shana

I was smoking all first semester of freshman year and I was gaining 25 pounds. But now I think, I won't eat that: I'll have a cigarette. And I don't binge like I used to. Every once in a while I'll binge. But the weirdest thing was when I had lost all my weight after sophomore year, and I was looking anorexic. Just to save myself, I would diet all week. Then Sunday was my day to eat everything in sight. And I'd do it to the point that I got sick. Then I wouldn't eat on Monday, and I'd diet, diet, diet until Sunday.

—June

I was in my room and I had to write this paper. It was due the next day. I had done my research on it. I had taken all my notes. All I had to do was to write the thing. You know, it wasn't a long paper, I knew what I was writing, but for some reason, I did not want to write this paper. I thought, maybe I just won't show up. Maybe I'll go to the infirmary in the morning. I don't know how many dumb things went through my head. I do this for almost every single test I have. I was sitting there in front of this computer and I did not finish the paper until 11:00. I just sat there, like "I can't do this!" That night I binged on two pieces of cake, and two cookies. The minute I got up to my room, I locked the door, binged on the food, and threw up. I finished the paper, and I didn't sleep at all. I went on the Stairmaster machine the next morning for 45 minutes.

—Melissa

You'd be sitting around, you'd skip dinner because you were studying or it just didn't look good or what ever the reason would be. And somebody would've gone down to the store, so it would just be a matter of having to starting munching on a few potato chips. And then we'd say "Oh, I've got a bag of something else" and pull those out. And the next thing, you'd say "Well this is crap, why don't we just get a pizza." But then when the pizza came you'd be on something else. There was always junk there to be eating.

—Ann

The type of disordered eating these students were engaged in was a way to cope with the stress. One female college student, Martha notes:

Food wasn't much of a problem in high school. Food became a psychological problem in college, and I would be bingeing and purging, because my boyfriend did something to me, because I had an exam the next day, because I felt really lonely at college, all by myself. It was a psychological issue.

We see how this semi-cloistered environment, where looks can matter most for women, not only amplifies a drive for thinness but offers food as a coping mechanism for college's new stressors.

I'd eat like a slob for a week and then the following week I'd stop eating all together. A binge for me is eating some type of three meals a day and then when I'm home I eat everything in sight. And it's not just eating dinner. It's eating maybe two or three of everything that's there. And on weekends, I just keep eating and eating. The following week I won't eat breakfast or lunch and all I'll eat for dinner is some broccoli or maybe I'll make an ice cream sundae. I don't care too much about nutrition.

—*Sara*

I remember my roommates all pigged out and then they all tried to make themselves throw up. They just all went into the bathroom and threw up. And I couldn't do it. I tried but it wouldn't happen. I thought, "This is stupid!" So I never did it again.

—*Dawn*

In this situation, it's important for parents, friends, coaches, and students to emphasize healthful ways to manage eating and weight.

Long-Term Impact

What remains unexplored by researchers is the long-range impact of college life on women's body image and eating patterns. In the transition from high school to college many young women struggle with independence, maturity, self-concept, and the dating/mating game, a vulnerability ripe for the onset of disordered eating.[63] I conducted several follow-up studies of women from their senior years in high school to their senior years in college. They reported plummeting self-esteem in terms of physical attractiveness, social self-confidence, assertiveness, and popularity, especially with the opposite sex. More disturbed eating patterns accompanied this decline.[64] In fact, those women whose eating patterns remained problematic throughout the 4 years of college showed a pattern of diminishing self-concept over time compared to those whose eating patterns were normal or whose eating issues improved.[65]

My self-esteem just went down. I went from a public school to this private college, where it seemed to me like everybody was really rich, and everybody had been to private schools. I'd been so protected before, when I surrounded myself with people like myself. I just went off the deep end.

—Miriam

I had a horrible experience that first year of college because of where I lived, who I lived with, and the alienation I felt. I gained weight, of course. I was living with three girls who had their own food issues, like everyone I have lived with. . . . On top of that, you have homework that probably wasn't being completed because you're thinking about your weight. Eating became, you know, how to get through the day.

—Irene

Several female students I interviewed told painful stories about feeling unattractive and unsuccessful in finding a boyfriend.

I liked this guy and we were friends and then I came out one day and made the stupid mistake of telling him. I said "You must know how I feel about you," and then he said "You'll never be Angelina Jolie." At the time I was horrified. Now I can laugh, because he's certainly no Brad Pitt. But I couldn't say this because I was so hurt at the time and so his comment really did a thing on my psyche. And in a matter of 18 weeks I lost 35 pounds.

—Ginger

There is no simple cause-and-effect relationship here, and it is difficult to generalize the findings from one study. More research could explore the reasons for these self-esteem declines during college and how this is specifically related to eating issues. Research so far shows that college reproduces traditional gender stereotypes of women, creating an opportunity for the Cult of Thinness to flourish. Some researchers have speculated that the coeducational college environment may act as a "null environment"[66] for its female students—where women are neither encouraged nor discouraged in the pursuit of any but the most traditional of roles. Depending on their previous socialization experiences, the lack of encouragement alone may have some devastating consequences for the developing self. As one researcher writes:

Even though men and women are presumably exposed to a common liberal arts curriculum and other educational programs during the undergraduate years, it would seem that these programs serve more to preserve, rather than to reduce, stereotypic differences between men and women in behavior, personality, aspirations, and achievement.[67]

Understanding the Cultural Context of Eating Disorders

In summary, disorderly eating is not a sign of psychopathology, but a strategy that is a "normal" part of the female existence. In a culture where obesity is becoming more and more common, it becomes increasingly easy to mock the seriousness of the disease.

While psychological trauma or even biochemical deficits may contribute to some of the eating problems occurring in the young college women I have described, psychological and biological theories fail to address the more general issues. The link between the cultural norms of thinness and a young woman is mediated by her family, school, and peer group, who, more often than not, translate and embellish society's thinness messages.

It would not be enough, for example, to get Barbara's father to be more aware of the impact of his "stay young and beautiful" message on his wife and daughters, or to counsel the family to deal with their emotional issues. Barbara's problem with her body image and her resulting eating disorder is reinforced at every turn by the world she lives in. As noted in chapter 1, biological, physiological, as well as psychological factors play an important role in determining one's position along this continuum. However, the argument is that one's micro and macro cultural environment—what happens especially in one's immediate community of family and peers and in the wider culture—has created a climate ripe for widespread development of a Cult of Thinness, which is enveloping a wider and wider population of women beyond white middle-class girls and women. It is beginning to spread, as we shall see in chapter 8, to other groups in the society—preteen girls, straight men, gays and lesbians, and women from other racial and ethnic groups.

Notes

1. Al Dubin and Harry Warren, Keep Young and Beautiful [Recorded by Annie Lennox], On *Diva* [CD], New York: RCA, 1992
2. See: A.E. Anderson, "Anorexia Nervosa and Bulimia in Adolescent Males," *Pediatric Annals,* 12 (1984): 901–904, 907.
3. K.M. Bemis, "Current Approaches to the Etiology and Treatment of Anorexia Nervosa," *Psychology Bulletin,* 85, no. 3 (1978): 593–617; H. Bruch, *Eating Disorders: Obesity, Anorexia and the Person Within* (New York: Basic Books, 1973).
4. H. Bruch, *Eating Disorders: Obesity, Anorexia and the Person Within* (New York: Basic Books, 1973), A.H. Crisp, "Some Aspects of the Evolution Presentation and Follow-up of Anorexia Nervosa," *Proceedings of the Royal Society of Medicine,* 58 (1965): 814–820; H.G. Morgan and G.F.M. Russel, "Value of Family Background and Clinical Features as Predictors of Long-Term Outcome in Anorexia Nervosa: Four-year Follow-up Study of 41 Patients," *Psychological Medicine,* 5 (1975): 355–371.
5. Figures are from Anorexia Nervosa and Related Eating Disorders, Inc. www.anred.com. Accessed May 25, 2005.

6. Even this number may be conservative; the real incidence is underreported because of the stigma attached to having an eating disorder.

7. Steven Levenkron, *Anatomy of Anorexia* (New York: W.W. Norton, 2001), 137. (See also: David Garner and Paul Garfinkel, *The Handbook of Treatment for Eating Disorders* (New York: Guilford Press, 1997), 222.

8. Nancy J. Kolodny, *The Beginner's Guide to Eating Disorders Recovery* (Carlsbad, CA: Gurze Books, 2004), 94.

9. See: Jennie Bristow, "Kelly Holmes: No Prizes for Confessing," *Spiked Risk*, June 2, 2005, http://www.spiked-online.com/Articles/0000000CAB88.htm

10. See: Tracey Gold, *Room to Grow: An Appetite for Life* (Beverly Hills, CA: New Millennium Press, 2003).

11. See: Jaime-Lynn Sigler and Sheryl Beck, *Wise Girl: What I've Learned about Life, Love, and Loss* (New York: Pocket Books, 2002).

12. See: *Us Weekly*, July 4, 2005.

13. Tracy Robinson and Janie Victoria Ward, "A Belief in Self far Greater Than Anyone's Disbelief." Cultivating Resistance Among African American Female Adolescents. Carol Gilligan, Annie G. Rogers, and Deborah L. Tolman, (eds.) *Women, Girls, and Psychotherapy: Reframing Resistance* (New York: Harrington Park Press, 1991), 95.

14. Sylvia Brody, *The Development of Anorexia Nervosa: The Hunger Artists* (Madison, CT: International Universities Press, 2002), 186.

15. Hilde Bruch, *Conversations with Anorexics: A Compassionate and Hopeful Journey through the Therapeutic Process* (Northvale, NJ: Basic Books, 1988), xvi, 44.

16. Hilde Bruch, *The Golden Cage: The Enigma of Anorexia Nervosa* (Cambridge, MA: Harvard University Press, 1978), 28.

17. Susie Orbach, *Hunger Strike: Starving amidst Plenty* (New York: Other Press, 2001), 95, 156.

18. The Eating Attitudes Test (EAT) was used as a measure for eating disorders. The EAT is a clinical test that has been used in other research with student populations. The test consists of 26 items designed to evaluate a broad range of behaviors and contains three scales: diet, bulimia, and oral control. The diet scale relates to an avoidance of fattening foods and a preoccupation with being thin. The bulimia scale consists of items reflecting a preoccupation with food as well as thoughts indicating bulimic behaviors. The third measure, oral control, relates to self-control about food. See: D.M Garner, M.P. Olmsted, Y. Bohr, and P.E. Garfinkel, "The Eating Attitudes Test: Psychometric Features and Clinical Correlates," *Psychological Medicine*, 12 (1982): 871–878. The EAT has been used as an outcome measure in many treatment studies and it has also been used as a screening instrument in nonclinical populations http://river-centre.org. River Centre Clinic Eating Disorder Program. Also see: http://www.river-centre.org/ED_Index.html

19. We found that women who followed a cultural ideal were also less satisfied with their body image and more concerned about their body weight. In addition, 34% of cultural followers reported feeling anxious, depressed, or repulsed by their bodies, compared with only 24% of medical followers. Finally, we learned that almost

half of the cultural-ideal followers (47%) reported significant to extreme concern about their body weight, compared with only approximately one fourth (26%) of medical followers.

20. See: R.A. Gordon, "A Sociocultural Interpretation of the Current Epidemic of Eating Disorders," in *The Eating Disorders: Medical and Psychological Basis of Diagnosis and Treatment*, ed. B.J. Binder, B.F. Chaitin, and R. S. Goldstein (New York: PMA Publishing, 1988), 151–164.

21. Mervat Nasser, *Culture and Weight Consciousness* (New York: Routledge, 1997), 13.

22. Kim Chernin, *The Hungry Self: Women, Eating, and Identity* (New York: HarperCollins, 1985), 186.

23. Nancy J. Kolodny, *The Beginner's Guide to Eating Disorders Recovery*, 33–34. (See n. 8)

24. J. Polivy and C.P. Herman, "Dieting and Binging: A Causal Analysis," *American Psychologist*, 40, no. 2 (1985). 193-201.

25. There is disagreement about the order of causality. It is difficult to ascertain whether depression leads to eating issues or problematic eating issues lead to depression. See: W.J. Swift, D. Andrews, and N.E. Barklage, "The Relation between Affective Disorder and Eating Disorders: A Review of the Literature," *American Journal of Psychiatry*, 143, no. 3 (1986): 290–299. Some researchers suggest that the onset of depression and eating issues in young women is a result poor body image. See: M. McCarthy, "The Thin Ideal, Depression, and Eating Disorders in Women," *Behavioral Research and Therapy*, 28, no. 3 (1990): 205–218. Also see the early work of J. Polivy & C.P. Herman, "Dieting and Binging: A Causal Analysis," *American Psychologist*, 40, no. 2 (1985): 193-201.

26. Levenkron notes the following additional personality traits associated with an eating disorder:

> failure to develop trusting dependence on a parent; turning inward toward self-reassurance when distressed; development of obsessive personality traits; development of perfectionism; problems with feelings of emptiness; lack of sense of developing identity (or a negative identity); a weak sense, if any, of their own femininity; remarkable ability in many cases to mask all of the above with charming, pleasing, outgoing behavior and success in school as well as social coping. (pp. 197–198)

Steven Levenkron, *Anatomy of Anorexia* (New York: W.W. Norton, 2001), 197–198.

27. D.M. Garner, M.S. Olmsted, and P.E. Garfinkel, "Does Anorexia Nervosa Occur on a Continuum? Subgroup of Weight-Preoccupied Women and their Relationship to Anorexia Nervosa," *International Journal of Eating Disorders*, 2, no. 4 (1983): 11–20; E.J. Button and A. Whitehouse, "Subclinical Anorexia Nervosa," *Psychological Medicine,* 11, no. 3 (1981): 509-516; Sharlene Hesse-Biber, "Report on a Panel Longitudinal Study of College Women's Eating Patterns and Eating Disorders: Noncontinuum versus Continuum Measures," *Health Care for Women International,* 13, no. 4 (1992): 375–391.

28. Marya Hornbacher, *Wasted* (New York: HarperCollins, 1998), 2.
29. WeightWatchers, "Online Achiever's Stories: Back to the Beach," WeightWatchersca. 2005, http://www.weightwatchers.ca/index.aspx. "Success Stories" Online Achiever Stories. "Didn't You Used to be Fat?"
30. Sharlene Hesse-Biber, "Report on a Panel Longitudinal Study. . . ." (See n. 27)
31. Kim Chernin, *The Hungry Self: Women, Eating, and Identity,* (New York: HarperCollins, 1985), 136 (See n. 22).
32. See: L.R. Furst and P.W. Graham (Eds.), *Disorderly Eaters: Texts in Self-Empowerment* (University Park: Pennsylvania State University Press, 1992). See also: Becky Thompson, "Food, Bodies, and Growing Up Female: Childhood Lessons about Culture, Race, and Class," in *Feminist Perspectives on Eating Disorders,* ed. P. Fallon, M. A. Katzman, and S.C. Wooley (New York: Guilford Press, 1994), 355–378. See also: M.L. Lawrence (Ed.), *Fed Up and Hungry: Women, Oppression and Food* (New York: Peter Bedrick Books, 1987).
33. Caroline Knapp, *Appetites: Why Women Want* (New York: Counterpoint, 2003), 9.
34. See: Kathleen M. Pike and Judith Rodin. "Mothers, Daughters, and Disordered Eating," *Journal of Abnormal Psychology,* 100, no. 2 (1991): 198–204; M. Strober and L.L. Humphrey, "Familial Contributions to the Etiology and Course of Anorexia Nervosa and Bulimia," *Journal of Consultative Psychology,* 55, no. 5 (1987): 654–659; M. Strober, C. Lampert, W. Morrell, J. Burroughs, and C. Jacobs, "A Controlled Family Study of Anorexia Nervosa: Evidence of Familial Aggregation and Lack of Shared Transmission with Affective Disorders," *International Journal of Eating Disorders* 9, no. 3 (1990): 239–253.
35. P.T. Keel, J. Harnden, J. Heatherton, and C. Hornig, "Mothers, Fathers, and Daughters: Dieting and Disordered Eating," *Eating Disorders,* 5, no. 3 (1997): 216–228; A. Moreno and M. H. Thelen, "Parental Factors Related to Bulimia Nervosa," *Addictive Behaviors,* 18, no. 6 (1993): 681–689.
36. L. J. Fabian and J. K. Thompson, "Body Image and Eating Disturbance in Young Females," *International Journal of Eating Disorders,* 8, no. 1 (1989): 63–74.
37. Margo Maine, *Father Hunger: Fathers, Daughters, and Food* (Carlsbad, CA: Gurze Books, 1991), 22.
38. Margo Maine writes, "Girls who enter puberty early may be a special risk to develop eating problems and body dissatisfaction. Early maturation is very disruptive to girls. They feel different from their peers and may worry whether they will be able to maintain friendships or if they will be ostracized for their unique bodies. These girls will be extremely self-conscious, fretting about how to cover up the signs of puberty—breasts and menstrual periods." See: Margo Maine, *Father Hunger: Fathers, Daughters, and Food,* 98. (See n. 37)
39. Caroline Knapp, *Appetites: Why Women Want,* 73. (See n. 33)
40. Caroline Knapp, *Appetites: Why Women Want,* 64. (See n. 33)
41. I. Attie and J. Brooks-Gunn, "Developmental Issues in the Study of Eating Problems and Disorders," in *The Etiology of Bulimia Nervosa: The Individual and Familial Context,* ed. J.H. Crowther, D.L. Tennenbaum, S.E. Hobfoll, and M.A. P. Stephens (London: Hemisphere Publishing, 1992), 43–45. See also: Suzanne Alexander, "Egged on by Moms, Many Teenagers Get Plastic Surgery," *Wall*

Street Journal, September 24, 1990, p. 1. For a good discussion of mother-daughter competition see especially: I. Attie and J. Brooks-Gunn, "Developmental Issues in the Study of Eating Problems and Disorders," 35–58 (see above); J. Rodin, R.H. Striegel-Moore, and L.R. Silberstein, "Vulnerability and Resilience in the Age of Eating Disorders," in *Risk and Protective Factors in the Development of Psychopathology*, ed. J. Rolf, A. Masten, D. Cicchetti, K.H. Nüchterlein, and S. Weintraub; (Cambridge, UK: Cambridge University Press, 1990), 366–390. One research study compared two sets of mothers: those whose daughters manifested high rates of eating disorders and those with low rates. Mothers whose daughters were in the high eating-disturbance group differed from mothers whose daughters were in the low eating-disordered group along the following factors. They had higher levels of unhappiness in their family lives, reported a more checkered eating-disordered career, were more concerned about their daughter's weight (wanting them to drop more weight), and felt that their daughters were less attractive compared to how their daughters rated their own attractiveness. Kathleen M. Pike and Judith Rodin, "Mothers, Daughters, and Disordered Eating," *Journal of Abnormal Psychology*, 100, no. 2 (1991): 198–204.

42. Susie Orbach, *Hunger Strike: Starving amidst Plenty* (New York: Other Press, 2001), 27, 61. In addition, Judi Hollis, Ph.D., writes:

> Mothers, daughters, and food—it's an obvious connection. Where else but in motherhood, childbirth, and eating are beings so closely bound, so merged? How do these beings separate into their own individual selves? What's fascinating is the questions we don't ask about the mother-daughter relationship. In essence, it's a relationship that's all about giving and getting nurturing. And this sets the stage for disordered eating. . . . Mothers have a powerful effect on their daughters' lives because girls watch their moms' every move. A mother's denied emotions are internalized by the daughter. No matter how much mothers try to cover up the pain, they still serve as models for womanhood, and their daughters have a keen and vigilant eye. Too often the mother-daughter wound is based on unconscious enmeshment, a blending of boundaries, a failure to see where you begin and your mother ends. This failure creates self-destructive behavior that is played out on the plate.

Judi Hollis, *Fat and Furious: Mothers and Daughters and Food Obsessions* (Lincoln, NE: Ballantine, 1994), xiv–xv.

43. A. Hall, "Family Structure of 50 Female Anorexia Nervosa Patients," *Australian and New Zealand Journal of Psychiatry*, 12, no. 4 (1978): 236–268.

44. Fay Murphy, Nicholas A. Troop, and Janet L. Treasure, "Differential Environmental Factors in Anorexia Nervosa: A Sibling Pair Study," *British Journal of Clinical Psychology*, 39, no. 2 (2000): 193–203.

45. Quotes excerpted from: Rachel Dobkin and Shana Sippy (Eds.), *Educating Ourselves: The College Women's Handbook* (New York: Workman Publishing, 1995), 278–284.

46. E.J. Button and A.Whitehouse, "A Subclinical Anorexia Nervosa," *Psychological Medicine*, 11, no. 3 (1981): 509–516; D.M. Garner and P.E. Garfinkel, "The Eating Attitudes Test: An Index of the Symptoms of Anorexia Nervosa," *Psychological Medicine*, 9, no. 2 (1979): 273–279; M. Tamburrino, K.N. Franco, G. A.A. Bernal, B. Carroll, and A.J. McSweeny, "Eating Attitudes in College Students," *Journal of the American Medical Women's Association*, 42, no. 2 (1987): 45–50; M.G. Thompson and D. Schwartz, "Life Adjustment of Women with Anorexia Nervosa and Anorexic-like Behavior," *International Journal of Eating Disorders*, 1, no. 2 (1982): 47–60.

47. J.J. Gray and K. Ford, "The Incidence of Bulimia in a College Sample," *International Journal of Eating Disorders*, 4, no. 2 (1985): 201–210; K.A. Halmi, J.R. Falk, and E. Schwartz, "Binge-eating and Vomiting: A Survey of a College Population," *Psychological Medicine*, 11, no. 4 (1981): 201–210; K.J. Hart and T.H Ollendick, "Prevalence of Bulimia in Working and University Women," *American Journal of Psychiatry*, 142, no. 7 (1985): 851–854; M.A. Katzman, S.A. Wolchik, and S.L. Braver, "The Prevalence of Frequent Binge Eating and Bulimia in a Nonclinical College Sample," *International Journal of Eating Disorders*, 3, no. 3 (1984): 53–62; R.L. Pyle, P.A. Halvorson, P.A. Neuman, and J.E. Mitchell, "The Increasing Prevalence of Bulimia in Freshman College Students," *International Journal of Eating Disorders*, 5, no. 4 (1986): 631–647; R.L. Pyle, J.E. Mitchell, E.D. Eckert, P.A. Halvorson, P.A.Neuman, and G.M. Goff, "The Incidence of Bulimia in Freshman College Students," *International Journal of Eating Disorders*, 2, no. 3 (1983): 343–348.

48. R.C. Hawkins and P.F. Clement, "Development and Construct Validation of a Self-Report Measure of Binge-eating Tendencies," *Addictive Behaviors*, 5, no. 3 (1980): 219–226; K.A. Halmi, J.R. Falk, and E. Schwartz, "Binge-Eating and Vomiting: A Survey of a College Population," *Psychological Medicine*, 11, no. 4 (1981): 697–706; P.A. Ondercin, "Compulsive Eating in College Women," *Journal of College Student Development*, 20, no. 2 (1979): 153–157; D. M. Zuckerman, A.C. Colby, N.C.Ware, and J.S. Lazerson, "The Prevalence of Bulimia among College Students," *American Journal of Public Health*, 76, no. 9 (1986): 1135–1137.

49. See: M. Boskind-Lodahl and W.C.White, Jr., "The Definition and Treatment of Bulimarexia in College Women," *Journal of the American College Health Association*, 27, no. 2 (1978): 84–86, 97. See also: Marlene Boskind-White and William C. White, Jr., *Bulimarexia: The Binge/Purge Cycle* (2nd ed.) (New York: W.W. Norton, 1987).

50. Steven Levenkron, *Anatomy of Anorexia* (New York: W.W. Norton, 2001), 99.

51. Mervat Nasser, *Culture and Weight Consciousness*, 7. (See n. 21)

52. R. Striegel-Moore, L. Silberstein, and J. Rodin, "Towards An Understanding of the Risk Factors for Bulimia," *American Psychologist*, 41, no. 3 (1986): 246–263; S. Squire, *The Slender Balance: Causes and Cures for Bulimia, Anorexia, and the Weight-Loss/Weight-Gain Seesaw* (New York: Putnam, 1983).

53. S.M. Dornbusch, J.M. Carlsmith, P.D. Duncan, R.T.Gross, J.A.Martin, P.L. Ritter, and B.Siegel-Gorelick, "Sexual Maturation, Social Class, and the Desire to Be

Thin among Adolescent Females," *Developmental and Behavioral Pediatrics*, 5, no. 6 (1984): 308–314; A. J. Stunkard, E.E. d'Aquili, S. Fox, and R.D.L. Filion, "Influence of Social Class on Obesity and Thinness in Children," *Journal of the American Medical Association*, 221, no. 6 (1972): 579–584.

54. See: R. Striegel-Moore, L. Silberstein, and J. Rodin, "Toward an Understanding of the Risk Factors for Bulimia," *American Psychologist*, 41, no. 3 (1986): 246–263.

55. C.S. Crandall, "Social Contagion of Binge Eating," *Journal of Personality and Social Psychology*, 55, no. 4 (1988): 588–598.

56. Nancy J. Kolodny, *The Beginner's Guide to Eating Disorders Recovery*, 81. (See n. 8)

57. C.S. Crandall, "Social Contagion of Binge Eating." (See n. 55)

58. J. Rodin, L. Silberstein, and R. Striegel-Moore, "Women and Weight: A Normative Discontent," in *Psychology and Gender: Nebraska Symposium on Motivation*, ed. T.B. Sonderegger (Lincoln: University of Nebraska Press, 1985), 267–307.

59. Dorothy C. Holland and Margaret A. Eisenhart, *Educated in Romance: Women, Achievement, and College Culture* (Chicago: University of Chicago Press, 1990), 201.

60. See: M.F. Hovell, C.R. Mewborn, Y. Randle, and J.S. Fowler Johnson, "Risk of Excess Weight Gain in University Women: A Three-Year Community Controlled Analysis," *Addictive Behaviors*, 10, no. 1 (1985): 15–28; R.H. Striegel-Moore, L.R. Silberstein, P. Frensch, and J. Rodin, "A Prospective Study of Disordered Eating among College Students," *International Journal of Eating Disorders*, 8, no. 5 (1989): 499–509.

61. S. Squire, *The Slender Balance*. (See n. 52).

62. There is debate about how much weight gain women experience, and some researchers note that for some it may be more of a myth of college life than a reality. See: C. N. Hodge, L.A. Jackson, and L. A. Sullivan, "The 'Freshman 15': Facts and Fantasies about Weight Gain in College Women," *Psychology of Women Quarterly*, 17, no. 1 (1993): 119–126.

63. M. Brouwers, "Depressive Thought Content among Female College Students with Bulimia," *Journal of Counseling and Development*, 66, no. 9 (1988): 425–428; P.R. Holleran, J. Pascale, and J. Fraley, "Personality Correlates of College-Age Bulimics," *Journal of Counseling and Development*, 66, no. 8 (1988): 378–381; L.P.F. McCanne, "Correlates of Bulimia in College Students: Anxiety, Assertiveness, and Locus of Control," *Journal of College Student Personnel*, 26, no. 4 (1985): 306–310; L.B. Mintz and N.E. Betz, "Prevalence and Correlates of Eating Disordered Behaviors among Undergraduate Women," *Journal of Counseling Psychology*, 35, no. 4 (1988): 463–471; M. Pertschuk, M . Collins, J. Kreisberg, and S.S. Fager, "Psychiatric Symptoms Associated with Eating Disorders in a College Population," *International Journal of Eating Disorders*, 5, no. 3 (1986): 563–568; J. Rodin, L. Silberstein, and R. Striegel-Moore, "Women and Weight: A Normative Discontent," in *Psychology and Gender: Nebraska Symposium on Motivation*, ed. T.B. Snoderegger (Lincoln: University of Nebraska Press, 1985), 267–307; S.A. Segal and C.B. Figley, "Bulimia: Estimate of

Incidence and Relationship to Shyness," *Journal of College Student Personnel*, 26, May (1985): 240–244; B. Silverstein and L. Perdue, "The Relationship between Role Concerns, Preferences for Slimness, and Symptoms of Eating Problems among College Women," *Sex Roles*, 18, no. 1-2 (1988): 101–106; R. Striegel-Moore, L. Silberstein, and J. Rodin, "Towards an Understanding of the Risk Factors for Bulimia," *American Psychologist*, 41, no. 3 (1986): 246–263.

64. Sharlene Hesse-Biber and M. Marino, "From High School to College: Changes in Women's Self-Concept and Its Relationship to Eating Problems," *Journal of Psychology*, 125, no. 2 (1991): 199–216.
65. Sharlene Hesse-Biber, "Report on a Panel Longitudinal Study. . . ." (See n. 27); Sharlene Hesse-Biber, M. Marino, and D. Watts-Roy, "A Longitudinal Study of Eating Disorders among College Women: Factors that Influence Recovery," *Gender and Society,* 13, no. 2 (1999): 385–408.
66. J. Freeman, "How to Discriminate against Women without Really Trying," in *Women: A Feminist Perspective*, ed. Jo Freeman (Palo Alto, CA: Mayfield, 1975).
67. J. Freeman, "How to Discriminate against Women without Really Trying," 216. (See n. 66)

Bibliography

"Alanis Morissette, In Her Own Words: How I Battled an Eating Disorder." *US Weekly.* July 4, 2005.

Alexander, S. "Egged on by Moms, Many Teen-agers Get Plastic Surgery." *Wall Street Journal*, September 24, 1990, p. 1.

Andersen, A.E. "Anorexia Nervosa and Bulimia in Adolescent Males." *Pediatric Annals,* 13, no. 12 (1984): 901–904, 907.

Anorexia Nervosa and Related Eating Disorders, Inc. *ANRED.* www.anred.com May 25, 2005.

Attie, I., & J. Brooks-Gunn. "Developmental Issues in the Study of Eating Problems and Disorders." In *The Etiology of Bulimia Nervosa: The Individual and Familial Context*, ed. J.H. Crowther, D.L. Tennenbaum, S.E. Hobfoll, & M.A.P. Stephens, pp. 43–45. London: Hemisphere Publishing, 1992.

Bemis, K.M. "Current Approaches to the Etiology and Treatment of Anorexia Nervosa." *Psychology Bulletin*, 85. no. 3 (1978): 593–617.

Boskind-Lodahl, M., & W.C.White, Jr. "The Definition and Treatment of Bulimarexia in College Women." *Journal of the American College Health Association*, 27, no. 2 1978: 84–86, 97.

Boskind-White, M., & W.C. White, Jr., *Bulimarexia: The Binge/Purge Cycle* (2nd ed.). New York: W.W. Norton, 1987.

Boston Women's Health Book Collective. *Our Bodies Ourselves.* New York: Simon & Schuster, 1998.

Bristow, J. "Kelly Holmes: No Prizes for Confessing." *Spiked Risk*, June 2, 2005. Accessed June 14, 2005, from www.spiked-online.com

Brody, S. *The Development of Anorexia Nervosa: The Hunger Artists.* Madison, CT: International Universities Press, 2002.

Brouwers, M. "Depressive Thought Content among Female College Students with Bulimia." *Journal of Counseling and Development*, 66, no. 9 (1988): 425–428.

Bruch, H. *Conversations with Anorexics: A Compassionate and Hopeful Journey through the Therapeutic Process*. Northvale, NJ: Basic Books, 1988.

Bruch, Hilde. *Eating Disorders: Obesity, Anorexia, and the Person Within*. Northvale, NJ: Basic Books, 1973.

Bruch, Hilde. *The Golden Cage: The Enigma of Anorexia Nervosa*. Cambridge, MA: Harvard University Press, 1978.

Button, E.J. & A. Whitehouse. "Subclinical Anorexia Nervosa." *Psychological Medicine*, 11, no. 3 (1981): 509–516.

Chernin, K. *The Hungry Self: Women, Eating, and Identity* New York: HarperCollins, 1985.

Crandall, C.S. "Social Contagion of Binge Eating." *Journal of Personality and Social Psychology*, 55, no. 4 (1988): 588–598.

Crisp, A.H. "Some Aspects of the Evolution Presentation and Follow-up of Anorexia Nervosa." *Proceedings of the Royal Society of Medicine*, 58, no. 10 (1965): 814–820.

Dobkin R. & S. Sippy (eds.). *Educating Ourselves: The College Women's Handbook*. New York: Workman Publishing, 1995.

Dornbusch, S.M., J.M. Carlsmith, P.D. Duncan, R.T. Gross, J.A. Martin, P.L. Ritter, & B. Siegel-Gorelick. "Sexual Maturation, Social Class, and the Desire to Be Thin among Adolescent Females." *Developmental and Behavioral Pediatrics*, 5 (1984): 308–314.

Dublin, A., & H. Warren. Keep Young and Beautiful. [Recorded by Annie Lenox]. On *Diva* [CD]. New York: RCA, 1992.

Fabian, L.J., & J.K. Thompson. "Body image and eating disturbance in young females." *International Journal of Eating Disorders*, 8, no. 1 (1989): 63–74.

Freeman, J. "How to Discriminate against Women without Really Trying." In *Women: A Feminist Perspective*, ed. Jo Freeman. Palo Alto, CA.: Mayfield, 1975: 194–208.

Furst, L.R., & P.W. Graham, (Eds.). *Disorderly Eaters: Texts in Self-Empowerment*. University Park, Pennsylvania State University Press, 1992.

Garner, D.M., & P.E. Garfinkel. "The Eating Attitudes Test. An Index of the Symptoms of Anorexia Nervosa." *Psychological Medicine*, 9, no. 2 (1979): 273–279.

Garner, D. & P. Garfinkel (Eds.). *The Handbook of Treatment for Eating Disorders*. New York. Guilford Press, 1997.

Garner, D.M., M.S. Olmsted, & P.E. Garfinkel. "Does Anorexia Nervosa Occur on a Continuum? Subgroup of Weight-Preoccupied Women and Their Relationship to Anorexia Nervosa." *International Journal of Eating Disorders*, 2, no. 4 (1983): 11–20.

Garner, D.M., Olmsted, M.S., Bohr, Y. & Garfinkel P.E. "The Eating Attitudes Test: Psychometric Features and Clinical Correlates." *Psychological Medicine,* 12, (1982): 871–878.

Gold, T. *Room to Grow: An Appetite for Life*. Beverly Hills, CA: New Millennium Press, 2003.

Gordon, R.A. "A Sociocultural Interpretation of the Current Epidemic of Eating Disorders." In *The Eating Disorders: Medical and Psychological Basis of*

Diagnosis and Treatment, ed. B.J. Binder, B.F. Chaitin, & R.S. Goldstein, p. 157–164. New York: PMA Publishing, 1988.

Gray, J.J., & K. Ford. "The Incidence of Bulimia in a College Sample." *International Journal of Eating Disorders*, 4, no. 2 (1985): 201–210.

Hall, A. "Family structure of 50 female anorexia nervosa patients." *Australian and New Zealand Journal of Psychiatry*, 12, no. 4 (1978): 236–268.

Halmi, K.A., J.R. Falk, & E. Schwartz. "Binge-Eating and Vomiting: A Survey of a College Population." *Psychological Medicine*, 11, no. 4 (1981): 697–706.

Hart K.J., & T.H Ollendick. "Prevalence of Bulimia in Working and University Women." *American Journal of Psychiatry*, 142, no. 7 (1985): 851–854.

Hawkins, R.C., & P.F. Clement. "Development and Construct Validation of a Self-Report Measure of Binge-eating Tendencies." *Addictive Behaviors*, 5, no. 3 (1980): 219–226.

Hesse-Biber, S. "Report on a Panel Longitudinal Study of College Women's Eating Patterns and Eating Disorders: Non-Continuum versus Continuum Measures." *Health Care for Women International*, 13, no. 4 (1992): 375–391.

Hesse-Biber, S., & M. Marino. "From High School to College: Changes in Women's Self-Concept and Its Relationship to Eating Problems." *Journal of Psychology*, 125, no. 2 (1991): 199–216.

Hesse-Biber, S., M. Marino, & D. Watts-Roy. "A Longitudinal Study of Eating Disorders among College Women: Factors That Influence Recovery." *Gender and Society*, 13, no. 2 (1999): 385–408.

Hodge, C.N., L.A. Jackson, & L.A. Sullivan. " The 'Freshman 15': Facts and Fantasies about Weight Gain in College Women." *Psychology of Women Quarterly*, 17, no. 1 (1993): 119–126.

Holland, Dorothy C., & M.A. Eisenhart. *Educated in Romance: Women, Achievement, and College Culture*. Chicago: University of Chicago Press, 1990.

Holleran, P.R., J. Pascale, & J. Fraley. "Personality Correlates of College Age Bulimics." *Journal of Counseling and Development*, 66 (1988): 378–381.

Hollis, J. *Fat and Furious: Mothers and Daughters and Food Obsessions*. New York Ballantine, 1994.

Hornbacher, M. *Wasted*. New York: HarperCollins, 1998.

Hovell, M.F., C.R. Mewborn, Y. Randle, & J.S. Fowler-Johnson. "Risk of Excess Weight Gain in University Women: A Three-year Community Controlled Analysis." *Addictive Behaviors*, 10, no. 1 (1985): 15–28.

Katzman, M.A., S.A. Wolchik, & S.L. Braver. "The Prevalence of Frequent Binge Eating and Bulimia in a Nonclinical College Sample." *International Journal of Eating Disorders*, 3, no. 3 (1984): 53–62.

Keel, P.T., J. Harnden, J. Heatherton, & C. Hornig. Mothers, fathers, and daughters: Dieting and disordered eating." *Eating Disorders*, 5, no. 3 (1997): 216–228.

Knapp, C. *Appetites: Why Women Want*. New York: Counterpoint, 2003.

Kolodny, N.J. *The Beginner's Guide to Eating Disorders Recovery* Carlsbad, CA: Gurze Books, 2004.

Lawrence, M.L. (Ed.). *Fed Up and Hungry: Women, Oppression and Food.* New York: Peter Bedrick Books, 1987.

Levenkron, S. *Anatomy of Anorexia.* New York: W.W. Norton, 2001.

Maine, M. *Father Hunger: Fathers, Daughters, and Food.* Carlsbad, CA: Gurze Books, 1991.

McCanne, L.P.F. "Correlates of Bulimia in College Students: Anxiety, Assertiveness, and Locus of Control." *Journal of College Student Personnel,* 26, no. 4 (1985): 306–310.

McCarthy, M. "The Thin Ideal, Depression, and Eating Disorders in Women." *Behavioral Research and Therapy,* 28, no. 3 (1990): 205–215.

Mintz, L.B., & N.E. Betz. "Prevalence and Correlates of Eating Disordered Behaviors among Undergraduate Women." *Journal of Counseling Psychology,* 35, no. 4 (1988): 463–471.

Moreno, A., & M.H. Thelen. "Parental Factors Related to Bulimia Nervosa." *Addictive Behaviors,* 18, no. 6 (1993): 681–689.

Morgan, H.G., & G.F.M. Russel, "Value of Family Background and Clinical Features as Predictors of Long-Term Outcome in Anorexia Nervosa: Four-Year Follow-up Study of 41 Patients." *Psychological Medicine,* 5, no. 4 (1975): 355–371.

Murphy, F., N.A. Troop, & J.L. Treasure. "Differential Environmental Factors in Anorexia Nervosa: A Sibling Pair Study." *British Journal of Clinical Psychology,* 39, pt. 2 (2000):193–203.

Nasser, M. *Culture and Weight Consciousness.* London: Routledge, 1997.

Ondercin, P.A. "Compulsive Eating in College Women." *Journal of College Student Personnel,* 20, no. 2 (1979):153–157.

Orbach, S. *Hunger Strike: Starving amidst Plenty.* New York: Other Press, 2001.

Pertschuk, M., M. Collins, J. Kreisberg, & S.S. Fager. "Psychiatric Symptoms Associated with Eating Disorders in a College Population." *International Journal of Eating Disorders,* 5 (1906): 563–568.

Pike, K.M., & J. Rodin. "Mothers, daughters, and disordered eating." *Journal of Abnormal Psychology,* 100 (1991): 198–204.

Polivy, J., & C.P. Herman. "Dieting and Binging: A Causal Analysis." *American Psychologist,* 40, no. 2, (1985): 193–201.

Pyle, R.I., P.A. Halvorson, P.A. Neuman, & J.E. Mitchell. "The Increasing Prevalence of Bulimia in Freshman College Students." *International Journal of Eating Disorders,* 5, no. 4 (1986): 631–647.

Pyle, R.L., J.E. Mitchell, E.D. Eckert, P.A. Halvorson, P.A. Neuman, & G.M. Goff. "The Incidence of Bulimia in Freshman College Students." *International Journal of Eating Disorders,* 2, no. 3 (1983): 343–348.

Robinson, T. & J.V. Ward. "A Belief in Self Far Greater than Anyone's Disbelief: Cultivating Resistance Among African American Female Adolescents." in C. Gilligan, A. Rogers, & D. Tolmam. (eds). Women, Girls, and Psychotherapy: Reframing Resistance. New York: Harrington Park Press, 1991.

Rodin, J., L. Silberstein, & R. Striegel-Moore. "Women and Weight: A Normative Discontent." In *Psychology and Gender: Nebraska Symposium on Motivation*, ed. B. Sonderegger, pp. 267–307. Lincoln: University of Nebraska Press, 1985.

Rodin, J., R.H. Striegel-Moore, & L.R. Silberstein. "Vulnerability and Resilience in the Age of Eating Disorders." In *Risk and Protective Factors in the Development of Psychopathology*, ed. J. Rolf, A. Masten, D. Cicchetti, K.H. Nüchterlain, & S. Weintraub. pp. 366–390. Cambridge, UK: Cambridge University Press, 1990.

Segal, S.A., & C.B. Figley. "Bulimia: Estimate of Increase and Relationship to Shyness." *Journal of College Student Personnel*, 26, May (1985): 240–244.

Sigler, J.-L., & S. Beck. *Wise Girl: What I've Learned about Life, Love, and Loss*. New York: Pocket Books, 2002.

Silverstein B., & L. Perdue. "The Relationship between Role Concerns, Preferences for Slimness, and Symptoms of Eating Problems among College Women." *Sex Roles*, 18, no. 1-2 (1988): 101–106.

Squire, S. *The Slender Balance: Causes and Cures for Bulimia, Anorexia, and the Weight-Loss/Weight-Gain Seesaw*. New York: Putnam, 1983.

Striegel-Moore, R.H., L.R. Silberstein, P. Frensch, & J. Rodin. "A Prospective Study of Disordered Eating among College Students," *International Journal of Eating Disorders*, 8, no. 5 (1989): 499–509.

Striegel-Moore, R., L. Silberstein, & J. Rodin. "Toward Understanding the Risk Factors for Bulimia." *American Psychologist*, 41 (1986): 246–263.

Strober, M., & L.L. Humphrey, "Familial Contributions to the Etiology and Course of Anorexia Nervosa and Bulimia." *Journal of Consultative Psychology*, 55, no. 5 (1987): 654–659.

Strober, M., C. Lampert, W. Morrell, J. Burroughs, & C. Jacobs, "A Controlled Family of Anorexia Nervosa: Evidence of Familial Aggregation and Lack of Shared Transmission with Affective Disorders." *International Journal of Eating Disorders*, 9, no. 3 (1990): 239–253.

Stunkard, A.J., E.E. d'Aquili, S. Fox, & R.D.L. Filion. "Influence of Social Class on Obesity and Thinness in Children." *Journal of the American Medical Association* 221, no. 6 (1972): 579–584.

Svec, C. "The Freshman 15, What to Do: Practical Tips for Preventing Weight Gain." *InteliHealth*. www.intelihealth.com (accessed June 10, 2005).

Swift, W.J., D. Andrews, & N.E. Barklage. "The Relation between Affective Disorder and Eating Disorders: A Review of the Literature." *American Journal of Psychiatry*, 143, no. 3 (1986): 290–299.

Tamburrino, M., K.N. Franco, G.A.A. Bernal, B. Carroll, & A.J. McSweeny. "Eating Attitudes in College Students." *Journal of the American Medical Women's Association*, 42, no. 2 (1987): 45–50.

Thompson, B. "Food, Bodies, and Growing Up Female: Childhood Lessons about Culture, Race, and Class." In *Feminist Perspectives on Eating Disorders,* ed. J. Horns & P. Johnson, p. 355–378. New York: Guilford Press, 1994.

Thompson M.G., & D. Schwartz. "Life Adjustment of Women with Anorexia Nervosa and Anorexic-like Behavior." *International Journal of Eating Disorders*, 1 (1982): 47–60.

Weight Watchers. "Online Achiever's Stories: Back to the Beach." Weight Watchers International, Inc. © 2005 WeightWatchers.com, Inc. http://www .weightwatchers.ca/success/art/index.aspx?sc=600&SuccessStoryID=3151

Zuckerman, D.M., A.C. Colby, N.C. Ware, & J.S. Lazerson. "The Prevalence of Bulimia among College Students." *American Journal of Public Health*, 76, no. 9 (1986): 1135–1137.

EIGHT

New Recruits for the Cult of Thinness: Preteen Girls, Adolescents, Straight Men, Gays, Lesbians, and Ethnic Women

Marketing the Cult to Preteen Girls

> When I see these twigs of people in the magazines and on TV, I say "I'm going to go on a diet." You almost want to get thin just so you can wear the right clothes. I watch my junior high friends—they look like something out of a magazine.
>
> —Darcey, age 12

Eating disorders are increasing in the United States. They are no longer confined to a particular class or ethnic group, and are affecting females at younger ages.[1]

The average fashion model is white, 5' 9" tall, and weighs 110 pounds[2]—approximately 32 pounds lighter and five inches taller than the average American woman.[3] Her good looks are relatively rare among the population, yet her image is so pervasive that it is difficult for girls to see themselves as anything but "wrong" in comparison. They are barraged with messages from beauty magazines and TV, and from classmates and parents and doctors, about the value of thinness and the liability of obesity. Many of them, by virtue of being female, white, and middle class, are already primed to join the Cult of Thinness. This population supplies new recruits, at ever-younger ages. Even preadolescents are joining the diet craze, and some are stunting their growth as a result.[4] In one national study, 45% of adolescent girls reported having been on a diet at some point, with 89% giving "to look better" as the reason for dieting.[5] Comparatively, only 20% of the boys indicated they had ever dieted, with 62% motivated by the desire to look better.[6] Why are they all so fearful of fat?

FIGURE 8.1 The Next Big Thing Collage, 2005.

As I have indicated, convincing certain vulnerable groups that they need to purchase goods and services to feel good about their bodies is very profitable. Advertising campaigns for fashion and beauty products are more frequently targeting children.[7] These industries are well aware of the purchasing power of preteens. One market researcher notes, "Today's parents spend more money on their children than any prior generation; children and adolescents have unprecedented amounts of money at their disposal, which they spend on fashion, beauty, and entertainment or leisure products; and children have gained increasing power in a wide range of purchasing decisions made by their parents."[8] Many of these products are directly aimed at promoting body insecurity. Am I fat? Does my hair lack body? Do I have blemishes? At a developmental point in their lives when they are highly sensitive to peer group pressure and media hype, kids seek out "how to" messages. As "guidelines about how to behave, young adolescents may be particularly susceptible to popular media stereotypes, especially those values and ideas presented by entertainment and fashion industries as vital elements of 'youth culture.'"[9] Teen magazines provide a seductive case for body obsession, defining what

FIGURE 8.2 "Get Noticed," "16 Dress Sizes 8 Hours of Surgery," "Get the Attention you Deserve." *(Nutrisystem, Discovery Health, Trimspa.)*

young girls are supposed to be doing with their lives—what is important and valued. The message is: You must be model beautiful, and attract a boyfriend, to be happy. These magazines exploit newfound interest in the opposite sex and youthful insecurities in order to market countless beauty and clothing trends.

One young woman I interviewed told me:

> Magazines were the big thing, especially in the teen years. There were always articles talking about how to become thinner and sexier and how to attract the opposite sex.

These media messages link thinness with love and happiness, often solely in terms of having the right body to attract the opposite sex. Diet and weight loss products fill the mail-order section of these magazines.

The slender ideal in magazines also shows up in educational materials. In a 1992 study of third-grade textbooks since l900, girls' body illustrations were progressively thinner in each decade. The study focused on depictions of the child's entire body, where gender could be clearly identified. Conversely, there was no significant trend for the images of boys' bodies.[10]

Fear of Fat

Some researchers suggest that young girls' problems with weight, body image, and eating are linked to puberty's onset, which brings a 20-30% increase in body fat.[11] Though it is critical to maturity and reproduction,[12] many young teenagers regard this normal increase with horror. My college interview subjects recalled this time in their lives with pain or embarrassment.

I was 12 when I started getting a chest. I hated it. My sisters weren't developing yet—even my older sister. I guess at first, I thought it was fat. I never wanted it.

The medical establishment may have helped trigger an excessive fear of childhood fat by casting doubt on the old image of a chubby, healthy baby.[13] With 65% of the U.S. population characterized as overweight,[14] adults' weight and dieting preoccupation is transferred to the younger generations. As Seid notes, fear of obesity has spawned a shelf of weight-loss books for younger children as well as kids' weight-loss camps.[15] The "fat camp" promotional literature shows how well they understand the social consequence of being fat—*the* primary issue for kids.

> Erica [15 years old], 215 pounds at 5 foot 4, has checked into Camp Camelot because she hated being fat. She hated being taunted, being called "fatso" and "lardo." She hated looking in the mirror, hated what she saw there so much that she would punch her pillowy face in a search for checkbones and scream at her self inside her head: "I HATE YOU! I HATE YOU! YOU ARE SO FAT!"

The 1995 comedy *Heavyweights*, set at a fat camp, earned box office bucks as adolescents paid to be reminded that fat is something to ridicule and get rid of. The reward of thinness is social acceptance, "a new image—a new you," and better feelings about one's "slimmer, trimmer self." But by binding self-esteem so closely to weight and physical appearance, this attitude may also set the stage for a psychologically damaging cycle of weight gain and self-hatred. The youngster who loses weight at summer camp and "improves her self-esteem" is in danger of feeling worthless if she regains some weight when she returns home.

Studies show how early the cultural mirror begins to distort girls' perceptions of their body size and weight: one study in 2000 found that 41% of girls ages 9-10 favored a slimmer body shape.[16] Another study asked girls and boys ages 5-11 to choose an "ideal" and an "aspired to" female and male body shape from a group of drawings.[17] Then they were asked to consider their own body shape and to associate different traits with different body shapes.[18] The results showed that "by the age of 5, girls already have a perception of the ideal female as being thin. By age 7 they recognize that this is the body shape they would like, as seen by their 'aspired to' choices. By the time the girls reach 9 years old, some have become aware of a mechanism for pursuing this aspiration and have begun dieting."[19] The study also concluded that "the children ascribed more feminine traits to the thinner female figure, whereas ascription of the masculine traits did not favor any one particular body type."[20]

While there have been some reported cases of preteen anorexia nervosa, eating disorders are not widespread in this younger population. Approximately 1% of adolescent females are anorectic.[21] Four percent of college women have bulimia.[22] Roughly 10% of all people with bulimia and anorexia are men.[23] Studies suggest that the majority of cases of anorexia begin between the ages of 15 and 19.[24] However, severe dieting practices are quite common among preteen girls.[25] In a study of almost 10,000 Connecticut students in their seventh, ninth, and eleventh years of school, 7.5% of the girls and 3.4% of the boys stated that they had made themselves vomit, or taken diet pills, laxatives, or diuretics in the previous week in order to control their weight.[26] Numerous research studies have documented fat fears among normal-size young girls.[27] This fear exists despite their knowledge of nutrition and their own "normal" body weight. More than 50% of the underweight adolescents in one study described themselves as extremely fearful of being fat, and said that they did not apply their basic nutritional awareness to their eating habits.[28] They have the fear without the behavior; this makes them a perfect target for marketing, because they are already susceptible at a young age, primed and ready to join the Cult. Another study found that at age 10, 19.6% of the young adolescent girls questioned indicated a fear of being overweight, and that that number increased to 58.8% by the age of 14.[29] There is also some evidence that young girls who practice extreme dieting risk "nutritional dwarfing"—short stature and delayed puberty.[30] Self-imposed malnutrition has become a health concern in clinical pediatric practice.[31]

Lauren, in one of my college interviews, recalled:

> I was big for my age and they called me Baby Huey, after the fat cartoon duck. That was always my impression of myself—a real clod. At 6 years old I can remember feeling big. It was horrible, because in ballet class I wanted to be like the other girls, petite and pretty. I look at those pictures now, and I looked fine. I was a beautiful little girl, but at the time I didn't feel that way.

While the mass media provides young children with images of the culturally desirable body, family members and peers also influence positive or negative self-image, as we saw in Chapter 6. The young women I interviewed often referred to criticism from friends, siblings, and parents, especially their mothers. In some cases it had a lasting effect on their self-esteem. One young woman, Sandra, reflected on her mother's critical attitude about her appearance when she was growing up and how this criticism still impacts her life.

> She was very critical. I was always the fat one and she was the thin one. She made sarcastic remarks like "you have the fattest thighs in the world." She was always saying "you better watch what you eat, you're going to get fat; you look chunky." This started when I was little. My mom said, "Thin down!" all my life. She's 5'1" and weighs about 100 pounds. She always fits into size 2 and size 4 clothes. And here I am and I can't fit size 2 on my elbow. I don't even eat dinner with them anymore.

A study of fourth and fifth graders and their parents [32] examines how parents' concerns about their own dieting and body dissatisfaction as well as their concerns about their child's weight and body image are important factors in determining their child's feelings about his or her body. Parents who commented on their child's weight negatively impacted how both daughters and sons felt about their bodies, especially their fear of becoming fat. While a father's attitude about his own weight issues is related to a daughter feeling too fat, it appears that the mother's influence is greater. Some research suggests that where the mother-daughter relationship lacks clear boundaries, and the mother is controlling her daughter's everyday routines, especially her food intake, the daughter may be at greater risk for developing eating issues.[33]

Eating disorders expert Michael Levine[34] stresses the importance of parental self-awareness. Parents should examine their own attitudes and stereotypes about weight and body image and whether they convey negativity about their child's body in what they say and do within the family. To what extent does a parent pressure a child to lose weight or to objectify his or her body? To what extent do parents discuss the unrealistic nature of body images in magazines and commercials, thereby teaching children media literacy skills?

Peers and Siblings

Another important influence on young girls' attitudes toward their weight and body image comes from their peer group. Peer group comparisons become especially important now, as bodies begin to change and develop. Many women I interviewed remarked that while they did not feel like "one of the boys" during this time, they certainly did not feel like one of the girls. They were simply girls who wanted to do boy things.

> When I was a kid I used to love hanging out with guys, much more than with the girls. I remember one day my mother came to school. I guess she got a call from a teacher. She yanked me off the slide, because I was playing with the guys. She told me never to play with them again. I asked her why, and she said, "Just because."

> She used to put me in dresses for parties, especially when it was my own party. I'd go back into my room, change into my favourite pants and by that time I knew that she couldn't do anything about it, because if she did it would make a scene.

Being a tomboy protects some young girls—it relieves them from being attentive to fashion and body image and from getting caught up in "boy appeal." For most of them it is a phase, a short delay before they succumb to being a "normal" female in this society.

Donna's young male peers sent her a powerful negative message about her body. She relates a specific trauma she experienced in seventh grade:

> I was going out with a guy who was very cute and I was feeling like the happiest person in the world. His friends started giving him a hard time because I was

fat and also the smartest girl in the school, and you don't go out with the fattest and smartest girl in the school. So he broke up with me—even though we had confessed love to each other. To this day, he was the only guy I ever felt that way for and he dumped me, totally unexpectedly. It was real hard because not only did he dump me but he convinced all his friends to give me a hard time, too, I guess so it didn't look like it was just him. So again, I was totally ostracized, this time for being smart and not just for being fat.

One 11-year-old told me "personality and body image" determines whether a guy will like you, and added that boys "don't like overweight people. They want pretty girls. When you're older they probably won't mind as much if you are a little overweight but right now they notice everything." This girl's perception of what males want seems to have been formed not just by magazines and television, but by her own experience.

There is also the pressure young girls feel from their older female peers, including older sisters. Amanda recalls her competitive feelings about her sister Gretchen.

I think my older sister influenced my attitudes about wanting to be thin. I always compared myself with her. She is now 5'5" but has a very small body frame. My mom is more like me, medium to large frame, well developed and well proportioned. And my father has a medium frame. I was always known as the little one. So I didn't have anything to worry about when I was very young. But then as I developed, I always had to watch my weight. I couldn't eat everything that I wanted; it would go to my stomach. I wanted to be like Gretchen, I always envied her. She had so many boyfriends. She could take on everything. In high school, she was a social butterfly, she had so many friends, yet Gretchen was the valedictorian; she could do it academically and socially. And I'm looking at her wishing I could do that. But . . . I never had the confidence in myself.

In comparison, Amanda felt she did not measure up. Some recent research suggests that young girls who are deeply involved in teen culture at a young age and are exposed to older girls in school or older sisters at home may be at greater risk for following the Cult of Thinness.[35] An older sister may adversely impact a younger sibling's attitude concerning weight and body image.

Although dieting and weight preoccupation are more common in young girls, many young boys are getting caught up as well. While females feel the pressure to be thin, young boys are increasingly urged to increase muscle size, shape, and tone.[36]

Adolescent Boys and Adult Males

Research on body image in adolescent boys reveals that at any one time, between 20% to 50% of boys want to lose weight, while 20% to slightly over

50% are trying to "bulk up."[37] Many spend time in body work because they link body image to success in their peer group relationships with both genders. One researcher notes: "It would appear that adolescent boys gain greater peer acceptance and popularity with both same-gender and other-gender peers by achieving a more muscular body that demonstrates physical strength and athletic success."[38] Young men often accomplish their desired body through excessive exercise.[39]

Men in general are less concerned with their appearance than women, and less convinced to alter their looks, but the number of men who are dissatisfied with their bodies is growing. In 1984 I interviewed two college-age men, Jim and Ken, and asked, "Do you think women are more weight-conscious than men?"

JIM: Women are more weight-conscious. Men have never had to worry—the only time I think men get really weight-conscious is when they're playing sports. When I swim, I have to be conscious of it, but otherwise I never think of my weight. When I'm not in swim season, I'll just grab a candy bar and not think about it I don't expect to marry because some woman thinks I look good. Hell, no.

KEN: Traditionally men are more active in athletics, so weight watching is not a problem. The media and models have placed a lot of pressure on women to be painfully thin, as opposed to the strong and muscular man.

Fifteen years later, their attitudes may not be shared by as many men. Today, the strong, muscular ideal has more guys packing the gyms, performing obsessive rituals of exercise, diet, and supplement use. Men have some rigorous standards when it comes to their bodies: rippled muscles from shoulders, arms, and chest, to six-pack, rock-hard abs, all the way to bulging thighs and calves. Toned, buff young men are used by the media to sell everything from paper towels to diet soda to luxury cars. Men struggling to express their masculinity are increasingly concerned about their body image.

The Rise of Male Consumers

As all Americans are becoming more consumer-oriented, "men as well as women will be evaluated increasingly in terms of how they measure up to media images of attractiveness rather than their achievement in work."[40] A 1994 study of men's magazine articles over a 12-year period notes "a statistical trend for an increase in weight-loss focus" and suggests that men are becoming more appearance conscious.[41]

FIGURE 8.3 How I Get My Body: A Focus on Abs. *(Ripped Fuel by Twinlab.)*

There is huge financial potential in promoting body obsession and anxiety in males, and it is no wonder that the market for men's body products has grown dramatically in recent years. The diet and cosmetics industries have developed marketing strategies that prey on men's weight and appearance insecurities. Certain diet soft drinks and weight-loss products are targeting the male market.[42] Women's cosmetics companies, like Estée Lauder, Inc., Elizabeth Arden, and others, have been offering men's skin care items for years.

Targeted media like *Men's Health* and *Men's Fitness* capitalize on the trend, urging men to "Build a Beach Ready Body: Sculpt Big Arms, Chisel a Muscle Chest, Carve Awesome Arms," and "Lose Your Gut for Good: 35 Fat-Burning Meals." Guys—you too can look like the hunky model on the cover.

Body Dissatisfaction

There is growing evidence that the market emphasis may be working, as body image surveys published every decade or so in *Psychology Today* attest. In 1972, 15% of the men surveyed were dissatisfied with their overall appearance.[43] In 1985 this number rose to 34%,[44] and in 1997 it reached 43%,[45] with 22% desiring weight gain.[46]

Men are spending hours in the gym lifting weights and trying to gain muscle and lose fat. I asked Tom, a trainer at a local gym, who these men compare themselves to, and he answered:

> Each other, I think. But no matter how much they look at others or themselves, in general, it's never good enough. They are never big enough; they are never "cut" enough, so they'll go to any extreme to get to their goals. Attraction is the main issue; sexual attraction to the opposite sex—or it's an ego thing . . . it's how you look at yourself compared to other people.

Interestingly, one study found that college males "believe females prefer larger male bodies than they actually do."[47] Similarly, the study also found that college women believed men preferred a much smaller female body than they in fact do.[48] So both college men and women are under the misconception that "model-skinny" and "bodybuilder-huge" are the looks that others find most appealing.[49] The changing nature of gender roles offers another reason for men's increasing attention to appearance. Traditionally, "the woman is supposed to be attracted to the man for his social achievements (wealth and power) and simply because he is a man, not because of any special effort on his part to make himself attractive to her."[50] Today, as women are gaining economic resources and positions of authority, they are starting to shift the balance of power within society. Noted psychologist and eating disorder specialist Judith Rodin writes:

> Men's appearance concerns also seem affected by shifting gender roles and expectations. Once a man could be assured of his masculinity by virtue of his occupation, his interests, or certain personality characteristics. According to historian Mark Gerzon in his book, *A Choice of Heroes: The Changing Faces of American Manhood*, there have been five traditional archetypes of masculinity throughout history: soldier, frontiersman, expert, breadwinner, and lord. Frontiersman and lord are no longer available roles for anyone, and expert and breadwinner are no longer exclusively male. Men may be grasping for the soldier archetype—the strong, muscle armored body—in an exaggerated, unconscious attempt to incorporate what possible options remain of the male images they have held since youth.[51]

Today women can be CEOs of top companies and high-ranking military officers, so men may feel that, more than ever, muscles define manhood.[52] This idea may be an important contributing factor to male eating disorders, muscle dysmorphia, supplement use, and male cosmetic surgery.

Dieting and Eating Disorders

Historically, Roberta Seid notes, "Men could not easily be sucked into dieting because of the persistent belief that a big, strong body was masculine and sexy. Even if it wasn't too strong, a big body gave the illusion of power and sexual vigor."[53] While most men who are dissatisfied with their weight deal with it through exercise,[54] there is evidence that others are taking to dieting.

Researchers in the early 1990s noted that "already diet soft drinks, light beers, and other diet products are being marketed by male movie stars and athletes. Men are finally getting hooked into feeling immoral if they eat the wrong foods." They suggested that if this trend continues, "the next ten years will see an explosion of weight problems in males."[55]

Indeed, the last 10 years has seen a pronounced jump in reported cases of male eating disorders. As the Cult continues to recruit new members and the gym culture expands, more cases can be predicted. Researchers Drewnowski and Yee found that 29% of men they studied had followed a reduced calorie diet during the previous month and that 66% of them reported more than 30 minutes of exercise per day.[56] This highlights a gender difference: Women tend to diet (64% had dieted in the previous month in the study just mentioned) more than men, while men tend to exercise more.[57] Thus, men who are dissatisfied with their abs (63% of men, according to a 1997 survey conducted by *Psychology Today*)[58] or their muscle tone (45% of men according to that same survey)[59] are sweating and pumping iron at the gym to achieve the ideal body, rather than watching food intake. The researchers agree. A 2001 study by Woodside and others found 2% of their male subjects had full or partial eating disorders, compared to 4.8% of their female subjects.[60] Braun et al. noted that males comprise about 5-10% of anorectics and 10-15 percent of bulimics.[61] Petrie notes that "approximately 10 percent of individuals with anorexia nervosa and bulimia nervosa and 25 percent of those with binge eating disorder are men."[62] This does not mean, however, that less prevalent male-eating disorders are less serious. Eating-disordered males live lives of secrecy and shame, like their female counterparts, but far fewer are receiving treatment due to the heightened stigma attached to a male eating disorder.

Woodside's study found the female to male ratio of patients with at least partial syndrome anorexia nervosa was 2.0:1, and the ratio for bulimia was 2.9:1.[63] Still, researchers are unsure if this number is completely accurate. Judith Rodin observes how men try to conceal their concern with physical appearance: "Perhaps they try to keep their body image concerns a secret. It's less socially acceptable for men to think and worry about their appearance than it is for women to do so. Men experience their body concerns as unmasculine, and therefore embarrassing and shameful."[64]

According to psychologist Harry Gwirtsman, "Bulimia may be more prevalent among males than we thought since it's an easy disease to hide and men are reluctant to come in for treatment."[65] In their study of males at the inpatient eating disorders unit at The New York Hospital, Cornell, Braun et al.

noted that although there was evidence of an increase in males with eating disorders, the percentage of males admitted into the unit increased from 1984 to 1997.[66] The researchers hypothesized this surge could be explained as "men are beginning to feel a greater degree of comfort in seeking treatment" and/or that "area professionals have become better able to detect eating disorders in males or are more readily referring them for treatment."[67]

When I asked Tom, the fitness trainer I interviewed, if he'd noticed eating disorders among men at his gym he said he felt eating disorders were mostly a female thing.

> I've seen bulimic behavior in one bodybuilder, in a competition. When he'd eat something right before he went on stage, I watched him throw it up . . . because they feel if they hold that water they are not going to be as "cut" on the stage; I've also seen wrestlers throw up to lose weight before going on the scale—I think that's a lot of pressure from the coach

Both examples Tom mentions come from sports with weight requirements and this suggests that men at the gym may be dealing with their body image insecurities more covertly. However, it would be erroneous to assume that such pressure does not also stem from the individuals themselves—who live in a culture where bigger is better (for men anyway). As a sports nutritionist, Nancy Clark notes:

> In our society, muscularity is commonly associated with masculinity. According to Olivardia, compared to ordinary men, muscular men tend to command more respect and are deemed more powerful, threatening and sexually virile. Muscular men perceive others as "backing off" and "taking them seriously." Not surprisingly, men's desire for muscles has manifested itself in a dramatic increase in muscle (and penile) implants.[68]

Some men experience a secret torment when they have an eating disorder. In their book, *The Adonis Complex*, psychiatrist Harrison Pope and his colleagues studied a variety of body image issues in men and boys, which they coin "The Adonis Complex." This term describes a number of body image distortions they find increasingly prevalent among boys and men. Adonis is a god depicted in Greek mythology as "half man and half god," who was idolized as the ideal masculine form. It was Adonis who gained the love of Aphrodite through his perfect physique. "The Adonis Complex" can present itself in several forms— as a preoccupation with fat that leads to the development of an eating disorder, as well as an obsession with muscle mass. Bill's situation, as recounted in *The Adonis Complex*, captures his lonely struggle with Binge Eating Disorder:

> On his way home from the gym, Bill will purchase two large Italian submarine sandwiches, two large bags of Doritos, two cans of onion dip, and a quart of

chocolate-chip cookie-dough ice cream. After shutting off the ringer on his phone, he'll begin to eat as fast as he can—sometimes even using both hands to feed himself, grabbing food with his left while eating with his right.[69]

Bill abuses food not to enlarge his physique, but rather to soothe psychological distress.

Muscle Dysmorphia

Some men with the Adonis Complex become fixated with muscle mass, obsessively bulking up, and being bigger than the next guy. This behavior is now a disorder classified as muscle dysmorphia, "in which individuals develop a pathological preoccupation with their muscularity."[70] In their book, *The Adonis Complex*, psychiatrist Harrison Pope and his colleagues also relate the story of Scott. Scott graduated from business school, but became a personal trainer because "it was the only job I could think of that gave me enough time to do my own training."[71] His body image, his exercise routine, and his diet consumed his life, "even on hot summer days, after getting a bad shot of myself in the mirror, I'll put on heavy sweatshirts to cover up my body because I think I don't look big enough."[72] He even lost his girlfriend: "I told her that when we first started living together: the gym comes first, my diet second, and she was third. I guess she couldn't take being in third place anymore."[73] But he thought she would probably leave him for a bigger guy anyway. He didn't see therapy as beneficial, "At first, it was a healthy thing, wanting to pursue a healthy lifestyle and be in shape. But now, it's gotten out of control. It's a trap. I can't get out of it."[74]

Tom, the certified trainer I interviewed, relates a similar story about himself:

> It's like I always had to be the best. So I would always train. Even in high school, I'd go to the gym in the morning, I'd go to school, I'd have practice, I'd go to the gym afterwards. I was probably one of the only kids that did that. . . . I was the only one that actually started to train directly off-season. I had coaches that would help me.

Men with muscle dysmorphia have a difficult life. They spend hours at the gym bulking up, but are so afraid that they are too small that they are embarrassed to even take off their shirts at the beach. They cling to their regime of weightlifting, much like an anorectic exercises extreme control over her food intake. To most onlookers, these bodybuilders appear leaner and much more muscular than the average man, yet they feel exactly the opposite. One study found that 71% of the bodybuilders they observed began their careers because they "felt too fat, too thin, and/or not sufficiently masculine."[75] Olivardia,

Pope, and Hudson found that 52% of the muscle dysmorphic bodybuilders they studied disagreed with the statement "I really like my body" and 46% of them stated that they were dissatisfied with their body proportion.[76]

Men with this disorder often, and quickly, turn to steroids or supplements to enhance and maintain their muscle. Tom, the trainer, revealed to me that he has used supplements.

I'm not going to say I've never taken ephedrine. I do now. I've taken it because I see the results. I'm not the type of person that says I need more, or more is better. I'll take the serving or half a serving; it speeds your metabolism up with just a little bit more energy, and makes you sweat a little bit more. So it's more of a charge, like having a coffee in the morning.

But Tom also knows the risks of using steroids to obtain more muscle.

A friend of my friend's just passed away at 23 years old. He gained 110 pounds of solid muscle in 1 year. That's almost impossible. He didn't understand that his heart is also a muscle that also built to a point where it just burst in his sleep.

Although steroids are illegal, they are attainable at the fringes of the gym scene. However, innumerable weight gain and protein products, diet pills, and supplements *are* legal, marketed, and sold to men yearning for the ideal muscular body. Some researchers note that "the muscular mesomorph is the ideal because it is intimately tied to cultural views of masculinity and the male sex role, which prescribes that men can be powerful, strong, efficacious—even domineering and destructive."[77]

What both these forms of the Adonis Complex—obsession with fat and fixation on muscle mass—share in common is the secrecy of these disorders. While more women have become open about their experiences with food and body image issues over the past several decades, few men are able to talk openly about their eating and body image problems because they perceive them to be "women's" concerns. As Harrison Pope, coauthor of *The Adonis Complex* notes, "Over the last 20 years, women with eating disorders have become more willing to disclose such problems, but men often remain too embarrassed to do so."[78]

Under the Knife

Body dissatisfaction has led some men to drastic measures. While women undergoing cosmetic surgery still outnumber men 7 to 1, men are beginning to take this route to good looks. According to the American Society for Aesthetic Plastic Surgery, men had almost 1.2 million cosmetic procedures in 2004, making up 8% of all procedures performed that year,[79] reflecting an 8%

increase from 2003.[80] The five most popular surgical procedures were lipo-suction, eyelid surgery, rhinoplasty, male breast reduction and hair transplan-tation.[81] As they age, men who were once secure about their bodies may fear the kind of devaluation aging women experience.

I asked a successful plastic surgeon why there has been an increase in the cosmetic surgery on men. He told me:

> The most common reason is economic. It's the male who is rising up the eco-nomic ladder and usually achieves his greatest success in his 50s and 60s. Now he needs a physical appearance that is consistent with his power and his place in society. He must stay physically trim, must not have loose skin, must not have anything that suggests infirmity. His looks maintain his power because we're all being judged by the vigor of our appearance. This is more true for men, because our society continues to economically reward them over women. Even though a 50-year-old woman entering my office might give the same reasons as a man—she wants to maintain a high position in her career and feels that without a youthful appearance, she would lose out—I think for most women it's an issue of self-esteem. With aging, they have diminished self-esteem and they want to regain something that they feel they've lost.

Male Subgroups

The greatest number of converts to the pursuit of muscular thinness occurs in particular subgroups. Men who are heavily involved in sports with required weight norms (e.g., wrestling, horse racing) may be more at risk for eating problems.[82] Some studies hint that gay males may be at even greater risk because of the importance of appearance (from body build to clothing) in their culture.[83] David Crawford, in his book *Easing the Ache: Gay Men Recovering from Compulsive Disorders*, highlights the importance of physical attractive-ness in gay society: "To some degree, we can identify with the image women have had thrust on them. Seeing ourselves in abject terms of physical attrac-tiveness, we—like many women—are extraordinarily self-conscious about our looks."[84] Some research also suggests there is greater body dissatisfaction among gay males. A research study comparing heterosexual and homosexual college men notes that "gay men expressed greater dissatisfaction with body build, waist, biceps, arms, and stomach than did heterosexual men. Homo-sexual men also indicated a greater discrepancy between their actual and ideal body shapes than did heterosexual men, and showed higher scores on mea-sures of eating regulation, and food and weight preoccupation."[85]

The impact of AIDS and its physical devastation may be changing gay emphasis on thin appearance. Some researchers suggest that instead, a more muscularly powerful body image may be emerging to "avoid the appearance of illness with AIDS. The illness has been described in slang usage as 'slims' in some countries."[86]

The Spread of the Cult of Thinness to Other Social Classes, Races, and Cultures

The Cult of Thinness occurs primarily in wealthy Western societies among white, upper-middle-class, educated females.[87] Their stories have comprised this book. The excessive pursuit of thinness has been rare among people of color in the United States (e.g., Blacks and Latinos)[88] and in non-Western developing societies such as in Asia, Africa, and South America.[89] In fact, traditionally these societies view obesity quite positively. As psychologist Esther Rothblum writes, "In developing countries, the major causes of death are malnutrition and infectious disease, and thinness is unlikely to be viewed with envy, rather, increased body weight is associated with health and wealth."[90] Furnham and Baguma also note: ". . . to a person living in a poor country an obese body may be considered a healthy body for two reasons: first, fat deposits laid down mean that people may survive 'lean' periods more effectively; second, because one has to be fairly wealthy to afford food and could equally use this wealth to acquire medical treatment."[91]

Emily Bradley Massara's 1989 study, *¡Que Gordita!*, looks at the role of obesity in the day-to-day lives of ethnic women.[92] She wanted to know the cultural causes of weight gain among a small sample of Puerto Ricans living in one Philadelphia neighborhood. Massara investigated the life histories of several first-generation women who "have a distinct sense of social identity as Puerto Ricans"[93] and who were defined as "medically obese." All were married and had children. She found that certain cultural definitions of overweight were important factors. Within this community, fat was not considered a sign of illness, but indicated "tranquility, good appetite and health."[94] Conversely, to be thin meant to be malnourished and diseased —an undesired condition. In fact, when given a series of photos of body types (thin to obese) to rank in terms of attractiveness, the women in her sample gave a narrower range of acceptable thin weights, but a wider range of acceptable heavier weights. As Massara notes, "one of the ways in which the 'good wife' and mother expresses her love for her husband and children is by presenting family members with large helpings of food and manifesting concern over amounts of food eaten."[95]

Women were expected to gain weight, especially upon marriage. It was a "sign, particularly to her family, that she was adequately provided for."[96] Women who lost weight got negative reactions. One woman whose weight declined from 170 to 140 pounds when she divorced her husband reported: "When I lost weight, people said: 'You're so skinny! What happened to you?' So many people told me fat didn't look bad and I looked better that way because I had a shape."[97]

Massara notes that:

> Linguistic terms, such as "pretty little plump one" (*gordita buena*), reinforce the notion that a certain degree of heaviness in women is positively valued. The plump (*gordita*) woman may also be referred to as a "total woman" (*mujer entera*) because she is considered to have a "beautiful body [shape]" and good health. . . . "How plump!" (*!Que gordita!*) is one expression which suggests shapeliness and health and is used in a highly complimentary manner.[98]

In Massara's sample, the men appeared more sensitive to their weight than the women, in part from the expectations of the provider role: "Both men and women expressed a belief that men should, as one informant explained, 'be in shape for the work they do,' or, 'they shouldn't let themselves go.'[99]

Massara found that the men were more likely to diet and were more concerned about their appearance. One man in her sample lamented, "Already I'm 'over the hill!' The girls like someone who is nice and slim."[100]

Massara also observed that American values of female thinness were beginning to appear within this group of first-generation women, as the process of acculturation spread to their children.[101] "For instance, many mothers showed an awareness of Western medical concepts about the dangers of heaviness in children. With regard to adult weight, some children encourage their mothers to reduce so that they will look more attractive. By the same token, some of the more acculturated women actively practiced eating restraint."[102]

What is happening in one Puerto Rican neighborhood is a microcosm of what is happening throughout nonaffluent classes and racial groups in American society, as well as in non-Western societies as a whole.[103]

Thinness and Black Culture

Some research findings suggest that "cultural loyalty and strong ethnic identity protects black women from the thin ideal standards of American culture."[104] Black women are likely to report feeling underweight, while white women are likely to report feeling overweight.[105] Although black women's ideal body image is larger than the ideal body image for white women, "one might expect that black women who are significantly overweight from their ideal body image might display similar dieting, bingeing, and purging symptoms as white women."[106] As one recent study suggests, "some black women are not buffered against eating disorders as suggested in previous research."[107]

The Cult of Thinness has a different context for a woman of color, whose hair texture, skin tone, and build do not conform to Anglo-Saxon standards. One black sociologist writes: "White feminists who write about body image, such as Naomi Wolf, often fail to acknowledge the particular concerns that black women face because of the combination of racism and the beauty myth."[108] She lists the important appearance issues that came up in discussions with other black women:

> African women are subject to the same pressures to attain an ideal of beauty as are white women in North American society, but efforts to approach the blonde, thin, young ideal are made at an even greater cost for black women. Weight pre-occupation is not a central concern for many black women,[109] but weight is one among many factors that preclude black women from attaining "beauty" according to the cultural archetype. Three issues came up again and again when I talked with other black women: skin color, hair texture, and body size.[110]

As one black researcher says, the defining of white beauty depends on the denigrating of what is not white: "Blue-eyed, blond, thin white women could not be considered beautiful without the Other—Black women with classical African features of dark skin, broad noses, full lips and kinky hair."[111]

Gladys Jennings, Associate Professor of Food Science and Human Nutrition at Washington State University, comments, "There's a cultural standard from our African heritage that allows for more voluptuousness and padding on black women."[112]

Traditionally, the African American community's ideal has been more realistic and sensual: "Women's bodies were substantial. They had breasts and hips and curves and softness."[113] Black psychologist Marva Styles notes that many black women have maintained strong bonds with their cultural roots through soul food: "The essence of Black culture has been handed down through oral history, generation after generation in the African tradition, through the selection and preparation of soul food. The determination to hold on to native foods by bringing seeds into this country may be symbolic of the ever-present determination to preserve the African culture through food."[114]

That preparation becomes a primary definer of a black woman's sense of herself: "The Black woman gains a sense of pride as she watches her extended family—her man, her children, and maybe her grandparents, sisters, nieces and friends—enjoy the soulful tastes and textures prepared by her skillful hands."[115]

As in the Puerto Rican community, plumpness is a sign of health and prosperity—telling the black woman she is doing a good job. Styles remarks on the generational differences in her attitude toward food compared with her mother's.

> Slimness, however, is not valued by middle aged and older black women. My mom worries about my slimness because at 5'4", I barely weigh 120, and I am a middle-aged woman. She asks me often, "Are you eating properly these days?" Maintaining my weight at 120 pounds is hard for me, because I was taught to enjoy eating and preparing food. If I ate the kind of food my mom prepares consistently, I would probably weigh 150 by now. . . . Staying slim is difficult in a culture that values cooking and eating.[116]

Yet there is reason to believe from current research studies that the Cult of Thinness is spreading beyond the white middle class.[117] Eating disorders are reportedly growing among the black American population.[118] One researcher speculated that "increasing affluence among some blacks, and thus their access to traditional white middle class values, and the homogenization of life style and priorities, perhaps as a result of the increasing influence of the media, have finally penetrated the black culture: the young black female (and perhaps the male) is getting fatter and is becoming more concerned about her fatness."[119] The problem appears particularly acute among persons of color who are upwardly mobile.[120] A case study of anorexia nervosa in seven middle-class black and Hispanic adolescent women elaborated:

> They encountered early our [white] society's conviction that thinness and trimness are the essential ingredients that lead to success. Thus, these girls, who were already feeling different and suffering from a low self-esteem and a powerful need to be accepted, sought integration with society through rigid dieting and an extremist adoption of the current societal standard of slimness.[121]

In general, the rate of obesity among black women is greater than among white women. Research indicates that black women are less concerned with being thin [122] and that eating disorders are less common in black women than in white women.[123] However, one recent study, which compared eating disorder symptoms in a group of black and white girls, found that "black girls had significantly higher bulimia scores than white girls." [124]

Women of color face double jeopardy—they are subject to racial as well as sexual discrimination. If we include discrimination based on social class, they suffer from "triple jeopardy."[125] In my interviews with women of color, I found they used food as a nurturing mechanism to cope with oppressive social and economic conditions. Bingeing can be a "cheap" way to find temporary relief from sexual abuse, poverty, racism, and sexism. Eating large quantities of food in a short time can serve to numb, soothe, and literally "shield" (with fat) some women from physical and emotional trauma.[126]

Compulsive eating was also a coping mechanism for white women in my sample who had experienced sexual abuse—their drive for thinness was secondary. This form of bingeing is an eating disorder, but also a perfectly rational means of dealing with the pain blacks and others also experience living in our society.

Lesbians

Some research suggests that gay men and straight women are the most likely groups to engage in eating-disordered behaviors.[127] Even though lesbians are often portrayed as uninterested in their physical appearance, a 1992 study that compares lesbians, heterosexual women, gay men, and heterosexual men notes that lesbians and heterosexual women were most discontented with their body image.[128] Lesbians dieted significantly more than gay or heterosexual males.[129] Although heterosexual women and gay men were found to be more preoccupied with weight than lesbians and heterosexual men, "gender was a more salient factor than sexual orientation on most variables."[130]

But other research suggests that while lesbians (compared to heterosexual females) are aware of the cultural pressures on women in heterosexual society to look thin, they do not appear to internalize this norm to the same degree.[131] As one lesbian in her early 20s told me,

> In straight communities, if a girl says "I'm too fat, I'm going to diet," there is support for that. In the queer community, there wouldn't be support. People would challenge it and confront it. I've never met a lesbian on a diet.

I conducted focus group interviews and intensive interviews with white middle-class college-age and postcollege lesbians about body image, weight concerns, eating issues, and general appearance and identity—all in the context of their lesbian lifestyle. They first discussed what it meant be a lesbian in today's society and that their body image seems to be central to their perception of themselves in relation to both the lesbian and heterosexual communities. Just as homosexual males, raised in a heterosexual world, get the clear message that the "real" men are macho and have big muscles, lesbian women are told that "real" women are slim and, in a male-driven world, submissive.

Martha, a white, lesbian, middle-class college student told me:

> I grew up listening to my mother and sister always being on diets. In the straight world, I am not like what every girl is supposed to want to look like. I don't want to say I'm not feminine but I'm not fitting into the mold. . . . I had the longest hair, but then two summers ago I chopped it off. A friend of my mother's commented that my hair was "just a bit too short."

Those lesbian women I interviewed who were now in the job market spoke about how they had to negotiate their appearance in their workplace. They were keenly aware of how the straight world would stereotype them if they did not conform to the dominant ideals of beauty. Natasha noted:

> People get jobs because of how they look . . . people identify you as pretty, "let's hire her because she'll sell things." . . . I mean, if you want income from the straight world, there's a certain price you pay for not conforming.

Although lesbians are not trying to attract men with their bodies or style of dress, they still may be Cult of Thinness practitioners in order to attract other women. Some of those I interviewed used their bodies as symbols of their rejection of the patriarchal society—refusing to shave their armpits or legs, wear high heels, or apply makeup. Some identify politically with feminists or take on a "butch" role, actively combating the oppressive thinking that torments women into believing they must be thin to be valued. Jennie, a white middle-class professional woman in her late 20s said, "I feel like being skinny has really been a struggle for me because it's hard to be a powerful woman."

The opposite stereotype is the "lipstick femme" lesbian, who follows the more traditional image of a thin heterosexual woman. Mary, a lesbian I interviewed, talked about lesbians who identify themselves along the butch-femme continuum. She pointed out that these categories are not mutually exclusive and are often imposed by straight culture:

> It depends on how you self-identify. There's an eroticism to a big, fat, butch/dike. . . . Or if you're femme, being big breasted and having voluptuousness can be like a way to be more feminine. I think there is a whole other side of the spectrum for those who don't identify in categories. While most lesbians self-identify as queer, that's probably the only commonality we have. In my opinion, queer doesn't necessarily mean I'm a lesbian, I'm a dike, I'm a butch and a this or that—it's all of those things.

Caroline noted that she does not want her own lesbian identity to be compartmentalized, but she also feels pressure to live up to her butch appearance when she is out with her lesbian friends:

> When I am out with my gay friends I still don't fit the lesbian mold because I . . . look like this. There is always going to be something, like my hair is not looking perfect, I don't match. I have this look, but I really am not the perceived as "butch," since I really don't have that kind of personality.

Dress and public behavior are self-expressions associated with gender. Whereas homosexual males may be judged as "twinks" because they are "flamey" or effeminate, in the lesbian community women feel safe to challenge or play with traditional gender roles. Some lesbians "pass" for men and enjoy the strength that image gives them. Weight-related issues may be a concern for some lesbians, but not for others, taking a back seat to these gender-role issues. Their different attitudes about weight-related issues in fact may reflect which role a lesbian primarily identifies with. Some research suggests lesbians who are on the "lipstick femme" end of lesbianism may experience lower body satisfaction than those who identify with the more masculine "butch" role.[132] These differences within lesbian culture help our understanding of the impact of the Cult of Thinness on the lesbian community. In addition, lesbian women who are dissatisfied with their bodies, but who are acutely aware that this dissatisfaction is culturally based, may deal with it in a healthier way than heterosexual women.

Globalization of Eating Issues

It appears that eating disorder rates are increasing in other Western and non-Western societies. According to a recent *Christian Science Monitor* article, anorexia rates in Argentina surpass those in the United States.

> In this beauty-conscious nation, which has the world's second-highest rate of anorexia (after Japan), many are partially blaming the country's clothing industry for offering only tiny sizes of the latest fashions. The result, say many health experts, is a dangerous paradox of girls and women adapting to the clothes rather than clothes adapting to them. Prompted by anecdotal evidence and expert testimony, the Argentine legislature is considering whether to force clothing manufacturers to cover "all the anthropometric measurements of the Argentine woman" up to size 54 (the equivalent of extra large in the United States).[133]

As globalization spreads Western values to other nations, American society's "Cult of Thinness" message promises to envelope these nations' young women in a complex web of eating disorders and eating problems.[134] Satellite television transmits these values across all cultures, regardless of race, class, and level of industrial advancement. Developing societies import Caucasian beauty ideals with every purchase of Western media, clothing styles, and beauty products. As non-Western women attempt to meet the ideal, they may deny the very features that give them their racial and ethnic identities—and their unique beauty.

Susie Orbach, author of *Fat Is a Feminist Issue*,[135] notes that

> if you want to measure a culture's engagement with globalism, go look at the level of eating problems. It's probably a better indicator than economic ones. In cultures in which a small group of people are allowed to be Westernised the immediate thing is that they try to create a Western body.[136]

A recent study analyzed Western culture's impact on the relatively isolated island of Fiji. Traditionally, Fijians view weight loss as a sign of illness and deteriorating health. When American television programming was introduced to the island in 1995, none of the girls surveyed reported that they practiced self-induced vomiting to lose weight.[137] After 3 years of American TV exposure, that number had jumped to 11.3%.[138] That same year, 1998, 74% of girls reported feeling "'too big or fat' at least some of the time" and 62% stated that they had dieted in the last month.[139] The island's cultural understanding of beauty is drastically changing. What has happened in Fiji may serve as a warning to other global economies that have embraced Western culture.[140]

Unless cultural globalization takes a different turn, rejecting the idealized Western body, the ultra-thin ideal and its effects on young women are likely to spread dangerously throughout the world.

Notes

1. See: Madeline Altabe, "Ethnicity and Body Image: Quantitative and Qualitative Analysis," *International Journal of Eating Disorders*, 23, no. 2 (1998): 153–159; Declan T. Barry, Carlos M. Grilo, and Robin Masheb, "Gender Differences in Patients with Binge Eating Disorder," *International Journal of Eating Disorders*, 31, no. 1 (2002): 63–70; Renee A. Botta, "The Mirror of Television: A Comparison of Black and White Adolescents' Body Image," *Journal of Communication*, 50, no. 3 (2000): 144–159; Jack Demarest and Rita Allen, "Body Image: Gender, Ethnic, and Age Differences," *Journal of Social Psychology*, 140, no. 4 (2000): 465–472.

2. Karen Schneider, "Mission Impossible," *People Weekly*, June 1996, p. 71.

3. Ibid.

4. L.M. Mellin, S. Scully, and C.E. Irwin, *Disordered Eating Characteristics in Preadolescent Girls*, Paper presented at American Dietetic Association Annual Meeting, Las Vegas, NV, October 28, 1986; David M. Stein and Paula Reichert, "Extreme Dieting Behaviors in Early Adolescence," *Journal of Early Adolescence*, l0, no. 2 (1990): 108–121.

5. Dianne Neumark-Sztainer and Peter J. Hannan, "Weight-Related Behaviors among Adolescent Girls and Boys," *Archives of Pediatrics and Adolescent Medicine*, 154, no. 6 (2000): 570–571.

6. Ibid.

7. R.H. Striegel-Moore, "Prevention of Bulimia Nervosa: Questions and Challenges," in *The Etiology of Bulimia Nervosa: The Individual and Familial Context*, ed. Janis H. Crowther, Daniel L. Tennenbaum, Stevan E. Hobfoll, and Mary Ann Parris Stephens (Washington, D.C.: Hemisphere Publishing, 1992), 203–223.

8. Ibid., 212.

9. I. Attie and J. Brooks-Gunn, "Weight Concerns as Chronic Stressors in Women," in *Gender and Stress*, ed. R.C. Barnett, L. Biener, and G.K. Baruch (New York: Free Press, 1987), 233. See Also: R.H. Striegel-Moore, "Prevention of Bulimia Nervosa: Questions and Challenges," 213. (See n. 7)

10. Jenifer Davis and Robert Oswalt, "Societal Influences on a Thinner Body Size in Children," *Perceptual and Motor Skills*, 74, no. 3 (1992): 697–698.
11. I. Attie and J. Brooks-Gunn, "Weight Concerns as Chronic Stressors In Women," 218–254 (see n. 9); See especially: M.P. Levine and L. Smolak, "Toward a Model of the Developmental Psychopathology of Eating Disorders: The Example of Early Adolescence," in *The Etiology of Bulimia Nervosa: The Individual and Familial Context*, eds. J.H. Crowther, D.L. Tennenbaum, S.E. Hobfoll and M.A.P. Stephens (London: Hemisphere Publishing, 1992), 69–70.
12. See: Deborah Dunlap Marino and Janet C. King, "Nutritional Concerns during Adolescence," *Pediatric Clinics of North America*, 27, no. 1 (1980): 125-139; M.P. Warren, "Physical and Biological Aspects of Puberty," in *Girls at Puberty: Biological and Psychosocial Perspectives*, ed. J. Brooks-Gunn and A.C. Petersen (New York: Plenum, 1983). A certain amount of fat on the body is required for reproduction. Adolescent girls undergo an increase in fat around puberty.
13. S. Shapiro, M. Newcomb, and T.B. Loeb. "Fear of Fat, Disregulated-Restrained Eating, and Body-esteem: Prevalence and Gender Differences among Eight- and Ten-Year-Old Children," *Journal of Clinical Child Psychology*, 26, no. 4 (1997): 358-365.
14. U.S. Department of Health and Human Services, "Prevalence of Overweight and Obesity among Adults: United States, 1999-2002," http://www.cdc.gov/nchs/products/pubs/pubd/hestats/obese/obse99.htm
15. Roberta Pollack Seid, *Never Too Thin: Why Women Are at War with Their Bodies* (New York: Prentice-Hall Press, 1989), 173.
16. Ellen A. Schur, Mary Sanders, and Hans Steiner, "Body Dissatisfaction and Dieting in Young Children," *International Journal of Eating Disorders*, 27, no. 1 (2000): 74.
17. Karen J. Pine, "Children's Perceptions of Body Shape: A Thinness Bias in Pre-Adolescent Girls and Associations with Femininity," *Clinical Child Psychology and Psychiatry*, 6, no. 4 (2001): 527,
18. Ibid., 528
19. Ibid., 534.
20. Ibid., 533.
21. Anorexia Nervosa and Related Eating Disorders, Inc. (ANRED), http://www.anred.com.
22. Ibid.
23. Ibid,
24. Cynthia M. Bulik, Lauren Reba, Anna-Marie Siega-Riz, and Ted Reichborn-Kjennerud, "Anorexia Nervosa: Definition, Epidemiology, and Cycle of Risk," *International Journal of Eating Disorders*, 37, no. S1 (2005): S2–S9.
25. L.M. Mellin et al., "Disordered Eating Characteristics in Preadolescent Girls." (See n. 4)
26. Dianne Neumark-Sztainer and others, "Disordered Eating among Adolescents: Associations with Sexual/Physical Abuse and Other Familial/Psychosocial Factors," *International Journal of Eating Disorders*, 28, no. 3 (2000): 252.

27. For a discussion of the research literature on "fear of fat" in young children, see: M.H. Thelen, C.M. Lawrence, and A.L. Powell, "Body Image, Weight Control and Eating Disorders among Children," in *The Etiology of Bulimia Nervosa: The Individual and Familial Context*, ed. J.H. Crowther, D.L. Tennenbaum, S.E. Hobfoll, and M.A.P. Stephens (London: Hemisphere Publishing, 1992.), 81–101. A note of caution must be voiced here. Some researchers note that while teenage girls may talk about fear of fat and dieting, these attitudes may not translate into severe dieting behaviors, as some research on adolescents suggests. A recent study by Mark Nichter and Mimi Nichter questioned adolescents about their dieting behavior by asking "What does being on a diet mean?" They noted that, for teens, being on a diet "often constitutes a ritual activity wherein the consumption of token foods is suspended." See: Mark Nichter and Mimi Nichter, "Hype and Weight," *Medical Anthropology*, 13, no. 3 (1991): 264. "Fat talk" among adolescents has important consequences even if these attitudes do not readily translate into severe dieting. Researchers Mimi Nichter and Nancy Vuckovic's longitudinal study of adolescent teens' "fat talk" suggests that "by engaging in fat talk, females present themselves to others as responsible beings concerned about their appearance. . . . Irrespective of what actions girls are taking to achieve their body goals, they are attempting to reproduce the cultural ideal through their discourse." See: Mimi Nichter and Nancy Vuckovic, "Fat Talk: Body Image among Adolescent Girls," in *Many Mirrors: Body Image and Social Relations*, ed. Nicole Sault (New Brunswick, NJ: Rutgers University Press, 1994), 127.

28. N. Moses, M. Banilivy, and F. Lifshitz, "Fear of Obesity among Adolescent Girls," *Pediatrics*, 83, no. 3 (1989): 393–398. Other research studies reveal similar results. For an excellent review of the literature on eating disorders among children see: M.H. Thelen, C.M. Lawrence, and A.L. Powell, "Body Image, Weight Control and Eating Disorders among Children," in *The Etiology of Bulimia Nervosa: The Individual and Familial Context*, ed. J. H. Crowther, D.L. Tennenbaum, S.E. Hobfoll, and M.A.P. Stephens (London: Hemisphere Publishing, 1992.), 81–101.

29. Gail McVey, Stacey Tweed, and Elizabeth Blackmore, "Dieting among Preadolescent and Young Adolescent Females," *Canadian Medical Association Journal*, 170, no. 10 (2004): 1560.

30. See: F. Lifshitz, N. Moses, C. Cervantes, and L. Ginsberg, "Nutritional Dwarfing in Adolescents," *Seminars in Adolescent Medicine*, 3 no. 4 (1987): 255–266; F. Lifshitz, N. Moses, "Nutritional Dwarfing: Growth, Dieting, and Fear of Obesity," *Journal of the American College of Nutrition*, 7, no. 5 (1988): 367–376.

31. See: F. Lifshitz et al., "Nutritional Dwarfing in Adolescents," 255. (See n. 30)

32. L. Smolak, M.P. Levine, and R. Schermer, "Parental Input and Weight Concerns among Elementary School Children," *International Journal of Eating Disorders*, 25, no. 3 (1999): 263–271.

33. J. Ogden and J. Steward, "The Role of the Mother-Daughter Relationship in Explaining Weight Concern," *International Journal of Eating Disorders*, 28, no. 1 (2000): 78–83.

34. Levine, Michael. "10 Things Parents Can Do to Help Prevent Eating Disorders," http://www.nationaleatingdisorders.org

35. See: Jane Wardle and Rachel Watters, "Sociocultural Influences on Attitudes to Weight and Eating: Results of a Natural Experiment," *International Journal of Eating Disorders,* 35, no. 4 (2004): 589–596.
36. See: Lina A. Ricciardelli, Marita P. McCabe, and Jennifer Finemore, "The Role of Puberty, Media and Popularity with Peers on Strategies to Increase Weight, Decrease Weight and Increase Muscle Tone among Adolescent Boys and Girls," *Journal of Psychosomatic Research,* 52, no. 3 (2002): 145–154.
37. Lina A. Ricciardelli and Marita P. McCabe, "A Longitudinal Analysis of the Role of Biopsychosocial Factors in Predicting Body Change Strategies among Adolescent Boys," *Sex Roles: A Journal of Research,* 48, nos. 7-8 (2003): 349–360.
38. Jacqueline N. Stanford and Marita P. McCabe, "Evaluation of Body Image Prevention Programme for Adolescent Boys," *European Eating Disorders Review,* 13, no. 5 (2005): 360–370.
39. See: Marita P. McCabe and Lina A. Ricciardelli, "Body Image and Body Change Techniques among Young Adolescent Boys," *European Eating Disorders Review,* 9, no. 5 (2001): 335–347.
40. M. Millman, *Such a Pretty Face: Being Fat in America* (New York: Berkeley, 1981), 224.
41. Carol J. Nemeroff, R. I. Stein, N.S. Diehl, and K.M. Smilack. "From the Cleavers to the Clintons: Role Choices and Body Orientation as Reflected in Magazine Article Content," *International Journal of Eating Disorders,* 16, no. 2 (1994): 167, 173.
42. See: M.E. Mishkind, J. Rodin, L.R. Silberstein, and R.H. Striegel-Moore, "The Embodiment of Masculinity: Cultural, Psychological, and Behavioral Dimensions," *American Behavioral Scientist,* 29 (1986): 545-562. See also: "You're So Vain," *Newsweek,* April 1986, pp. 48–55.
43. David M. Garner, "The 1997 Body Image Survey Results," *Psychology Today,* 30, no. 1 (1997). 42.
44. Ibid.
45. Ibid.
46. Ibid., 35.
47. Gordon B. Forbes, Leah E. Adams-Curtis, Brooke Rade, and Peter Jaberg. "Body Dissatisfaction in Women and Men: The Role of Gender-Typing and Self-Esteem," *Sex Roles,* 44, no. 7/8 (2001): 471.
48. Ibid.
49. Ibid.
50. D. MacCannell and J.F. MacCannell, "The Beauty System," in *The Ideology of Conduct: Essays in Literature and the History of Sexuality,* ed. N. Armstrong and L. Tennenhouse (New York: Methuen, 1987), 207.
51. J. Rodin, *Body Traps: Breaking the Binds That Keep You from Feeling Good about Your Body* (New York: William Morrow, 1992), 38–39.
52. Harrison G. Pope, Katherine A. Phillips, and Roberto Olivardia, *The Adonis Complex* (New York: Free Press, 2000), 23–24.
53. Roberta Pollack Seid, *Never Too Thin,* 116. (See n. 15)

54. Adam Drewnowski and Doris K. Yee, "Men and Body Image: Are Males Satisfied with Their Body Weight?" *Psychosomatic Medicine*, 49, no. 6 (1987): 626–634.

55. Rodin, *Body Traps: Breaking the Binds That Keep You from Feeling Good about Your Body* (New York: William Morrow, 1992), 181.

56. Adam Drewnowski and Doris K. Yee, "Men and Body Image: Are Males Satisfied with Their Body Weight?" *Psychosomatic Medicine,* 49, no. 6 (1987): 632.

57. Ibid.

58. David M. Garner, "The 1997 Body Image Survey Results," 42. (See n. 43)

59. Ibid.

60. D. Blake Woodside et al., "Comparisons of Men with Full or Partial Eating Disorders, Men without Eating Disorders, and Women with Eating Disorders in the Community," *American Journal of Psychiatry,* 158, no. 4 (2001): 570–574.

61. Devra L. Braun, Suzanne R. Sunday, Amy Huang, and Katherine A. Halmi, "More Males Seek Treatment for Eating Disorders," *International Journal of Eating Disorders*, 25, no. 4 (1999): 515.

62. Trent A. Petrie and Rebecca Rogers, "Extending the Discussion of Eating Disorders to Include Men and Athletes," *The Counseling Psychologist*, 29, no. 5 (2001): 475.

63. D. Blake Woodside et al., "Comparisons of Men with Full or Partial Eating Disorders. . . , 571. (See n. 60)

64. J. Rodin, *Body Traps,* 88. (See n. 51)

65. Harry Gwirtsman, cited in Judy Folkenberg, "Bulimia: Not for Women Only." *Psychology Today*, 18 (March 1984): 10.

66. Devra L. Braun et al., "More Males Seek Treatment for Eating Disorders," 421. (see n. 61)

67. Ibid.

68. Nancy Clark, "Mirror, Mirror on the Wall . . . Are Muscular Men the Best of All? The Hidden Turmoil of Muscle Dysmorphia—Nutrition," *American Fitness*, January-February, 2004, http://www.looksmartfitness.com/p/articles/mi_m0675/is_1_22/ai_112408511

69. H.G. Pope, Jr., K.A. Phillips, and R. Olivardia, *The Adonis Complex: The Secret Crisis of Male Body Obsession* (New York: Free Press, 2000), 13–14.

70. Roberto Olivardia, Harrison G. Pope, and James I. Hudson, "Muscle Dysmorphia in Male Weightlifters: A Case-Control Study," *American Journal of Psychiatry*, 157, no. 8 (2000): 1291.

71. H.G. Pope, Jr., et al., *The Adonis Complex*, 8. (See n. 69)

72. Ibid., 9.

73. Ibid., 10.

74. Ibid.

75. B. Mangweth et al., "Body Image and Psychopathology in Male Bodybuilders," *Psychotherapy and Psychosomatics*, 70, no. 1 (2001): 41.

76. Roberto Olivardia, Harrison G. Pope, and James I. Hudson, "Muscle Dysmorphia in Male Weightlifters: A Case-Control Study," *American Journal of Psychiatry*, 157, no. 8 (2000): 1294.

77. Marc E. Mishkind, Judith Rodin, Lisa R. Silberstein, and Ruth Striegel-Moore. "The Embodiment of Masculinity: Cultural, Psychological, and Behavioral Dimensions," *American Behavioral Scientist*, 29, no. 5 (1986): 549.
78. Harrison G. Pope, "Unraveling the Adonis Complex," *Psychiatric Times*, 18, no. 3 (March 2001), http://www.psychiatrictimes.com/p010353.html
79. American Society for Aesthetic Plastic Surgery (ASAPS), http://www.surgery.org.
80. Ibid.
81. Ibid.
82. See: M.B. King and G. Mezey, "Eating Behavior of Male Racing Jockeys," *Psychological Medicine*, 17 (1987): 249–253; S.N. Steen, R.A. Oppliger, and K.D. Brownell, "Metabolic Effects of Repeated Weight Loss and Regain in Adolescent Wrestlers," *Journal of the American Medical Association*, 260 (1988): 47–50.
83. Millman, *Such a Pretty Face: Being Fat in America* (New York: Berkeley, 1981), 225.
84. David Crawford, *Easing the Ache: Gay Men Recovering from Compulsive Disorders* (New York: Dutton, 1990), 126.
85. Marc E. Mishkind et al., "The Embodiment of Masculinity," 455. (sec n. 77)
86. A.D. Mickalide, "Sociocultural Factors Influencing Weight among Males" in Arnold M. Andersen, *Males with Eating Disorders* (New York: Brunner/Mazel, 1990), 30–39.
87. See: D. Garner and P.E. Garfinkel, "Socio-Cultural Factors in the Development of Anorexia Nervosa," *Psychological Medicine*, 10, no. 4 (1980): 647–656; D.M. Garner, P.F. Garfinkel, D. Schwartz, and M. Thompson. "Cultural Expectations of Thinness in Women," *Psychological Reports*, 47, no. 2 (1980): 483–491; E.D. Rothblum, "Women and Weight: Fad and Fiction," *Journal of Psychology*, 124, no.1 (1990): 5–24.
88. See: M.P. Warren and R.L. Vande Wiele, "Clinical and Metabolic Features of Anorexia Nervosa," *American Journal of Obstetrics and Gynecology* 117, no. 3 (1973): 435–449; H. Bruch, "Anorexia Nervosa and Its Differential Diagnosis," *Journal of Nervous Mental Disease*, 141 (1966): 555–566; D.J. Jones, M.M. Fox, H.M. Babigian, and H.E. Hutton. "Epidemiology of Anorexia Nervosa in Monroe County, New York: 1960-1976," *Psychosomatic Medicine*, 42, no. 6 (1980): 551–558.
89. See: Elizabeth Rieger, Stephen Touyz, Tony Swain, and Peter Beaumont. "Cross-Cultural Research on Anorexia Nervosa: Assumptions Regarding the Role of Body Weight," *International Journal of Eating Disorders*, 29, no. 2 (2001): 205–215; G.A. German, "Aspects of Clinical Psychiatry in Sub-Saharan Africa," *British Journal of Psychiatry*, 121, no. 564 (1972): 461–479; J.S.Neki, "Psychiatry in South East Asia," *British Journal of Psychiatry*, 123, no. 574 (1973): 257–269; B. Dolan, "Cross-Cultural Aspects of Anorexia Nervosa and Bulimia," *International Journal of Eating Disorders*, 10 (1990): 67–78. See also: A. Furnham and P. Baguma, "Cross-Cultural Differences in the Evaluation of Male and Female Body Shapes," *International Journal of Eating Disorders*, 15, no.1 (1994): 81–89.

90. E.D. Rothblum, "Women and Weight: Fad and Fiction," *Journal of Psychology*, 124, no.1 (1990): 5. See also: P.S. Powers, *Obesity: The Regulation of Weight* (Baltimore, MD: Williams & Wilkins, 1980).

91. Adrian Furnham and Peter Baguma, "Cross-Cultural Differences in the Evaluation of Male and Female Body Shapes," *International Journal of Eating Disorders*, 15, no. 1 (1994): 88. Sobal and Stunkard note: "Obesity may be a sign of health and wealth in developing societies, the opposite of its meaning in developed countries." They also note the importance of evolution: "Through the millennia, obesity was probably not a possibility for most people. Limited supplies of food characterized the lives of many of our ancestors and are present in many developing societies today." See: J. Sobal and A.J. Stunkard, "Socioeconomic Status and Obesity: A Review of the Literature," *Psychological Bulletin*, 105, no. 2 (1989): 266–267.

92. Emily Bradley Massara, *!Que Gordita! A Study of Weight among Women in a Puerto Rican Community* (New York: AMS Press, 1989).

93. Ibid., 19.

94. Ibid., 12.

95. Ibid., 171.

96. Ibid., 293.

97. Ibid., 141.

98. Ibid., 145.

99. Ibid., 161.

100. Ibid.

101. It is important to point out that the extent of the spread of the Cult of Thinness depends on a variety of factors within a given ethnic community. Within this community there are the beginnings of intracultural variations in terms of the degree of assimilation. As the second generation of Puerto Ricans in this community comes to gain upward mobility, their susceptibility to the Cult of Thinness may grow as well. As one researcher notes: "Among the African-American and Latina women I interviewed, the degree to which thinness was imposed on them as girls depended upon whether their families' class had changed, the families' geographical location, the schools the children attended, and nationality." See: B. Thompson, "Food, Bodies, and Growing Up Female: Childhood Lessons about Culture, Race, and Class," in *Feminist Perspectives on Eating Disorders*, ed. P. Fallon, M.A. Katzman, and S.C. Wooley (New York: Guilford Press, 1994), 371.

102. Emily Bradley Massara, *!Que Gordita!* 145. (See n. 92)

103. Regarding American society, see: J. E. Smith and J. Krejci, "Minorities Join the Majority: Eating Disturbances among Hispanic and Native American Youth," *International Journal of Eating Disorders*, 10, no. 2 (1991): 179–186; L.K.G. Hsu, "Are the Eating Disorders Becoming More Common in Blacks?" *International Journal of Eating Disorders*, 6 (1987): 113–124. Regarding non-Western societies as a whole, see: M. Nasser, "Comparative Study of the Prevalence of Abnormal Eating Attitudes among Arab Female Students of Both London and Cairo Universities," *Psychological Medicine*, 16, no. 3 (1986): 621–625; J. Sobal

and A.J. Stunkard, "Socioeconomic Status and Obesity: A Review of the Literature," *Psychological Bulletin*, 105, no. 2 (1989): 260–275; A. Furnham and B. Baguma, "Cross Cultural Differences in the Evaluation of Male and Female Body Shapes," *International Journal of Eating Disorders*, 15, no. 1 (1994): 81–89; T. Furukawa, "Weight Changes and Eating Attitudes of Japanese Adolescents under Acculturative Stresses: A Prospective Study," *International Journal of Eating Disorders*, 15, no. 1 (1994): 71–79; L.L. Osvold and G.R. Sodowsky, "Eating Disorders of White American, Racial and Ethnic Minority American, and International Women," *Journal of Multicultural Counseling and Development*, 21, no. 3 (1993): 143–154.

104. Marisol Perez and Thomas E. Joiner, Jr., "Body Image Dissatisfaction and Disordered Eating in Black and White Women," *International Journal of Eating Disorders,* 33, no. 3 (2003): 343.

105. Ibid., 342.

106. Ibid., 343.

107. Ibid., 342.

108. K.S. Buchanan, "Creating Beauty in Blackness," in *Consuming Passions: Feminist Approaches to Weight Preoccupation and Eating Disorders,* ed. C. Brown and K. Jasper (Toronto, Ontario, Canada: Second Story Press, 1993), 37.

109. K.K. Abrams, L.R. Allen, and J.J. Gray, "Disordered Eating Attitudes and Behaviors, Psychiatric Adjustment, and Ethnic Identity: A Comparison of Black and White Female College Students," *International Journal of Eating Disorders*, 14, no. 1 (1993): 49–57.

110. K.S. Buchanan, "Creating Beauty in Blackness," 37. (See n. 108)

111. P. Collins, *Black Feminist Thought: Knowledge, Consciousness and the Politics of Empowerment* (Boston: Unwin Hyman, 1990), cited in K.S. Buchanan, "Creating Beauty in Blackness," 79. (See n. 108)

112. E. White, "Unhealthy Appetites," *Essence*, September 1991, p. 28. See also: C.S.W. Rand and J.M. Kaldau, "The Epidemiology of Obesity and Self-Defined Weight Problems in the General Population: Gender, Race, Age, and Social Class," *International Journal of Eating Disorders*, 9, no. 3 (1990): 329–343.

113. R. Bray, "Heavy Burden," *Essence*, January 1992, p. 54.

114. M.H. Styles, "Soul, Black Women and Food," in *A Woman's Conflict: The Special Relationship between Women and Food*, ed. Jane Rachel Kaplan (New York: Prentice Hall, 1980), 161—162. The roots of plants are the primary ingredients of soul food, for example, yams, sweet potatoes, turnips, and "greens" such as collards.

115. Ibid., 163.

116. Ibid., 174–175.

117. I. Attie, and J. Brooks-Gunn, "The Development of Eating Regulation across the Life Span," In D. Cicchetti and D. Cohen (Eds.), *Developmental Psychopathology: Vol. 2: Risk, Disorder, and Adaptation* (New York: Wiley, 1995): 332–368.

118. R. Streigel-Moore and L. Smolak, "The Role of Race in the Development of Eating Disorders," in L. Smolak and M.P. Levine (Eds.), *The Developmental*

Psychopathology of Eating Disorders: Implications for Research, Prevention, and Treatment (Mahwah, NJ: Lawrence Erlbaum, 1996), 259–284.

119. L.K. George Hsu, "Are Eating Disorders Becoming More Common in Blacks?" *International Journal of Eating Disorders*, 6 (1987): 122.

120. See: Jalmeen K. Makkar and Michael J. Strube, "Black Women's Self-Perceptions of Attractiveness following Exposure to White versus Black Beauty Standards: The Moderating Role of Social Identity and Self-Esteem," *Journal of Applied Social Psychology*, 25, no. 17 (1995): 1547–1566.

121. T. J. Silber, "Anorexia Nervosa in Blacks and Hispanics," *International Journal of Eating Disorders*, 5, no. 1 (1986): 127.

122. Marisol Perez and Thomas E. Joiner, Jr., "Body Image Dissatisfaction and Disordered Eating in Black and White Women," 343. (See n. 104)

123. Ibid., 342.

124. Ruth H. Striegel-Moore et al., "Eating Disorder Symptoms in a Cohort of 11 to 16-Year-Old Black and White Girls: The NHLBI Growth and Health Study," *International Journal of Eating Disorders*, 27, no 1. (2000): 62.

125. J. A. Ladner, *Tomorrow's Tomorrow: The Black Woman* (New York: Doubleday, 1971).

126. See: Becky Thompson, *A Hunger So Wide and So Deep: A Multiracial View of Women's Eating Problems* (Minneapolis: University of Minnesota Press, 1994). Thompson writes,

> Talking with Latina, African-American, and white women—including both heterosexual and lesbian women—reveals that the origins of eating problems have little or nothing to do with vanity or obsession with appearance. In fact, eating problems begin as survival strategies—as sensible acts of self-preservation—in response to myriad injustices including racism, sexism, homophobia, classism, the stress of acculturation, and emotional, physical, and sexual abuse. (12)

Later Thompson describes bingeing as "a creative coping mechanism in the face of terrible odds. . . . As a drug, food worked quickly to help her [respondent] 'stuff back emotions'" (61). For another respondent of Thompson's, bingeing "made her 'disappear,' which made her feel protected; it began as a way to numb and block painful feelings" (61).

127. Tory DeAngelis, "Body-Image Problems Affect All Groups," *Monitor on Psychology*, 28, no. 3 (1997): 45.

128. Pamela A. Brand, Esther D. Rothblum, and Laura J. Solomon, "A Comparision of Lesbians, Gay Men and Heterosexuals on Weight and Restrained Eating," *International Journal of Eating Disorders*, 11, no. 3 (1992): 253.

129. Ibid.

130. Ibid.

131. Ibid., 103.

132. Maryanne R. Ludwig and Kelly D. Brownell, "Lesbians, Bisexual Women, and Body Image: An Investigation of Gender Roles and Social Groups Affiliation," *International Journal of Eating disorders*, 24 (1997): 89–97.

133. Kelly Hearn, "Which Came First, Thin Women or Tiny Sizes?" *Christian Science Monitor* [Electronic version], http://www.csmonitor.com/2005/0224/p12s02-lihc .html. 02/24/2005

134. See: Amelia J. Lake, Petra K. Staiger, and Huguette Glowinski, "Effect of Western Culture on Women's Attitudes to Eating and Perceptions of Body Shape," *International Journal of Eating Disorders*, 27, no. 1 (2000): 83–89. See also: K.M. Pike and B.T. Walsh, "Ethnicity and Eating Disorders: Implications for Incidence and Treatment," *Psychopharmacology Bulletin*, 32, no. 2 (1996): 265–274; Katzman, M.A., and Lee, S. "Beyond Body Image: The Integration of Feminist and Transcultural Theories in the Understanding of Self Starvation." *International Journal of Eating Disorders*, 22, no. 4 (1997): 385–394; Pate, J.E., Pumariega, A.J., Hester, C., and Garner, D.M. "Cross-cultural Patterns in Eating Disorders: A Review," *Journal of the American Academy of Child and Adolescent Psychiatry*, 31, no. 5 (1992): 802–809.

135. See: Susie Orbach, *Fat Is a Feminist Issue* (New York: Berkeley Press, 1978).

136. Susan Flockhart, "Diet Industry Blamed for Obese Society," *Sunday Herald*, September 15, 2002, http://www.sundayherald.com/print27674

137. Anne E. Becker, Rebecca A. Burwell, Stephen E. Gilman, David B. Herzog, and Paul Hamburg, "Eating Behaviors and Attitudes following Prolonged Exposure to Television among Ethnic Fijian Adolescent Girls," *British Journal of Psychiatry*, 180, no. 6 (2002): 510.

138. Ibid.

139. Ibid., 511

140. M.N. Miller and A.J. Pumariega, "Culture and Eating Disorders: A Historical and Cross-cultural Review," *Psychiatry: Interpersonal and Biological Processes*, 64, no. 2 (2001): 93–110.

Bibliography

Abrams, K.K., L.R. Allen, & J.J. Gray. "Disordered Eating Attitudes and Behaviors, Psychiatric Adjustment, and Ethnic Identity: A Comparison of Black and White Female College Students." *International Journal of Eating Disorders*, 14, no. 1 (1993): 49–57.

Altabe, M. "Ethnicity and Body Image: Quantitative and Qualitative Analysis," *International Journal of Eating Disorders*, 23, no. 2 (1998). 153–159

American Society for Aesthetic Plastic Surgery. "ASAPS." http://www.surgery.org

Anorexia Nervosa and Related Eating Disorders, Inc. "ANRED." http://www.anred .com

Attie, I., & J. Brooks-Gunn. "The Development of Eating Regulation across the Life Span." In *Developmental Psychopathology: Volume 2. Risk, Disorder, and Adaptation*, ed. D. Cicchetti & D. Cohen, pp. 332–368. New York: Wiley, 1995.

Attie, I., & J. Brooks-Gunn. "Weight Concerns as Chronic Stressors in Women." In *Gender and Stress*, ed. R.C. Barnett, L. Biener, & G.K. Baruch, p. 218–254. New York: Free Press, 1987.

Barry, D.T., C.M. Grilo, & R. Masheb. "Gender Differences in Patients with Binge Eating Disorder." *International Journal of Eating Disorders*, 31, no. 1 (2002): 63–70.

Becker, A.E., R.A. Burwell, D.B. Herzog, P. Hamburg, & S.E. Gilman. "Eating Behaviors and Attitudes Following Prolonged Exposure to Television among Ethnic Fijian Adolescent Girls." *British Journal of Psychiatry*, 180, no. 6 (2002): 509–514.

Botta, R.A. "The Mirror of Television: A Comparison of Black and White Adolescents' Body Image." *Journal of Communication*, 50, no. 3 (2000): 144–159.

Brand, P.A., E.D. Rothblum, and L.J. Solomon. "A Comparision of Lesbians, Gay Men and Heterosexuals on Weight and Restrained Eating." *International Journal of Eating Disorders*, 11, no. 3 (1992): 253–259.

Braun, D.L., S.R. Sunday, A. Huang, & K.A. Halmi. "More Males Seek Treatment for Eating Disorders." *International Journal of Eating Disorders*, 25, no. 4 (1999): 415–424.

Bray, R. "Heavy Burden," *Essence*, January 1992, p. 52–54, 90.

Bruch, H. "Anorexia Nervosa and Its Differential Diagnosis." *Journal of Nervous and Mental Disease*, 141 (1966): 555–566.

Buchanan, K.S. "Creating Beauty in Blackness." In *Consuming Passions: Feminist Approaches to Weight Preoccupation and Eating Disorders*, ed. C. Brown & K. Jasper pp. 36–52. Toronto, Ontario, Canada: Second Story Press, 1993.

Bulik, C.M., L. Reba, A.-M. Siega-Riz, & T. Reichborn-Kjennerud. "Anorexia Nervosa: Definition, Epidemiology, and Cycle of Risk." *International Journal of Eating Disorders*, 37, no. S1 (2005): S2–S9.

Clark, N. "Mirror, Mirror on the Wall . . . Are Muscular Men the Best of All? The Hidden Turmoil of Muscle Dysmorphia—Nutrition." *American Fitness*, January-February 2004. http://www.looksmartfitness.com/p/articles/mi_m0675/is_1_22/ai_112408511

Collins, P. *Black Feminist Thought: Knowledge, Consciousness and the Politics of Empowerment* (Boston: Unwin Hyman, 1990), cited in K.S. Buchanan, "Creating Beauty in Blackness," in *Consuming Passions: Feminist Approaches to Weight Preoccupation and Eating Disorders*, eds. C. Brown and K. Jasper (Toronto, Ontario, Canada: Second Story Press, 1993), 79.

Crawford, D. *Easing the Ache: Gay Men Recovering from Compulsive Disorders*. New York: Dutton, 1990.

Davis, J., & R. Oswalt. "Societal Influences on a Thinner Body Size in Children." *Perceptual and Motor Skills*, 74, no. 3 (1992): 697–698.

DeAngelis, T. "Body-Image Problems Affect All Groups." *Monitor on Psychology*, 28, no. 3 (1997): 45.

Demarest, J. & R. Allen. "Body Image: Gender, Ethnic, and Age Differences." *Journal of Social Psychology*, 140, no. 4 (2000): 465–472.

Dolan, B. "Cross-Cultural Aspects of Anorexia Nervosa and Bulimia." *International Journal of Eating Disorders*, 10 (1990): 67–78.

Drewnowski, A., & D.K. Yee. "Men and Body Image: Are Males Satisfied with Their Body Weight?" *Psychosomatic Medicine*, 49, no. 6 (1987): 626–634.

Flockhart, S. "Diet Industry Blamed for Obese Society." *Sunday Herald*, September 15, 2002 [Electronic version]. http://www.sundayherald.com/print27674

Folkenberg, J. "Bulimia: Not for women only." *Psychology Today*, 18 (March 1984): 10.

Forbes, G.B., L.E. Adams-Curtis, B. Rade, & P. Jaberg. "Body Dissatisfaction in Women and Men: The Role of Gender-Typing and Self-Esteem." *Sex Roles*, 44, no. 7/8 (2001): 461–484.

Furnham, A. & P. Baguma. "Cross-Cultural Differences in the Evaluation of Male and Female Body Shapes," *International Journal of Eating Disorders*, 15, no. 1 (1994): 81–89.

Furukawa, T. "Weight Changes and Eating Attitudes of Japanese Adolescents under Acculturative Stress: A Prospective Study," *International Journal of Eating Disorders*, 15, no. 1 (1994): 71–79.

Garner, D.M. "The 1997 Body Image Survey Results." *Psychology Today*, 30, no. 1 (1997): 30–44.

Garner D., & P.E. Garfinkel, "Socio-Cultural Factors in the Development of Anorexia Nervosa," *Psychological Medicine*, 10, no. 4 (1980): 647–656

Garner D.M., P.E. Garfinkel, D. Schwartz, & M. Thompson. "Cultural Expectations of Thinness in Women." *Psychological Reports*, 47, no. 2 (1980): 483–491.

German, G.A. "Aspects of Clinical Psychiatry in Sub-Saharan Africa." *British Journal of Psychiatry*, 121, no. 564 (1972): 461–479.

Hearn, K. "Which Came First, Thin Women or Tiny Sizes?" *The Christian Science Monitor* [Electronic version]. http://www.csmonitor.com/2005/0224/p12s02-lihc.html (accessed February 24, 2005).

Hsu, L.K.G. "Are the Eating Disorders Becoming More Common in Blacks?" *International Journal of Eating Disorders*, 6, no. 1 (1987): 113–124.

Jones, D.J., M.M. Fox, H.M. Babigian, & H.E. Hutton, "Epidemiology of Anorexia Nervosa in Monroe County, New York: 1960-1976." *Psychosomatic Medicine*, 42, no. 6 (1980): 551–558.

Katzman, M.A., & S. Lee. "Beyond Body Image: The Integration of Feminist and Transcultural Theories in the Understanding of Self Starvation." *International Journal of Eating Disorders*, 22, no. 4 (1997): 385–394.

King, M.B. & G. Mezey. "Eating Behavior of Male Racing Jockeys," *Psychological Medicine*, 17, no. 1 (1987): 249–253.

Ladner, J.A. *Tomorrow's Tomorrow: The Black Woman*, New York: Doubleday, 1971.

Lake, A.J., P.K. Staiger, and H. Glowinski. "Effect of Western Culture on Women's Attitudes to Eating and Perceptions of Body Shape." *International Journal of Eating Disorders*, 27, no. 1 (2000): 83–89.

Levine, M. "10 Things Parents Can Do to Help Prevent Eating Disorders." http://www.nationaleatingdisorders.org

Levine, M.P., & L. Smolak, "Toward a Model of the Developmental Psychopathology of Eating Disorders: The Example of Early Adolescence." In *The Etiology of Bulimia Nervosa: The Individual and Familial Context*, ed. J.H. Crowther, D.L. Tennenbaum, S.E. Hobfoll, & M.A.P. Stephens, pp. 59–80. London: Hemisphere Publishing, 1992.

Lifshitz, F., & N. Moses. "Nutritional Dwarfing: Growth, Dieting, and Fear of Obesity." *Journal of the American College of Nutrition*, 7, no. 5 (1988): 367–376.

Lifshitz, F., N. Moses, C. Cervantes, & L. Ginsberg, "Nutritional Dwarfing in Adolescents." *Seminars in Adolescent Medicine*, 3, no. 4 (1987): 255–266.

Ludwig, M.R., & K.D. Brownell. "Lesbians, Bisexual Women, and Body Image: An Investigation of Gender Roles and Social Groups Affiliation." *International Journal of Eating Disorders*, 25, no. 1 (1999): 89–97.

MacCannell, D., & J.F. MacCannell. "The Beauty System." In *The Ideology of Conduct: Essays in Literature and the History of Sexuality*, ed. N. Armstrong & L. Tennenhouse, pp. 206–238. New York: Methuen, 1987.

Makkar, J.K. & M.J. Strube. "Black Women's Self-Perceptions of Attractiveness Following Exposure to White versus Black Beauty Standards: The Moderating Role of Racial Identity and Self-Esteem." *Journal of Applied Social Psychology*, 25, no. 17 (1995): 1547–1566.

Mangweth, B., H.G. Pope, Jr., G. Kemmler, C. Ebenbichler, A. Hausmann, C. De Col, B. Kreutner, J. Kinzl, & W. Biebl. "Body Image and Psychopathology in Male Bodybuilders." *Psychotherapy and Psychosomatics*, 70, no. 1 (2001): 41.

Marino, D.D. & J.C. King, "Nutritional Concerns during Adolescence." *Pediatric Clinics of North America*, 27, no. 7 (1980): 125–139.

Massara, E.B. *!Que Gordita! A Study of Weight among Women in a Puerto Rican Community*. New York: AMS Press, 1989.

McVey, G., S. Tweed, & E. Blackmore. "Dieting among Preadolescent and Young Adolescent Females." *Canadian Medical Association Journal*, 170, no. 10 (2004): 1559–1561.

Mellin, L.M., S. Scully, & C.E. Irwin. *Disordered Eating Characteristics in Preadolescent Girls*. Paper presented at American Dietetic Association Annual Meeting, Las Vegas, NV, October 28, 1986.

Mickalide, A.D. "Sociocultural Factors Influencing Weight among Males" In *Males with Eating Disorders*, ed. A.M. Andersen, pp. 30–39. New York: Brunner/Mazel, 1990.

Miller, M.N., & A.J. Pumariega. "Culture and Eating Disorders: A Historical and Cross-Cultural Review." *Psychiatry: Interpersonal and Biological Processes*, 64, no. 2 (2001): 93–110.

Millman, M. *Such a Pretty Face: Being Fat in America*. New York: Berkeley, 1981.

Mishkind, M.E., J. Rodin, L.R. Silberstein, & R.H. Striegel-Moore. "The Embodiment of Masculinity: Cultural, Psychological, and Behavioral Dimensions." *American Behavioral Scientist*, 29, no. 5 (1986): 545–562.

Moses, N., M. Banilivy, & F. Lifshitz. "Fear of Obesity among Adolescent Girls." *Pediatrics*, 83, no. 3 (1989): 393–398.

Nasser, M. "Comparative Study of the Prevalence of Abnormal Eating Attitudes among Arab Female Students of Both London and Cairo Universities," *Psychological Medicine*, 16, no. 3 (1986): 621–625.

Neki, J.S. "Psychiatry in South East Asia." *British Journal of Psychiatry*, 123, no. 574 (1973): 257–269.

Nemeroff, C.J., R.I. Stein, N.S. Diehl, & K.M. Smilack. "From the Cleavers to the Clintons: Role Choices and Body Orientation as Reflected in Magazine Article Content." *International Journal of Eating Disorders*, 16, no. 2 (1994): 167–176.

Neumark-Sztainer, D., & P.J. Hannan. "Weight-Related Behaviors among Adolescent Girls and Boys." *Archives of Pediatrics and Adolescent Medicine*, 154, no. 6 (2000): 569–577.

Neumark-Sztainer, D., M. Story, P.J. Hannan, T. Beuhring, & M.D. Resnick. "Disordered Eating among Adolescents: Associations with Sexual/Physical Abuse and Other Familial/Psychosocial Factors." *International Journal of Eating Disorders*, 28, no. 3 (2000): 249–258.

Nichter, M., & M. Nichter. "Hype and Weight." *Medical Anthropology*, 13, no. 3 (1991): 249–284.

Nichter, M. & N. Vuckovic. "Fat Talk: Body Image among Adolescent Girls." In *Many Mirrors: Body Image and Social Relations*, ed. N. Sault, pp. 109–131. New Brunswick, NJ: Rutgers University Press, 1994.

Ogden, J., & J. Steward. "The Role of the Mother-Daughter Relationship in Explaining Weight Concern." *International Journal of Eating Disorders*, 28, no. 1 (2000), 78–83.

Olivardia, R., H.G. Pope, & J.I. Hudson. "Muscle Dysmorphia in Male Weightlifters: A Case-Control Study." *American Journal of Psychiatry*, 157, no. 8 (2000): 1291–1296.

Urbach, S. *Fat is a Feminist Issue.* New York: Berkeley Press, 1978.

Osvold, L.L., & G.R. Sodowsky. "Eating Disorders of White American, Racial and Ethnic Minority American, and International Women." *Journal of Multicultural Counseling and Development*, 21, no. 3 (1993): 143–154.

Pate, J.E., A.J. Pumariega, C. Hester, & D.M. Garner. "Cross-cultural patterns in eating disorders: A review." *Journal of the American Academy of Child and Adolescent Psychiatry*, 31 no. 5 (1992): 802–809.

Perez, M., & T.E. Joiner, Jr. "Body Image Dissatisfaction and Disordered Eating in Black and White Women." *International Journal of Eating Disorders*, 33, no. 3 (2003): 342–350.

Petrie, T.A., & R. Rogers. "Extending the Discussion of Eating Disorders to Include Men and Athletes." *Counseling Psychologist*, 29, no. 5 (2001): 743–753.

Pike, K.M., & B.T. Walsh. "Ethnicity and Eating Disorders: Implications for Incidence and Treatment." *Psychopharmacology Bulletin*, 32, no. 2 (1996): 265–274.

Pine, K.J. "Children's Perceptions of Body Shape: A Thinness Bias in Pre-Adolescent Girls and Associations with Femininity." *Clinical Child Psychology and Psychiatry*, 6, no. 4 (2001): 519–536.

Pope, H.G. "Unraveling the Adonis Complex," *Psychiatric Times*, 18, no. 3 (March 2001) [Electronic version]. http://www.psychiatrictimes.com/p010353.html

Pope, H.G., K.A. Phillips, and R. Olivardia. *The Adonis Complex: The Secret Crisis of Male Body Obsession.* New York: Free Press, 2000.

Powers, P.A. *Obesity: The Regulation of Weight.* Baltimore, MD: Williams & Wilkins, 1980.

Rand, C.S.W., & J.M. Kuldau. "The Epidemiology of Obesity and Self-Defined Weight Problems in the General Population: Gender, Race, Age, and Social Class." *International Journal of Eating Disorders*, 9, no. 3 (1990): 329–343.

Random House of Canada, Ltd. "Pamela Paul: Author Spotlight," 2005. http://www.randomhouse.ca/catalog/author.pperl?authorid=23378

Ricciardelli, L.A., & M.P. McCabe. "A Longitudinal Analysis of the Role of Biopsychosocial Factors in Predicting Body Change Strategies Among Adolescent Boys." *Sex Roles: A Journal of Research*, 48, nos. 7-8 (2003): 349–360.

Ricciardelli, L.A., & M.P. McCabe. "Body Image and Body Change Techniques among Young Adolescent Boys." *European Eating Disorders Review*, 9, no. 5 (2001): 335–347.

Ricciardelli, L.A., M.P. McCabe, & J. Finemore. "The Role of Puberty, Media and Popularity with Peers on Strategies to Increase Weight, Decrease Weight and Increase Muscle Tone among Adolescent Boys and Girls." *Journal of Psychosomatic Research*, 52, no. 3 (2002): 145–154.

Rieger, E., S.W. Touyz, T. Swain, & P.J.V. Beumont. "Cross-Cultural Research on Anorexia Nervosa: Assumptions Regarding the Role of Body Weight." *International Journal of Eating Disorders*, 29, no. 2 (2001): 205–215.

Rodin, J. *Body Traps: Breaking the Binds That Keep You from Feeling Good about Your Body*. New York: William Morrow, 1992.

Rothblum, E.D. "Women and Weight: Fad and Fiction." *Journal of Psychology*, 124, no. 1 (1990): 5–24.

Schneider, K. "Mission Impossible." *People Weekly*, June 1996, pp. 65–73.

Schur, E.A., M. Sanders, & H. Steiner. "Body Dissatisfaction and Dieting in Young Children." *International Journal of Eating Disorders*, 27, no. 1 (2000): 74–82.

Seid, R.P. *Never Too Thin: Why Women Are at War with Their Bodies*. New York: Prentice-Hall Press, 1989.

Shapiro, S., Newcomb, M., & Loeb, T.B. "Fear of Fat, Disregulated-Restrained Eating, and Body-Esteem: Prevalence and Gender Differences among Eight- to Ten-Year-Old Children." *Journal of Clinical Child Psychology*, 26, no. 4 (1997): 358–365.

Silber, T.J. "Anorexia Nervosa in Blacks and Hispanics." *International Journal of Eating Disorders*, 5, no. 1 (1986): 121–128.

Smith, J.E. & J. Krejci. "Minorities Join the Majority: Eating Disturbances among Hispanic and Native American Youth." *International Journal of Eating Disorders,* 10, no. 2 (1991): 179–186.

Smolak, L., M.P. Levine, & R. Schermer. "Parental Input and Weight Concerns among Elementary School Children." *International Journal of Eating Disorders*, 25, no.3 (1999): 263–271.

Sobal, J., & A.J. Stunkard. "Socioeconomic Status and Obesity: A Review of the Literature." *Psychological Bulletin*, 105, no. 2 (1989): 260–275.

Stanford, J.N. & M.P. McCabe. "Evaluation of Body Image prevention Programme for Adolescent Boys." *European Eating Disorders Review*, 13, no. 5 (2005): 360–370.

Steen, S.N., R.A. Oppliger, & K.D. Brownell, "Metabolic Effects of Repeated Weight Loss and Regain in Adolescent Wrestlers." *Journal of the American Medical Association*, 260, no. 1 (1988): 47–50.

Stein, D.M., & P. Reichert. "Extreme Dieting Behaviors in Early Adolescence." *Journal of Early Adolescence*, 10, no. 2 (1990): 108–121.

Striegel-Moore, R.H. "Prevention of Bulimia Nervosa: Questions and Challenges." In *The Etiology of Bulimia Nervosa: The Individual and Familial Context*, ed. J.H. Crowther, D.L. Tennenbaum, S.E. Hobfoll, & M.A.P. Stephens, pp. 203–223. Washington, DC: Hemisphere Publishing, 1992.

Striegel-Moore, R.H., G.B. Schreiber, A. Lo, P. Crawford, E. Obarzanek, & J. Rodin. "Eating Disorder Symptoms in a Cohort of 11 to 16-Year-Old Black and White Girls: The NHLBI Growth and Health Study." *International Journal of Eating Disorders*, 27, no 1. (2000): 49–66.

Striegel-Moore, R., & L. Smolak, "The Role of Race in the Development of Eating Disorders." In *The Developmental Psychopathology of Eating Disorders: Implications for Research, Prevention, and Treatment*, ed. L. Smolak & M.P. Levine, pp. 259–284. Mahwah, NJ: Lawrence Erlbaum, 1996.

Styles, M.H. "Soul, Black Women and Food." In *A Woman's Conflict. The Special Relationship between Women and Food*, ed. J.R. Kaplan pp. 161–176. New York: Prentice-Hall, 1980.

Thelen, M.H., C.M. Lawrence, & A.L. Powell. "Body Image, Weight Control and Eating Disorders among Children." In *The Etiology of Bulimia Nervosa: the Individual and Familial Context*, ed. J.H. Crowther, D.L. Tennenbaum, S.E. Hobfoll, & M.A.P. Stephens, pp. 81–101. London: Hemisphere Publishing, 1992.

Thompson, B. "Food, Bodies, and Growing Up Female: Childhood Lessons about Culture, Race, and Class." In *Feminist Perspectives on Eating Disorders*, ed. P. Fallon, M.A. Katzman, & S.C. Wooley, pp. 355–378. New York: The Guilford Press, 1994.

Thompson, B. *A Hunger So Wide and So Deep: A Multiracial View of Women's Eating Problems*. Minneapolis: University of Minnesota Press, 1994.

U.S. Department of Health and Human Services. "Prevalence of Overweight and Obesity among Adults: United States, 1999-2002." http://www.cdc.gov/nchs/products/pubs/pubd/hestats/obese/obse99.htm

Wardle, J., & R. Watters. "Sociocultural Influences on Attitudes to Weight and Eating: Results of a Natural Experiment." *International Journal of Eating Disorders*, 35, no. 4 (2004): 589–596.

Warren, M.P. "Physical and Biological Aspects of Puberty." In *Girls at Puberty: Biological and Psychosocial Perspectives*, ed. J. Brooks-Gunn & A.C. Petersen, pp. 3–28. New York: Plenum, 1983.

Warren, M.P., & R.L. Vande Wiele. "Clinical and Metabolic Features of Anorexia Nervosa." *American Journal of Obstetrics and Gynecology*, 117, no. 3 (1973): 435–449.

White, E. "Unhealthy Appetites." *Essence*, September 1991, p. 28.

Woodside, D.B., P.E. Garfinkel, E. Lin, P. Goering, A.S. Kaplan, D.S. Goldbloom, & S.H. Kennedy. "Comparisons of Men with Full or Partial Eating Disorders, Men without Eating Disorders, and Women with Eating Disorders in the Community." *American Journal of Psychiatry*, 158, no. 4 (2001): 570–574.

"You're So Vain." *Newsweek*, April 1986, pp. 48–55.

nInE

Breaking Free from the Cult of Thinness

I think it's a state of the heart. I don't think there's anything in particular that, for example, the fitness industry or the diet industry can do because that's going from the outside in. It has to be a question of where we arrive within ourselves.

—Fitness trainer, Boston

I don't think social change happens from the inside out. I don't think people have inner children somewhere inside waiting to be nurtured, reparented, and their natural goodness released into the world . . . our inner selves are constructed by the social and political contexts in which we live, and if we want to alter people's behavior it is far more effective to change the environment than to psychologise individuals.

—Celia Kitzinger[1]

"The personal is political."[2]

—Carol Hanisch

Does change come from "inside out" or do we have to change society to change individuals? Can one escape the Cult of Thinness by means of self-help books and programs, and various therapies? Or is what has happened to women's bodies a political issue, inseparable from our personal concern?

From the Inside Out: Self-Help Books and Treatments

Nancy, a college sophomore, commented:

I think it's wrong to say "I've got to look this certain weight" for anyone else but yourself. If you can feel comfortable the way you are then it will make you a more positive person.

Nancy's advice about "feeling comfortable with the person you are" echoes the philosophy of self-help literature. Starting in the 1980s, self-help books

FIGURE 9.1 Get Real, Full Voice Collage, 2005.

replaced the 1970s feminist movement's consciousness-raising groups, except that now all the talk is about personal issues with little analysis of the "personal as political."[3]

This literature's prevailing message is that you can change your state of mind by adopting the "right" attitude. One very popular book, *Making Peace with Food*,[4] is intended as a resource for those women who are weight preoccupied, dissatisfied with their body image, or have an eating disorder. The author, Susan Kano, points out the risks of dieting and the body's tendency to reach its "natural" weight. She offers exercises for finding a more positive body image and a better sense of self, as well as for dealing with stress and anxiety. *Bodylove*,[5] another book in this genre, emphasizes body acceptance through a range of beauty techniques, such as the artful use of cosmetics. *Transforming Body Image*[6] relies on imaginative exercises to help women love the body they have. More recent books include Margo Maine's *Body Wars: Making Peace with Women's Bodies. An Activist's Guide*,[7] and Patricia Foster's *Minding the Body: Women Writers on Body and Soul*.[8]

Advocating self-acceptance and suggesting ways to reclaim self-esteem, these books can assist individual women in overcoming body insecurity and hatred. They also help women "tap into a community of sorts; they 'feel less alone' when they read."[9] As one self-help therapy analyst notes: "They do some of what the consciousness-raising movement did twenty years ago: They let us share our deepest, perhaps most shameful pain with people in the same boat, and they provide examples of how others have extricated themselves from similar situations."[10]

Gloria Steinem, who wrote *Revolution from Within*, says that after a "previous dozen years working on external barriers to women's equality, [I] had to admit there were internal ones too."[11] Her book suggests that abuse or some type of deprivation has damaged many women's self-esteem. In this view, rejecting the Cult of Thinness begins with recovery and reclaiming your "inner child," the authentic self. The research of Carol Gilligan and others shows that around the age of 11-14, girls begin to lose their authenticity, their confident and self-assured childhood selves. They "go underground," find less direct ways to speak, become more concerned about what others think of them, and lose faith in their own opinions. Their self-esteem diminishes, and depression increases. They start to worry about weight and how they look to others, especially boys. They become concerned about competitiveness within their peer group, and their academic performance, especially in math and science, may begin to decline.[12] The "revolution within" refers to the process of regaining what women lost in their preteen years. As one therapist working with eating-disordered women says, "young teenagers encounter enormous conflicts when joining the cultural definitions of adult womanhood, in which they are forced to risk their authentic self. For many girls, going underground begins with their bodies as they struggle to fit into culturally defined molds."[13]

To get a sense of what life is like for preteens on the brink of losing their "authentic" selves, I interviewed three 9-year-old girls: Beth, Monica, and Willa. Beth and Monica have sisters who are 5 years older; Willa is the eldest child in her family. I asked them to tell me what it is like to be 9, and what they did with each other in their free time. They remarked, "Just playing and having a lot of fun hanging around." When I asked them to elaborate they chorused, "We play with Barbie dolls."[14]

A "Barbie Doll" Tale

Beth has nearly two dozen Barbie dolls in her collection. (First she told me she had only 12, but her older sister, who overheard this part of our conversation, reported that in fact she had 23.) I asked the girls what type of games they played with the Barbies. They replied, "We play the Mean Sisters."

The Mean Sisters game is a reenactment of the identity conflicts pre-pubescent girls go through. Beth put it this way:

> When you get older you start liking boys, wanting to be skinny, and you want to get dates and stuff like that. When my sister Amelia was young she just got dressed, washed up, combed her hair, ate her breakfast and left for school. Now it is different. She gets out of bed, she washes up, then she starts fiddling with her hair and making it into ponytails and seeing what she likes, then she dresses up for a really long time 'cause she wants to make sure she looks really, really good, then finally she goes down and eats breakfast. Probably it will happen to me. It's natural. Because as you get older you like boys.

As Beth and Monica stand on the brink of adolescence, they are worried. Beth said: "I'm afraid that if I'm very beautiful and I wore high heels and stuff then I couldn't go out and play sports anymore. I'd be putting on make-up and fixing my hair, if I end up like my sister."[15]

They want to hang onto the selves they have, but also realize they will need to confront what their older sisters have become. In their play, they act out their ambivalence.

> We split the Barbies into groups. First there is the mother. We pretend the father is away on vacation or got divorced or died. We split the mother's children into little kids and big sisters. The Skipper [Barbie's younger sister] dolls are the little kids. They don't have big boobs. Then we divide the Barbies into mean sisters and nice sisters. The nice sisters treat the little kids nicely and the mean sisters usually try to kill the nice sisters because they want to have all the power and the nice sisters prevent that. The mean sisters don't want the Skipper kids nagging them and stuff.

I asked these preteens what the nice girls usually talk about. They replied, "They talk about opera and dancing. The mean girls talk about boys, plans to kill the little sisters, and they talk about being beautiful. They talk about big breasts, their beautiful eyes and hair."

"What made the sisters mean?" I asked. They said, "They only care about how beautiful they are; they don't care about anybody else; they are snob sisters; they like to get all the power. The nice sisters don't care about how they look. They just want the boys to like them for their selves and personality."

At the height of the game the bad girls kill off all the nice girls and the little kids. (Apparently the mother has gone out when this takes place.) They sometimes kill them by stabbing, or drowning the nice sisters and kids. When the good girls are dead, the bad girls have a celebration:

Like a party, where they jump up and down, and make a lot of noise, and usually get sent to their rooms by their mother. Once all the good girls are dead the bad girls use their power on boys. The boys like the mean sisters because they are beautiful and they are rich. They spend their money on good food. They get their money from the nice sisters' allowances, which they are saving up for a college education. The bad girls sneak out in the middle of the night and walk out with boys.

There is revenge, however. The nice sisters and little kids come back either from the grave or from the hospital. The mother then abandons the bad sisters (sends them to their rooms). And the game ends.

For now, Willa, Beth, and Monica are letting their dolls bear the burden of society's expectations.

Strengthening Self and Spirituality

> *History, despite its wrenching pain, cannot be unlived, but*
> *if faced with courage, need not be lived again.*
>
> —Maya Angelou
> "On the Pulse of the Morning"

Feminist writers offer other avenues to strengthen women's selfhood, from forging stronger mother-daughter bonds to developing one's spiritual life.

In the hopeful vision of *The Mother-Daughter Revolution: From Betrayal to Power*, mothers and their daughters form a new kind of alliance. Its authors believe that mothers' influence is of primary importance in shaping their daughters' future lives. But they need to recover their own lost selves —the ones that went underground at adolescence in the face of patriarchal culture. By finding and reintegrating their truthful, assertive childhood voices, mothers can help prevent the same thing from happening to their vulnerable daughters. They can initiate a process of validation for young girls. The authors claim: "Not only does an authorizing mother validate her daughter's reality, but she adds her authority as a mother, as a woman who has experience in this culture, to amplify and harmonize with her daughter."[16] The ultimate goal is to have a community alliance of mothers and daughters and discerning males who, together, would resist the devaluation of women's selfhood.

bell hooks, a noted black feminist, stresses the importance of spirituality in "becoming your own person." She feels that it is imperative to move the individual from being an "object" to being a "subject:"

> There is such perfect union between the spiritual quest for awareness, enlightenment, self-realization, and the struggle of oppressed people, colonized people to change our circumstance, to resist—to move from object to subject; much of

what has to be restored in us before we can make meaningful organized protest is an integrity of being. In a society such as ours it is in spiritual experience that one finds a ready place to establish such integrity.[17]

The Role of Therapy

In chapter 1 we mentioned depression, anxiety, and dysfunctional families[18] as often-cited factors in eating disorders. A number of "disease" models have been used to explain why women join the Cult of Thinness. One of them is the addiction model, which labels women's eating and body image problems as an illness. Like the views expressed in the self-help literature, this model of behavior places responsibility for the cure with the individual, assisted by medical treatment, psychotherapy, or self-help programs. Overeaters Anonymous, one of the largest self-help groups for weight and eating problems, is based on the same principles as the original quasi-religious 12-step program, Alcoholics Anonymous. The core assumption is personal accountability. Recovery comes with accepting one's lack of power over eating issues and embracing a belief in a "higher power." Twelve-step organizations take pride in their apolitical character; in fact, they go out of their way to avoid identification with any political group. Rather than looking at women's empowerment as a solution to the problem, they suggest that women admit "powerlessness" over their "disease." The emphasis on the individual totally ignores the social, cultural, political, and economic context of women's problems with weight obsession. For instance, psychologist Jane Ogden notes that this perspective fails to take into account that "eating behavior takes place within a social context which offers a strong basis for what is considered normal and abnormal. These social norms are central to the creation and perpetuation of many eating-related attitudes and behaviors."[19] Social context is an important catalyst that influences and sustains weight obsessions and eating disorders.

Although they charge no fees and are therefore outside of the market economy, 12-step programs still fuel the medicalization[20] of women's obsession with weight. They replace a focus on women's oppression and exploitation with the apolitical perspective of addiction, suggesting that therapy, rather than political action, will provide the "cure." Women in these programs are locked into depending on others, who repeat messages of powerlessness.

Some therapy programs *can* help women recover from an eating disorder by alleviating stress and offering help coping with body and food issues. Treatment may range from a hospital stay, to drugs, to individual therapy, group therapy, family therapy, or hypnotherapy. But the focus is primarily on the individual or family unit, with little emphasis on wider cultural factors. And although many therapy programs do not address a disorder's sociocultural context, they provide tools to help the individual feel empowered. They teach patients to analyze past experiences and recognize the choices available in similar experiences. Recognition, knowledge, and active change can improve the problem. For example, Judi Hollis, author of *Fat and Furious*, suggests thinking about life as a four-act play:

ACT I   I walk down a street.
           I see a hole.
           I fall in.
           I am lost and helpless, but it is not my fault.
           I have great difficulty getting out.

ACT II   I walk down a street.
           I see a hole.
           I fall in.
           I see an old habit, and I take responsibility.
           I get out faster and with less difficulty.

ACT III   I walk down a street.
           I see a hole.
           I walk around the hole.

ACT IV   I walk down a different street.[21]

The "play" metaphor is a therapeutic tool in the sense that it reaffirms individual agency. An individual's sense of power, which may have been lost in the "addiction" model, returns when growth and change are possible. However, the play metaphor fails to address the limitations of individual power. One response to the preceding "Acts" might be to ask how to prevent falling into the "hole"; how to get to work if navigating holes is inevitable; how to avoid stepping in "holes" that appear to be stepping-stones; how to renegotiate your sense of self, of femininity, when your identity depends on stepping in holes; and how to mitigate the uncertainty of traveling down "a different street." There are some important ways to think beyond the body by re-envisioning how it is that you think about being a body and how you come to develop a sense of personal body image.

Tips on how you might begin to transform your own body image

HOW DO YOU MEASURE YOUR SELF? Many people, (especially females), use quantitative measures of self-worth, such as weight or clothing size. If we do not measure up, we believe we are not worthy.

Instead of centering your entire day on what you can do to get thinner, focus on what you want to accomplish *today.*

TRANSFORM BAD MEMORIES THAT CONTINUE TO EAT AT YOU. Many of us can remember an early moment of feeling badly about our bodies—a sibling calling you "thunder thighs" or your mother saying "You're too fat to wear that."

Reclaim those early memories that haunt you. You may need to journal and really come to terms with that part of yourself. For instance, maybe you were called "thunder thighs," but think about what a strong soccer player those thighs helped you to be. Begin to locate all the accomplishments you have masked with shame.

YOU ARE MORE THAN THE SUM OF YOUR PARTS. Women tend to think of their bodies in parts—"I hate this but I love that."

Tearing yourself into body parts is not helpful. Instead, look at yourself holistically. Think about all the things you like about your body—and how it helps you to be so many things—a mother, a daughter, a teacher, a doctor, an athlete, a musician, a considerate friend, and so on.

FIND A NEW MEASURING STICK. Many people judge themselves against unrealistic images, such as celebrities.

Instead, think about who you admire most, and for what qualities other than looks?

THE BODY IS FOR MORE THAN ADORATION. Do you see your body as disappointing instead of empowering?

Maybe you will never look like Angelina Jolie—but maybe you can write like Maya Angelou. Perhaps you will run a marathon, author a book, give birth to a child, enjoy walks with your dog, or relax in the sun. See your body as empowering and enjoyable. If you have arms and legs, be grateful. Don't just put in an appearance in life—live it!

DISCONNECT OBLIGATION FROM EXERCISE. For many of us, exercise is something we *have* to do, not something we *like* to do. We feel guilty if we do not exercise—particularly if we feel we must "make up for" consuming calories.

Instead, focus on the exercise that you most enjoy rather than the one that burns the most calories. Maybe you will do it more often, and feel better and happier in the process. And if you have never exercised, begin slowly. You do not need a fancy gym membership or a personal trainer to get started. Why not begin by going for a walk with a friend?

BUT EVERY/BODY'S DOING IT. Not everyone hates her body or takes drastic measures like crash dieting or plastic surgery—but increasingly, many of us do. Body hatred is not just an individual problem; it is a collective, social problem. And while patriarchal and capitalist systems profit from our body hatred, we need to examine our own roles and ask what we are doing to raise the next generation. What messages are mothers sending to their daughters when they are getting plastic surgeries together? What messages are you sending to your friends when you talk about how much weight you need to lose? What messages might you be sending to a daughter when you criticize your own body?

Change has to happen incrementally—you cannot expect it to change overnight. You cannot expect that you will change overnight. But think about how you affect people in your life and how they affect you. Consider the case of a young girl. The people in her sphere of influence—parents, relatives, teachers—have to talk to her . . . about her accomplishments more than just how beautiful she is. It is fine to adorn our bodies and be beautiful, but if that is all you hear, it is a problem. So in our everyday interactions with our children, with our peers, what messages do we send to one another—intentionally and unintentionally?

There are also a number of feminist therapies, which begin to make the links between women's eating issues and cultural oppression.[22] Some feminist therapists who support a broader social perspective conduct self-help groups offering some alternatives to the continued obsession with patriarchal beauty standards. These groups encourage women to give up perpetual diets and to examine the food's meaning for them. Other therapists advocate "fat liberation." Their goal is to change the individual's attitude by helping her feel good about her present body weight.[23]

Perhaps feminism's inability to provide solutions for attaining "the longing for personal transformation that its successes have awakened in women"[24] helped create the self-help market. For example, in the 1960s and 1970s, feminist health activists promoted the idea of self-help. In this context it meant women learned and shared information about a range of issues, from body image to women's social and economic conditions. Self-recovery inspired women to question their own conditions and to take action in dealing with them.

Today, therapists and self-recovery authors do not attempt to change the "outside," but resort to individualistic "inside" treatments. Since the purpose of self-help books and therapeutic intervention is to treat the eating disorder or the body image disturbance, they rarely look at the causes connecting the individual with society. These treatments, in effect, do not challenge existing domination and power structure in our culture. Instead, they tacitly accept these oppressions, including the pressures on women to look attractive, and even address ways in which women can strive to attain a more culturally accepted body image. There is also a prevailing attitude that women who put a great deal of their energy into their own growth and development are "hurtful and destructive to others." As psychologist Harriet G. Lerner notes:

> Women tend to feel so guilty and anxious about any joyful assertion of self in the face of patriarchal injunctions that each small move out from under is invariably accompanied by some unconscious act of apology and penance. . . . Recovery then, to my mind, is a sort of compromise solution. It teaches women to move in the direction of "more self" while it sanitizes and makes change safe, because the dominant group culture (never fond of "those angry women") is not threatened by sick women meeting together to get well.[25]

Individual solutions may be the only recourse for those who, because of their age, gender, race or class, are not in a position to effect societal change. And societal change—obviously a long-term process—is not going to help the anorectic who needs emergency intervention. Since women are rewarded or punished for having the culturally correct or incorrect body image, for some, giving up the pursuit of thinness may be unwise.

Employing a "social/psychological lens" can help us comprehend how mass media images influence the development of eating disorders in women. Much of the research in this area looks at the amount of exposure of women have to the thin ideal through various media (i.e., TV, magazines, advertisements, articles, etc.). Not until recently have studies begun to look at the varying levels of *awareness* and *internalization* of these messages. Not all women develop eating disorders, despite being exposed to these widely popularized images. Additional factors, such as the individual's self-esteem, and the degree to which she has already objectified her body, account for mass media's additional impact.[26]

Social Change from the Outside In

If we recognize the social, political, and economic forces that help support and sustain the Cult of Thinness, then it is clear that simply helping individual women deal with their weight and body image will not resolve these issues on a broad scale. Every day, what we eat, what we wear, and how we view our bodies are very much shaped by the outside forces of our cultural environment. These forces are not only associated with institutions like government or the education system, but are central components in how we perceive our personal lives.[27] A different way to escape the Cult of Thinness focuses on the structural features of society rather than on the individual. These solutions aim to change the climate in which the Cult of Thinness flourishes, and chop at its very roots.

Addressing the Political Economy of the Cult of Thinness through Social Activism

In this book, we have examined the sociocultural and political-economic framework that supports the Cult of Thinness. We observed how capitalistic interests, such as the diet, cosmetic, beauty, and health industries, and the mass media, benefit from promoting women's body insecurity. An ultra-slender body ideal also helps controlling patriarchal interests, since it requires women to divert money, time, and energy away from more empowering activities.

To address these issues demands a critical examination of *capitalism and patriarchy*—even a boycott of those industries involved. One activist strategy organizes women at the grass-roots level to target and boycott consumer goods whose advertising is offensive to women's body image. Boston-area women who are against the use of overly thin models in advertising formed a group known as Boycott Anorexic Marketing (BAM). Their purpose is to "curtail the practice of featuring waif-like, wafer-thin models in ads for a variety of products by identifying companies considered to be culprits and asking consumers not to buy their wares." As the founder of the group explained: "So many women in this group felt powerless at the way our culture applauds anorexia [or, at least, anorexic-*looking* women] and we thought of this boycott as a way to talk back."[28] They successfully targeted a Diet Sprite advertisement that depicted a very thin model who, the copy told us, as a teenager was nicknamed "Skeleton." Their effort prompted the sponsor to retract the commercial. Making women aware that they have the power to change societal attitudes through their purchasing decisions could diminish the Cult of Thinness. While this group's activities have not continued in the recent years, other groups and websites have taken up the boycotting message. There are a range of popular websites, such as "About-Face,"[29] that combat the negative portrayal of women's body image in the mass media by presenting "galleries of Offenders/Winners" in a move to challenge and reward those advertisers who market their goods and services to young women. This website offers specific advocacy resources for those who want to empower themselves and make their voices heard in order to combat and prevent offensive advertising and programming around women's body image issues.

The *tobacco industry* is another important boycott target. Over the last 35 years, this industry has created a female market by feminizing cigarette brands such as Virginia Slims and Capri. Their advertisements strongly suggest smoking as a way to help women lose weight and imply that women who quit cigarettes will gain weight. Even though cigarette smoking accounts for about one quarter of the cancer deaths in women each year, a growing number of teenage girls are taking up smoking.[30] The American Cancer Society currently estimates that 30% of all cancer deaths result from cigarette smoking. According to the Centers for Disease Control and Prevention (CDC),

> 44.5 million American adults are smoking and this translates into 20.9% of all adults (23.4% of men, 18.5% of women)—more than 1 out of 5 people. . . . About 87% of lung cancer deaths are caused by smoking. Lung cancer is the leading cause of cancer death among both men and women, and is one of the most difficult cancers to treat. . . . About half of all Americans who continue to smoke will die because of the habit. Each year, about 438,000 people die in the U.S. from tobacco use. Nearly 1 of every 5 deaths is related to smoking. Cigarettes kill more Americans than alcohol, car accidents, suicide, AIDS, homicide, and illegal drugs combined. . . . Based on data collected from 1995 to 1999, the CDC estimated that adult male smokers lost an average of 13.2 years of life and female smokers lost 14.5 years of life because of smoking.[31]

In addition, while cigarette smoking is declining among most age groups, young women remain resistant to this downward trend. The reason most often cited by young women is a fear of gaining weight if they stop smoking.[32] It appears that an early smoking-related death is far less frightening than failing to be thin.

We must also look into the controlling role of the *medical industry*. Currently, anorexia and bulimia are classified as illnesses, requiring medical or psychotherapeutic interventions. Eating disorder clinics promise to be big money-makers. One might question whether labeling an eating disorder as primarily a medical problem serves the economic interests of the drug companies, who have developed an antidepressant drug (fluoxtine) for bulimic women. Their theory is that a chemical imbalance in the brain is the root cause of bulimia and other eating disorders in women.[33] Yet a current review of the link between depression and bulimia finds "inadequate support" for this relationship.[34] While some women experience positive effects from taking pre-

FIGURE 9.2 A Bicycle Built for one? *Bicycle built for one . . . but light enough for two—with the help of Newport cigarettes. (Newport Pleasure and Newport Spimaker.)*

scription drugs (such as Zoloft) for their eating disorder; drug companies and medical researchers who explain women's problems with food solely in terms of depression, and who market a profitable "cure for eating problems," should have their motives examined.

Social activism within our own communities is another route to social change, and there are many activist opportunities for challenging the Cult of Thinness. I asked the 9-year-old Barbie owners what could be done to change older girls' concerns about how they look. They immediately made the connection between their toys, their body image fears, and the greater population of children. They wanted to take action. Beth said, "I would like to change the Barbie doll's shape. I'd like to make her normal, not big boobed, just like a normal person." Monica decided to write a letter to the Mattel toy company.

Dear Mattel:
Make your Barbie dolls less adorable or stop selling them because little kids and older kids and even younger sisters and brothers play with Barbie dolls and in one second they will want to look as skinny as them. So either stop selling them

or make them more normal, a little chubbier, not as big boobed and not standing on their tippy toes. Make more pants, and not only shirts with puffy shoulders which come down to their belly button. Make full bathing suits, not only
bikini bathing suits.

Some women advocate combining our enthusiasm for getting our bodies in
shape with social activism.

Women I talked with suggested organizing a 10K walk/run in which
women of all sizes and shapes were encouraged to participate, to challenge
cultural attitudes regarding ultra-thinness. Some mentioned a 1-day bike ride
to promote awareness of eating disorders and to advocate insurance coverage
for the treatment of these problems. Others liked the idea of women enjoying
a long distance run on their own, choosing where, when, and at what pace,
serving as a time of self-reflection and relaxation.

Social Activism through Education

Public education is also critical. The medical community—physicians, dieti-
tians, and mental health professionals, as well as educators, coaches, and athletes sponsor Eating Disorders Awareness Week (EDAW). Its purpose is to
raise public awareness about eating disorder prevention and treatment, and promote healthy body image attitudes. The organization has challenged cultural
pressures toward thinness, especially those pressures from the multibillion-
dollar diet and fashion industries, and links these pressures to the outbreak of
eating problems. It questions cultural beauty standards beauty with the idea
that "it's what's inside that counts."

Educational programs on eating disorders are part of school curricula. One
private school in Boston requires all eighth- and ninth-grade girls to take a 10-
week course on anorexia, bulimia, and compulsive overeating.[35] At Harvard
University, the telephone hotline known as Echo (Eating Concerns Hotline
and Outreach)[36] provides a forum for men and women who have eating issues
or are concerned about a friend who has an eating problem. They also sponsor speakers and films to educate the wider community. The Center for the
Study of Anorexia and Bulimia has put together curriculum materials for
grades 7-10 dealing with such topics as emotions and eating, body image, and
the cultural pressures on women.[37] A new interactive and step-by step program titled "Full of Ourselves"[38] is a school-based wellness program designed
to "inoculate" young girls against negative body image by helping preteens
develop media literacy, nutritional information, and coping skills to combat
the Cult of Thinness.

There are also several national associations that are educating the population. The National Association to Aid Fat Americans was founded in 1969. It

provides its members with "tools to be happy with yourself as you are, to fight discrimination and stereotyping and to understand the effects that dieting can have on the body and mind." The association has gone out of its way to fight fat discrimination, from launching a write-in campaign against greeting cards offensive to the obese to educating physicians about the problems of undertaking surgery to cure obesity.[39] The National Association of Anorexia Nervosa and Associated Disorders is another self-help and educational organization that aims to promote healthy body image and eating attitudes.

A New Vision of Femininity: Breaking Down the Mind/Body Dichotomy

Western society's prescription of what it means to be feminine needs a rewrite. Current definitions of femininity are dictated by a social system that gains control over women by defining them primarily in terms of their bodies. The split between mind and body is central to our idea of what it means to be male and female—and our culture values mind over body. But dichotomous thinking is a powerful mechanism of social control and oppression. It separates groups into "we" and "they," instead of allowing diversity to flourish.

In order to break down the mind/body dichotomy, our institutions must change. They must acknowledge and reward a broader view of "the feminine" which includes aspects of both mind and body. Truly eradicating the Cult of Thinness will ultimately require women to become politically active in changing basic institutions—educational, economic, family, legal, political, and religious. Women must challenge the industries that feed on body insecurity. They need to change the messages girls and women absorb from families, schools, and jobs—all places where women are rewarded or punished daily for being in the "right" or "wrong" body.

To effect change in the economic arena for example, women must continue to demand equal opportunity in the workplace. Sexual harassment, ageism, and weightism must be included with issues of salary equity and job promotion. Our legal institutions must address gender discrimination as well as the growing violence against women, which continues to undermine feminine power and authority. In education, it is important to close the gender gap in mathematics and science, and to build awareness of gender bias within and outside the classroom. This will require teachers and counselors to change male-based teaching environments and provide positive encouragement to female students to overcome years of anxiety about taking advanced math and science courses.

In the sense that the body is a cultural construction, perhaps we can begin to build another culture—one that offers alternatives to Madison Avenue messages. In the social arena, we need a re-envisioning of femininity, where women look hard at current cultural norms and free themselves from these definitions. Groups of women are beginning to do this.

In *Female Sexualization: A Collective Work of Memory*, Frigga Haug describes a group of German feminists who undertook an exciting project using their own bodies as objects of study.[40] The goal was to "unravel" how gender socialization created and molded bodies over time. In this process, each woman chose a body part—hair, legs, and so on—and then asked the others to recollect events in their lives that focused on this area. They circulated their written memories among the group, where body socialization stories were "discussed, reassessed and rewritten."[41]

Photography has been an important influence in the control and definition of feminine appearance, from advertising images to the family photo album. Another new way to revision femininity is photo therapy, through a technique known as "reframing." The idea behind photo therapy is that "each of us has sets of personalized archetypal images 'in memory,' images which have been produced through various photo practices—the school photo . . . is one example."[42] These photos are often "surrounded by vast chains of connotations and buried memories."[43] The reframing process[44] involves a challenge or description of "visual discourse" by parody and reversal. Through playing with photo images of themselves, women "retake" old images and thereby gain some control over how they define their physical appearance and sense of self.

Still other strategies of re-envisioning femininity require women to become politically active, even on the smallest personal level.

I interviewed a group of women ranging from their 30s to 60s and asked them what advice or solutions they might offer to the younger generation. What would help younger women to promote social change around women's problems with body image? They agreed that changing society would most likely happen in small increments, on a small group and peer group level. In the words of one woman in her 40s, a school administrator, social change starts with our "significant others." She commented:

> A person's life extends out, like an embrace. I know I can work on myself, but I also know the impact that I have with my stepchildren and my siblings and friends. I think we all have that sphere of influence to work on. It's all of our daughters that we need to make aware of the Cult of Thinness. I think demonstrating some of my changed behaviors and attitudes toward my body has made a difference to my stepdaughter, my younger sisters, my best friend. They've watched me gain weight and not freak out about it too much. I mean, not get crazed as I would have in my 20s, where 2 pounds was cause for terrible alarm and self-abuse. I think by just living the way I'm living and calling their attention to it enough, it's made an impression on them.

Ellen, a writer, noted how she has tried to influence her extended family by asking them to not pay so much attention to her 8-year-old daughter's looks:

> My relatives can never greet one another without saying, "Hi, you lost weight! Don't you look good!" That's hello, the first thing. I'm not terribly assertive with my family, but they know they can't pull that around my daughter. They can't talk about her figure, or what she's eating. I won't let them comment on her appearance. They can't do that, because to me, it takes her away from her childhood.

In their own ways, older women can reach out to the next generation to change the culture within which young women grow up. Maybe it happens when a teacher pays attention to how she talks about weight and body image in the classroom. Perhaps it is when a mother stops dieting to demonstrate to her daughters that she is breaking free of the cultural demands she has had to endure in "becoming a certain body." Maybe it is in a family's attitudes at the dinner table. As Miranda, one the students I interviewed, told me:

> My parents never used food as a temptation or a weapon, like "you won't get dessert if you do something," or "you are being sent to bed without dinner." Food was never a reward and it was never a punishment.

These personal gestures are important examples of how social change can start within our own close circle of friends, relations, coworkers, or students. The appendix to this book also provides some more specific ways you might think about changing the Cult of Thinness culture, starting with those who you embrace in your everyday life.

Making a Life: Becoming Your Own Person

Although I began this chapter by suggesting social change as an either/or phenomenon—"outside in" or "inside out"—*both* types of change are fundamental to extricating young women from the Cult of Thinness. Finding the space to develop the self appears critical to the healthy maturity of young women.

In fact, the process of self-making is crucial to moving beyond the Cult of Thinness. I asked Anna, the religious cult member quoted earlier, what enabled her to leave the cult after 12 years. She had entered her 30s, gone through an arranged marriage with a fellow member, and had begun raising a child within the cult community. She told me she began to question her guru's rigid rules, and to reject his controlled version of reality, especially when he sent her young son away to school in India:

> I reached a level of strength where I knew that it was time to go on and have a life of my own. I finally felt like I could figure out on my own who I was and what I wanted to do and that I didn't need to live inside that prison.

A heightened sense of self-esteem characterized those college-age women I interviewed who felt they had put the Cult into perspective. They had begun to feel good about who they were as individuals. To some extent, they had reclaimed the "self" of early childhood. I sensed that these young women were beginning to make a life for themselves that did not involve concentrating solely on their bodies, but encompassed both the mind and the body.

Tips for Integrating Mind and Body

HOW DO YOU *FEEL*—NOT WHAT DO YOU *WEIGH*? Self-esteem is not about a number on a scale, but about how you feel about *yourself.* You can show a commercial featuring unrealistically thin women to two girls—one who feels good about herself and one who does not. One knows how to manage the messages the commercial sends—the other succumbs to self-hatred. So it's not just about the commercials, it's about what's going on in the family, in peer groups, in a girl's head. What's going on to make you more than just a body?

We know you are doing body work, but what are you doing to nurture your mind and soul? Self-esteem, feeling positive, feeling good *enough, are strong antidotes to disordered eating.*

DIETS DO NOT WORK. Almost all people who diet gain the weight back—and sometimes even more weight than they lost! In most circumstances, putting yourself on a diet equals setting yourself up to fail.

Instead of dieting, you need to make lifestyle changes. The issue here is incremental—things you can fit into your life and know you can handle, so that failure does not become inevitable. What can you do to make more nutritious choices in your diet? Eating better should lead you to feeling healthier—not hungrier.

LESS IS NOT MORE. Eating less does not mean that you are eating better.

Focus on quality *of food before* quantity. *While moderate portion sizes are important to keep in mind, nutritious food choices should come first. Conveniently, foods that are high in nutrition are likely to satisfy your hunger more quickly than junk foods.*

A PIECE OF CAKE WILL NOT MAKE YOU FAT. Lots of people think of diets in "all or nothing" terms.

One piece of anything, an occasional treat here or there, is not going to make you fat. Most people need to consume 3,500 calories in order to gain a single pound. Eating a single piece of cake is not going to make you gain weight, nor is avoiding that piece of cake going to make you lose weight.

IT IS NOT ABOUT THE CAKE. Many people eat or abstain because of how they feel *emotionally*, not in response to *physical* hunger or satiety.

Ask yourself whether you are eating because you are really hungry or because you are emotionally hungry? The same applies to whether you are not eating —is your lack of appetite physical or emotional? To get a reading of why you are eating (or not eating), think about the emotional issues surrounding food intake and/or food restriction. If it is helpful, keep a notebook of what you are eating and record how you are feeling before and after you eat. Afterwards, notice times when you were eating out of hunger, stress, obligation, and so on. How do these instances compare to when you sit down for a meal because your stomach is growling? However, if recording what you eat is going to create a greater source of stress, begin with simply reflecting on why you might continually eat when you're not hungry—or why you continually do not allow yourself to eat when you are hungry. Perhaps this reflection will help you make changes when you are confronted with food.

IT IS ABOUT CONTROL. It is not about food, it is about control. Food often becomes the way to control the body and to seemingly control one's life, to make life manageable.

Friends and family members of people with eating disorders have to understand that you cannot just ask an anorectic or bulimic to eat normally. You have to get at the root of the problem. Culturally induced eaters—those who can mimic anorectic or a bulimic behavior, but not the psychological mechanisms—are more interested in thinness than in control. On the other hand, asking an eating-disordered individual to give up coping, controlling behavior is asking them to give up their life.

WHAT CAN BE DONE TO HELP THOSE WITH EATING DISORDERS?

First, help prevent them from getting so ill that they die, or so hopeless that they want to die. Get them help—to build up their self-esteem, to let go of food controlling their lives. Be supportive without setting deadlines for getting well or withholding love and respect until improvement is evident.

SOME PEOPLE NEVER GET WELL. While a very small minority of people believe that they have recovered from an eating disorder, the overwhelming majority only partially recover, or never get well at all.

If you have an eating disorder, focus on making it more manageable before you entertain the prospect of completely overcoming it. If you are part of this (nonrecovered) majority, then know that you will possibly never completely *be over it. However, it* can *become a manageable chronic condition—like diabetes—always there, but under control. Improvement should always be the first goal for the eating-disordered person. Continual love and support should be the goal for an eating-disordered person's friends and family. Finally, know that* some people do get well.

Evelyn described her ability to resist the Cult of Thinness by learning more about her feelings and focusing not on "What am I going to eat today, but what am I going to do today." She said:

The more confidence I had in myself, the more self-esteem I got. I would say it comes with experience. Probably learning about life, knowing how I feel about certain things and really feeling sure about how I felt. The more I was sure of my feelings, the more I didn't care what anybody else thought. So then I had self-esteem because I felt good about who I was and where I was coming from. If I were 10 or 20 pounds overweight now I feel that it wouldn't bother me as much because I'm happy with the person that I am. I have a younger cousin who is very overweight and a lot of the problem with the girls that I know is that they don't like themselves. And eating is a diversion from thinking about what's going on in their lives or what they should be doing. Whereas I'm directing attention to doing things that I want to accomplish.

Jennifer is also making a life that does not buy into the mind/body dualism. She is the youngest of five siblings from a white, middle-class, intact family. Jennifer's mother was in her early 40s when Jennifer was born, and stayed home when she was growing up. Jennifer is a highly independent and self-confident young woman. She recently graduated from college, is looking for her own apartment, and is embarking on her career. I asked her to define her "sense of self:"

> Everything I do, I do for me, not to please other people. If I decide to exercise I do it not because I want to lose weight. And if it were to lose weight it would not be because my boyfriend would look differently towards me. I exercise because it feels good, it releases tension.

I asked Jennifer what quality most characterized her. She replied·

> Probably that I'm my own person. I won't do something because that's what the crowd is doing. Recently I broke up with my boyfriend. We'd been going together for a while. We became friends first, and then it grew into a relationship and we had a lot of good times together. And I guess, although it was never really mentioned, marriage was sort of kicked around. It was sort of like "well, what do you want in the marriage?" and stuff like that. I discovered that he wanted a wife like what my mother was and what his mother was. I don't want that, I want to work. A career is very important to me. He wanted a homemaker.
> My ideal package would be to have a career, meet a guy, and date him a year, be engaged for about a year, and then get married. All this still having my career, being married for several years so that we could be together and get to know each other and then start a family. And then I'd probably take time off, about a year or two and then go back to work. I know I would go crazy staying home.

I asked Jennifer if she sometimes felt it would be difficult to attain her "ideal package."

> I can't say it hasn't crossed my mind because it has. But then again when I see my friends getting married and what they are getting into and I can see that they are not going to last. I have plenty of time. I don't want to be content with just being married. Your life does go on. I really feel like I have to accomplish so much more. I want to do more—travel, kind of test my limits, even though I'm scared to do it because I'm scared of failure. But I'm not going to settle.

In order for women to "make a life" there must be space for them to forge an identity that is not bound by traditional definitions of what it means to be female. Working for a new femininity, based on integrating the mind *and* body, and creating a society which values women, is the best antidote to the Cult of Thinness.

APPENDIX: RESOURCES THAT ARE JUST A CLICK AWAY: WEB-BASED SITES FOR EATING AND BODY IMAGE ISSUES

Activist opportunities: You can make difference!

(These are great ways to make incremental change. This what each website has to say about how to make change happen.)

- **"International No-Diet Day"**:[45] Participate in a day where you vow not to diet, to eat when you are hungry, and stop when you are full.

- **"International Size Acceptance Day"**:[46] Participate in a day where you help vocalize the importance of acceptance for a diversity of body types.

- Nominate a woman for **"Women's Healthy Weight Day."** "Woman's Healthy[47] Weight Day is an attempt to change media conceptions of beautiful women—hollow-cheeked, self-absorbed, and extremely thin. It is a stereotype that starts 9-year-olds dieting and teaches teenage girls that their bodies will never be good enough.

- Participate in **National Eating Disorders Awareness Week.** "Held annually since 1987, NEDAW is the nation's largest eating disorders outreach effort. During NEDAW, health care providers, teachers, social workers, students, and eating disorder professionals work to promote healthy body image and prevent eating disorders by distributing educational materials and organizing awareness raising events on their campuses and in their communities."[48]

- Get involved in **"The Media Watchdog Program."** This website provides ways (1) to take social action and "involves letter-writing campaigns to either celebrate advertisers who promote diversity in body sizes and shapes, or (2) to help educate those who send negative body image messages about the impacts of their campaigns. To date, more than 1,000 signatures from Watchdogs worldwide accompany each letter. More than half of the negative advertisements targeted have been discontinued!"[49]

- Bring **"Go Girls"** to your school. Go Girls is "a high school curriculum created by the National Eating Disorders Association. The website notes that its mission involves: "giving girls inspiration and resources for lasting self-esteem." "Through facilitated discussions, students in the program explore their own body image issues, general principles about eating disorders and prevention, and the connection between the media and body image. Go Girls! teams take an in-depth look at how advertisements are developed, and, in the process, gain an ability to analyze their underlying messages."[50]

Website Resources Organized by Issue

EATING DISORDERS, OBESITY AND BODY IMAGE ISSUES

EDAP (Eating Disorders Awareness and Prevention). www.edap.org

National Eating Disorder Information Centre (Canada). www.nedic.ca

Childhood and Adolescent Obesity in America: What's a Parent to Do? (Betty Holmes, MS, RD) http://www.uwyo.edu/ces/PUBS/b1066.pdf

Gurze Books. www.gurze.com

Council on Size and Weight Discrimination. www.cswd.org

National Association to Advance Fat Acceptance (NAAFA). www naafa.org

Dads and Daughters. www.dadsanddaughters.org

AABA. American Anorexia/Bulimia Association. www.aabainc.org

ANAD. Association of Anorexia Nervosa and Related Disorders. http://www.anad.org /site/anadweb or www.anad.org

ANRED. Anorexia Nervosa and Related Disorders www.anred.com

NEDO. National Eating Disorders Organization. http://www.nationaleatingdisorders.org

Mirror-Mirror. http://www.mirror-mirror.org/eatdis.htm

HEALTH

Healthy Weight Network: www.healthyweight.net

National Women's Health Information Center: www.4women.gov

Women's Health Initiative: Department of Health & Human Services National Institutes of Health, National Heart, Lung, & Blood Institute. http://www.nhlbi .nih.gov/whi

US Department of Health & Human Services. Office of Minority Health Resource Center: www.omhrc.gov

NUTRITION

USDA Food and Nutrition Information Center. http://www.nal.usda.gov/fnic

National Network for Childcare Nutrition. http:www.nncc.edu

Oregon Dairy Council. www.oregondairycouncil.org

PHYSICAL ACTIVITY

President's Council on Physical Fitness Sports. http://www.fitness.gov

Girls on the Run. http://www.girlsontherun.com

American Alliance for Health, Physical Education, Recreation, and Dance. www .aahperd.org

NAGWS: National Association for Girls & Women in Sport. http://www.aahperd .org/nagws/

MEDIA LITERACY

Media Education Foundation: http://www.mediaed.org

Center for Media Literacy: www.medialit.org
In the Mix: Reality Television for Teens (PBS). http://www.pbs.org/inthemix

Notes

1. Celia Kitzinger, "Depoliticising the Personal: A Feminist Slogan in Feminist Therapy," *Women Studies International Forum*, 16, no. 5 (1993): 487–496.
2. This phrase originated with Carol Hanisch. See Carol Hanisch, "The Personal Is Political," in *The Radical Therapist*, ed. J. Aget (New York: Ballantine, 1971).
3. Cynthia D. Schrager, "Questioning the Promise of Self-Help: A Reading of Women Who Love Too Much," *Feminist Studies*, 19, no. 1 (1993): 188.
4. See Susan Kano: *Making Peace with Food: Freeing Yourself from the Diet/Weight Obsession* (rev. ed.) (New York: Harper & Row, 1989).
5. Rita Freedman, *Bodylove: Learning to Like Our Looks—and Ourselves* (New York: Harper & Row, 1988).
6. Marcia Germaine Hutchinson, *Transforming Body Image: Love the Body You Have* (Freedom, CA: Crossing Press, 1985).
7. See: Margo Maine, *Body Wars: Making Peace with Women's Bodies. An Activist's Guide* (Carlsbad, CA: Gurze Books, 2000).
8. See: Patricia Foster, *Minding the Body: Women Writers on Body and Soul* (New York: Anchor Books, 1994).
9. Wendy Simonds, *Women and Self-Help Culture: Reading between the Lines,* (New Brunswick, NJ: Rutgers University Press, 1992), 227.
10. Elayne Rapping, "Hooked on a Feeling," *The Nation*, March 5, 1990, p. 317.
11. Gloria Steinem, *Revolution from Within: A Book of Self-Esteem* (Boston: Little Brown, 1992).
12. Carol Gilligan, Nona P. Lyons, and Trudy J. Hanmer. (eds.), *Making Connections: The Relational Worlds of Adolescent Girls at Emma Willard School.* (Cambridge, MA: Harvard University Press, 1990). See also: R.G. Simmons, D.A. Blyth, E.F. Van Cleave, and D. Bush, " Entry into Early Adolescence: The Impact of School Structure, Puberty and Early Dating on Self Esteem," *American Sociological Review*, 44, no. 6 (1979): 948–967; Lyn Mikel Brown and Carol Gilligan, *Meeting at the Crossroads: Women's Psychology and Girls' Development* (New York: Ballantine Books, 1992), 2, 16, 86, 99–100, 164, 168, 122; Gilligan, Rogers, and Tolman, *Women, Girls, and Psychotherapy: Reframing Resistance* (New York: Harrington Park Press, 1991). Readers may also be interested in: Peggy Orenstein, *School Girls: Young Women, Self-Esteem, and the Confidence Gap* (New York: Doubleday, 1994).
13. Catherine Steiner-Adair, "The Politics of Prevention," in *Feminist Perspectives on Eating Disorders*, ed. Patricia Fallon, Melanie A. Katzman, and Susan C. Wooley (New York: Guilford Press, 1994), 381.
14. For an interesting read on how Barbie collectors engage in "cultural reappropriations" of Barbie through play, and how Barbie is "a great political and pedagogical tool" see Erica Rand, *Barbie's Queer Accessories* (Durham, NC: Duke University Press, 1995), 195.

15. See: Collete Dowling, *The Frailty Myth: Redefining the Physical Potential of Women and Girls* (New York: Random House, 2000), 57, 161. Dowling writes that in the United States two out of three girls do not participate in school athletic programs. Dowling's central argument counters the idea that women are too weak for sports, which she calls "the frailty myth." She notes:

> The frailty Myth is not just about women being excluded from "the world of sport," or women "not being allowed to compete," or even about women being discriminated against. It is about women actually being kept from using their bodies—and for a reason. When physically weakened, women become socially and politically weakened. It is not so much that men want women to be frail and incompetent, and certainly individual men have no consciousness of such a wish. What men want, simply, is to keep on being the ones with the power to make the big decisions, and this is easier to pull off when the other—the other race or the other gender—is economically weakened, intellectually weakened, physically weakened, or ideally all three. . . . For this reason society has gone to great lengths to control girls' and women's physical development and to keep them out of the game—a game that is much larger than just the game of sport. (161)

16. E. Debold, M. Wilson, and I. Malave, *Mother-Daughter Revolution: From Betrayal to Power* (New York: Addison-Wesley, 1993), 129.

17. bell hooks, *Yearning: Race, Gender and Cultural Politics* (Boston, MA: South End Press, 1990), 219. Also See: bell hooks, "Feminism: A Transformational Politic," in *Talking Back: Thinking Feminist Thinking Black* (Boston: South End Press, 1989), 19–27. More recent books by bell hooks, exploring similar inquiries, include *Feminism Is for Everybody, Teaching Community,* and *Rock My Soul.*

18. See, for example: Johan Vanderlinden, Jan Norre, and Walter Vandereycken, *A Practical Guide to the Treatment of Bulimia Nervosa* (New York: Brunner/Mazel, 1992); Kelly D. Brownell and John P. Foreyt (Eds.), *Handbook of Eating Disorders: Physiology, Psychology, and Treatment of Obesity, Anorexia and Bulimia* (New York: Basic Books, 1986); David M. Garner and Paul E. Garfinkel (Eds.), *Handbook of Psychotherapy for Anorexia Nervosa and Bulimia* (New York: Guilford Press, 1985).

19. Jane Ogden, *The Psychology of Eating: From Healthy to Disordered Behavior* (Malden, MA: Blackwell Publishing, 2003), 245.

20. It is interesting to note that as early as 1874, "anorexia nervosa was understood in medical literature in the context of the ideology of femininity and was seen as an extension of female irrationality." See: Julie Hepworth, *The Social Construction of Anorexia Nervosa* (Thousand Oaks, CA: Sage, 1999), 29. Thus, we can see how direct links can often be discerned between the medicalization and the pathologization of women.

21. Excerpted from: Judi Hollis, *Fat and Furious: Mothers and Daughters and Food Obsessions* (Lincoln, NE: iUniverse, 1994, 2003), 290.

22. See: Patricia Fallon, Melanie A. Katzman, and Susan C. Wooley (Eds.), *Feminist Perspectives on Eating Disorders* (New York: Guilford Press, 1994).

23. Mary Bergner, Pam Remer, and Charles Whetsell, "Transforming Women's Body Image: A Feminist Counseling Approach," *Women and Therapy*, 4, no. 3 (1985): 25–38. Orlando Wayne Wooley, Susan C. Wooley, and Sue R. Dyrenforth, "Obesity and Women II: A Neglected Feminist Topic," *Women's Studies International Quarterly*, no. 2 (1979): 81–92.

24. Cynthia D. Schrager, "Questioning the Promise of Self Help: A Reading of Women Who Love Too Much," *Feminist Studies*, 19, no. 1 (1993): 189. Schrager refers to the important work of feminist theorist bell hooks, who suggested this idea in her book, *Talking Back* (Boston: South End Press, 1989).

25. H.G. Lerner, "12 Stepping It: Women's Roads to Recovery," *Lilith*, Spring 1991, p. 16. no. 2.

26. (Cusumano and Thompson, 1997; Hesse-Biber et. al., 2006; Morry and Staska, 2001; Stice et al., 1994.)

27. Celia Kitzinger, "Depoliticising the Personal: A Feminist Slogan in Feminist Therapy," *Women's Studies International Forum*, 16, no. 5 (1993): 487–496.

28. Alison Bass. "Boycott Called on 'Anorexic' Ads," *Boston Globe*, April 25, 1994, p. 16.

29. See the About-Face website at http://www.about-face.org/. See also: http://www.mediawatch.org. Media Watch's mission is noted as follows:

> Our goal is to challenge abusive stereotypes and other biased images commonly found in the media. Media Watch, which began in 1984, distributes educational videos, media literacy information and newsletters to help create more informed consumers of the mass media. We do not believe in any form of censorship, especially the silencing of marginalized groups. We believe education will help create a more active citizenry who will take action against commercial media pap.

30. Virginia L. Ernster, "Women, Smoking, Cigarette Advertising and Cancer." *Women & Health*, 11, no. 3–4 (1986): 217–235.

31. American Cancer Society, "Prevention and Early Detection: Cigarette Smoking," 2005, http://www.cancer.org/docroot/PED/ped_10.asp

32. Marius Griffin, "Building Blocks for Children's Body Image," *Radiance Online: The Magazine for Large Women* (2004), http://www.radiancemagazine.com/kids_project/body_image.html

33. Harrison G. Pope and James I. Hudson, *New Hope for Binge Eaters: Advances in the Understanding and Treatment of Bulimia* (New York: Harper & Row, 1984).

34. Alan B. Levy, Katherine N. Dixon, and Stephen L. Stern, "How Are Depression and Bulimia Related?" *American Journal of Psychiatry*, 146, no. 2 (1989): 162–169.

35. See: Mary C. Franklin, "Eating Disorders a Topic for Girls," *Boston Globe*, May 8, 1994, p. 43.

36. Freshman Dean's Office. "Yard Bulletin, Freshman Dean's Office, April 29, 2004." http://lists.fas.harvard.edu/pipermail/yard-bulletin-list/2004-April/000029.html. Also: ECHO: Eating Concerns Hotline and Outreach http://hcs.harvard.edu/~echo/

37. Center for the Study of Anorexia and Bulimia. *Teaching about Eating Disorders: Grades 7-12*. New York: 1983. For a fuller discussion of the range of eating disorder prevention programs, see: C.M. Shisslak and M. Crago, "Toward a New Model for the Prevention of Eating Disorders," in P. Fallon, M.A. Katzman, and S.C. Wooley (Eds.), *Feminist Perspectives on Eating Disorders* (New York: Guilford Press, 1994), 419–437.

38. Catherine Steiner Adair and Lisa Sjostrom, *Full of Ourselves: A Wellness Program to Advance Girl Power, Health, and Leadership.* (New York: Teachers College Press, 2006). See also: *Full of Ourselves: Advancing Girl Power, Health, and Leadership.* McLean Hospital: a Harvard Medical School Affiliate. http://www.mclean.harvard.edu/education/youth

39. This quotation was taken from a recent advertisement for NAAFA, which appeared in *Dimensions* magazine. The national address for NAAFA is: National Association to Advance Fat Acceptance (NAAFA), P.O.B. 188620, Sacramento, CA 95818.

40. Frigga Haug (Ed.), *Female Sexualization: A Collective Work of Memory* (London: Verso, 1987).

41. Ibid, 13.

42. Rosy Martin and Jo Spence, "New Portraits for Old: The Use of the Camera in Therapy," in Rosemary Betterton (Ed.), *Looking On: Images of Femininity in the Visual Arts and Media* (London: Pandora, 1987), 268.

43. Ibid.

44. Rosemary Betterton (Ed.), *Looking On: Images of Femininity in the Visual Arts and Media* (London: Pandora, 1987), 209.

45. For more information, contact: The Council on Size and Weight Discrimination, Inc., P.O. Box 305, Mt. Marion, NY 12456. Also see: http://www.bodypositive.com/

46. For further information, contact the International Size Acceptance Association (ISAA). See http://www.size acceptance.org. Also see: http://www.bodypositive.com/

47. Body Positive. "Nominations for Women's Healthy Weight Day Awards—2002," http://www.bodypositive.com/

48. National Eating Disorders Association, "NEDAW 2005," www.nationaleatingdisorders.org

49. National Eating Disorders Association, "The Media Watchdog," www.nationaleatingdisorders.org

50. National Eating Disorders Association, "GO GIRLS!" www.nationaleatingdisorders.org

Bibliography

About Face. http://www.about-face.org

American Cancer Society, "Prevention and Early Detection: Cigarette Smoking" (2005), http://www.cancer.org/docroot/PED/ped_10.asp

Anderson, A., L. Cohn, & T. Holbrook. *Making Weight: Healing Men's Conflicts with Food, Weight, and Shape.* Carlsbad, CA: Gurze Books, 2000.

Bass, A. "Boycott Called on 'Anorexic' Ads. *Boston Globe*, April 25, 1994, p. 16.

Bergner, M., P. Remer, & C. Whetsell. "Transforming Women's Body Image: A Feminist Counseling Approach." *Women and Therapy*, 4, no. 3 (1985): 25–38.

Betterton, R. (Ed.). *Looking on: Images of Femininity in the Visual Arts and Media.* London: Pandora, 1987.

Body Positive. "Nominations for Women's Healthy Weight Day Awards—2002." www.bodypositive.com/activism.htm

Brown, L.M., & C. Gilligan. *Meeting at the Crossroads: Women's Psychology and Girls' Development.* New York: Ballantine Books, 1992.

Brownell, K.D., & J.P. Foreyt (Eds.). *Handbook of Eating Disorders: Physiology, Psychology, and Treatment of Obesity, Anorexia and Bulimia.* New York: Basic Books, 1986.

Cash, T. *The Body Image Workbook: An Eight-Step Program for Learning to Love Your Body.* Oakland, CA: New Harbinger Workbooks, 1998.

Center for the Study of Anorexia and Bulimia. *Teaching about Eating Disorders: Grades 7-12.* New York: Author, 1983.

Chianese, R. "The Body Politic." *Utne Reader*, May/June 1992, p. 69.

Cohen, P., & S. Pierson. *You Have to Say I'm Pretty, You're My Mother: How to Help Your Daughter Learn to Love Her Body and Herself.* New York: Simon & Schuster, 2003.

Council on Size and Weight Discrimination, Inc. www.bodypositive.com

Cusumano, D.L., & J.K. Thompson, "Body Image and Body Shape Ideals in Magazines: Exposure, Awareness, and Internalization," *Sex Roles: A Journal of Research*, 37, no. 9–10 (1997).

Debold, E., M. Wilson, & I. Malave. *Mother-Daughter Revolution: From Betrayal to Power.* New York: Addison-Wesley, 1993.

Dowling, C. *The Frailty Myth: Redefining the Physical Potential of Women and Girls.* New York: Random House, 2000.

ECHO: Eating Concerns Hotline and Outreach. http://hcs.harvard.edu/~echo

Ernster, V.L. "Women, Smoking, Cigarette Advertising and Cancer." *Women & Therapy*, 6 (1987): 217–237.

Fallon, P., M.A. Katzman, & S.C. Wooley (Eds.). *Feminist Perspectives on Eating Disorders.* New York: Guilford Press, 1994.

Foster, P. *Minding the Body: Women Writers on Body and Soul.* New York: Anchor Books, 1994.

Franklin, M.C. "Eating Disorders a Topic for Girls." *Boston Globe*, May 8, 1994, p. 43.

Freedman, R. *Bodylove: Learning to Like Our Looks—and Ourselves.* New York: Harper & Row, 1988.

Freshman Dean's Office. "Yard Bulletin, Freshman Dean's Office, April 29, 2004." http://lists.fas.harvard.edu/pipermail/yard-bulletin-list/2004April/000029.html. Accessed May 18, 2006.

Full of Ourselves: Advancing Girl Power, Health, and Leadership. McLean Hospital: a Harvard Medical School Affiliate. http://www.mclean.harvard.edu/education/youth

Garner, D.M., & P.E. Garfinkel (Eds.). *Handbook of Psychotherapy for Anorexia Nervosa and Bulimia.* New York: Guilford Press 1985.

Gilligan, C., A.G. Rogers, & D.L. Tolman, *Women, Girls, and Psychotherapy: Reframing Resistance.* New York: Harrington Park Press, 1991.

Gilligan, C., N.P. Lyons, & T.J. Hanmer. (Eds.). *Making Connections: The Relational Worlds of Adolescent Girls at Emma Willard School.* Cambridge, MA.: Harvard University Press, 1990.

Green, B., & O. Winfrey. *Make the Connection: Ten Steps to a Better Body–and a Better Life.* New York: Hyperion, 1996.

Griffin, M. "Building Blocks for Children's Body Image." *Radiance Online: The Magazine for Large Women* [The Body Image Task Force, 2004]. Accessed from http://www.radiancemagazine.com/kids_project/body_image.html

Hanisch, C. "The Personal is Political." In *The Radical Therapist,* ed. J. Agel, p. 152–155. New York: Ballantine, 1971.

Haug, F. (Ed.). *Female Sexualization: A Collective Work of Memory.* London: Verso, 1987.

Hepworth, J. *The Social Construction of Anorexia Nervosa.* Thousand Oaks, CA: Sage, 1999.

Herrin, M. *How to Help a Friend with an Eating Disorder.* [handout]. Dartmouth Program Nutritional Education Program, Eating Disorders Awareness, Inc. http://www.gettysburg.edu/college_life/counseling/HelpFriend.pdf

Hesse-Biber, S., P. Leavy, C.E. Quinn, & J. Zoino, "The mass marketing of disordered eating and Eating Disorders: The social psychology of women, thinness, and culture," *Women's Studies International Forum,* 29, no. 2 (2006): 96–114.

Hill-Collins, P. *Black Feminist Thought: Knowledge, Consciousness, and the Politics of Empowerment* (2nd ed.). New York: Routledge, 2000.

Hirschman, J.R. *When Women Stop Hating Their Bodies: Freeing Yourself from Food and Weight Obsession.* New York: Ballantine Books, 1995.

Hollis, J. *Fat and Furious: Mothers and Daughters and Food Obsessions.* Lincoln, NE: iUniverse, 1994, 2003.

hooks, bell. "Feminism: A Transformational Politic." In *Talking Back: Thinking Feminist Thinking Black,* Boston: South End Press, 1989: p 19 27.

hooks, bell. *Talking Back.* Boston. South End Press, 1989.

hooks, bell. *Yearning: Race, Gender and Cultural Politics.* Boston, MA: South End Press, 1990.

hooks, bell. *Rock My Soul: Black People and Self Esteem.* New York: Atrra, 2002.

hooks, bell. *Feminism is for Everybody: Passionate Politics.* Boston, MA: South End Press, 2000.

hooks, bell. *Teaching Community.* New York: Routledge, 2003.

Hutchinson, M.G. *Transforming Body Image: Learning to Love the Body You Have.* Freedom, CA: Crossing Press, 1985.

International Size Acceptance Association (ISAA). http://www.size-acceptance.org

Johnson, C.A. *Self-Esteem Comes in All Shapes and Sizes: How to Be Happy and Healthy at Your Natural Weight* (rev. ed.). Carlsbad, CA: Gurze Books, 2001.

Kano, S. *Making Peace with Food: Freeing Yourself from the Diet/Weight Obsession* (rev. ed.). New York: Harper & Row, 1989.

Kitzinger, C. "Depoliticising the Personal: A Feminist Slogan in Feminist Therapy." *Women Studies International Forum*, 16, no. 5 (1993): 487–496.

Lerner. H.G. "12 Stepping It: Women's Roads to Recovery." *Lilith*, Spring 1991, p. 16.

Levine, M. "10 Things Parents Can Do to Help Prevent Eating Disorders." National Eating Disorders Association. www.NationalEatingDisorders.org

Levine, M., & M. Maine. "Eating Disorders Can Be Prevented!" National Eating Disorders Association. www.nationaleatingdisorders.org

Levine M., & L. Smolak. "10 'Will-Powers' for Improving Body Image." National Eating Disorders Association. www.NationalEatingDisorders.org

Levy, A.B., K.N. Dixon, & S.L. Stern. "How are Depression and Bulimia Related?" *American Journal of Psychiatry*, 146, no. 2 (1989): 162–169.

Maine, M. *Body Wars: Making Peace with Women's Bodies: An Activist's Guide.* Carlsbad, CA: Gurze Books, 2000.

Maine, M., & J. Kelly. "The Women We Admire." *The Body Myth*. Hoboken, NJ: John Wiley & Sons, Inc. 2005.

Martin, R., & J. Spence. "New Portraits for Old: The Use of the Camera in Therapy." In *Looking On: Images of Femininity in the visual Arts and Media*, ed. R. Betterton, p. 267–279. London: Pandora, 1987.

Media Scope. "Mediascope Issue Briefs—Body Image and Advertising." Accessed from www.mediascope.org/pubs/ibriefs/bia.htm

Morry, M.M. & S.L. Staska, "Magazine exposure: Internalization, self-objectification, eating attitudes, and body satisfaction in male and female university students," *Canadian Journal of Behavioral Science*, 33, no. 4 (2001): 269–279.

National Association to Advance Fat Acceptance (NAAFA; Sacramento, CA). *Dimensions Magazine*. Shardco, Inc., 1983-current.

National Eating Disorders Association. "GO GIRLS!" www.nationaleatingdisorders.org

National Eating Disorders Association. "NEDAW 2005." www.nationaleatingdisorders.org

National Eating Disorders Association. "The Media Watchdog." www.nationaleatingdisorders.org

National Eating Disorders Association Media Watchdog Program. "What Should I Look For?" www.nationaleatingdisorders.org

Ogden, J. *The Psychology of Eating: From Healthy to Disordered Behavior.* Malden, MA: Blackwell, 2003.

Orenstein, P. *School Girls: Young Women, Self-Esteem, and the Confidence Gap.* New York: Doubleday, 1994.

Pipher, M. *Hunger Pains: The Modern Women's Tragic Quest for Thinness.* New York: Ballantine Books, 1995.

Pope, H.G., & J.I. Hudson. *New Hope for Binge Eaters: Advances in the Understanding and Treatment of Bulimia.* New York: Harper & Row, 1984.

Rand, E. *Barbie's Queer Accessories.* Durham, NC: Duke University Press, 1995.

Rapping, E. "Hooked on a Feeling." *The Nation*, March 5, 1990, p. 317.

Satter, E. *How to Get Your Kid to Eat . . . But Not Too Much.* Boulder: Bull Publishing Co., 1987.

Schrager, C.D. "Questioning the Promise of Self-Help: A Reading of Women Who Love Too Much." *Feminist Studies*, 19, 1 (1993): 177–192.

Shanker, W. *The Fat Girl's Guide to Life.* New York: Bloomsbury, 2004, 2005.

Shisslak, C.M., & M. Crago. "Toward a New Model for the Prevention of Eating Disorders." In P. Fallon, M.A. Katzman, & S.C. Wooley (p. 419–437). *Feminist Perspectives on Eating Disorders* ed. New York: Guilford Press, 1994.

Simmons, R.G., D.A. Blyth, E.F. Van Cleave, & D. Bush, "Entry into Early Adolescence: The Impact of School Structure, Puberty and Early Dating on Self Esteem." *American Sociological Review*, 44, no. 6 (1979): 948–967.

Simonds, W. *Women and Self-Help Culture: Reading Between the Lines.* New Brunswick, NJ: Rutgers University Press, 1992.

Something Fishy Website on Eating Disorders, The. "Tips for Doctors." www .something-fishy.org

Steinem, G. *Revolution from Within: A Book of Self Esteem.* Boston: Little Brown, 1992.

Steiner-Adair, C. "The Politics of Prevention." In *Feminist Perspectives on Eating Disorders*, ed. P. Fallon, M.A. Katzman, & S.C. Wooley. New York: Guilford Press, 1994.

Steiner-Adair, C., & L. Sjostrom. *Full of Ourselves: A Wellness Program to Advance Girl Power, Health, and Leadership.* New York: Teachers College Press, 2006.

Stice, E. & Shaw, H.E. "Adverse effects of the media portrayed thin-ideal on women and linkages to bulimic symptomatology," *Journal of Social and Clinical Psychology*, 13, no. 3 (1994): 288.

Vanderlinden, J., J. Norre, & W. Vandereycken. *A Practical Guide to the Treatment of Bulimia Nervosa.* New York: Brunner/Mazel, 1992.

Wann, M. *Fat!So?: Because You Don't Have to Apologize for Your Size.* Berkeley, CA: Ten Speed Press, 1998.

Wooley, O.W., S.C. Wooley, & S.R. Dyrenforth. "Obesity and Women II: A Neglected Feminist Topic." *Women's Studies International Quarterly*, 1 (1979): 81–92.

"York County Turn Beauty Inside Out, Maine." www.umaine.edu/umext/ genderproject/TBIO.htm

Index

DATE DUE